American Ethnicity

American Ethnicity

The Dynamics
and Consequences
of Discrimination

SEVENTH EDITION

Adalberto Aguirre, Jr. and *Jonathan H. Turner*
University of California, Riverside

McGraw Hill

Connect
Learn
Succeed™

AMERICAN ETHNICITY: THE DYNAMICS AND CONSEQUENCES OF DISCRIMINATION, SEVENTH EDITION

Published by McGraw-Hill, a business unit of The McGraw-Hill Companies, Inc., 1221 Avenue of the Americas, New York, NY 10020. Copyright © 2011 by The McGraw-Hill Companies, Inc. All rights reserved. Previous editions © 2009, 2007 and 2004. No part of this publication may be reproduced or distributed in any form or by any means, or stored in a database or retrieval system, without the prior written consent of The McGraw-Hill Companies, Inc., including, but not limited to, in any network or other electronic storage or transmission, or broadcast for distance learning.

Some ancillaries, including electronic and print components, may not be available to customers outside the United States.

This book is printed on acid-free paper.

2 3 4 5 6 7 8 9 0 DOC/DOC 1 0 9 8 7 6 5 4 3 2 1

ISBN   978-0-07-811158-7
MHID 0-07-811158-7

Vice President & Editor-in-Chief: *Michael Ryan*
Vice President EDP/Central Publishing Services: *Kimberly Meriwether David*
Publisher: *William Glass*
Senior Sponsoring Editor: *Gina Boedeker*
Executive Marketing Manager: *Pamela S. Cooper*
Managing Editor: *Meghan Campbell*
Project Manager: *Erin Melloy*
Design Coordinator: *Margarite Reynolds*
Cover Designer: *Carole Lawson*
Photo Research: *Sonia Brown*
Cover Image: *PhotoLink/Getty Images*
Buyer: *Nicole Baumgartner*
Media Project Manager: *Sridevi Palani*
Compositor: *Glyph International*
Typeface: *10/12 Palatino*
Printer: *R.R. Donnelley*

All credits appearing on page or at the end of the book are considered to be an extension of the copyright page.

Library of Congress Cataloging-in-Publication Data

Aguirre, Adalberto.
   American ethnicity: the dynamics and consequences of discrimination / Adalberto Aguirre, Jr. and Jonathan H. Turner. — 7th ed.
         p. cm.
      Includes bibliographical references and index.
      ISBN 978-0-07-811158-7 (acid-free paper)
   1. United States—Race relations.   2. United States—Ethnic relations.   3. Discrimination—United States.   4. Ethnicity—United States. I. Turner, Jonathan H. II. Title.

E184.A1A38   2010
305.800973—dc22
                                                                                          2010038426

www.mhhe.com

About the Authors

ADALBERTO AGUIRRE, JR. is Professor of Sociology, University of California at Riverside. He is the author of over eleven books and many articles in professional journals. Among his books related to this effort are *Race, Racism and the Death Penalty in the United States; Perspectives on Race and Ethnicity in American Criminal Justice; Chicanos in Higher Education: Issues and Dilemmas for the 21st Century; Chicanos and Intelligence Testing;* and *Women and Minority Faculty in the Academic Workplace.*

JONATHAN H. TURNER holds the title of University Professor in the University of California system and Distinguished Professor of Sociology at University of California, Riverside. He is the author of thirty-one books and many articles in professional journals. Among his books related to this effort are *Oppression: A Sociohistory of Black-White Relations; American Society: Problems of Structure, Social Problems in America;* and *Inequality: Privilege & Poverty in America.*

To Our Wives,
Carmen Alicia Aguirre
Alexandra Maryanski

Brief Contents

Contents

Preface

In the twenty-first century, American society continues to be shaped by the so-cial forces associated with growing numbers of racial and ethnic populations. American society was shaped by waves of European immigrants who forged ethnic identities within the Anglo-Saxon core over the last four decades of the twentieth century, and an increasing number of immigrants arriving in the United States from Asia, Mexico, and Central America have made diversity more noticeable in the so-cial fabric of American society. Increasing diversity not only has become more no-ticeable but also has become more volatile in the social relations of everyday life.

The tragic events of September 11, 2001, transformed America's aware-ness of persons noticeably different from the Anglo-Saxon core. "Suspicious" became a term for describing anyone who dressed differently, spoke a lan-guage other than English, or professed different religious beliefs. "Terrorist" became a label for restricting the freedom of anyone who sounded or looked un-American. Unsurprisingly, after September 11, racial, ethnic, and religious minorities became perceived as suspected terrorists in American society.

As we close on the first decade of the twenty-first century, racial and ethnic diversity is no longer emerging in American society; diversity has become readily identifiable in America's social institutions and everyday life. The public discourse on racial and ethnic diversity in U.S. society has become more intense as the dom-inant Anglo population perceives itself under attack from diverse populations. The increasing racial and ethnic diversity in American society is making native-born white Americans consider their racial identity and their growing minority status. It is our contention that tensions between ethnic populations and the dominant Anglo population represent the core of *ethnic stratification* in American society.

Conceptual Framework

Our goal is to understand how social dynamics, such as prejudice and discrim-ination, have affected the participation of ethnic minorities in American society. To this end, we employ a conceptual framework incorporating key ideas from theories about ethnic stratification in an effort to organize historical and census data pertaining to ethnic populations in the United States. The great virtue of using a unified conceptual framework to organize the data is that it facilitates comparison between the ethnic populations in the United States on the same social dimensions.

Our analysis of each ethnic group in America begins with a few simple questions:

1. What share of resources does the ethnic group receive?
2. What are the major resource outcomes for ethnic groups in the United States in terms of income, education, health care, housing, and other valued resources?

We then explore how past and present discrimination can account for inequality in the distribution of resources among various ethnic groups.

In examining the dynamics of discrimination, we call attention to important factors, such as the sense of threat experienced by those who discriminate, the varying degrees of identifiability of people as targets of discrimination, the negative stereotypes that are created to legitimize discrimination, and—most important—the institutionalization of discrimination in economic, political, legal, educational, and housing patterns. These forces, as they have fueled and shaped discrimination, have created a system of ethnic stratification that reinforces the very discriminatory social forces that created this system of stratification in the first place. A major challenge for American society in the twenty-first century is to attack the discriminatory social forces that produce ethnic stratification. This challenge, however, is especially difficult given the rapid growth of ethnic populations in American society and the increasing and inevitable threat perceived by the dominant Anglo population as it confronts their rapid growth.

New to the Seventh Edition

In each chapter we have updated statistics and data tables with the most recent data available from public use data sources such as the U.S. Census Bureau, especially the American Community Survey. We chose not to update statistics or data tables if we could not find new data that matched the statistics and data tables already in the sixth edition. Because the U.S. Census Bureau and other public use data collection agencies often change the types of data they collect from one period to another, a problem arises if one desires to examine the same data over different time periods. The ability to do this is particularly important here because we compare racial and ethnic populations on the same variables over different time periods. However, where possible, we supplement discussion of statistics and data tables by incorporating new data to illustrate how social conditions have changed for each racial and ethnic population.

Other Changes/Additions

- We have expanded the conceptual framework guiding the organization of chapters to include the concept of social identity as part of the dynamics of discrimination.

- We have tried, where possible (given the uneven data available) to highlight the intersection of ethnicity and gender in patterns of ethnic stratification.

Supplements

Visit our companion website at **www.mhhe.com/aguirre7e** for dynamic resources for both instructors and students.

The **student center** on the website provides an overview of the text, chapter quizzes, discussion questions, a glossary, key concepts, and Web exercises.

The **password-protected instructor center** includes the instructor's manual and test bank. The instructor's manual is organized to correspond to the ten chapters in the text. Each chapter offers a chapter overview, a chapter outline, a list of key terms and concepts, discussion questions, suggested readings, and suggested Web links. The test bank offers multiple-choice, true-false, fill-in-the-blank, and essay questions for each chapter.

Acknowledgments

We have amassed a large number of debts in writing this book. First, we wish to thank the reviewers of the seventh edition, who provided many helpful comments and suggestions: David Allen, Temple University; Brian Baker, California State University–Sacramento; Celestino Fernandez, University of Arizona; Jamie Harazmus, Western Technical College; Jeremy Hein, University of Wisconsin–Eau Claire; Eric Patton, Southern State Community College; Ralph Pyle, Michigan State University; Mary Anna E. Townsend, State Fair Community College.

We also want to acknowledge once again those who reviewed previous editions and those whose contributions helped us lay the groundwork for this book: Peter Adler, University of Denver; E. M. Beck, University of Georgia; Joel D. Bloom, University of Oregon; Larry Carps, Northwestern Michigan College; Richard M. Cramer, University of North Carolina at Chapel Hill; Timothy Evans, Community College of Allegheny County; Jan Fiola, Moorhead State University; Charles Green, CUNY–Hunter College; Emily Noelle Ignacio, Loyola University; Meg Wilkes Karraker, University of St. Thomas; Jessica L. Kenty-Drane, Southern Connecticut State University; Peter Kivisto, Augustana College; M. Wibrod Mazura, Normandale Community College; Judith McDonnell, Bryant University; Peter Melvoin, Bellevue Community College; Joan M. Morris, University of Central Florida; Richard N. Pitt, Jr., Vanderbilt University; Luis Alfredo Posas, Minnesota State University–Mankato; Ralph Pyle, Michigan State University; Ernest Quimby, Howard University; Peter I. Rose, Smith College; Ellen Rosengarten, Sinclair Community College; Peter Singelmann, University of Missouri–Kansas City; Robert Speel, Penn State Erie; Becky Thompson, Simmons College; Chikwendu Christian Ukaegbu, University of Wyoming; George Wilson, University of Miami; and S. Rowan Wolf, Portland Community College. The following individuals have been invaluable in assisting us with the research for population statistics: Manuel de la Puenta and Edna Paisano at the

U.S. Bureau of the Census; Ruth McKay at the U.S. Department of Labor Statistics; Tony Hernandez at the Hispanic Resarch Center, Arizona State University; and Georges Vernez at the RAND Corporation.

Our special thanks go to Clara Dean for helping us bring coherency to the manuscript. Other individuals have offered their insights and suggestions at one time or another: David Baker, Shoon Lio, Janet Hill, and Jacque Godsey. Finally, we give our heartfelt thanks to our families for giving us the space and time to complete this book.

Our purpose in writing this book continues to be one of providing students and teachers in the social sciences with a "working text"—an information tool that provides both students and teachers with the resources needed to build around it. For example, many of you have commented on your ability to use supplementary materials, such as journal articles, to enhance the utility of this text in your classes. We are encouraged by your comments, because they tell us that the conceptual and comparative organization of the text serves as a valuable tool in the teaching and learning process. For those of you who have shared your thoughts and suggestions about *American Ethnicity* with us, we encourage you to continue doing so. We have been especially encouraged by those faculty who have shared with us student comments about the book or student reviews of the book. We hope others will also be encouraged to share their thoughts and suggestions with us. Please feel free to contact either one of us at:

adalberto.aguirre@ucr.edu   jonathan.turner@ucr.edu

Adalberto Aguirre, Jr.
Jonathan H. Turner

American Ethnicity

CHAPTER 1

Ethnicity and Ethnic Relations

*E*thnic strife exists everywhere in the world today. People hate each other with a passion that is sometimes difficult to understand, and in many places, the protagonists seem to be locked in a cycle of mutually escalating violence. People are often proud of their ethnic heritage, and equally often they are suspicious of the heritage of others, seeing another ethnic population as a potential threat to their well-being. Thus, we must reluctantly conclude that ethnicity is a force that mobilizes people's emotions ranging from a sense of ethnic pride, on the one side, to fear and hatred of other ethnics, on the other. In very few places are tolerance and mutual understanding of ethnic differences accepted as normal, or even as desirable. True, ideologies often preach ethnic tolerance and celebration of diversity, but in actual practice, most of the world reveals ethnic tensions, open conflict, and in a few cases, efforts to exterminate others who are seen as different. Tensions are often so profound that societies are de-evolving, breaking apart along ethnic lines. The Soviet Union collapsed around old ethnic lines; Yugoslavia disintegrated into episodes of ethnic cleansing; Czechoslovakia is now two nations; French-speaking Canadians want to break away from the union; and India and Pakistan stand ready to use their nuclear weapons as they dispute the borders that were created to partition ethnic subpopulations. For those populations who cannot be split into new nations, the tensions persist, often erupting into violence and almost always producing systematic efforts at discrimination. And when ethnics migrate to new lands, they almost always encounter discrimination and, at times, violence. Thus, the world is filled with ethnic tension and outright conflict. Noisy and threatening protests, long-term oppression, terrorist bombings, mass killings, and war can be found around the globe. Ethnicity is one of the most volatile forces of the twenty-first century.

Why do ethnic tension and racial hatred persist in patterns of human organization? Why did the early white settlers in North America, for example, kill so many Native Americans? Why did slavery exist? Why are neo-Nazi hate groups emerging in Germany? Why are churches attended by African Americans arson targets? Why do Catholics and Protestants in Northern Ireland wall themselves off from each other? Why do ethnic jokes about Polacks, Wops, Japs, Jews, and others persist in America? Why do European-origin Americans so fear Latinos? And so the questions go.

Our goal in this book is to answer these and many related questions that can be asked about ethnicity. Our emphasis is on American ethnic tensions, and compared to the violence and killings in many parts of the world, the dynamics of ethnicity in America can appear rather muted. This is not to say, however, that tensions among American ethnics are not severe. On the contrary, the existing divisions among ethnics in the United States are at a critical phase; America will either become a viable multiethnic society, or it will degenerate into patterns of hatred and violence so evident in our nation's past and so clear in much of the world today. The task before us, then, is to understand American ethnic antagonisms; and with this understanding, perhaps we can better appreciate what needs to be done to reduce the conflicts among ethnic groups in America.

In this chapter, we begin this task by clarifying basic concepts. To understand a phenomenon like ethnicity, we need to define key terms that are used to explain how the phenomenon operates. So let us begin with a conceptual mapping of our subject; in Chapter 2 we can turn to theorizing about the dynamic properties of American ethnic relations.

RACE AND ETHNICITY

The term **race** connotes biological differences among peoples—skin color, facial features, stature, and the like—that are transmitted from generation to generation. As such, these biological differences are seen as permanent characteristics of people. The notion of race does not make much sense as a biological concept, however, because the physical characteristics that make people distinctive are trivial. A few alleles on genes are what account for these differences, and, most important, these alleles are on genes that are not determinative of basic biological functions. These biological differences are, in essence, superficial. Moreover, they do not mark clear boundaries: Where does "black" end and "white" begin? Is the child of an Asian mother and a European father more Asian or more European?

Even though biological differences are superficial and difficult to use as markers of boundaries between peoples, they are important sociologically. For if people believe that others are biologically distinctive, they tend to respond to them as being different. And when people associate superficial biological differences with variations in psychological, intellectual, and behavioral makeup, they may feel justified in treating members of a distinctive group in discriminatory ways. For example, if some individuals in a society consider dark skin an important distinction, and this distinction becomes associated in their minds with differences in the behavior of "black people," then this superficial biological difference will influence how dark-skinned people are treated in that society.

How, then, should we conceptualize the notion of "race" if it does not make much biological sense? Our answer is to subordinate and incorporate the idea of

Box 1.1
Race and the Biology of Humans

The concept of "race" does not have great meaning in biology because the genetic differences among humans are not great. Just a small amount of genetic material accounts for differences in skin color, eye folds, hair color and texture, and other markers of "racial differences." Still, social scientists, census takers, newscasters, and the general public continue to denote people by "their race." Race is thus a *social construction*, denoting some rather superficial physical differences among humans.

To put this tendency to denote humans as genetically part of racial groups into evolutionary perspective, the genetic diversity of humans is less than any primate on earth. Why should this be so? The answer is that the human species almost went extinct at two points in its history, the most significant being the decline in humans in Africa to perhaps only a few hundred individuals and certainly not more than a few thousand. Only by migrating out of Africa were these early humans, who came very close to extinction, able to pass on their genes and sustain the species. This fact means that this small "breeding stock" for all modern humans did not reveal much variation, especially compared to other primates and, indeed, most other mammals. Since humans are so closely related genetically, notions of race seem overblown, at least in a biological sense. There are no "races" among chimpanzees, for example, with whom we share 99 percent of our genetic material (although a 1 percent difference in genes can, as is obvious, produce very different-looking and- acting species).

Yet, despite this biological closeness among the over 6.5 billion people on earth, we tend to codify minor differences that represent adaptations of populations to unique ecological locations as "racial." When a biological-sounding label is used to denote such minor differences, these differences take on more *social* significance—as the history of ethnic relations in America and elsewhere so clearly documents.

race into a broad definition of **ethnicity.** When a subpopulation of individuals reveals, or is perceived to reveal, shared historical experiences as well as unique organizational, behavioral, and cultural characteristics, it exhibits its ethnicity. For instance, when country of origin, religion, family practices, interpersonal style, language, beliefs, values, and other characteristics are used to demark a population of individuals from others, then ethnicity is operating. The more visible the characteristics marking ethnicity, the more likely it is that those in an ethnic category will be treated differently.

Here is where race or presumptions of biological differences become a part of ethnicity. Physical features like skin color and facial features can be used as highly visible markers of organizational, behavioral, and cultural differences among individuals. When someone is labeled "black," more than skin color is involved; whole clusters of assumptions about historical experiences, behavior, organization, and culture are associated with this label. The same is true for labels such as "white," "Asian," "Mexican," "Jew," and "Indian."

In fact, as we will come to see, labels are often self-fulfilling in creating and sustaining ethnicity. If people are given a label because of their skin color and then discriminated against as if they were different, they will react to such treatment by behaving and organizing in ways that are indeed distinctive. Once behavioral and organizational differences exist and are elaborated culturally into norms, beliefs, and other systems of symbols, they become an additional marker of differences, both justifying the earlier label and the distinctive treatment of these others as somehow "different." So if biological distinctiveness can become a part of the label for denoting populations, then biology becomes an aspect of the social dynamics producing and sustaining ethnicity. Indeed, racial labels are like turbochargers in ethnic relations: They escalate the heat and power of emotions and tensions.

The notions of race and ethnicity are thus social constructions. They are conceptions, often inaccurate, that people have about what makes certain people different and unique. Over the last twenty years in America, especially in the last decade, ethnicity appears to have taken on greater significance. Why should this be so? One reason is perhaps obvious: American society is one of the most ethnically diverse in the world, and it is natural for people to notice this simple fact of life. But more is involved. An additional force raising perceptions of ethnicity has been social movements that draw attention to discrimination against a particular group, especially as laws and other policies like "affirmative action" have been designed to compensate for past patterns of discrimination against a particular ethnic population. Another reason is the rapidly changing proportions of various ethnic groups in America, some increasing as a proportion of the total population while others are declining. Such shifts in the ethnic composition often make people aware of ethnic differences, particularly if they feel threatened by demographic changes. Still another reason is the widespread attention paid to ethnicity in schools and the media. When ethnicity gains publicity, and particularly if it becomes a hot-button political issue, it becomes more salient in people's minds. And finally, the U.S. Census Bureau, which collects data on the characteristics of the American population, emphasizes ethnicity; indeed, many of the questions on the census forms are devoted to a person's ethnic background. The Census Bureau increasingly uses the concept of race, especially in its efforts to discover "mixed-race" segments of the population (see Box 1.2).

It is difficult, therefore, to not be aware of ethnicity in American society. As attention is called to ethnicity, it takes on more reality and shapes how Americans think about themselves and others around them. While some of this reflection can be positive, much of what individuals think about ethnicity is negative, involving perceptions of others as somehow different and threatening. In the end, when ethnic differences are on people's minds, tensions among ethnic groups inevitably increase.

ETHNIC GROUPS

What is a group? Sociologists generally define a group as a gathering of individuals in face-to-face interaction. According to this definition, an ethnic "group" would be a number of interacting individuals distinguished by their ethnicity. Not every one of these individuals interacts face to face, but they may

Box 1.2
The Increasing Significance of "Race"

Despite the fact that "race" has no real meaning in a biological sense, the U.S. Census Bureau has increased its use of the term to denote ethnicity. In so doing, the Bureau is implicitly suggesting that people are biologically different, although this is far from its intent. In the 2000 census, for example, the Bureau asked questions about "mixed" ancestry and race, placing everybody in a "race" and constructing summary data in terms of "race" rather than "ethnicity." Persons responding to the question on "race" in both the 2000 and 2010 censuses chose from the following five categories: (1) White, (2) Black or African American, (3) American Indian and Alaska Native, (4) Asian, and (5) Native Hawaiian and Other Pacific Islander. A sixth racial category, "some other race," was provided for those persons unable to identify with one of the five racial categories. In an effort to document the number of multiracial persons in the U.S. population, persons could also respond to the "race" question by selecting one of the following categories: "race alone" or "race in combination." Persons in the "race alone" category reported only one race category, while persons in the "race in combination" category reported two or more race categories.

One result of the treatment of "race" in the census is that the Census Bureau now tabulates the population by "race," downplaying the notion of ethnicity, which, we feel, is the more appropriate label. Curiously, "Hispanics" are often separated from other whites, and one frequently finds tables with labels denoting the distribution of "races" for the non-Hispanic population. In this way, Latinos who are seen as part of the "white race" are separated in calculations on "Hispanics," resulting in the cumbersome categories of "non-Hispanic white" and "white Hispanics." This partitioning of whites into two categories only highlights the insignificance of race as a marker of difference and the importance of ethnicity.

The intent of the Bureau was, no doubt, benign; it simply needed a label for people of mixed ethnic backgrounds. But in using the term "race," the Bureau suggests that the offspring of people from different ethnic groups are of a "mixed race," which makes no sense biologically. They are, in reality, of mixed ethnic ancestry rather than race. In the end, this kind of tabulation makes "race" ever more salient in people's minds, and as ethnic differences become perceived as "racial differences," the lines dividing ethnic subpopulations can harden.

With the 2010 census, the movement to emphasize "race" at the expense of ethnicity will gain traction. For all those who report being "white" or "black," no further questions on their ancestry will be asked. This reverses the policy from the first census conducted in 1790. Thus, we will have no data on the ancestry of all those designated as white or black, while the salience of other ethnicities may increase. For example, if persons identify themselves as Latino or Asian, then there will be further questions about their specific ancestry, especially their national origins. True, the ancestry questions for those categorized as white always represented a problem because of uneven reporting of ancestry, especially as the salience of being Irish, Scottish, Swedish, Italian, and the like declined. Yet, such data are still useful. Indeed, Arab Americans and others from the Middle East are categorized as "white," but their country of origin (e.g., Egypt, Syria, Iran) is still salient to them and is also useful information to have. But, as we will see in various tables in this book, the 2000 census will be the last one where more detailed data about white ancestry will be available.

interact in various social settings. Obviously, when we use the term "ethnic group," we have something much bigger, broader, and more inclusive in mind. **Subpopulations** of individuals in a society can be distinguished by their history as well as their distinctive behavior, organization, culture, and, perhaps, superficial biological features. An **ethnic group** is a subpopulation of individuals who are labeled and categorized by the general population and, often, by the members of the group itself as being of a particular type of ethnicity. They share a unique history as well as distinctive behavioral, organizational, and cultural characteristics, and, as a result, they often are treated differently by others. In addition to the term "ethnic group," in this text we use the terms **ethnic subpopulation** and **ethnic population,** which more accurately describe the groups that we are discussing.

MINORITY GROUPS

What is a **minority group?** Louis Wirth (1945:347) long ago offered the basic definition, the general thrust of which is still used today: "A group of people who, because of their physical or cultural characteristics, are singled out from others in the society in which they live for differential and unequal treatment and who therefore regard themselves as objects of collective discrimination." There are many problems with this definition, however. First, it is not a group but members of a larger subpopulation who are singled out for unequal treatment. Second, the label "minority" is not always accurate; sometimes it is a majority, as was the case historically in South Africa, that is discriminated against. Thus, we should begin to revise this traditional definition of "minority group" by acknowledging what it really means: an ethnic subpopulation in a society subject to discrimination by members of *more powerful ethnic subpopulations*. Usually the victimized subpopulation is a numerical minority, and the more powerful discriminators are in the majority. Since this is not always true, however, the important issue is this: Which ethnic subpopulation has the power to discriminate? The more powerful subpopulation is the dominant or *superordinate* ethnic group, and the less powerful ethnic subpopulation is the *subordinate* group. The latter terminology, which revolves around dominance and subordination, more accurately frames the issues that were once classified as "minority group relations."

ETHNIC DISCRIMINATION

Phrases like "unequal treatment" and "distinctive treatment" have been used rather loosely thus far. These and related terms can be consolidated by one key term: "discrimination." In general, **discrimination** is the process by which an individual, group, or subpopulation of individuals acts in ways that deny another individual, group, or subpopulation access to valued resources. So, in the context of ethnic relations, **ethnic discrimination** is the process by which the members of a more powerful and dominant ethnic subpopulation deny the members of another, less powerful and subordinate ethnic subpopulation full access to valued resources—such as jobs, income, education, health, prestige, power, or anything else that the members of a society value.

Today, the term **reverse discrimination** is often used to emphasize that programs designed to overcome the effects of past discrimination against members of a subordinate subpopulation often deny some members of the dominant subpopulation equal access to valued resources. What makes these programs so controversial is that those denied access to resources—say, particular classes of jobs—are usually not the ones who engaged in discrimination in the past. Thus, they feel cheated and angry—emotions that the victims of discrimination almost always feel. The phrase "reverse discrimination" is pejorative in that it emphasizes the net loss of resources for those who may no longer discriminate but whose forefathers did, so they ask: Is this fair? On the other side, those who must live with the legacy of past discrimination ask: How are the effects of past discrimination to be overcome? There is no easy answer to either of these questions, but one thing is clear: The term "discrimination" often becomes the centerpiece of ideological and political debate over ethnic tensions (Feagins, 1990; Kinder and Sanders, 1990; Ross, 1990; Thomas, 1990).

The process of discrimination is the most important force sustaining ethnicity in a society. Discrimination denies some people access to what is valued, making it a highly volatile process. Because discrimination varies in nature, degree, and form, we need to identify some of its dimensions.

Types of Discrimination

The ways in which discrimination is perpetrated against an ethnic population vary considerably. The most intense form is **genocide,** when members of an ethnic subpopulation are killed or, potentially, an entire ethnic group is exterminated. The Nazi death camps with their gas chambers constituted an effort at genocide; the exposure of Native Americans to diseases and then the carnage of the Indian wars resulted in the near-genocide of the original population in America. More recently, the systematic attempt at **ethnic cleansing** by the Serbs in the former Yugoslavia is another example of genocidal behavior. The dominant Serbs tried to rid—"cleanse"—Yugoslavia of Muslims and ethnic Albanians.

Expulsion is a somewhat less intense form of discrimination because those who are exiled from a society retain access to at least one highly valued resource: life. Expulsion is a common form of discrimination. For example, during the time of slavery in the United States, several American presidents, including Abraham Lincoln, contemplated the creation of a black state in Africa to which "free" black people would be sent. Expulsion is usually forced, but it is often the case that one group makes life so miserable for another that the latter leaves "voluntarily." Thus, the concept of expulsion has ambiguity: If we confine its use only to cases in which people are thrown out of a country by direct coercion, the importance of *indirect* expulsion—people packing up and leaving because their lives have been made so miserable—is underemphasized.

Segregation is a process of spatially isolating members of an ethnic subpopulation in areas where they cannot have the same access to valued resources as

A Mexican mother and her children.

do people who are not isolated. For instance, as we will see in Chapter 5, most African Americans were confined to the decaying cores of large cities during the post–World War II era by governmental and private housing policies; and as a result, they were denied access to the jobs, schools, and housing enjoyed by white Americans who moved to suburbia (see Box 1.3). The black townships and various rules of residence in South Africa mark another segregation pattern that historically denied access to resources. The Indian reservations that dot the American landscape are yet another form of segregation.

Exclusion is a pattern of discrimination that denies members of an ethnic group certain positions, independent of the effects of segregation. Slaves were denied basic citizenship rights. Only a few decades ago, African Americans were excluded from most craft unions; even in industrial unions, they were allowed to rise only to certain grade levels and not beyond. For many decades, African Americans and Latinos in the Southwest were excluded from the political arena through poll taxes, literacy tests, gerrymandering of districts, and other exclusionary tactics. Exclusion in the job sphere is especially harmful because it denies members of an ethnic group the money they could use to buy other valued resources—health care, housing, education, and political power. Exclusion from the political arena denies an ethnic group the power to move out of its subordinate position.

Box 1.3
Residential Segregation

Over the years, a series of statistical procedures have been developed to calculate the degree of residential segregation among various ethnic populations. The details of these calculations need not concern us here, but in essence, the higher the number for the "index of dissimilarity" the less likely are members of various ethnic groups to live in the same neighborhoods. A number of zero would mean no segregation, while a score approaching 100 would signal complete segregation. The index is calculated for all metropolitan areas and for cities that have more than 25,000 residents; each area or city is given an index score for any two ethnic groups. The average index scores between non-Hispanic whites and other ethnic groups are as follows for cities and metropolitan areas:

	Cities	Metropolitan Areas
White–Black	45	59
White–Asian	32	45
White–Hispanic	35	43
White–American Indian	39	59

Segregation is higher in metropolitan areas than in cities, a finding that should not be surprising, since non-Hispanic whites were the first to move out of the cities to suburbia. It should be emphasized that these are only averages; the range of scores varies enormously. For example, the score for blacks and whites reveals a high of 87 in Chicago and a low of 18 in Newark, California. The number 87 means that 87 percent of whites in Chicago would have to move to a new neighborhood for whites to be evenly distributed throughout the city. Even when cities reveal a high proportion of African Americans, the index can still be high. For instance, New York is 25 percent African American but still has a score of 85; Philadelphia is 43 percent black with a score of 81; Boston is 24 percent black and has a score of 76. The highest score for non-Hispanic whites and Hispanics is 77, and the lowest score is 12. In New York, which is 27 percent Hispanic, the index score is still 70; in Los Angeles with 47 percent Hispanic, the score is 67. For whites and Asians, the highest score is 69 and lowest is 15. New York and Los Angeles, which are both 10 percent Asian, have, respectively, scores of 54 and 49.

Thus segregation is still very evident in American society, and African Americans are the most segregated. When people are segregated, they are typically denied access to valued resources, such as adequate housing, good schools, health care, and better-paying jobs.

Source: Frey and Myers, 2002.

Selective inclusion is the process of allowing members of ethnic subpopulations into certain positions while at the same time excluding them from other positions. For instance, Jews in Europe historically were excluded from most economic, social, and political positions but were included in the world of finance. In the United States, early Asian immigrants were allowed access to some positions—the Chinese were laborers on the railroads and later ran small service businesses. According to Takaki (1993), the Japanese were denied access to the industrial labor market in California during the 1920s; as a result, many moved into the agricultural labor market, in which they used their entrepreneurial skills to become successful farmers and landowners. Today, many Asian immigrants are given easy access to ownership of small retail businesses but are excluded, to some degree, from white- and blue-collar positions in large companies. In the past and still today, Mexican American laborers were included in the low-wage farm labor workforce and, later, in other low-paying jobs in light industry, but they were excluded from better-paying economic positions as well as positions in the political and educational arena. Thus, *exclusion* and *selective inclusion* tend to operate simultaneously, in a pincerlike movement that denies access to some positions and opens access only to those areas that are often (though not always) financially unrewarding or lacking in power and prestige.

Abusive practices are patterns of action against the victims of discrimination by members of other ethnic groups and particularly by those charged with enforcement of the law. These practices may be intentional, but often they are not. However, for their victims it makes little difference because they must suffer. For example, in the United States it is typically in neighborhoods inhabited by poor and relatively powerless ethnic groups that environmental problems are, literally, dumped. Disposal sites are generally near the poor, causing some to label this process **environmental racism** (Bullard, 2000; Farhat, 2002). Or, to take another example, what is now labeled **racial profiling** occurs every single day in American cities when officers use ethnic markers to assess the likelihood of potential crime. The result is that members of particular ethnic populations are likely to be singled out for special surveillance and potential harassment by police officers (Johnson, 2000; Russell, 2001). These kinds of practices typically make the difficult lives of the ethnic poor even more difficult, and in so doing, they ensure that it will be hard for members of these ethnic groups to gain a greater share of resources.

The intensity of discrimination varies according to its type: from genocide and expulsion to physical segregation to exclusion, selective inclusion, and abuse. None is pleasant if you are on the receiving end. These patterns of discrimination have been implemented in various ways, but the underlying mechanisms of discrimination are much the same, as discussed below.

The Institutionalization of Discrimination

Acts by individuals to deny others access to valued resources are the most salient form of discrimination. When a white refuses to sell a house to an Asian, when a police officer physically abuses a member of a minority group, or when a supervisor refuses to promote an ethnic worker and these actions are taken simply because a person is a member of an ethnic group, discrimination is at work. These examples are *isolated* acts of discrimination if (1) they are not sanctioned by cultural values, beliefs, and norms; (2) they are not performed as a matter of policy within an organized structure such as a corporation, police department, board of realtors, school, or factory; and (3) they are not frequent and pervasive in the informal contact among people within an organization. In contrast, **institutionalized discrimination** exists when these individual acts are sanctioned by cultural values, beliefs, laws, and norms; when they are part of the way a social structure normally operates; and when they are a pervasive and persistent feature of the contact among people.

The distinction between isolated acts of discrimination and institutionalized discrimination is easier to make in a definition than in practice. For example, when discrimination is institutionalized in one sphere—say, housing practices—it becomes easier to commit acts of discrimination in other arenas, such as schooling, politics, or jobs. If enough people practice such isolated acts of informal discrimination, these acts become institutionalized. In the United States, civil rights laws and cultural beliefs do not condone discrimination as they once did; indeed, they demand that all individuals be given equal access to schools, jobs, housing, and other important resources. They even mandate punishments for those who discriminate, and they have led to the creation of watchdog and enforcement agencies. Yet individual acts of informal discrimination are so widespread in many communities that discrimination is informally institutionalized even in the face of formal prohibitions.

Thus, the process of institutionalized discrimination is subtle and complex. It can operate at formal and informal levels, and these two levels can even be in contradiction. Isolated acts of discrimination can increase in frequency when they constitute a normatively sanctioned and, hence, institutionalized form of discrimination.

The subtlety and complexity of institutionalized discrimination is demonstrated in the lingering effect of past patterns of discrimination that are now formally banned and no longer practiced. The legacy and cumulative effects of past discrimination can be so great that they prevent ethnic subpopulations from gaining equal access to resources. Many blacks (and Native Americans, Latinos, and others) are systematically denied by their present circumstances the same access to valued resources as whites have. Even if we could assume that no employer, real estate agent, teacher, or police officer currently acts in a discriminatory way, many African Americans and other ethnic groups would not have the same degree of access to resources as white Americans have because of their present location in segregated slums with a long history of exclusion from most spheres of mainstream life in America. Many African Americans today live in urban slums away from decent schools, housing, and jobs because of past patterns of discrimination. In this environment, they do not acquire the education, job skills, or motivation that would enable them to leave the slums and take advantage of new opportunities that were not available even thirty years ago.

An example of slum housing.

Thus, sometimes the legacy of the past operates as a barrier in the present and constitutes a pervasive pattern of discrimination. We must acknowledge that institutionalized discrimination has a lag effect beyond the period in the past when individuals and organizations practiced discrimination routinely.

Another facet of institutionalized discrimination is that it is often unintentional. This is certainly the case with the holdover effects of past discrimination, but more is involved. To take the most obvious example in the United States today—schools—it is now clear that the school curriculum, testing procedures, and classroom activities place some ethnic students at a disadvantage in comparison with other students. This type of discrimination is not intentional, at least in most instances; and it could be argued (albeit problematically) that schools facilitate the acquisition of the critical skills necessary for success and for overcoming the effects of past discrimination. Yet if the schools are organized in ways that are, for example, alien to students, that are unresponsive to the problems of poor children or immigrant children, and that are insensitive to the distinctive culture of a minority population, then the schools can become a source of discrimination. Students will have difficulty adjusting and will become discouraged—dropping out and finding themselves with few prospects for jobs and income. The school may not have intended this to occur—indeed, just the opposite—but the very nature of its structure and operation has worked to discourage students and, in so doing, has subtly and inadvertently discriminated against students whose access to resources is dramatically lowered when they drop out (Hilliard, 1988; McCarthy, 1990; Medina, 1988; Miller & Porter, 2007; Suh-Ruu, 2008; Trueba, 1986). In a society that uses educational credentials as a quick and easy way to sort people out in a labor market, the consequences for members of ethnic subpopulations who find the school experience unrewarding extend to all spheres of their life—job, home, income, and health.

Thus, the institutionalization of discrimination is an important force in ethnic relations. The pattern of institutionalization affects the type of segregation, exclusion, selective inclusion, and abuse that a subordinate ethnic subpopulation experiences, if it is not killed off or sent away. As the pattern of institutionalized discrimination changes, so do patterns of segregation, exclusion, selective inclusion, and abuse.

ETHNIC STRATIFICATION

Discrimination, as it operates to segregate, exclude, and selectively include members of a subordinate ethnic subpopulation within a society, produces a system of ethnic stratification. Because discrimination determines how many and which types of valued resources the members of an ethnic subpopulation are likely to have, it establishes the location of an ethnic subpopulation within the stratification system of a society. Moreover, discrimination also determines the patterns of mobility, if any, across social class lines.

For our purposes, **ethnic stratification** refers to several interrelated processes:

1. The amount, level, and type of resources—such as jobs, education, health, money, power, and prestige—an ethnic subpopulation typically receives.
2. The degree to which these **resource shares** locate most members of an ethnic subpopulation in various social hierarchies.
3. The extent to which these resource shares contribute to those distinctive behaviors, organizations, and cultural systems that provide justification to the dominant group for making the ethnic subpopulation targets of discrimination.

We can take almost any ethnic group—Latinos, for example (see Chapter 7)—and determine their average income, their level of political representation, and their average years of education. In performing this exercise, we soon find that, on the whole, many Latinos in America have relatively low incomes, are underrepresented in the halls of political power, and attain less education than Anglo-Americans. The statistics can be determined by simple counts of average income, years of education, and number of political offices held. The numbers show the share of resources that Latinos possess in American society.

One often finds, in addition, differences in the shares of resources *within* an ethnic subpopulation. There are affluent Latinos as well as very poor ones; their average level of affluence, power, and prestige tends to vary according to which subpopulation—Mexican American, Cuban, Puerto Rican, South or Central American—is being addressed. Yet when ethnic stratification is in evidence, a majority of a subpopulation does reveal a particular level and configuration of resource shares. On various social hierarchies—power, income and wealth, prestige, and education—a profile of resource shares locates a majority of the ethnic group at a particular place in the broader system of stratification. There are always deviations, of course, but when ethnic stratification is in force, these deviations apply to a minority of cases. Some Latinos, such as Mexican Americans, are located near the bottom of the power, income and wealth, prestige, and education hierarchies, thereby occupying the lower and working classes. There are middle- and upper-class Mexican Americans, to be sure, but they are a tiny minority of this subpopulation as a whole. This profile of resource shares and the resulting location on various social hierarchies contribute to the distinctiveness of Mexican Americans and, as a consequence, justify new and continuing prejudices and discrimination against them, thereby perpetuating the ethnic dimensions of social stratification.

In general, discrimination causes members of an ethnic subpopulation to be (1) overrepresented in lower and working classes or (2) overrepresented in a narrow range of middle-class positions, usually in small businesses of various kinds. As discrimination lessens, mobility to other classes and positions within classes occurs, but a holdover effect persists that limits such mobility for many.

Institutionalized discrimination, as it segregates, excludes, and selectively includes, determines the kinds and shares of resources received by members of an ethnic subpopulation; these shares locate them on society's hierarchies. By virtue of its pattern of resource shares and location on various social hierarchies, an ethnic subpopulation's distinctiveness is created and sustained. Thus, the principal consequence of ethnic discrimination is to give the broader stratification system in a society an ethnic dimension, one that is often more tension producing and volatile than the normal antagonisms between members of different social classes.

One rough measure of the effects of ethnic discrimination is the rate of poverty among various ethnic groups. The higher the poverty rate, the more an ethnic population has been subject to discrimination. Members of this population have been denied equal access to quality education and, thereby, jobs and income.

Table 1.1 summarizes the percentages of all persons, dual-headed families, female-headed families, and unattached individuals whose income falls below the official poverty line in 2008, the last year for which data are available from the Census Bureau's *American Community Survey* (2009). It is clear that non-Hispanic whites have the lowest levels of poverty of all ethnic subpopulations, except for the dual-head category where Asians/Pacific Islanders have a lower rate of poverty. In 2008, 13.2 percent of all persons in the United States were defined as poor, but as is also very clear, Latino, African American, and Native American/Alaskan Natives poverty rates are almost three times those for

TABLE 1.1 Percentages of Persons, Families and Family Types, and Unattached Individuals below Poverty Line, 2008

| | All Persons | Percentage in Poverty | | |
		Dual-Headed Families	Female-Headed Families	Unattached Individuals
All ethnicities	13.2%	11.5%	31.4%	20.8%
Non-Hispanic whites	8.6	6.4	21.5	17.7
Whites	11.2	9.4	27.2	19.1
Latinos/Hispanics	23.2	22.3	40.5	29.1
African Americans	24.7	23.7	40.5	28.8
Asians/Pacific Islanders	10.2	8.1	14.8	23.4
Native Americans/ Alaska Natives	22.5	22.5	—	—

Dashes represent data not reported by survey.
Source: U.S. Bureau of the Census, *Current Population Survey: Annual Social and Economic Survey*, 2009.

non-Hispanic whites and over double those for Asian Americans/Pacific Islanders. Marriage consistently reduces rates of poverty for whites (including Hispanics), non-Hispanic whites, and Asians/Pacific Islanders, but for Latinos, African Americans, and Native Americans/Alaska Natives, there is little difference between the overall rates of all persons and those in stable families. Thus, poverty is not simply the result of unstable families and a single source of income, but instead, it is built into the economic system and the ability of certain ethnics to secure adequate income for themselves and their families. Data such as these indicate that discrimination, or, at the very least, the legacy of past discrimination, is at work, pushing certain ethnics into poverty. For all ethnic categories, single-parent households headed by a female have dramatically increased rates of poverty, as might be expected by the fact that there is, at best, only one source of income and, in all likelihood, dependence upon income assistance from welfare agencies. Indeed, for most ethnic populations, the rate of poverty almost doubles for female-headed families. Interestingly, unattached individuals have high poverty rates for all ethnic subpopulations, clearly indicating that being free of family obligations does not make an individual immune to poverty.

Ethnic stratification is generated by discrimination whereby one or more ethnic subpopulation(s) act(s) in ways to deny other ethnic subpopulations access to valued resource such as income, power, prestige, education, health care, or anything that people value. As we reviewed earlier, discrimination can take many forms. We have discussed the more blatant forms, but as we will come to appreciate, discrimination can often be subtle and even unintended. Still, discrimination decreases people's access to resources throughout the world today, and it has been part of American society since its founding.

Rates of poverty are only a rough proxy for assessing ethnic discrimination and stratification. When people lack income to buy the necessities of life, this fact usually signals that they cannot get a job or, if they have a job, it does not pay enough. The ability to secure a job is often related to the amount of education that people have been able to secure, for, in a society where educational credentials determine who gets, and does not get, jobs that carry income, prestige, and even power, those without much education are doomed to low incomes; and as Table 1.1 emphasizes, many fall into poverty.

When children grow up in poverty, they are at a great disadvantage in the school system, which in turn means they will have difficulty in the job market. And when children do not have sufficient education and cannot, as adults, secure well-paying jobs, they often will not be able to make sufficient incomes to meet basic needs. We can see these mutually reinforcing consequences of education, jobs, and income by reviewing briefly the fate of ethnic subpopulations in their ability to generate access to education, jobs, and income. Thus, rates of poverty signal a chain of causes: Lack of education leads to poor job prospects that lead to low incomes, which ensure poverty. To anticipate the data that will be presented for each ethnic subpopulation, let us follow this causal chain in more detail.

TABLE 1.2 Median Family Income for Ethnic Subpopulations, 2007

Ethnic Subpopulation	Median Family Income
Non-Latino white	$65,652
Latino	42,074
African American	40,259
Native American/Alaska Native	40,310
Asian	77,046
Native Hawaiian/Other Pacific Islander	58,990
All households	**$61,173**

Source: 2010 *Statistical Abstract,* Table 36.

Table 1.2 reports the median family income of key ethnic subpopulations in the United States. Total median family income in 2007 varied considerably by ethnic group. The median income for all families was $61,173, with non-Latino whites and Asians evidencing incomes considerably above the median. In contrast, Latinos, African Americans, and Native Americans/Alaska Natives show median incomes significantly below the figure for the total population and even farther below the incomes of non-Latino whites and Asians. Since the median is a statistic that divides a population equally above and below a given distribution, this means that one-half of all Latinos, African Americans, and Native Americans/Alaska Natives earn incomes below the median. As a result, some portion of this lower half must live in poverty, for the median figure is not dramatically above the income figures that establish the poverty line for families of five or more individuals (and many poor families are large).

Table 1.3 reports the mean earnings of selected racial and ethnic populations by sex. One can see in the table that black and Latino mean earnings lag behind the earnings of white persons, 77 percent and 69 percent, respectively. Black men earn 69 percent of the mean earnings of white men, while Latino men earn 64 percent. Black women earn 95 percent of the mean earnings of white

TABLE 1.3 Mean Earnings by Race/Ethnicity and Sex, 2007

	Total	Percentage of White Income
White	$43,139	
Male	51,781	
Female	32,899	
Black	$33,333	77%
Male	35,668	69*
Female	31,317	95†
Latino	$29,910	69%
Male	33,040	64*
Female	25,262	77†

*Percentage of white male income.
†Percentage of white female income.
Source: 2010 *Statistical Abstract,* Table 227.

women, while Latino women earn 77 percent. Comparatively speaking, the mean earnings of black and Latino women are closer to the mean earnings of white women than those of black and Latino men relative to white men. However, the earnings differential between whites, blacks, and Latinos can serve as a constraint on the economic well-being of blacks and Latinos.

Income comes from work, and so a low income means that certain individuals cannot get higher-paying jobs. Table 1.4 presents the occupational distribution of selected ethnic subpopulations in the United States. As is evident, African Americans and Latinos are underrepresented in the best-paying occupational category, "Management/Professional." In contrast, whites and Asians are much more likely to be in managerial and professional occupations. Latinos and African Americans reveal much higher rates of employment in low-paying service jobs. Whites, African Americans, and Asians approximate the total population in sales and office jobs, which generally do not reveal a high-wage structure. Thus, the higher rate of poverty for particular ethnic subpopulations reflects low pay at work and, in many cases, periodic unemployment.

Low pay generally means that individuals do not have the educational credentials to qualify for higher-paying jobs. Table 1.5 summarizes the educational attainment of key ethnic subpopulations in the United States. As is immediately evident, Latinos and Native Americans/Alaska Natives have noticeably lower high school graduation rates than the rest of the population—a fact that condemns them to marginal economic success. About 28 percent of working adults have a college degree, but this too varies by ethnic group. Whites (29 percent with degrees) and Asians (50 percent with degrees) are much more likely to have educational credentials that give them access to better-paying jobs, whereas Latinos (13 percent with college degrees), African Americans (17 percent), and Native Americans/Alaska Natives (13 percent) are much less likely to have a college degree that can open up job opportunities.

Table 1.6 reports dropout rates from high school for 1990, 2000, and 2008. Although all dropout rates have declined somewhat between 1990 and 2008, rates for certain ethnic groups are still very high. The rates for Latinos and American Indian/Alaska Natives are dramatically higher than for the white population. These dropouts severely limit opportunities for jobs and income, and indeed, many who drop out are likely to be chronically unemployed. They have few chances for success, and they are likely to pass these lowered chances on to their children, who will be more likely to drop out of high school.

Without sufficient money and income or secure employment, individuals cannot gain access to other valued resources in American society. They cannot buy homes or cars; they cannot take interesting vacations; they cannot buy decent clothes; and they often do not have access to health care. Indeed, as Table 1.7 documents for selected ethnic groups, health insurance and, hence, access to the health care system is like any resource: It is unequally distributed. In 2004–2006, 15.3 percent of the population did not have health insurance, but this percentage is much higher for Latinos, Native Americans/Alaska Natives, and Native Hawaiians/Pacific Islanders. And while the rate for African Americans and Asians is lower than the rate for Latinos, Native Americans/Alaska Natives, and

TABLE 1.4 Occupational Distribution of Ethnic Subpopulations, 2007

	Percentage of Adults Employed in:				
	Management/ Professional	Service	Sales/Office	Construction/ Extraction/ Maintenance	Production/ Transport/ Materials Moving
Ethnic Subpopulation					
White	36.6%	15.0%	25.9%	10.0%	11.9%
Latino	17.7	24.3	21.5	16.1	18.0
African American	26.8	24.1	20.6	6.1	16.1
Asian	46.9	15.7	23.0	3.7	10.4
American Indian/ Alaska Native	25.3	22.4	22.9	13.5	14.3
Native Hawaiian/ Pacific Islander	21.9	22.9	29.5	10.5	14.8
Total U.S. labor force	**34.6%**	**16.7%**	**25.6%**	**9.7%**	**12.7%**

Source: 2010 *Statistical Abstract*, Table 36.

TABLE 1.5 Educational Attainment of Ethnic Subpopulations, 25 Years Old and Older, 2007

Ethnic Subpopulation	Percentage with High School Diploma or More	Percentage with Undergraduate Degree or More
White	81.0%	29.1%
African American	80.1	17.3
Native American	76.2	12.7
Asian	85.8	49.5
Latino	60.6	12.5
Total U.S. population	**84.5%**	**27.5%**

Sources: 2010 *Statistical Abstract*, Table 36.

TABLE 1.6 High School Dropout Rates by Ethnic Subpopulation, Ages 16–24, 1990–2008

Ethnic Subpopulation	Percentage Who Drop Out		
	1990	2000	2008
White	9.0%	6.9%	4.8%
Latino	32.4	27.8	18.3
African American	13.2	13.1	9.9
Asian/Pacific Islander	4.9	3.8	4.4
American Indian/Alaska Native	12.1	10.9	8.0
All persons 16–24	**12.1%**	**10.9%**	**8.0%**

Source: 2008 *Statistical Abstract*, The Condition of Education 2010, Indicator 20.

TABLE 1.7 Percentage of Ethnic Subpopulations without Health Insurance, Three-Year Average for 2004–2006

Ethnic Subpopulation	Percentage without Health Insurance
White	14.5%
Latino	32.7
African American	19.4
Native American/Alaska Native	31.4
Asian	16.1
Native Hawaiian/Pacific Islander	21.7
Total U.S. population	**15.3%**

Source: U.S. Bureau of the Census, *Current Population Survey, 2005 to 2007 Annual Social and Economic Supplements.*

Native Hawaiians/Pacific Islanders, it is still significantly higher than the rate for whites. Health insurance and access to medical care can be a life-and-death issue, as those who cannot easily enter the health care system have a much greater chance of being denied the ultimate resource: life and health. Indeed, along with difficulties in securing adequate health care, the persistence of prejudice, discrimination, and poverty increases both the physical and the psychological burdens on individuals, which, in turn, leads to shortened life spans and chronic health problems. For example, African Americans, who have probably endured more extreme discrimination than any other minority subpopulation, live, on average, five to six years less than white Americans; they have the highest infant mortality rate of all ethnic subpopulations (indeed, a rate that approaches the rates of impoverished nations); and they are more likely to suffer from heart disease, malignant neoplasms (cancers), influenza and pneumonia, diabetes, and unintentional injuries (their death rate from homicide is five times higher than that of whites). Thus, like any valued resource, health and life are unequally distributed in the United States (Spalter-Roth, Lowenthal, and Rubio, 2005).

One consequence of not having access to adequate health care is higher rates of infant mortality: Infants of some ethnic subpopulations are more likely to die soon after birth than those of other ethnic groupings. Overall, the United States has a very high infant mortality rate compared to other post-industrial nations. The reason for this is that a higher percentage of the American population is poor than in other post-industrial societies and a much higher percentage of Americans do not have health care insurance (indeed, virtually all post-industrial societies mandate health insurance or provide it through a government-sponsored program). Table 1.8 reports the infant mortality rates per 1,000 live births; and as is immediately evident, there are large differences. Black non-Hispanics and American Indians/Alaska Natives—the poorest of ethnic subpopulations in the United States—have the highest rates, with Hawaiians and part-Hawaiians also having very high rates. Another way to look at these rates is to ask: How many times greater than the non-Hispanic white rate is the rate of any particular ethnic population? This can be done by a simple ratio of infant mortality for each ethnic population against the non-Hispanic white rate. Looking down the right column in Table 1.8, it is evident that the very young children of black non-Hispanics, American Indians/Alaska Natives, Native Hawaiians, and Puerto Ricans are

TABLE 1.8 Infant Mortality Rates According to Race: United States

Race of Mother and Hispanic Origin of Mother	Rates*	Nonwhite/White Ratio
White, non-Hispanic	6.0	
Black, non-Hispanic	13.9	2.32
American Indian or Alaska Native	9.3	1.55
Asian or Pacific Islander	5.2	0.87
Chinese	3.4	0.57
Japanese	4.3	0.72
Filipino	5.9	0.98
Hawaiian and part-Hawaiian	8.2	1.37
Other Asian or Pacific Islander	5.5	0.92
Hispanic origin	5.9	0.98
Mexican	5.8	0.97
Puerto Rican	8.1	1.35
Cuban	4.7	0.78
Central and South American	5.2	0.87
Other and unknown Hispanic	6.8	1.13

*Infant deaths per 1,000 live births.
Source: National Center for Health Statistics, 2001, p. 153, as cited in Rubio and Williams, 2004.

much more likely to die than the very young children of non-Hispanic whites and other minority subpopulations. Thus, once again, the ethnic stratification system is a matter of life and death.

These kinds of data are presented throughout this book. Even though data often seem dry and dull, they are essential to the analysis of discrimination and ethnic stratification (see Box 1.4). They tell us where people stand in the class system and what opportunities are available to them. When certain minority subpopulations are consistently overrepresented in poverty categories, in low-paying jobs, and in low educational attainment categories, we can easily see how ethnic stratification works. Young people find school alienating; they drop out; they have dramatically lowered job prospects and, indeed, have few job prospects in a society that values education; they have low incomes or no income when unemployed; and as a result, they are much more likely to be in poverty, which, if chronic, destroys educational and occupational opportunities for the next generation while increasing the health risks for all members of poor families.

These kinds of data, however, give us only the outcome of ethnic stratification. They do not tell us *how discrimination actually works* to produce this outcome. Our goal in the next chapters is to explain the specific discriminatory processes that have worked to generate ethnic stratification in America. One of the processes sustaining ethnic stratification is ethnic prejudice.

ETHNIC PREJUDICE

The terms "prejudice" and "discrimination" are often uttered together, for it is presumed that prejudiced people discriminate, and vice versa. **Prejudice** is a set of beliefs and stereotypes about a category of people; hence, **ethnic prejudices** are beliefs and stereotypes about designated subpopulations who share certain identifying characteristics—biological, behavioral, organizational, or cultural— or at least are perceived to share these identifying characteristics. Those prejudices that lead to, and are used to justify, discrimination are negative, emphasizing the undesirable features of a subpopulation.

Does prejudice invariably lead to discrimination? In a classic study in the early 1930s, Richard La Piere (1934) observed in his travels with a Chinese couple that, despite a climate of hostility toward Asians in the United States at that time, the couple was served and treated courteously at hotels, motels, and restaurants. He was puzzled by this observation because all the attitude surveys at that time revealed extreme prejudice by white Americans toward the Chinese. La Piere sent a questionnaire to the owners of the establishments where he and his Asian companions had experienced courteous service, asking if they would "accept members of the Chinese race as guests in [their] establishment." More than 90 percent said no, thus demonstrating that prejudice and discrimination do not always go together.

Robert Merton (1949) defined four categories of people in his analysis of the relationship between prejudice and discrimination:

1. **All-weather liberals** who are not prejudiced and do not discriminate.
2. **Reluctant liberals** who are unprejudiced but will discriminate when it is in their interest to do so.

Box 1.4
The Intersection of Dimensions of Stratification: Ethnicity and Gender

Just as ethnic inequality intersects with class stratification, so do other dimensions of stratification. As the figures below document, males and females within an ethnic subpopulation do not receive the same levels of income. In general, women earn less than men—a fact that is accounted for by their distribution in different kinds of occupations. Men are overrepresented in higher-paying jobs, but there is considerable difference among ethnic subpopulations. As the figures below document, the median incomes of males and females differ, but to varying degrees. This variability is captured by computing the percentage of male income earned by females within ethnic subpopulations (see column 3 in the figures below). For all income earners, women earn on average about 77 percent of what males earn. Among all whites, including white Hispanics, this figure drops somewhat to about 75 percent, and drops a bit more among non-Hispanic whites, with women earning only about 73 percent of the income of males. Asians fall within the range of whites, with women earning about 77 percent as much as their male counterparts. Among the lowest-income ethnics, however, there is more convergence in the incomes of males and females. Latino and Native Hawaiian/Pacific Islander women earn about 90 percent of what Latino males earn; African American women earn about 88 percent as much as their male counterparts; and American Indian/Alaska Native women earn about 84 percent as much as their male counterparts. Moreover, if women's income is compared to that of white males, the differences across ethnic groups are even more pronounced. For example, among all income earners, women earn only 67 percent of the income of men. Latino women earn only 52 percent as much as white males; American Indian/Alaska Native women earn about 58 percent of what white males do; African American women earn about 62 percent; and Asian women earn the most—75 percent of the income of white males (Institute for Women's Policy Research, 2007, Table 2, p. 7). There is, then, both a gender and ethnic basis to class stratification.

	Median Income		Female Income as a
	Males	Females	Percentage of Male Income
All income earners	$42,210	$32,649	77.4%
Whites	45,727	34,133	74.7
Non-Hispanic whites	47,814	35,151	73.5
Latinos	27,494	24,737	90.0
African Americans	34,480	30,398	88.2
American Indians/ Alaska Natives	32,684	27,370	83.7
Asians	50,159	38,613	77.0
Native Hawaiians/ Pacific Islanders	34,641	31,171	90.0

Source: U.S. Bureau of the Census (2007), Table 7, p. 16.

3. **Timid bigots** who are prejudiced but afraid to show it.
4. **Active bigots** who are prejudiced and quite willing to discriminate.

In the study of motel owners, then, La Piere encountered timid bigots who, in face-to-face contact with an ethnic group, did not implement their prejudices.

Even though prejudice does not always translate into discrimination, it is an important force in ethnic relations, for several reasons. First, prejudicial beliefs and stereotypes highlight, usually unfairly and inaccurately, certain characteristics of an ethnic subpopulation. By spotlighting these characteristics, they make ethnic group members more identifiable, alerting others to their existence, separating them from the majority, and potentially making them easier targets for discrimination. Second, prejudices present negative images of an ethnic group, legitimizing discrimination against such "undesirable" persons. Third, prejudices arouse fears about, and anger toward, an ethnic group, placing members of the ethnic group in constant tension with those who are prejudiced and often making them vulnerable to unprovoked acts of discrimination. Fourth, prejudice creates a general climate of intolerance for differences exhibited not only by members of a selected ethnic group but other categories of individuals as well (such as individuals who are disabled or elderly).

Prejudice may generate potential or actual discrimination, but the reverse is also true. Acts of discrimination can generate prejudice or, as is often the case, reinforce existing prejudices. Most people feel they must justify their acts of discrimination; in a society like the United States, where cultural values emphasize equality and freedom, discrimination violates these values and must be rationalized and made to seem appropriate. Prejudice is one mechanism for doing this because it makes the denial of freedom and equality seem acceptable "in this one case" since "after all, these people are so . . . [fill in the prejudice]." Those who are victims of discrimination react in different ways: sometimes passively and other times aggressively. The results of people's reaction against prejudice and discrimination vary—prejudicial stereotypes are sometimes reinforced, other times changed or eliminated.

Thus, prejudicial beliefs based on negative and stereotypical portrayals of an ethnic subpopulation stimulate and sustain ethnic tensions. Such beliefs do not always translate into direct discriminatory action, but they target and highlight negative beliefs that arouse fear and anger, and create a culture of intolerance that can erupt into discriminatory acts or legitimate those that have been practiced in the past. Prejudice provides the rationale for discrimination, either before or after the fact, and is thus central to understanding discrimination and patterns of ethnic stratification.

ADAPTATIONS TO PREJUDICE AND DISCRIMINATION

When confronted with discrimination, members of a subordinate subpopulation respond. Usually, they seek to make the best of a difficult situation. Depending on the nature and magnitude of discrimination, as well as on other social conditions, several responses are possible: (1) passive acceptance, (2) marginal participation,

(3) assimilation, (4) withdrawal and self-segregation, (5) rebellion and revolt, (6) organized protest, and (7) ethnogenesis. Different segments of a minority population may resort to several of these adaptations at the same time, or a population may pass through different patterns of adaptation.

Passive Acceptance

If the power of an ethnic group is small and the magnitude of the discrimination great, members of the group may have no choice but to accept the discrimination. During the slavery era in the United States, it was nearly impossible for African slaves to do anything but accept subjugation. Yet even under severely oppressive conditions, populations acquire interpersonal techniques for dealing with their oppressors while maintaining their sense of identity and dignity. The stereotypical slave, as portrayed in Harriet Beecher Stowe's *Uncle Tom's Cabin,* offers a vivid example of such techniques. Bowing and scraping and repeated use of the phrase "Yes sir, yes sir" allowed Uncle Tom to gain favor with white people and to enjoy some degree of privilege. **Passive acceptance,** then, is often not passive but, rather, active manipulation of a situation. Some slaves were able to develop their own culture and to enjoy some of the basic pleasures of life through the appearance of passive acceptance. Of course, such a pattern of adjustment tends to perpetuate itself; the subordinate population does not initiate change, and the majority is not pressured to cease its discriminatory practices.

Marginal Participation

At times, subordinate ethnic subpopulations can find a niche where they can use their creative resources and prosper. In essence, these subpopulations are allowed **marginal participation.** For example, Jews have often been able to find business opportunities and to prosper in societies that actively discriminated against them. From the turn of the twentieth century to the present, many Chinese Americans have been able to prosper in small businesses providing services to the white American majority. Such marginal niches are created when the majority is not inclined to enter a specialized field. Marginal participation tends to be most successful when the minority population is small and does not enter areas dominated by the majority. It is probably for this reason that African Americans and Latinos have been unable to find specialized niches; their numbers are simply too great.

Assimilation

Assimilation is the process by which the members of an ethnic group become part of the broader culture and society, losing their distinctive character. Minorities that are less identifiable biologically and culturally are more readily assimilated. Ethnic populations that can be easily identified, however, have greater difficulty assimilating. It is for this reason that white ethnic groups in

Civil rights March on Washington for jobs and freedom, Washington, DC.

America, such as the Protestant Irish and Germans, have become largely assimilated, although enclaves are thriving in some large eastern cities. Other Caucasian migrants, such as Poles, Italians, and Catholic Irish, have also tended to assimilate, although the East and Midwest have cohesive ethnic cultures of these populations. African Americans, in contrast, have had a more difficult time assimilating because of their visibility and the resulting ease with which the majority can locate them as targets of discrimination.

Withdrawal and Self-Segregation

Another adaptation to discrimination is withdrawal and the creation of a self-sustaining "society" within the broader society. Such **self-segregation** enables a population to create and support their own communities, businesses, schools, leadership, churches, and other social forums. For example, the early Black Muslim movement in America advocated a separate African American community, self-supporting and isolated from "white" institutions. Urban communities as well as rural communes were established and still prosper, although there has been a clear trend away from complete withdrawal and isolation among many Black Muslims. Self-segregation is a difficult adaptation to maintain. Opportunities are necessarily limited compared to those in the broader society. As a result, some seek these outside opportunities. Moreover, economic, political, and social isolation is often difficult to sustain in urban, media-dominated societies, in which alternatives and options constantly present themselves.

Rebellion and Revolt

Subordinate ethnic subpopulations do not always accept, assimilate, withdraw, or marginally participate. Frequently they rebel. Such **rebellion** can take a number of forms, one being general hostility and aggressive behavior toward the majority. Few white Americans would feel comfortable walking through a black ghetto or a Chicano barrio, because they fear that there is some likelihood of intimidation and assault. Another form of rebellion is rioting, such as the widespread urban riots in the United States in the 1960s and the turmoil associated with the Rodney King beating in Los Angeles in the early 1990s. All forms of rebellion involve minorities' "striking back" and venting their frustrations, and at times, these revolts become extremely violent, mobilizing people for mass killings.

Organized Protest

Rebellious outbursts are often part of a larger social movement and, hence, may become **organized protests** when subordinate ethnic groups become organized to make broad-based and concerted efforts to change patterns of discrimination. The civil rights movement represents one such effort. Beginning with sit-ins and freedom rides in the 1960s, progressing to large-scale demonstrations (sometimes boiling over into riots), and culminating in creation of successful national organizations that effectively changed many legal and social patterns, the civil rights movement of African Americans successfully challenged pervasive discriminatory practices. The movement has been far from totally successful, however, since substantial integration of African Americans into the American mainstream has not occurred. But when an ethnic population is large and organized, it can generate political power and initiate some degree of social change. When minorities become majorities in cities and regions, as was the case in the late twentieth century in the United States, they can wield additional power and can force changes in old patterns of discrimination.

Ethnogenesis

At times, prejudicial beliefs and patterns of discrimination assume that individuals from diverse cultural and ancestral backgrounds are "all alike." For example, Asians as an ethnic subpopulation are a very diverse mix of persons who have very little in common, except an eye fold that makes them an easy target for prejudice and discrimination. Indeed, Asian Americans come from a broad range of societies with vastly different cultures—to name just a few: Korea, Japan, China, Vietnam, Philippines, Cambodia, and Laos. Similarly, Arab Americans also come from diverse societies and possess different religious affiliations. Historically, Native Americans or "Indians" as an ethnic category represented diverse cultures across the North American landmass. Yet despite their differences, prejudice and discrimination often treat target ethnics *as if* they are all the same. Asian Americans, Native Americans, and Arab Americans are portrayed by prejudicial beliefs as the same, justifying common forms of discrimination against them.

In fact, the Census Bureau's classification of ethnic groups implicitly reaffirms—in a manner certainly not intended—the lumping of individuals with very different backgrounds and cultures into one "ethnic category." The same thing could be said for chapters in a book on ethnicity, such as the one you are now reading.

One result of this process of categorization is for discrimination and prejudicial beliefs to "fulfill their own prophecy." Victims of discrimination who are lumped into the same ethnic category may have little in common except their similar treatment by the majority of a population. At times, this common experience leads to the creation of a new ethnic identity among the victims of discrimination who share common experiences as a result of prejudice and discrimination. This process of creating a new ethnic identity can be termed **ethnogenesis,** and it represents a final type of reaction to prejudice and discrimination.

The concept of ethnogenesis is often used to explain how ethnic subpopulations reveal a mix of characteristics, some involving assimilation into the dominant culture and others unique to their particular backgrounds (Greeley, 1974). We are using the term in a somewhat different way: to address the process whereby new ethnic identities are created as a response to prejudice and discrimination. The most dramatic example of this process is the fate of Arab Americans, examined in Chapter 9, who are divided by their countries of origin and religion (Islam, Christianity, and Judaism) but must endure prejudices that assume that they "are all alike" and that lead to similar experiences with discrimination. As a result of their common experiences, Arab Americans appear to be developing a new kind of ethnic identity, built around certain common traditions and around similar experiences with prejudice and discrimination by non-Arabs. To a lesser degree, Asians have also generated a certain level of common ethnic identity based on their common experiences with prejudices and discrimination, as have Native Americans. The same can be said for African Americans who, as slaves, came from diverse cultures but who, over centuries of prejudice and discrimination, have developed a unique "black" culture that unites all African Americans.

SUMMARY

Ethnic antagonism is one of the oldest and most pervasive dimensions of human social organization. To study this phenomenon, it is necessary to define terms and key concepts. The term "race" is of little importance biologically, but it is relevant sociologically. For if people perceive and believe others to be biologically distinctive and different, superficial biological traits become an important consideration in the formation of ethnicity. For our purposes, "ethnicity" refers to the history as well as the behavioral, organizational, and cultural features of people that make them distinctive and distinguishable from others. People can be distinguished on the basis of superficial biological traits, but these traits are associated with presumed behavioral, organizational, and cultural features—that is, with ethnicity.

The term "ethnic group" is commonly used, but we prefer "ethnic subpopulation." The latter term emphasizes the fact that people who are distinguished on the basis of an interrelated cluster of characteristics—biological, cultural, behavioral, and organizational—constitute a population more than a closed group. They are not all necessarily engaged in face-to-face contact, as the notion of "group" implies. To be sure, people's involvement in local groups and other structures sustains their distinctive patterns of organization, but these do not embrace the population as a whole. Ethnic subpopulations exist, instead, within a larger, more inclusive population. This point is not merely semantic; it is fundamental to an understanding of the dynamics of ethnicity.

The term "minority group" is also limited. Not all ethnic subpopulations subject to discrimination are minorities. They can constitute the majority in a community or in a nation as a whole. The underlying issue is *power*. Which groups have the power to limit the activities of other groups? More accurate terms are *"super*ordinate ethnic subpopulations" and *"sub*ordinate ethnic subpopulations."

Discrimination is the process of denying others access to valued resources. Ethnic discrimination occurs when members of a superordinate ethnic subpopulation are able to limit or deny members of a subordinate ethnic population access to valued resources—jobs, income, education, power, health care, and anything else that is valued and prized in a society. Ethnic discrimination surfaces in several different forms: genocide, or the systematic killing of members in a subordinate ethnic population; expulsion, or the exiling of all or selected members of an ethnic population; segregation, or the spatial confinement or isolation of members of an ethnic group so that they have difficulty gaining access to resources; exclusion, or the denial of rights to positions in a society that provide access to valued resources; and selective inclusion, or the confinement of members of an ethnic subpopulation to a narrow range of positions in the society. In addition to these forms of discrimination are a wide range of abusive practices against targeted ethnics. These types of discrimination gain effectiveness as discrimination becomes institutionalized. We define "institutionalized discrimination" as individual acts of discrimination that are (1) pervasive; (2) culturally supported in norms, beliefs, and values; and (3) lodged in social structures as matters of policy and practice. The more institutionalized the discrimination is, the more a subordinate ethnic subpopulation is segregated, excluded, and selectively included, while being vulnerable to genocide and expulsion. Discrimination is thus the central process underlying ethnic problems in society.

Institutionalized discrimination produces ethnic stratification. When members of a subordinate ethnic subpopulation receive only certain types and levels of valued resources, it becomes possible to establish their location on the social hierarchy of society. On the basis of this location, the distinctiveness of an ethnic group is retained, thereby making it a target of further prejudice and discrimination.

"Prejudice" refers to negative and stigmatizing beliefs, concepts, and stereotypes about people; "ethnic prejudice" is based on negative beliefs, conceptions, and stereotypes about members of a subpopulation distinguishable in their history and biological, behavioral, cultural, and organizational features. Prejudice and discrimination are not perfectly correlated, but discrimination cannot be easily institutionalized without widespread prejudice among dominant ethnic subpopulations.

Prejudice and discrimination force their targets to respond and adapt. Assimilation, or the elimination of ethnically distinct characteristics and adoption of those of the superordinate ethnic population, is one method of adaptation. At the other extreme are rebellion and revolt against superordinate ethnic groups, with the goal being redistribution of power and, hence, changes in the patterns of discrimination. Another response to discrimination is organized protest, often arising out of or even prompting acts of rebellion, in which ethnic groups and their allies organize to change patterns of discrimination. Yet another response is withdrawal and self-segregation of the subordinate ethnic group in order to isolate itself from the discriminatory acts of others. Members of an ethnic group may choose to accept their position passively, or they may participate marginally, finding narrow niches in which they can secure resources.

This chapter presents many useful terms and distinctions that will deepen our understanding of and provide a perspective on ethnic relations in America. These terms and distinctions do not explain ethnic relations; they merely describe them. We also need to know *why* people focus on perceived ethnic differences, *why* they discriminate, *why* they hold prejudices, and *why* superordinate populations force subordinate groups to adapt in certain ways. Explaining these "why" issues is the job of theory. Within the framework of definitions and distinctions developed in this chapter, we can now move on to explore the theories that have been used to explain ethnicity, prejudice, discrimination, and other aspects of ethnic relations.

POINTS OF DEBATE

In any society where distinct ethnic subpopulations exist, the issue of ethnicity is a subject of debate and controversy. No society revealing ethnic differences has ever been able to organize itself in ways that avoid the tension and conflict accompanying ethnic identity. The United States is not an exception; indeed, American society is one of the few in history that has sought to integrate so many large and diverse ethnic subpopulations into its cultural core. The problems of ethnicity in the United States have stimulated and continue to create many points of debate. When reading the coming chapters, keep in mind the following controversial issues.

1. The "first American dilemma": How can a society that values equality and freedom engage in systematic discrimination against minority subpopulations? This question is rhetorical because the evidence is irrefutable that discrimination has occurred, and continues to occur, on a massive and long-term scale. Can the accumulated effects of such discrimination be undone?
2. The "second American dilemma": Can the values of freedom and equality be used to justify efforts to compensate the descendants of past discrimination? An affirmative answer to this question has many implications, all of which

are debatable: (a) Are Americans willing to spend billions of tax dollars to create jobs, housing, and educational programs to overcome the effects of past discrimination? (b) Is private enterprise willing or able to participate on a massive scale in creating jobs for members of particular ethnic groups who have been the victims of this legacy of discrimination? (c) Are white Americans willing to give up some of their access to valued resources so that disadvantaged minority groups can increase their access, or is such action simply going to encourage accusations of "reverse discrimination"?

3. If Americans are unwilling to meet the challenges posed by the second American dilemma, what is the alternative? Conflict and violence among ethnic groups are escalating; poverty among ethnic groups is on the rise; out-of-wedlock childbearing is reaching epidemic proportions (now 63 percent among African Americans); substance abuse and other social problems among minority groups are growing; the number of crimes committed by minority group members is increasing; and innumerable problems are arising from the accumulated effects of past discrimination. This reality confronts Americans in their daily lives. What is to be done? Nothing? Build more prisons? Hire more police? Actively try to address the problems at enormous cost? What are the viable options? Such questions are ultimately part of any discussion of ethnicity in America.

KEY TERMS

abusive practices, 10
active bigots, 24
all-weather liberals, 22
assimilation, 25
discrimination, 6
environmental racism, 10
ethnic cleansing, 7
ethnic discrimination, 6
ethnic group, 6
ethnic population, 6
ethnic prejudices, 22
ethnic stratification, 13
ethnic subpopulation, 6
ethnicity, 3
ethnogenesis, 28
exclusion, 8
expulsion, 7

genocide, 7
institutionalized discrimination, 11
marginal participation, 25
minority group, 6
organized protests, 27
passive acceptance, 25
prejudice, 22
race, 2
racial profiling, 10
rebellion, 27
reluctant liberals, 22
resource shares, 13
reverse discrimination, 7
segregation, 7
selective inclusion, 10
self-segregation, 26
subpopulations, 6
timid bigots, 24

Visit our text-specific website at www.mhhe.com/aguirre7e for valuable resources for both students and instructors.

CHAPTER 2

Explaining Ethnic Relations

*T*here are many ways to understand social events and processes. One is by reviewing the history of events leading up to a present situation of interest. Another is by simply describing in detail what is occurring in a situation. Thus, reviewing the history of discrimination against selected ethnic subpopulations will inevitably increase our understanding of discrimination. Similarly, a detailed description of who is discriminating against whom in the present will further help us understand ethnicity and the process of ethnic discrimination. A third means of understanding events is to see them as manifestations of more general and universal social forces. Science always seeks to develop abstract theories outlining the relations among social forces that produce certain outcomes, not only in the present but also in the past and into the future. The goal of scientific **theory** is to explain with more general and abstract concepts a wide range of empirical events. Discrimination is not unique to the United States, nor is it unique in history. Humans have long discriminated against those who were "different"; and so, while the history and present dynamics of ethnic discrimination may have some unique features tied to American history and present circumstances, *the underlying dynamics of prejudice and discrimination* have been occurring for most of the time that humans have lived on earth.

In the popular mind, a theory is often portrayed as mere speculation, but in science, a theory is an *explanation of why and how whole classes of events occur*—in our case in this book, how and why ethnic discrimination has been so prominent in the history of American society. A theory is not wild-eyed speculation, but instead, a very precise and sober outline of the forces in play as they feed off each other and produce an outcome not only here in the United States but elsewhere in the world and back in time, and on into the future. Theory must be abstract to have this kind of explanatory power; it must rise above unique, historical, and contextual, particular empirical events—which can be fascinating in themselves—and examine what is *generic, universal,* and *timeless.* Theory produces a different kind of knowledge than history and description; and as will become evident, we use a relatively simple theory to organize our portrayal of the history of ethnic discrimination and our descriptions of the causes and consequences of discriminating against particular ethnic populations. A theory, then, can help us understand why history played out along a particular path, and why present conditions currently exist. Theory does not answer all questions that we may have, but it helps explain how and why events like prejudice and discrimination have consistently occurred in history, how and why they can still be found in the present-day world, and for our purposes, how and why they operate in the United States.

Many different theories exist concerning ethnic relations. Our goal in this chapter is to pull these theories together so that we have a coherent framework within which to examine specific ethnic groups in America—African Americans, Latinos, Native Americans, Asian Americans, Arab Americans, and European-origin white ethnics. The first step is to review the range of diversity in existing theories; later we can incorporate the strengths of each theory into a more general one that can guide us throughout our review of ethnic relations in America.

THEORIES OF ETHNIC RELATIONS

Assimilation Theories

Part of the early American creed was a belief that successive waves of ethnic immigrants could be incorporated into the mainstream of social life. Robert Park, one of the earliest American theorists on ethnic relations, saw such assimilation as "a process of interpenetration and fusion in which persons and groups acquire the memories, sentiments, and attitudes of other groups, and, by sharing their experience and history, are incorporated with them into a common cultural life" (Park and Burgess, 1924:735).

Park proposed stages of assimilation, beginning with contact among diverse ethnic groups. Out of such contact comes a **competitive phase,** in which ethnic populations compete over resources, such as jobs, living space, and political representation. The next stage is an unstable **accommodation,** in which immigrants and their descendants are forced to change and adapt to their new environment. During this phase, there is some degree of stabilization of relations between immigrants and those in the host society, even if this accommodation forces migrants into lower social strata. Moreover, once ethnic stratification exists, the pace of assimilation is dramatically reduced, although Park believed that, ultimately, even a lower-class, subordinate ethnic subpopulation could be assimilated. It might take hundreds of years, but eventually assimilation would occur. Thus, the last phase in Park's theory is assimilation in which the migrant ethnic merges with other ethnic groups (Park, 1950).

More recent assimilation theories have been more explicit about (1) the nature of the host society and culture to which migrant ethnic groups must adapt and (2) the various types, levels, and degrees of assimilation that can develop. For instance, as Milton Gordon (1964) emphasizes, it is to "the middle class cultural patterns of . . . white, Anglo-Saxon" culture that immigrants to the United States have had to adapt. Various ethnic subpopulations may evidence, however, different degrees of progress in adapting to the dominant Anglo-Saxon culture. **Cultural assimilation** occurs when the values, beliefs, dogmas, ideologies, language, and other systems of symbols of the dominant culture are adopted. Most ethnic groups become, to varying degrees, culturally assimilated. In contrast to cultural assimilation, **structural assimilation** occurs when migrant ethnic groups become members of the primary groups within dominant ethnic subpopulations—their families, close friends, cliques within clubs, and groups within organizations. Gordon emphasizes that structural assimilation is more difficult to achieve than cultural assimilation because it involves penetration into the close interactions and associations of dominant ethnic groups. Even when members of ethnic groups penetrate more secondary and formal organizational structures—schools, workplaces, and political arenas—they may still lack more primary and personal ties with members of dominant ethnic groups.

Other types of assimilation are based on the degree of cultural and structural assimilation an ethnic group is able to achieve: **marital assimilation,** or the emergence of high rates of intermarriage between the migrant and dominant ethnic groups; **identification assimilation,** in which individuals no longer see themselves as distinctive and, like members of dominant groups, stake their personal identities to participation and success in the mainstream institutions of a society; **attitude-receptional assimilation,** or the lack of prejudicial attitudes and stereotyping on the part of both dominant and migrant ethnic groups; **behavioral-receptional assimilation,** or the absence of intentional discrimination by dominant ethnic groups against subordinate ethnic groups; and **civic assimilation,** or the reduction of conflict between ethnic groups over basic values and access to the political arena.

According to Gordon, assimilation occurs over generations in the United States. By the third generation, a considerable amount of assimilation has occurred, especially among white ethnic groups. They have become culturally assimilated; they have made inroads into the primary groups or, at the very least, into the organizations of the Anglo-Saxon core; they have begun to intermarry with members of other ethnic groups; they identify with the institutional system; they are victims and perpetrators of fewer prejudices, stereotypes, and acts of discrimination; and they are engaged in less conflict over values and political rights. But what about nonwhite ethnic groups? For them, the assimilation process, Gordon (1981) admits, is slower, but he is optimistic that even the most identifiable subordinate ethnic groups in America—African Americans and Native Americans—are on the path to further assimilation.

Assimilation theories probably paint an overly benign view of ethnic relations, viewing assimilation as inexorable. Yet they provide us with a way to measure how far an ethnic group has moved into the dominant culture along various dimensions—cultural, structural, marital, identification, attitude, behavioral, political. Indeed, the amount and pace of assimilation along these dimensions provide clues about how much and what type of discrimination has been working against an ethnic subpopulation. For example, if we find that, after hundreds of years of coexistence with the dominant Anglo-Saxon society,

African Americans and Native Americans are structurally unassimilated and only partially assimilated in terms of culture, reveal low rates of intermarriage with other ethnic groups, identify only partially with the society and its institutions, suffer many prejudicial stereotypes, experience acts of discrimination, and remain partially disenfranchised from the political arena, then it is likely that massive informal and institutional discrimination still exists. Assimilation theories do not explain how these discriminatory forces operate, but they provide a sense of what their consequences are.

Pluralism Theories

Partially in reaction to the "melting pot" assumption underlying most assimilation theories are those theories that stress the process of maintaining patterns of ethnicity. Indeed, the maintenance of distinctive cultural, organizational, and behavioral characteristics is often a way of coping with discrimination. A distinct ethnic identity provides sources of support and guidance in a sometimes hostile world. When ethnic identity is nurtured, a pluralistic and permanent mosaic of ethnic subpopulations becomes evident.

Most scholars who subscribe to this more pluralistic view do not deny that some assimilation into the dominant segments of a society occurs. Rather, they argue, ethnicity remains a powerful force, even among white ethnic groups who are often presumed to be fully assimilated. Nathan Glazer and Daniel Moynihan (1970) were among the first to emphasize that even as many of their customs are replaced with those of the dominant Anglo-Saxon society, white ethnic groups continue to reveal residential, behavioral, organizational, and cultural patterns that mark their distinctive ethnic identity, one that subtly separates them from the middle-class, Anglo-Saxon Protestant core.

The term **ethnogenesis** is often employed to describe this process of creating a distinctive ethnicity as a means of adapting to discrimination, even as some degree of assimilation occurs. Andrew Greeley (1971, 1974) has been one of the most forceful advocates of this position, arguing that there is considerable ethnic diversity in America that simply cannot be explained by assimilation models. Ethnic groups not only retain elements of their past, but they also construct and create new ways of adjusting to discrimination. As generations pass, and ethnic groups come to share many characteristics with the dominant white, Anglo-Saxon Protestant segments of society, they selectively retain elements of their ethnic heritage and they create new elements. For example, third- and even fourth-generation Irish Americans, Poles, and Italians continue to display their ethnic identities; moreover, they often strive to create new symbols to mark with pride their ethnic heritage.

Pluralistic theories offer an important corrective to assimilation theories, but they do not explain adequately the broader social forces that cause and sustain discrimination. If ethnic pluralism is, to some degree, a consequence of discrimination, these theories have little to say about those forces producing such discrimination. They are, instead, concerned with ethnogenesis, per se, rather than the external structures in the society that set ethnogenesis in motion.

Biological Theories

The spectacular rise of sociobiology in recent decades has produced another kind of theory of ethnogenesis. This theory is different from pluralist theories in its emphasis on the biological underpinnings of ethnicity. What are these biological underpinnings? The basic position of early sociobiology was that the units of natural selection are the genes, rather than the individual. The individual is, from a sociobiological point of view, only a temporary house or vessel for genes that seek to survive in the gene pool. Thus, genes are seen as "selfish" and as driven to maximize their fitness, or their capacity to remain in the gene pool. Sociobiological theories of ethnicity, then, start with these assumptions and see them as a driving force operating to produce and sustain ethnicity (Turner and Maryanski, 1993). How do these evolutionary and biological forces operate? Pierre van den Berghe (1981) has provided the most forceful argument from a sociobiological perspective; let us examine his answer to this question.

According to van den Berghe and most sociobiologists, social structures are merely "survival machines" that exist to maintain the fitness of genes. Sociobiologists have introduced two concepts to explain why "selfish genes" create social structures or "survival machines." One concept is **kin selection** or **inclusive fitness,** which holds that family structures are a strategy allowing males and females to maximize their fitness by keeping as much of their genetic material as possible in the gene pool. Moreover, when family members help each other, they are ensuring that a portion of their genes remains in the pool (since brothers, sisters, parents, and offspring all share 50 percent of the same genes; grandparents, half siblings, uncles, aunts, nieces, and nephews share 25 percent of their genes; and first cousins, half nephews, and great grandchildren share 12 percent of their genes). Thus, familism is simply a strategy that allows genes to stay in the pool. The other concept is **reciprocal altruism,** which was developed to explain why nonfamily members help each other survive; for if maximization of fitness is the goal of genes, an explanation is needed for the fact that people help others with whom they do not share any genes. Reciprocal altruism seeks to provide this explanation: People offer assistance to nonkin because they know that at some future time their acts of altruism will be reciprocated by those they help. Such reciprocation promotes fitness and, thereby, enables individuals to keep their genes in the pool.

Van den Berghe uses these two concepts—kin selection and reciprocal altruism—to explain ethnicity. He extends the idea of kin selection to a larger subpopulation. Historically, larger kin groups (composed of lineages) constituted a breeding population of close and distant kin who sustained trust and solidarity with one another and mistrusted other breeding populations. Van den Berghe coins the term **ethny** for "ethnic group." An ethny is an extension of these more primordial breeding populations, a cluster of kinship circles created by endogamy (in which mate selection is confined to specific groups) and territoriality (physical proximity of its members and relative isolation from nonmembers). An ethny represents a reproductive strategy for maximizing fitness beyond the narrower confines of kinship, because by forming an ethny—even a very large one of millions of people—individuals create bonds with those who can help preserve their fitness, whether by actually sharing genes or, more typically, by reciprocal acts of altruism with fellow ethnys. An ethny is, therefore, a manifestation of more basic "urges" to help "those like oneself." Although ethnys become genetically diluted as their numbers increase and become subject to social and cultural definitions, the very tendency to form and sustain ethnys is the result of natural selection, which produced biological tendencies for people who share genetic material to help each other.

Thus, sociobiology provides an evolutionary explanation—a highly controversial one, we might add—for why members of an ethnic group band together and maintain distinctiveness. While this perspective has not gained a wide following among sociologists, sociobiology has taken center stage in the field of biology; as a result, we need to be aware of theories emanating from this quarter.

Psychological Theories

The most prominent psychological approach to ethnic relations is **social identity theory** (Hogg, 2006; Tajfel and Turner, 1979; Turner, 1975; Turner et al., 1987). Individuals have many potential identities revolving around their perceptions of themselves as persons. These perceptions are a cluster of cognitions, emotions, and self-evaluations that operate at many different levels. One level is the identities that individuals have of themselves in specific roles, or *role-identities*, such as student, father, mother, and worker. For each role that they play, people have a set of cognitions and emotions about who they are when playing a role, and they generally evaluate themselves by their ability to play a role successfully. Another level of identity is a more global *self-conception* that people carry with them to all roles; this is a more general identity that once again involves cognitions, emotions, and evaluations that people make about their "whole self." A third level, and the one most relevant to ethnic relations, is a *social identity* that emerges when people see themselves as members of a social category vis-à-vis other social categories. One kind of social identity, for example, is the identity of being male or female; this identity emerges by virtue of being categorized as a male or female, with the categories taking on greater definition when males and females see themselves as belonging to opposite categories. The same can be true for ethnicity as a social category: when people see themselves as a member of a particular category—say, African American—they become attuned to a set of beliefs, rules, and practices typical of those so categorized. Moreover, this categorization takes on greater salience and power when it is juxtaposed with other ethnic categories—say, white ethnics. It is this juxtaposition of categories and the different rules, practices, and beliefs of people belonging to these categories that give them power to shape how individuals see themselves, how they evaluate themselves, and how they are prepared to act.

A long tradition of research and theorizing on social identities emphasizes certain properties of such identities (see Hogg, 2006, for a brief review). First, social identities are collective; individuals see themselves as members of a category and others as members of another category. Social identities almost always involve an "us vs. them" orientation. Second, there is an evaluation of the membership in a social category (that is, the worth of those in this category), and this evaluation is compared to the evaluation of people in other categories. Third, there is a kind of depersonalization of members in social categories. This is not to say that people are dehumanized, but the attributes of individuals in a category are not tied to specific individuals; rather, they are typifications about the nature of *all who are in a given category.* Fourth, by virtue of this categorization, people become aware of templates or *prototypes* about the nature of people in a given category, how these people behave, what they believe, and how worthy they are. The prototype for members of one category—say, Latinos—takes on greater salience when it is juxtaposed with the presumed prototype governing people in another ethnic category—say, African Americans.

Psychological theories emphasize social identities as part of a natural cognitive process of placing self and others in categories. Individuals are motivated to see themselves and others as representatives of social categories because categorization reduces uncertainty, enhances self-feelings and esteem, and makes them feel part of a larger collectivity. As we have just seen, biological theories often argue that there is a biological basis to ethnic categorization, but most psychological theories do not go this far. More sociological approaches emphasize that when people can be distinguished by ethnic markers (speech, culture, superficial biological features) and when they compete for resources, these markers take on greater significance. And, as we will see shortly, when ethnicity is associated with unequal distribution of resources among ethnic subpopulations, the differences between ethnics are given added force.

The end result is for members of ethnic categories to develop a social identity of themselves and to adopt the template or prototype of beliefs, rules, and behaviors associated with membership in a particular social category. And, the more conflict, competition, and stratification exists among ethnic categories, the more salient social identities become and the more individuals with these identities will see themselves as being engaged in an "us vs. them" struggle.

Once social identities are formed, they take on a life of their own. Individuals are born into families whose members carry these identities, with the result that the young are socialized into the prototype of beliefs, norms, and behaviors appropriate to this identity. And, if the young have high rates of interaction with non-family members who hold this same identity, socialization moves beyond the family to peers and neighborhood organizations. So, as individuals acquire other types of identities—that is, their role-identities and more global self-conceptions—they also learn a *social identity* revolving around cognitions, feelings, and evaluations of self as a member of a distinctive social category.

Human Ecology Theories

Also drawing inspiration from biology are ecological theories stressing the forces of competition, selection, and "speciation" of distinctive ethnic groupings.

Robert Park's assimilation theory was couched in a larger ecological framework for analyzing urban areas (Park, 1916; Park and Burgess, 1924). This framework emphasized that living patterns in urban areas are produced by competition for scarce resources—land, housing, and jobs. Human groups exist in a kind of Darwinian struggle for survival, each trying to find a viable social niche. Thus, as populations migrate to urban areas, they accelerate the level of competition for resources with those already present and, Park believed, set in motion the processes of accommodation and assimilation.

More recent ecological theories stress that competition for resources often escalates the level of conflict between ethnic subpopulations, forcing subordinate ethnic groups into segregated housing niches and a narrow range of economic positions. Once members of an ethnic group find such niches, their boundaries and distinctiveness are preserved, thereby making them easier targets of discrimination. Susan Olzak (1986, 1992) is one of several scholars working in the human ecology tradition. Her theory holds that violence between ethnic subpopulations, especially attacks by members of the dominant group on subordinate groupings, occurs when members of subordinate ethnic subpopulations move into the occupational and housing niches of superordinate groups. Acts of violence against these mobile subordinates increase as members of the dominant subpopulation feel threatened. For example, Olzak (1992) has documented Anglo-Saxon Protestant attacks on nineteenth- and twentieth-century European immigrants in two scenarios: (1) when the number of immigrants expanded and (2) when economic recessions occurred. She concludes that under these conditions European immigrants were seen as a threat to the housing and occupational niches occupied by Anglo-Saxon Protestants (Roediger, 1991). These two conditions could provide reasons for the dramatic intensification of white violence against African Americans as they began to leave the rural South in the early decades of the twentieth century and to emigrate to northern cities as a low-wage labor force in tight labor markets, although it should be emphasized that African Americans and white Americans had come into conflict as early as the 1830s (Roediger, 1991). As greater numbers of African-origin people migrated north, European immigrants who had recently secured a foothold in American society felt threatened and, as a result, attacked blacks and developed intense prejudices, some of which persist to this day.

These ecological theories emphasize the relative size of ethnic subpopulations, their patterns of migration, their movement into various social niches, and their competition with other ethnic groups in markets for housing and jobs. Out of such competition come conflicts, often violent, that maintain prejudices and boundaries between antagonistic ethnic subpopulations. Thus, competition does not always lead to easy assimilation, as Park (1950) hoped, but to partitions and pluralism, punctuated by tension and conflict.

Power and Stratification Theories

Stratification theories emphasize how the process of discrimination produces overrepresentation of members of ethnic subpopulations in various social classes. All of these theories place considerable emphasis on the mobilization of power in order to control where ethnic groups are placed in the class system. Yet each stresses a somewhat different aspect of how power is used to create systems of ethnic stratification.

Caste Theories   In the early 1940s, W. Lloyd Warner and colleagues described black–white relations as constituting a **caste system** in which African Americans were confined to lower socioeconomic positions, denied access to power, prevented from intermarriage, and segregated in their own living space (Warner, 1941; Warner and Srole, 1945). African Americans thus constituted a distinctive caste that white Americans maintained to protect their own privileges.

Oliver C. Cox (1948) added a Marxist twist to this argument, emphasizing that the capitalist class of owners and managers of industry has been crucial to the castelike subordination of African Americans. The importation of slaves was a business enterprise in which European capitalists bought and sold cheap labor—slaves—to capitalistic plantations in the South. Once capitalists set this pattern of using Africans as a source of cheap labor and higher profits, it needed to be legitimated by highly prejudiced beliefs and stereotypes based on the biological characteristics of the "black race." Thus, exploitive practices are tied to the actions and interests of economic elites who mobilize power and ideologies in order to have a ready, desperate, and low-cost labor pool available for exploitation. From these early caste theories, the emphasis on power and stratification has taken a number of directions. Let us examine some representative theories.

Colonialism Theories   Colonialism theories draw inspiration from the analysis of the dynamics of European colonialism in the past. **External colonialism** is the process by which one nation controls the political and economic activities of another, less developed and less powerful society. Robert Blauner (1969:396) has identified four components of what he terms the **colonization complex:** (1) forced entry into a territory and its population, (2) alteration or destruction of the indigenous culture and patterns of social organization, (3) domination of the indigenous population by representatives of the invading society, and (4) justification of such activities with highly prejudicial, racist beliefs and stereotypes.

This basic theory has also been used to study **internal colonialism** (Blauner, 1969, 1972), in which the dynamics of the colonization complex are seen to operate *within* a society. From the internal colonization perspective, much of the history of ethnic relations in America has involved the establishment of successive internal colonies of people who are not white and who are dominated by descendants of the original Anglo-Saxon Protestant colonists. For example, African Americans constitute a colony within white America because institutionalized discrimination maintains white control over the economic, educational, and political opportunities of many African Americans. This situation, it is argued, is little different from that in South Africa, where until recently a white minority, made up of the descendants of British, Dutch, and German colonists, exerted institutional control over the black population.

The motivations behind internal colonialism in the United States were twofold: (1) the need for cheap labor to increase profits and (2) the desire to take and control land, first from Native Americans and later from Mexicans. As Robert Blauner (1969) notes, the desire for inexpensive labor led to the creation of slavery; the desire to control the agricultural base and land of Mexicans in the Southwest was the reason white Americans pushed Mexicans into a low-wage labor pool. Similarly, the attempted genocide of Native Americans was a way for Europeans to take their land, forcing those who survived to live on reservations—a very visible type of internal colony.

In order to create internal colonies, government must actively participate. It must provide the coercive force needed to control those who are "colonized," while legitimating patterns of domination with laws. Thus, by virtue of their control of the state, the descendants of early European white immigrants have been able to create and sustain internal colonies for long periods of time.

Split-Labor Market Theories   Split-labor market theories are much like ecological theories in their emphasis on competition between ethnic groups for resources, but they bring the mobilization and use of power to the forefront. Indeed, split-labor market theories make up for what is often considered a deficiency in ecological theories: the lack of sufficient attention to power and how the dominant class in society uses power to foster ethnic antagonism for its own benefit. **Split-labor market theories** emphasize that markets for labor become partitioned, with members of certain ethnic groups confined to some jobs in the labor market and not allowed to work in other, typically higher-paying jobs. The pressure to split the labor market comes from those in the more powerful ethnic populations who fear that they might lose their advantage if the labor market were to be opened up to other groups who would be willing to work for less and who would increase the supply of labor relative to the market's demand, thereby driving wages down as more workers competed for jobs.

Edna Bonacich (1972) has developed the most important split-labor market theory. This theory has been applied to black–white relations in America (Bonacich, 1976) and to ethnic populations in other societies. The basic argument is that capitalists, or those who own and manage large businesses, have an interest in high profits. One way to raise or maintain profits is to keep labor costs low; so capitalists try to import cheap labor in order to undercut higher-wage labor. Thus, for example, low-wage African American workers were imported from the South by northern industrialists as "strike breakers" in the 1920s and 1930s in order to undermine the efforts of white workers to unionize and to develop a power base for securing higher wages and better working conditions (Bonacich, 1976). And just as ecological theory would have predicted, acts of violence against African Americans increased dramatically in the 1920s.

Threatened workers sometimes react not only violently to efforts at undermining their wages but also politically and economically. At times they enlist government to exclude an ethnic group, but this is almost always impossible when powerful capitalists have an interest in supporting and sponsoring an influx of low-wage workers. A fallback strategy is for threatened workers to create formal and informal ways of "splitting the labor market" such that a subordinate minority is excluded from the more privileged positions in this market. As a result, members of the subordinate ethnic group often find themselves forced to compete with each other for a narrow range of less privileged and less secure positions. For example, as we will see in later chapters, for more than a century after the Civil War African Americans were excluded from most skilled craft unions and included in only some positions in industrial unions, creating a split in the labor market between its white and black sectors.

Thus, competition involves more than two antagonistic ethnic groups; it also involves third parties who wield power and who wish to maximize profits by stimulating competition between ethnic groups in labor markets. Such actions fuel both competition and threat, leading to discrimination ranging from acts of violence to institutionalization of a split-labor market.

Split-Class Theories Class theories emphasize economic exploitation of the lower classes by those in the higher classes. Added to this dynamic, however, is the recognition that each class includes segments or sectors that are isolated and hence subject to discriminatory practices. Theories of this sort, such as one developed by Mario Barrera (1979), generally begin with a Marxian view of the class system composed of (1) capitalists who control the investment of capital and who thereby regulate production and the purchase of labor; (2) managers who do the administrative work for capitalists and who, thereby, have control of workers; (3) petite bourgeoisie who own small businesses and buy labor; and (4) members of the working class who constitute the majority of workers and who sell their labor for salaries and wages. Aside from the conflicts of interest among these classes, Barrera argues, there are splits *within* each class along ethnic lines. Members of some ethnic subpopulations are subordinate within a class and are often relegated to the less desirable, lower-paying, and less secure jobs within this class. Moreover, these members can become a reserve labor force within a class, especially the large working class, in which they constitute a pool of excess labor that can be hired when needed for low wages and thrown back into the pool when not needed.

For example, within the working classes, subordinate ethnic minorities were until recently almost always excluded from the most desirable jobs—unionized craft positions (carpenters, plumbers, electricians, sheet metal workers, welders, machine workers, and the like)—and dramatically overrepresented in low-skill, low-pay, and low-job-security positions (day laborers, seasonal workers, and domestics). This is still the case, though somewhat less so, for African, Latino, and Native Americans. In Europe, Jews were historically confined to a few positions (trade, finance); even today in the United States, Jews are overrepresented in certain middle-class occupations and businesses (retail sales in certain spheres such as clothing, as well as accounting, finance, college teaching, and medicine), but they tend to be underrepresented in other spheres. Many Asian groups—Koreans, Vietnamese, and Chinese, for example—are confined to small retail and service businesses and underrepresented in other middle-class occupations and professions. Thus, there are splits in social classes, just as there are in labor markets. Indeed, splits in labor markets may extend beyond lower-paying jobs and operate in other, more affluent and privileged spheres.

Middleman Minority Theories   One process that creates splits in the middle class is described by **middleman minority theories.** Not all ethnic groups occupy lower castes and classes, nor are all confined to internal colonies. In fact, some are overrepresented in the petite bourgeoisie, or small businesses that often rely on family labor and ethnic networks (for credit, customers, and other needed aspects of doing business). They are middleman minorities along several potential dimensions: (1) They have middle, or moderate, levels of resources; (2) they serve as distribution links between producers of goods and those who buy them; and (3) in Marxist terms (Bonacich, 1973), they are the "go-betweens" (as small retail store owners) between members of elite classes and subordinate classes.

The various explanations for the formation of middleman minorities are basically the same (Blalock, 1967; Bonacich, 1973; Turner and Bonacich, 1980): Certain minorities bring to a host society entrepreneurial skills and perhaps some capital. Ironically, these very attributes pose a threat to dominant groups, and so these minorities are excluded from many middle-class positions and allowed to operate only those businesses that serve their own ethnic group, other oppressed ethnics, and, occasionally, more elite ethnic groups. Once these "middlemen" become lodged in these middle niches, movement to economic niches controlled by dominant groups is threatening and, hence, likely to engender discrimination, which keeps its ethnic victims confined. The clients of middleman minorities, especially those in the lower social classes, also tend to exhibit hostility toward the petite bourgeoisie, who are viewed as mercenary and exploitive. For example, tensions have emerged between African American residents and Korean business owners in ghetto areas. As demonstrated by the attacks on these businesses during the rioting in Los Angeles in the early 1990s, this hostility can translate into violence. At other times, boycotts against a middleman minority—as in the case of certain Korean stores in New York—are initiated as a way to vent hostility against perceptions of maltreatment. Such hostilities from potential competitors and clients force the members of a middleman minority to withdraw into an ethnic enclave and to be perceived as "clannish," thereby perpetuating hostility toward them.

We have now presented in very general terms the range of theories on ethnic relations. There are many variations of the theories discussed, but the basic types of theoretical approaches have been summarized. As is evident, each theory stresses some processes while ignoring others. Some appear to apply to a single ethnic group in America, whereas others seem more general and generic. How, then, can this theoretical diversity be pulled together in an analysis of ethnicity in America? Our answer to this question is to create an even more general theory that can incorporate the strong points of existing theories, while simplifying the explanation of ethnic relations. Good theory should not be complicated; rather, it should be simple and parsimonious.

A UNIFIED THEORY OF ETHNIC RELATIONS

Let us begin by emphasizing the central force in ethnic relations: **discrimination** against a subordinate subpopulation. The greater the level of discrimination and the more it is institutionalized across many social arenas, the more likely is a subpopulation to develop and retain a distinctive ethnic identity. Thus, if forms of discrimination, such as violence, exclusion, selective inclusion, abusive practices, and segregation, are practiced against a subpopulation, its members will become a clearly identifiable ethnic group. Conversely, the less the discrimination practiced against an identifiable subpopulation, the less distinctive will be its ethnicity and the more likely it will be to assimilate.

Of course, at times elements of ethnicity are retained without the threat of discrimination. Many white ethnic groups—Irish Catholics, Poles, Italians, and others in America—have tried to maintain elements of their ethnicity, such as holidays, festivals, churches, and community organizations. These ethnic elements are not immediately apparent, and, hence, they do not define and distinguish these subpopulations in a highly visible way. Moreover, all these ethnic groups were at one time victims of discrimination; and so the effort to retain ethnicity is a holdover effect of past discrimination, in which members of the subpopulation selectively retain certain symbols and rituals of the past. Other ethnic groups, such as the Basques in America, have retained a considerable number of their ethnic traditions without ever having experienced high levels of overt discrimination. This maintenance of ethnicity has been accomplished by retaining Basque communities, patterns of intragroup marriage, important rituals and festivals, and language. Even here, though, assimilation is slowly occurring because there is relatively little outside discrimination to force Basques to retreat into their ethnic traditions. Thus, ethnicity can be retained, to an extent and for a while, without discrimination; ultimately, however, the intensity of discrimination determines whether a subpopulation remains distinctively ethnic in culture, behavior, and organization or becomes assimilated into the societal mainstream.

Another force involved in creating and maintaining ethnicity is the degree of **identifiability** of members of a subpopulation. To be targets of discrimination, members of a subpopulation need to be visible and readily identified. And so, the more distinctive members of a subpopulation are, the more likely they are to become targets of discrimination.

There are several bases for distinctiveness. One is biological, and thus the more members of a subpopulation can be singled out in terms of biological features, such as skin color and eye shape, the more readily they can become targets of discrimination. It should come as no surprise, then, that the two ethnic groups most discriminated against in American society have been African Americans and Native Americans; after all, they can be identified biologically. Asians and Latinos have had a similar experience. Identifiability is also cultural—language, religious beliefs, normative practices, and other symbol systems. For example, if an American subpopulation uses a language other than English, has distinctive religious practices that deviate from Judeo-Christian traditions, and reveals norms that sanction behaviors and demeanors that are at odds with the

American mainstream, that subpopulation becomes distinctive and identifiable. As a consequence, they are likely targets of discrimination. Behavioral and organizational characteristics also create identifiability. When members of an ethnic population have a noticeable interpersonal demeanor (such as speech styles, body language, or dress) and when they have unusual organizational structures (such as deviant kinship patterns, church practices, and business arrangements), they can become targets of discrimination.

Discrimination and identifiability are mutually reinforcing. If people can be identified and singled out for discrimination, then such acts of discrimination and their institutionalization force their victims to "remain with their own kind," among whom they interact, intermarry, and maintain their distinctive cultural, organizational, and behavioral patterns. Sometimes this maintenance of ethnic patterns is a defensive reaction, and other times it is merely the only option for segregated and excluded peoples. Most typically, however, it is a mixture of the two. Once a subpopulation is forced to maintain its identity as a result of discrimination, ironically it becomes an easier target for further discrimination. This is particularly likely to be the case if rates of marriage within the ethnic group maintain biological distinctiveness, but other bases of distinctiveness—cultural, behavioral, and organizational—are also important. As biological, cultural, behavioral, and organizational features of a subpopulation become intertwined and intercorrelated, then the members of a subpopulation become ever more visible targets of discrimination. This cycle of identifiability, discrimination, maintenance of identifiability, and further discrimination is often difficult to break—as has certainly been the case for African Americans, Native Americans, most Latinos, and some Asians (Aguirre and Baker, 1993). In contrast, for ethnic groups that are not biologically distinguishable because of skin color or facial features, it has been easier to break the cycle and to filter into the mainstream, as has been the case for members of most white European ethnic groups.

Identifiability and discrimination affect the **resource shares**—the levels and types of valued resources—available to an ethnic subpopulation, such as income, power, and prestige. Resources such as human capital (skills and education) and financial capital (savings) that ethnics bring with them when they come to America are also important. But ultimately discrimination determines which resources members of a population can have and how those resources can be used. Discrimination shapes how and where immigrants who bring human and financial resources with them may use their imported resources, and as a consequence, it will affect the kinds and levels of resources they can accumulate. Discrimination keeps existing ethnic groups in the lower socioeconomic strata and those immigrants who do not bring human or financial capital with them from acquiring resources. Whether channeling the further acquisition of resources among those with some capital or denying resources to those without capital, discrimination works to maintain identifiability indirectly because the levels and types of resources that members of a population possess influence their behavioral, cultural, and organizational characteristics. When a population has little money, low levels of education (and hence lack of prestige in a credentialed society like the United States), and few channels of acquiring power, it develops distinctive characteristics which, in turn, make its members easier targets for further discrimination. For example, African Americans, Native Americans, and most Latinos have become even more visible as targets of discrimination because of their low shares of valued resources. Or when a population uses its financial resources to make more money but is excluded from positions of power and prestige, it also becomes distinctive, often arousing hostility over its wealth. As a result, it also can become a target of discrimination. For instance, most Asian middleman minorities have experienced this phenomenon, as have Jews over centuries of persecution in Europe and discrimination in the United States.

Figure 2.1 shows the relationships among *discrimination, identifiability,* and *resource shares.* If a population can be easily identified, it is likely to be a target of discrimination; if there is discrimination, this population develops a typical share of resources, which in turn increases its identifiability. We have added to this cycle another feature: *degree of ethnic stratification.* If a pattern of resource shares becomes discernible, then it usually creates distinctive pockets of ethnicity within the strata of society. For example, if African Americans are consistently overrepresented in the lower social strata, this situation increases their identifiability as somehow "not measuring up" to societal standards, and, as a result, it provides a further basis for discrimination which, in turn, perpetuates their meager shares of resources and their location in the stratification system.

As discrimination denies people access to resources, it limits their capacity to fight back or to move away from their situation. If a subpopulation does not have access to channels of power, how can it fight discrimination? If it does not have access to a good education, which leads to job opportunities and prestige, how does it become upwardly mobile? If it does not have money, how does it improve? Thus, resource shares also determine how people respond to discrimination; if their options are limited, they are more likely to accept their plight and, as a consequence, remain identifiable targets of further discrimination.

Once an ethnic subpopulation is identified and targeted for discrimination, this identity becomes a key element in each individual's psychology and personality. As we emphasized earlier, individuals always have identities of themselves in roles—for example, the identity of being a student, father, mother—and they also have a more global self-conception of themselves as a certain kind of person—as competent, shy, smart, and so forth. People also acquire a *social identity* of themselves as belonging to a category of persons, and once people are identified as members of an ethnic category and treated as such, they begin to internalize this social identity and use it to evaluate themselves and fellow ethnics and to structure their behaviors and interactions not only with fellow ethnics but with other ethnic subpopulations. And if members of an ethnic subpopulation are victims of discrimination and, as a result, are forced to live in ghettoes, to assume a limited range of roles, to interact primarily with fellow ethnics, and to marry within their ethnic category, this social identity becomes even more powerful among fellow ethnics. This social identity is learned early through interaction with parents, siblings, and peers, and as it becomes part of the psychological structure of a person, it organizes an increasingly greater

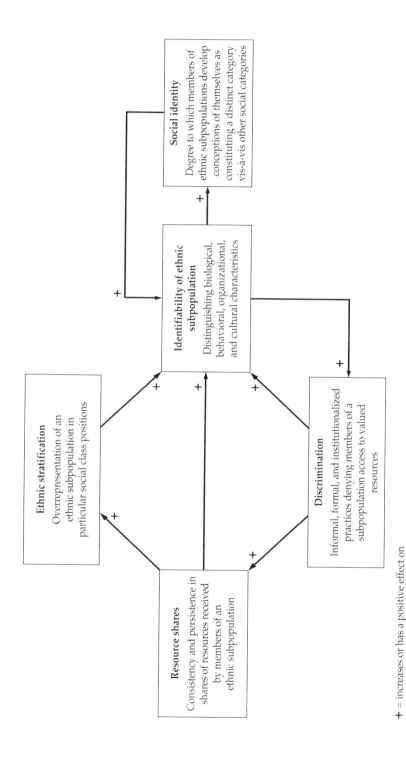

Social identity

Degree to which members of ethnic subpopulations develop conceptions of themselves as constituting a distinct category vis-à-vis other social categories

Identifiability of ethnic subpopulation

Distinguishing biological, behavioral, organizational, and cultural characteristics

Ethnic stratification

Overrepresentation of an ethnic subpopulation in particular social class positions

Discrimination

Informal, formal, and institutionalized practices denying members of a subpopulation access to valued resources

Resource shares

Consistency and persistence in shares of resources received by members of an ethnic subpopulation

+ = increases or has a positive effect on

FIGURE 2.1 Cycles of discrimination, identifiability, resource shares, and stratification.

share of that person's conception of self, cognitions, emotions, and behaviors. In so doing, the social identity sustains the identifiability of a person not only for fellow ethnics but also for other ethnics who may be disposed to discriminate. Thus, people become identifiable by virtue of their shares of resources, their superficial biological variations, and their experiences with discriminatory acts by others; at the same time, individuals often develop a social identity of themselves as a member of an ethnic category, and this social identity orders a person's cognitions, emotions, and behaviors—often in ways that sustain this person's identifiability for members of other ethnic subpopulations who are disposed to discriminate.

Figure 2.1 illustrates the reinforcing dynamics in the cycle of discrimination, identifiability, resource shares, and stratification—as denoted by the positive signs on the arrows. Each one increases the values of the other in the direction specified by the arrows. If these were the only processes involved in the cycles, they would be difficult to break. But other forces are involved, some of which work to intensify these cycles, a few to mitigate their effects.

Why do people discriminate? Is identifiability the only reason? Ethnic identifiability alone is not enough to generate the high levels of discrimination that perpetuate the cycles portrayed in Figure 2.1. At least one additional force is needed: a **sense of threat.** If a subordinate ethnic group is perceived as threatening the political power, the economic well-being, the cultural symbols (language, customs, values, and beliefs), the social structures (community organization, social clubs, rituals, and holidays), and/or the basic institutions (economy, politics, family, church, school, and medicine) of a dominant ethnic group, this perception will translate into hostility, fueling the fires of discrimination. For example, slavery may have persisted long after its economic viability had diminished because there was great fear about the social, economic, and political consequences of a large mass of freed slaves. This fear mobilized considerable hostility toward black people in the decades before and after the Civil War, resulting in violent acts (hangings, shootings) and efforts to reinstitutionalize in law and practice the oppression of African Americans (Singleton and Turner, 1975; Turner and Singleton, 1978; Turner, Singleton, and Musick, 1984). A more recent example is how the large influx of Latinos, especially Mexicans, into the United States has aroused fears about its effects on the economy, the existing balance of power, and schools. This fear has resulted in hostility and discriminatory practices. Recent Asian immigrants—Koreans and Vietnamese, for instance—are sometimes seen as a threat to small-business owners because many of them possess both human and financial capital and are willing to work long hours with pooled family labor. They are, in essence, more successful than some white ethnic groups in many entrepreneurial niches, thereby arousing hostility. Moreover, their success in these niches limits opportunities for other ethnic groups— African Americans and Latinos, for example—who may wish to start small businesses as a way to rise from their particular place in the system of ethnic stratification. The result is hostility and discrimination against these middleman minorities. Thus, the greater the sense of threat experienced by superordinate ethnic groups (and, at times, subordinate ones as well) over the influx or existence of another ethnic subpopulation, the greater is their hostility toward this subordinate population and the more likely they are to engage in discriminatory acts and to institutionalize these acts.

Which forces create a sense of threat? Is distinctiveness enough? Our sense is that two additional features of an ethnic subpopulation operate to generate hostility. One is the **size** of an ethnic population. A large number of immigrants or a large subordinate ethnic group poses a threat because they might (1) work for less money than the dominant ethnic groups (out of desperation for job opportunities), (2) upset the balance of political power if they become enfranchised, and (3) change existing cultural and organizational patterns if they influence the mainstream. Thus, African Americans and Latinos pose a threat to the dominant Anglo-Saxon population because of their large numbers, and as a result, they are discriminated against in order to preserve what white ethnic groups see as "the American way of life." When an ethnic group is large, intense discrimination, fueled by a sense of threat, will usually force them to the bottom of the stratification system because there are too many people to be channeled into a narrow range of middleman minority niches and because they cannot be allowed to "dilute" the dominant culture and its institutions. Of course, when ethnic groups are denied access to resources and pushed into a lower socioeconomic group, they maintain their ethnicity, which increases the identifiability that poses a threat—often more imagined than real. But more is involved: Large numbers of oppressed ethnic subpopulations sometimes become hostile, which causes the dominant ethnic groups to experience an escalated sense of threat. Intense discrimination against a large ethnic population only exacerbates the level of threat that prompted the discrimination; hence the cycle of threat, discrimination, hostile reaction to discrimination, escalated threat, and renewed discrimination is perpetuated.

Another force that creates a sense of threat is the **entrepreneurial resources**—occupational skills, education, money, and organizational abilities—that an ethnic population possesses. Usually, however, ethnic groups with entrepreneurial resources are small; hence, through discrimination, it is possible to channel them into a narrow range of middleman minority niches or a limited number of professions. The ability of these ethnic groups to outperform segments of the dominant population in economic enterprises is threatening and arouses hostility, which results in efforts to confine them to niches and positions that reduce head-to-head competition with the members of the dominant population and, perhaps, places them in competition with other subordinate minorities. Under these conditions, the resentment of the victims of discrimination is reduced because they can enjoy economic success in at least some activities, thus weakening the cycle. Because many Asian immigrants in America possess entrepreneurial resources, they have been shunted into middleman minority niches or selected professions. Yet, over time, it is difficult to maintain this kind of confinement because these ethnic groups, and their successive generations of offspring, possess skills, capital, and education that make them valuable in the mainstream; and if they can acquire at least the veneer of the cultural mainstream, they can often penetrate mainstream institutions. Because of their relatively small numbers coupled with increased rates of intermarriage with members of the dominant ethnic subpopulation, their penetration is less threatening and arouses less hostility than would be the case with larger ethnic populations.

Thus, the level of threat perceived by superordinate ethnic groups is increased not only by subordinate groups' distinctiveness but also by their *size* and *entrepreneurial resources*. Large numbers of ethnic groups threaten to "overrun" the mainstream, and the possession of entrepreneurial resources among ethnic groups threatens entrenched small businesses and professions.

How is this sense of threat and hostility sustained over time? The answer resides in another central aspect of ethnic relations: **negative beliefs** and **stereotypes.** Here is where prejudice becomes a significant force in ethnic relations (Allport and Postman, 1947; Fentress and Wickman, 1994; Rydgren, 2007). When dominant ethnic groups feel threatened, they develop prejudices and portray those who threaten them in a negative light. If the sense of threat is severe, these negative portrayals are codified into a series of beliefs and stereotypes about the perceived undesirable characteristics and qualities of a subordinate ethnic population. Ironically, such portrayals tend to heighten the potential "menace" of the ethnic group, thereby escalating the sense of threat, which, in turn, leads to more negative portrayals. For example, the initial justification for not freeing slaves in America was that they were "childlike" and hence incapable of "managing for themselves" (Turner and Singleton, 1978). But as the abolitionist movement gained momentum, and as the sense of threat experienced by some white Americans increased correspondingly, these portrayals became ever more vicious, shifting to a view of black males as sexually aggressive and as lusting after white women whom they were prepared to rape if ever set free. Such portrayals escalated the sense of threat in the minds of white southerners, resulting in ever more aggressive discrimination against African Americans. According to Jordan (1968:151), the perception that "Negro men lusted after white women" intensified white prejudice.

Prejudicial beliefs are facilitated by the formation of *social identities* among targeted subpopulations and among those who would discriminate against these subpopulations. When both the victims and perpetrators of discrimination view themselves as members of distinctive and different ethnic categories, an "us vs. them" psychological orientation often emerges. Each subpopulation portrays the other in highly negative terms and is prepared to act, often violently, to sustain the purity of their respective social identities. Among those with the power to be discriminators and to propagate prejudicial stereotypes, these negative beliefs are used to legitimate discrimination—often of the most vicious kind. We can see these dynamics unfolding all over the world—for example, between Muslims and Jews in the Middle East or Protestants and Catholics in Northern Ireland—but closer to home, they have been very much a part of the American ethnic experience. For example, the vicious portrayals of Native Americans as "savages" were used to commit virtual genocide against the indigenous population of the Americas; the extreme portrayals of slaves and, after the Civil War, of freed slaves were used to bolster Jim Crow practices, including lynching of "uppity" blacks; and the portrayal of early Irish immigrants as the "missing link" between apes and humans were used to ghettoize these immigrants and to deny them places of employment. Thus, social identities of ethnic subpopulations hardens prejudicial beliefs and solidifies social identities that distinguish ethnic subpopulations. The end result is typically more intense forms of discrimination by those with the power to discriminate.

Codified beliefs and stereotypes not only escalate the sense of threat, which then ratchets up the level of discrimination, but also legitimize discrimination: If an ethnic group is seen to have "undesirable" qualities, it is only appropriate that its members be segregated and excluded from the mainstream. And as discrimination sets in motion the cycles outlined in Figure 2.1, it appears to justify itself because the victims of discrimination tend to maintain those biological, behavioral, cultural, and organizational features that are portrayed in a negative light by stereotypes. As a consequence, the failure of ethnic groups to "change" (ignoring the obvious fact that discrimination prevents change) escalates the sense of threat and organizes the negative beliefs and stereotypes into a codified dogma. For example, Jews in Europe were denied access to many positions and forced into a narrow range of retail, finance, and professional niches; as they operated successfully in these niches and did not change their ethnic characteristics, the stereotypes about them—clannish, anti-Christian, financially ruthless, and so on—became ever more codified, thereby justifying more hostility, discrimination, and prejudice.

Figure 2.2 summarizes dynamics escalating discrimination. People discriminate when they feel threatened by the presence of an ethnic group. This sense of threat increases when the threatening ethnic group is large and/or when it has entrepreneurial or educational resources. When threatened, those who would discriminate justify their actions by formulating negative beliefs and stereotypes about the undesirable qualities of their victims. Ironically, as they formulate these stereotypes, the negative portrayal makes discriminators perceive their victims as more threatening, thus making them even more disposed to discriminate. Moreover, discriminating against an ethnic group makes it more threatening, because discriminators implicitly know that their victims will be hostile. This hostility, whether or not fully acknowledged by discriminators, will always make an ethnic group more menacing, thereby justifying abusive practices and other types of discrimination to "keep them in line," which, of course, arouses more resentments that make the ethnic minority even more threatening. As the positive arrows in Figure 2.2 underscore, these processes are self-reinforcing and, indeed, can become self-escalating. Threat escalates discrimination, and discrimination increases the sense of threat. As negative stereotypes are developed to justify discrimination, these negative portrayals make people more threatening and thereby justify negative beliefs and further discrimination.

We are now in a position to put the cycles portrayed in Figures 2.1 and 2.2 together so that we can see how discrimination, as fueled by threat and negative stereotypes, leads to ethnic stratification. In Figure 2.3, we have blended the first two figures. Threat increases with growing size and entrepreneurial/educational resources of an ethnic minority, setting into motion the formation of negative

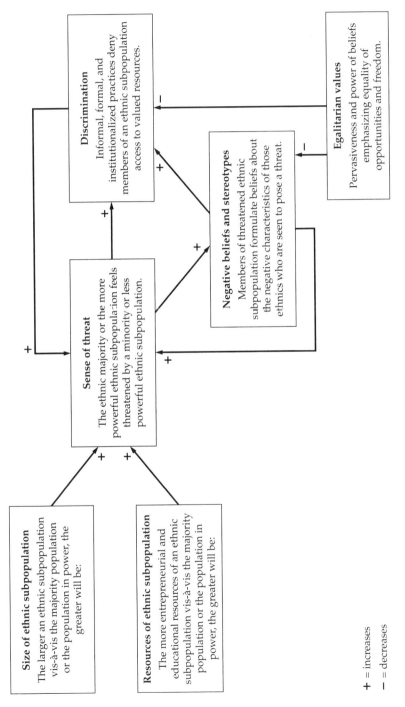

Size of ethnic subpopulation
The larger an ethnic subpopulation vis-à-vis the majority population or the population in power, the greater will be:

Resources of ethnic subpopulation
The more entrepreneurial and educational resources of an ethnic subpopulation vis-à-vis the majority population or the population in power, the greater will be:

Sense of threat
The ethnic majority or the more powerful ethnic subpopulation feels threatened by a minority or less powerful ethnic subpopulation.

Discrimination
Informal, formal, and institutionalized practices deny members of an ethnic subpopulation access to valued resources.

Negative beliefs and stereotypes
Members of threatened ethnic subpopulation formulate beliefs about the negative characteristics of those ethnics who are seen to pose a threat.

Egalitarian values
Pervasiveness and power of beliefs emphasizing equality of opportunities and freedom.

+ = increases
− = decreases

FIGURE 2.2 Forces increasing and decreasing ethnic discrimination.

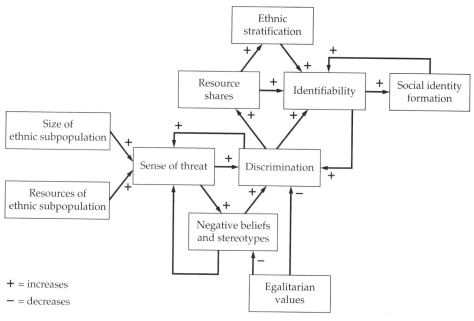

FIGURE 2.3 A general model of ethnic relations.

beliefs that, along with the fear that threat generates, pushes people to discriminate against an ethnic minority. As discrimination occurs, members of ethnic groups are denied resources and are generally segregated, forcing them to live with and marry "their own kind." As a result of their shares of resources that confine them to a given stratum in the stratification system as well as their high rates of interaction and intermarriage, both biological and cultural patterns are sustained, thereby making an ethnic group more identifiable and, hence, an easier target of discrimination.

As can be seen with all of the positively signed arrows, these dynamics, once unleashed, are self-reinforcing. Each one sets the others into motion, and it is for this reason that it is often difficult to break these vicious cycles revolving around discrimination. In American society, however, there has been one force working against discrimination and negative stereotyping: powerful **egalitarian values.** The arrow coming up from the bottom of Figures 2.2 and 2.3 emphasizes this important force that can act to reduce discrimination and stereotyping. Americans believe that people should be treated equally and be given equal opportunities, and these core values have always stood in opposition to ethnic discrimination. Obviously, Americans have often been willing to live with this contradiction between their values and their acts of discrimination, but the existence of these values has served historically as a rallying point for civil rights movements designed to eliminate discrimination (see Box 2.1).

The model in Figure 2.3 will guide our organization of each chapter on an ethnic group. We will begin by asking about the *resource shares* of an ethnic group. Are they overrepresented in poverty? What kinds of jobs do they have?

Box 2.1
Breaking the Hold of Prejudicial Beliefs and Discrimination

Egalitarian values represent one important source of pressure to reduce discrimination. These values can be used to make people feel guilty or ashamed of their prejudices and discriminatory acts, but as Box 2.2 emphasizes, Americans have a very nuanced and narrow view about what egalitarianism means. The result is that it is often difficult to use cultural beliefs to break the power of negative stereotypes about members of an ethnic subpopulation and the discrimination that such stereotypes engender and justify.

There are more structural routes to eroding the power of prejudicial beliefs. One is to increase rates of interaction among individuals from different ethnic backgrounds. If social structures can place individuals from various ethnic subpopulations at similar locations, the individuals are more likely to interact. And, as they interact, they will come to know one another as persons rather than as members of a threatening ethnic category. Of course, this was part of the logic of school integration, and of antidiscrimination laws, especially the civil rights acts of the 1960s. These acts gave members of ethnic subpopulations access to locations in social structures—such as schools, jobs, churches, sports activities, and public facilities—that not only provided these individuals with new opportunities, but equally significant, ensured that they would inevitably come into face-to-face interaction with members of other ethnic subpopulations, especially those that had practiced discrimination and held prejudicial beliefs for so long. The result has been a rather dramatic reduction in prejudicial beliefs in Americans over the last four decades. Negative stereotypes still exist, as do blatant and subtle forms of discrimination, but the fact that the vast majority of the population has interacted with members of other ethnic subpopulations has worked to reduce the intensity of ethnic stereotypes and the pervasiveness of discrimination.

Another route to eroding negative stereotypes comes through the visibility of members of ethnic subpopulations in public roles. The prominence, for example, of African Americans in sports and entertainment has increased their visibility in roles that bring prestige and, hence, has decreased the power of negative stereotyping, even though some media venues still perpetuate older stereotypes. Martin Luther King, through the eloquence of his voice and words, also dispelled many of the older stereotypes about African Americans. And, more recently, the election of Barack Obama as president of the United States signals not only that older prejudices have declined in salience, but more importantly, his visibility at the macro level of national and international politics can help micro-level interactions between African Americans and members of other subpopulations in local encounters. Often, macro-level power has large effects on micro-level social relations because the visible roles played by those in power erode prejudices that lead others to be less fearful about interactions with those who have seemed "different" and "unworthy" of attention.

Box 2.2
What Do Americans Mean by Egalitarian?

Affirmative action policies have, over the last two decades, generated so much controversy that it is reasonable to ask: Why the controversy? The answer ultimately resides in two approaches for realizing egalitarian values. The first, clearly stated in the Declaration of Independence, stresses equality for individuals rather than social categories; and as this value has become translated into social policies, the goal has been to equalize **opportunities for individuals.** The second approach, initiated under Richard Nixon's presidency in the 1970s, emphasizes equality for groups; and as this policy has been implemented under more recent affirmative action programs, the focus has been on **equality of results.**

As Seymour Martin Lipset (1991:209) has argued, these policies represent a clash of two basic American values: egalitarianism versus individualism. **Individualism** stresses that people get ahead through their own efforts and hard work; and when combined with **egalitarianism,** the result is a commitment to providing compensatory help to those individuals whose circumstances keep them from realizing their full potential for hard work and success. But, when equality is stressed over individualism, the commitment is to ensuring that certain categories of people—minorities and women, for example—achieve proportionate representation and results when compared to those who have been more advantaged. In this latter commitment, emphasis is on giving preferences to certain categories of individuals in order to compensate for past discrimination.

Public opinion polls in the United States have been consistent and overwhelming in their endorsement of individualistic egalitarianism. The American public is opposed to group-preference approaches; and even among minorities, who could be helped by these approaches, a clear majority is opposed to them as well. Yet Americans are strongly in support of programs that will help individuals, *as individuals* rather than as a social category, overcome the disadvantages that come with present and past discrimination. It should not be surprising, then, that affirmative action—when seen as group preferences—should be so hotly debated, and that Americans have come to disagree with virtually all policies based upon a group-preference interpretation of egalitarianism. Whether this feeling on the part of the American public is good, bad, right, or wrong in some ultimate moral sense is less relevant than the fact that Americans view group preferences as unfair. In contrast, they do not feel that compensatory efforts—special programs in education and job training, for example—are unfair; indeed, Americans see these kinds of efforts as necessary to overcome present, as well as the legacy of the past, discrimination.

Another basic American value is **humanitarianism**—that is, those who have suffered through no fault of their own should be helped. In the minds of most Americans this value is mixed with individualism and egalitarianism to produce a clear desire for programs to help individuals realize more opportunities, regardless of their social category. Those who are poor and who have been victims of discrimination need compensatory help *as individuals* to realize their potential. This is as far as Americans appear to be willing to go in their humanitarianism; relatively small percentages of Americans believe that categories of individuals should be given preferential treatment. Indeed, programs that are perceived to give preferential

(continued)

treatment to social categories—whether this perception is accurate or not is another matter—are seen as undesirable. Hence, efforts on the part of policy makers to overcome the effects of present and past discrimination will need to be careful in constructing these programs; if they are not, programs will encounter negative evaluation by the conditional humanitarianism of most Americans: Equality of opportunity is okay; equality of outcome through group preferences is not okay.

Yet it can be asked: Without group preferences, can the cumulative effects of discrimination over hundreds of years really be overcome? Can any compensatory educational program, for example, overcome the effects of being raised in a graffiti- and bullet-marked public housing project infested by gangs and drug dealers? Or can women ever overcome discrimination by anything but group preferences in ensuring their access to job categories dominated by men? In reality, the answer to these questions is probably no, but Americans think otherwise, or think group preferences won't work either; and, it is reasonable to assume, programs to realize egalitarian values in the face of past and present discrimination will always be limited by what the public perceives as fair and unfair.

How much education do they receive? How long do they live? Answers to these questions tell us about the respective shares of resources of an ethnic population and are a good indicator of present or past discrimination. Present resource shares tell us about the past. Has a subpopulation been denied access to valued resources and forced to live at the bottom or in a narrow range of middle slots in the stratification system of American society?

Next, we can review the history of *discrimination* against this ethnic group, paying particular attention to its institutionalization in the economic, governmental, and educational structures. We should also understand how and why an ethnic group remains *distinctive* or *identifiable* and, as such, an easy target for discrimination. We must then delve into questions about the *sense of threat* engendered by an identifiable ethnic population and how this sense of threat is related to its size and entrepreneurial resources. Then we can turn to the *negative beliefs* and *stereotypes* to see how they have legitimized discrimination while escalating the sense of threat. Finally, we need to examine the impact of *egalitarian values* imposing challenges to prejudicial beliefs and stereotypes about an ethnic group and to patterns of institutionalized discrimination that have denied this group access to resources. In this context, we can assess political and social movements that have arisen in recent years or that are likely to emerge in the future.

How can these self-reinforcing processes be broken? Rebellion and revolt, political mobilization, formation of a social movement, and other acts may force dominant ethnic groups to make concessions? Also, as noted earlier, the existence of egalitarian values, as portrayed in the lower portion of Figures 2.2 and 2.3, may stimulate change. The negative arrows pointing to prejudicial and negative beliefs as well as to discrimination indicate that such values stand in contradiction to prejudice and discrimination. Of course, in societies without such values, the cycles portrayed in Figure 2.3 are allowed to operate, up to the point of revolt and conflict. But in the United States, where values of equality and freedom are pervasive, they legitimize opposition movements to discriminatory practices—for example, the abolitionist movement that denounced slavery and the civil rights movement that culminated in a series of federal laws in the 1960s formally outlawing discrimination. Without the existence of such egalitarian values in the dominant culture, oppressed ethnic groups must accept discrimination, migrate to a more favorable environment, or incur the risks of rebellion. Historically, acceptance and migration have been the most common responses of subordinate ethnic groups; protest by a subordinate minority is usually crushed, unless the population is large and the dominant groups weak, or unless the ethnic group has allies within or outside the society. Only recently in world history have egalitarian values become a powerful force; patterns of discrimination and ethnic stratification have been a prominent feature of human societies for millennia. Since egalitarian values are hardly universal in the world today, ethnic stratification and tensions will remain part of human society in the future. This is assuredly the case when one considers that the United States, which subscribes to powerful egalitarian values, has yet to break the cycles portrayed in Figure 2.3.

The definitions in Chapter 1, coupled with the theoretical explanation offered in this chapter, provide us with a means for examining ethnic relations in America. More specifically, the model depicted in Figure 2.3 can serve as a springboard for discussion about each ethnic subpopulation to be examined in the chapters to follow.

When noticeable differences of an ethnic subpopulation are perceived to pose a threat, they lead to discrimination. Large ethnic populations or smaller ones with entrepreneurial skills are most likely to generate a sense of threat among dominant ethnics. This sense of threat leads people to construct negative beliefs and stereotypes about ethnics; and these beliefs are used to legitimize discrimination.

Discrimination itself also encourages beliefs that can make such discrimination seem legitimate; and once codified, these beliefs encourage further discrimination. The effects of additional discrimination are to limit resource shares of ethnic groups, maintain their identity and vulnerability to discrimination, and force them into habitual locations in the stratification system; as these effects occur, a renewed cycle of threat, prejudice, and discrimination is unleashed against ethnic groups who "refuse to change" (again, ignoring the obvious reasons why change is difficult).

The forces delineated in the theoretical model portrayed in Figure 2.3 become the chapter headings and sections in subsequent discussions. They provide a framework for systematically reviewing the past, present, and future of the most prominent ethnic subpopulations in America. And they do more. Because these headings are derived from a theoretical model, they contribute to an explanation of *why* an ethnic subpopulation and members of the dominant Anglo-Saxon Protestant culture have formed a particular pattern of tension-provoking relations. By examining how the forces portrayed in Figure 2.3 have operated and interacted for a particular ethnic population, we will be able to explain what has occurred in the past, what is going on today, and what will be likely to happen in the future.

SUMMARY

Theories attempt to explain why a phenomenon exists and how it operates. Theories explaining ethnicity are diverse, each capturing an important dynamic but none incorporating all the key forces in ethnic relations. Assimilation theories emphasize the process by which members of an ethnic population become part of the mainstream of a society, but they do not adequately account for the persistence of ethnic differences and the conflicts these differences generate. Theories of ethnic pluralism arose in reaction to the "melting pot" basis of assimilation theories, arguing that the maintenance of ethnicity is often a way of coping with discrimination. More recent biological theories propose the possibility of humans' genetic tendencies to identify with and support members of their distinctive ethnic heritage. These biological theories are as controversial as earlier and often ethnocentric, if not racist, theories. Ecological theories emphasize that competition for scarce resources is a key force in creating and sustaining ethnic relations and that patterns of domination and subjugation among ethnic groups reflect this competition over valued resources such as jobs, incomes, and housing.

All stratification theories argue that ethnic groups are overrepresented in particular social strata because of the unequal distribution of power. Caste theories stress that many minority groups have been historically pushed to the bottom of the class system with rigid barriers preventing mobility out of this position. Colonialism theories emphasize that minority populations often become exploited "colonies" within a society—much like their international counterparts, the overseas colonies of one nation that subjugates the members of others and extracts their resources without a proportionate return. Split-labor market theories draw attention to the fact that patterns of discrimination are often created and sustained through the partitioning of labor markets so that dominant subpopulations can continue to enjoy their privilege while denying subordinate ethnic groups access to jobs and income. Split-class theories argue that divisions and partitions *within* social classes exist, with the least powerful typically confined to a lower class in order to maintain the privilege of the dominant sector within a class. Middleman minority theories use elements from split-labor market and split-class theories to explain how small pockets within ethnic subpopulations, mostly in a narrow range of business and entrepreneurial positions, emerge and succeed in the socioeconomic mainstream.

Finally, this chapter seeks to take the main tenets of each theory and synthesize them into a general model of ethnic discrimination in America. This model stresses several interrelated factors: ethnic identifiability, the threat that an ethnic population poses, prejudicial stereotypes that are articulated, resources possessed by an ethnic population, size of an ethnic population, and position of a subpopulation in the stratification system.

POINTS OF DEBATE

Each of the theories summarized in this chapter suggests points of debate, some of which are enumerated here.

1. Is assimilation the desired outcome of ethnic relations? Today, many argue that America must be a "pluralistic society," but this raises the question: How much pluralism is possible? Historically, no society has endured without a cultural core that absorbs elements of diverse ethnic populations while remaining intact. When "ethnic pluralism" translates into competing cultural cores, history has shown that societal disintegration follows. When "ethnic pluralism" refers to a limited range of traditions such as religious beliefs and rituals, distinctive ceremonies and holidays honoring a cultural heritage and important figures in this heritage, and even maintenance of a secondary language, the disintegrative potential of ethnicity is reduced. Can the cultural core, which is examined in Chapter 3, absorb important components of diverse ethnic populations? Must ethnic groups assimilate, and, if so, to what degree? What are the consequences for society if assimilation does not occur? To what degree are members of the dominant Anglo-Saxon cultural core willing to accommodate change?

2. Stratification theories emphasize that discrimination forces some ethnic groups into lower-class positions or a narrow range of middleman positions. Inequality is one of the most volatile forces in human organization; when inequality takes on an ethnic dimension, it is doubly volatile. Because the socioeconomic position of many ethnic groups in America is the result of discrimination, it is reasonable to ask: How can the remaining patterns of discrimination be eliminated, or at least reduced? What can be done to compensate descendants of those who have experienced the most discrimination and those who live with the legacy of such discrimination? To the "second American dilemma," discussed in the Points of Debate section in Chapter 1, we now add a caveat: People who have been subjugated for a long time become angry and strike back. Americans need to consider how to avoid the dangers of ethnic violence as a form of retaliation by those in lower socioeconomic positions.

3. Ethnic stratification is sustained by mutually reinforcing cycles (see Figures 2.1 through 2.3); how can these cycles be broken? The identifiability cycle, especially when based on physical features, can be broken by intermarriage. How willing are the members of both subordinate and dominant ethnic groups to accept this type of assimilation? When members of the dominant culture, as well as other subordinate ethnic groups, feel threatened, discrimination and prejudice emerge. How can this cycle be broken, especially as competition for resources (as emphasized by ecological theories) intensifies? Are there enough jobs, houses, or educational credentials to go around? Are those who have these resources willing to see others acquire them if it costs them some of their own privilege? How much, if anything, are people willing to give up in the name of ethnic peace and egalitarianism? What are the consequences if privileged Americans are not willing to give up anything?

KEY TERMS

accommodation stage of
   assimilation, 33
assimilation theories, 33
attitude-receptional assimilation, 34
behavioral-receptional
   assimilation, 34
biological theories, 36
caste system, 40
caste theories, 40
civic assimilation, 34
colonialism theories, 40
colonization complex, 40
competitive phase of assimilation, 33
cultural assimilation, 34
discrimination, 44
egalitarian values, 53
egalitarianism, 55
entrepreneurial resources, 49
equality of results, 55
ethnogenesis, 35
ethny, 36
external colonialism, 40
human ecology theories, 38

humanitarianism, 55
identifiability, 44
identification assimilation, 34
individualism, 55
internal colonialism, 40
kin selection (inclusive fitness), 36
marital assimilation, 34
middleman minority theories, 43
middleman minorities, 43
negative beliefs, 50
opportunities for individuals, 55
pluralism theories, 35
psychological theories, 37
reciprocal altruism, 36
resource shares, 45
sense of threat, 48
social identity theory, 37
split-class theories, 42
split-labor market theories, 41
stereotypes, 50
stratification theories, 39
structural assimilation, 34
theory, 32

 Visit our text-specific website at www.mhhe.com/aguirre7e for valuable resources for both students and instructors.

CHAPTER 3

The Anglo-Saxon Core and Ethnic Antagonism

Relations between ethnic groups almost always involve elements of domination and subordination: One ethnic subpopulation is able to impose its culture and institutional arrangements on another. In the United States, this process of cultural and institutional domination is complex because of the immigration of so many diverse ethnic groups, but one fact is clear: Anglo-Saxon culture and institutions often dictate and define what other ethnic populations must become (Gordon, 1964; Vargas, 1998). Each ethnic minority in America has been expected to adapt to this Anglo-Saxon core, and each has experienced discrimination by those who have sought to maintain the cultural symbols and institutional structure of this core. Thus, before exploring the lives of the most prominent ethnic minorities in the United States, let us explore the history of those dominant sociocultural traditions that have been imposed on other ethnics.

EARLY COLONIZATION OF AMERICA

The Anglo-Saxons

The term "Anglo-Saxon" is a bit of a misnomer; it derives from northern Germanic tribes—the Saxons and Angles—that invaded England in the fifth and sixth centuries, displacing other tribes whose lives had already been disrupted by the invasions of the Celts from continental Europe and later the Romans. Other invaders followed, such as the Normans from France; and as a result, a considerable amount of mingling among continental and English cultures ensued. Thus, the English settlers who came to America were themselves a product of a long history of conquest and blending of ethnic subpopulations. And not only were Scots and Welsh (the remnants of the old Celts) part of the early "English" settlements, but in some areas significant numbers of Germans (as many as one-third in Pennsylvania) and Scandinavians were to follow, blending together with these "English Americans" to form the cultural core of America.

The term **Anglo-Saxon** (or one of its variants, **White Anglo-Saxon Protestant [WASP]**) denotes a northern European cultural and institutional complex

The white Anglo-Saxon core, clearly represented in this scene of the signing of the Declaration of Independence, was the dominant group that established the cultural and institutional agenda of the United States.

of ethnic traditions fused with, and dominated by, the English who were the first to settle North America in large numbers and to begin the process of colonization. We use the terms *Anglo-Saxon* and *WASP,* therefore, to denote an ethnic complex consisting of northern European ethnic stock with light, "white" skin; Protestant religious beliefs; Protestant-inspired values based on individualism, hard work, savings, and secular material success; and English cultural traditions (language, laws, and beliefs) and institutional structures (politics, economics, and education).

The Early Colonists

Although the early colonizers were predominantly English, there were significant numbers of Welsh and Scots. At first, the Welsh maintained their own communities, and even language traditions, but by the late 1600s, they were assimilated into the English core. Scots constituted a much larger population, coming from both the Highlands and the Lowlands as well as from Ireland (where many Scots had earlier migrated). Like the Welsh, they were almost fully assimilated into English culture by the end of the seventeenth century. A few Irish also lived in the early settlement communities, but the flood of Irish immigrants was to come much later.

Germans constituted the largest of the non–British Isle segment of early colonists, with almost all coming from the Protestant north. Later German immigrants were Catholics and Jews, but the early Germans were close to the English in culture and institutional practices. Thus, it was not difficult for these Germans to change in ways compatible with English culture, although some distinctive German traditions remained in isolated communities. Other northern Europeans, such as Scandinavians, were not as prominent as Germans; their peak period of immigration was not to come until the late nineteenth century. Continental Europeans, such as the Dutch and French (who were settling in larger numbers in Canada), also immigrated, but again, they did not come to the early colonies en masse.

Thus, by the close of the eighteenth century in the aftermath of the Revolutionary War and in the early phases of the emergence of the United States as a nation, the American Historical Association (1932) estimates that 60.1 percent of the free, nonslave population was English, 14.0 percent Scotch and Scotch-Irish, 8.6 percent German, 3.6 percent Irish, 3.1 percent Dutch, 3.0 percent French or Swedish, and 7.6 percent other ethnic nationalities. The English dominated numerically for the first two centuries, especially if one includes other ethnic groups from the British Isles. This dominant group established the cultural and institutional agenda of the United States.

THE CULTURAL AND INSTITUTIONAL LEGACY OF EARLY COLONIZATION

The Core Culture

Language Perhaps the single most important cultural legacy of the early settlers was the English language. Language was to become a litmus test for subsequent immigrants' right to be "American," for the early settlers demanded that English be spoken and that other immigrant populations adopt this language or suffer the consequences. Indeed, there was great agonizing over the "mongrelization" of the white, Anglo-Saxon culture by immigrants who spoke other languages. These concerns exist today, as is clearly evident in the "English-as-the-official-language" campaigns in Congress and some states.

Basic Values Many of the core values of America come from English Protestantism, as Max Weber [1905–1906 (1930)] emphasized in his famous analysis. As Weber stressed, the British brought with them to the Americas **ascetic Protestantism,** as personified in **Puritanism,** which emphasized salvation, hard work, abstinence from temptation, and religiosity. Weber's portrayal of asceticism—discipline, hard work, efficient use of time, rationality, accumulation and profit without moral temptation—can be seen in the core values of America. These values, in turn, have been used as a yardstick to see if ethnic immigrants "measure up." Those ethnic groups who have not been deemed hardworking, efficient, and disciplined have become targets of prejudicial beliefs and discriminatory practices.

Legal Tenets The basic tenets of American law owe much to British traditions, as modified by the colonists' adoption of ideas from eighteenth-century French philosophies. Law is to rule; people are to be equal before the law; laws are to be enacted by representatives of the people; and concentrations of power are to be limited or held in check by law. Despite the blending of French and British philosophical and legal traditions, much of the actual substance of early law in the colonies was English in origin. For example, the specific rights of property holders and obligations established by contracts were considered as important in the actual wording of substantive laws as the broader philosophical and constitutional concerns about equality, freedom, and justice. This disjunction between general constitutional principles, on the one hand, and state and local laws protecting property rights, on the other, enabled patterns of legally sanctioned discrimination to persist until the latter decades of the twentieth century.

The dominant systems of symbols in America—language, values, and laws—derive from the early English settlers. These core cultural components have, of course, been intermingled with those of other cultures and altered with changing circumstances, but more noticeable is the continuity of these symbols and their capacity to define how members of ethnic groups must speak, think, and behave.

The Core Institutional Structures

Economic Institutions The early American settlers came primarily for economic reasons. Colonial settlement was geared to the extraction of raw materials for English commerce and the creation of new markets for English goods. Other reasons for settlement—to escape religious persecution, to reduce the population, to arrest the Spanish and French advance in the hemisphere, and to search for a quicker passage to India—were secondary to the desire of the English Crown and commercial interests to develop America in ways that increased England's prosperity. The chartering of companies and granting of territory were the initial vehicles for transporting commercial capitalism to the colonies. Here, emphasis was placed on private property, contracts, and markets. The drive to take land, develop farms, kill or displace Native Americans, and import slaves was fueled by the effort to create markets that sent raw materials across the Atlantic and brought back finished goods from commercial and emerging industrial interests in England.

The Revolution freed this market-oriented economy from the chartered companies of the English Crown and created what eventually was to be a dynamic form of capitalism that relied on disadvantaged and inexpensive ethnic labor. The enslavement of Africans was the first manifestation of this use of ethnic populations to extract profits; the mass killing of Native Americans was ultimately for the economic gains that came with their land and resources; the conquest of Mexican Americans in the Southwest marked a similar appropriation of land and subordination of an ethnic group for economic gain; finally, the large-scale importation of white ethnic groups from other parts of continental Europe and of Asians was used to sustain further expansion of industrial development.

Thus, the legacy of early British commercial capitalism evolved into a system that depended on subordinated ethnic labor—a situation that persists to the present day.

Political Institutions   As with legal tenets, the structure of government in the United States reflects the blending of seventeenth-century British political traditions (Huntington, 1966) and eighteenth-century French social philosophy. The early colonists' concepts of decentered nationhood, representative government, decentralized power, and rule by law were greatly supplemented in the post-Revolutionary era by French thinking on equality, justice, individual rights, representative democracy, and checks and balances among legislative, judicial, and administrative branches of government. The result was a constitutional democracy that expounded high principles involving justice, equality, and freedom but also gave much political autonomy to local communities and the states.

In actual practice, this decentralized system allowed for considerable disjunction between lofty constitutional principles—freedom, equality, and justice—and the actual operation of government. Both local and state laws perpetuating slavery, justifying land appropriation from Native Americans and Mexican Americans, and encouraging discrimination against ethnic groups employed as inexpensive laborers existed alongside egalitarian constitutional tenets. Moreover, these highly discriminatory laws and political practices were often sanctioned by all branches of the federal government in the name of territorial expansion, industrial and commercial development, private property rights, and, most important, **states' rights.** This same system existed within a democracy that attacked discrimination on the political and legal battlefields. The result was that ethnic groups and their allies from the dominant core gradually overcame the most blatant and formal patterns of discrimination by making appeals to constitutional principles, by taking power at the local level, and by forcing legislative changes in the laws at all levels of government.

Educational Institutions   Before the Revolution, schooling was private and available only to affluent, mostly Anglo-Saxon citizens. Education was based largely on the tenets of English Protestantism, the core values that Protestantism spawned, the culture of western and northern Europe, and the views of commerce and politics held by the early English settlers. This early private system did not reach a large proportion of the population, but it became the model for the public schools, which later proliferated as an explicit and acknowledged means to "Americanize" newer and non-Protestant immigrants in the latter part of the eighteenth century and throughout the nineteenth and twentieth centuries. What typified these early schools and many public schools thereafter was an Anglo-Saxon Eurocentric curriculum. And even as a system of private Catholic schools, along with other religious institutions, began to emerge, the substance of the secular curriculum in these schools contained the core values and beliefs of the early northern European settlers. Only recently has this curriculum begun to accommodate the realities of non-European immigration and of the legacy of slavery and Native American genocide. In many instances, however, this new material is viewed as a supplement to the core white, Anglo-Saxon, middle-class thrust of the school culture and curriculum. These new materials are designed as supplements to efforts at Americanizing those who were unsuccessfully assimilated, such as those Native Americans and African Americans who remain at the fringes of society, those who have resisted full assimilation, such as Mexicans and other Latino individuals, and those newer immigrants, such as various Asian and Arab groups, who **must learn** Western and American ways.

Religious Institutions   The English brought with them Anglican and Congregational Protestantism, although these religions were not dominant by the Revolutionary era. The religious tone of the society was decidedly Protestant, however, with other religions, particularly Catholicism and Judaism, viewed most suspiciously. In fact, Will Herberg (1960) has argued that Catholicism, Judaism, and non-British Protestantism all accommodated themselves in the language used in their services, the organization of their religious schools, and the format of their rituals. As increasing numbers of non-English Protestants and non-Protestants immigrated to America in the post-Revolutionary era, tolerance for religious pluralism became evident; yet this was a pluralism among unequal partners, for English religious traditions dictated how each religion was to be tolerated. To this day, hostility exists toward those religions that do not conform to the style and format of Protestantism.

ANGLO-SAXON HEGEMONY AND THE DYNAMICS OF ETHNICITY

The Domination of the Anglo-Saxon Core

We can conclude, then, that the core cultural and institutional structures of the United States have been disproportionately influenced by the early English settlers. As founders of America, the English did not have to compete with rival cultural symbols and institutions from another equally developed population. For although Native Americans helped many European settlers survive the early winters, their institutional structures were unlikely to survive those of peoples from a much more technologically developed society. Unless the first settlers wanted to return to hunting and gathering or simple horticulture, Native American institutions could not out-compete those brought by an economically and militarily more developed population. Native Americans and their institutional structures were destroyed and displaced, as was their culture.

Once Anglo-Saxon culture and institutional structures were in place, Anglo-Saxons could set the terms of competition among ethnic groups—the nature of the playing field, the rules of the game, and the players who would be allowed in the game. In so doing, they could force other cultures and institutional systems to adapt to and adopt Anglo-Saxon ways. A conquering ethnic group, which has conquered and displaced the founding native stock, can usually establish itself before other ethnic migrants arrive and, as a consequence, will almost always be able to dominate.

Today, with 200 years of immigration to complement the ancestors of African slaves, Latinos, and Native Americans, the descendants of Anglo-Saxons still hold a disproportionate number of elite positions (see Feagin, 1989:75–78, for a brief review). Not only are core cultural and basic institutional structures Anglo-Saxon but the elite members of this group are overrepresented by the descendants of those who came before the Revolution. Because these elite members have the power to influence beliefs and policy, Anglo-Saxons can disproportionately determine the cultural climate and institutional policies of American society today. We are not concluding that there is a concerted conspiracy to do so; rather, the elite Anglo-Saxons and their many assimilated allies from other ethnic groups, especially later European immigrants, simply view certain symbols and arrangements as more desirable, workable, and fair. Indeed, they are likely to believe that these symbols and arrangements offer the best chance for the disadvantaged to do better in American society.

Table 3.1 reassembles the Census Bureau's data on reported ancestries. The actual numbers of individuals from various ancestral backgrounds, as presented in Table 3.1, are interesting and reflect the continued dominance of European ancestry in people's self-reports. Forty-four percent of the total number of respondents who specified their first ancestry reported that they are of European origin. Some 26 percent reported ancestries that correspond to the founding generations of northern Europeans—that is, the Anglo-Saxon core. The other 14 percent reported ancestries from the large immigrant pools that came to the United States in the middle to late nineteenth century and early twentieth century. About 10 percent of the American population reports that it is of Mexican origin.

The dominance of white ethnic groups, especially those in the Anglo-Saxon core as well as others who have adopted this core culture, is reflected in their economic well-being, as can be seen in a review of tables in Chapter 1. White ethnic groups have lower rates of poverty and higher levels of wealth than Native Americans, African Americans, and Latinos (Farley, 1990:238; U.S. Bureau of the Census, 1991a, b, and c). Some Asians match or exceed non-Latino white

TABLE 3.1 Ancestries Reported by Americans,* 2008

Ancestry	Percentage Who Report
European	44.24%
Early European core[†]	25.77
Later European immigrants[‡]	14.11
African	0.90
American	5.90
Mexican	10.11

*First ancestry reported.
[†]Respondents who reported their ancestry as German, English, French, Scottish, Scots-Irish, Dutch, Norwegian, or Swedish.
[‡]Respondents who reported their ancestry as Irish, Italian, or Polish.
Source: 2008 American Community Survey, People Reporting Ancestry.

Americans in income and wealth (see Chapter 8), but this fact does not detract from the basic point: White ethnic groups from the original core and later white immigrants who suffered enormously *until* they were absorbed into the core do well compared to those who were brought as slaves (African Americans), those who were killed by European diseases or instruments of violence (Native Americans), and those who were displaced by conquest in the Southwest (Mexican Americans). Other Latinos and Asians have also suffered, but not to the same degree as those whose human and material resources were taken away or used to build the society.

The Anglo-Saxon Core and the Dynamics of Discrimination

The imposition of the Anglo-Saxon core has not always been benign in the past, nor is it today. The dominance of the Anglo-Saxon core has led to patterns of ethnic antagonism along the lines discussed in Chapter 2. As each new ethnic group arrived, it posed a threat to this core: These ethnic groups tended to be non-Protestant, sometimes non-Christian; they were willing to work for less; they

Bird's-eye view of a Ku Klux Klan parade.

were sufficiently numerous to tip local balances of political power; they placed new burdens on schools and housing; and they brought different languages, values, beliefs, and other symbol systems. This threat led to negative and prejudicial stereotyping of these newly arrived ethnic groups based on their inability to conform to the Anglo-Saxon core; these prejudicial beliefs legitimized discrimination in jobs, housing, education, and politics. Such discrimination was relatively easy to practice because recently arrived ethnic groups are identifiable in culture (language, beliefs, traditions, values), behavior, imported institutions (religion, family), and, for many, physical appearance (skin color, facial features). Those who could adapt to Anglo-Saxon culture by changing their cultural or behavioral norms experienced less discrimination, especially if they were white (see Box 3.1). Groups who remained identifiable, but were small, and possessed entrepreneurial skills, tended to find middleman minority niches, even in the face of intense discrimination. Groups who were identifiable, large, and without skills or other resources tended to occupy lower socioeconomic positions.

As with each wave of immigration, the emancipation from slavery of African Americans and the mere survival of Native Americans and Mexicans set in motion these discriminatory dynamics. In the early years of settlement, in the seventeenth and eighteenth centuries, Africans were enslaved and Native Americans conquered; however, with the "freedom" and partial emergence of these populations, the Anglo-Saxon core had to adjust to the perceived threat against their predominance.

Germans and Scandinavians began to migrate to America in the late eighteenth century and continued to do so throughout the nineteenth century, as did many English. Their presence posed less threat to the Anglo-Saxon core than other ethnic populations, however, because of their Protestant and northern European heritage. But for the other ethnic groups, the dynamics of discrimination were always accelerated by the perception of new threats.

Abolitionist pressures to free slaves heightened the sense of threat in the South and also in the North. As the country expanded westward, nations of Native Americans were successively conquered in the Indian Wars of the 1800s and shunted to various reservations. The Indians were viewed as a constant threat by the white settlers who had taken their land and destroyed their culture. Irish Catholics, the first of the non-Protestant Europeans, came between the 1830s and 1860s. Their large numbers unsettled the Anglo-Saxon core in America's key cities. The Chinese—the first Asian ethnic population—came in the 1850s to 1870s as railroad workers. Their non-Western ways posed a threat to the western extensions of the Anglo-Saxon core. The Mexicans of the Southwest were colonized and thrown off their land beginning in the 1850s. Those who remained in the United States were relegated to low-wage jobs—a condition that continued and was exacerbated in the Mexican migration into the Southwest throughout the twentieth century. From the 1880s through the first decades of the twentieth century, Italians, Jews from eastern Europe, and Poles entered in large numbers. The Japanese and Filipinos also arrived at this time, coming as agricultural workers, often via Hawaii, to the West Coast and bearing with them the "threat" of Asian and South Asian cultures.

Box 3.1
The Changing Ethnic Composition of America

In addition to counting the current number of people in various ethnic groups, the Census Bureau also runs projections on the ethnic composition of America in the future. In the figures below, the actual proportion of the population represented by an ethnic group is reported for 2004, the most recent year available, and then the projections for 2025 and 2045 are made. What is immediately evident is that the non-Latino white core will decline from around 70 percent of the population today to around 55 percent in less than fifty years; African Americans will increase only a little, about 1 percent over the next forty years; and Native Americans will remain less than 1 percent of the total population. The decline of the white core is the result of an increase in the Asian/Pacific Islander population from 4 percent to over 8 percent and, more dramatically, in the Latino population from 14 percent to 23 percent. There is, then, a clear "Latinoization" of America under way, and particularly in certain regions of the country such as the Southwest, the eastern seaboard, and south Florida. As this transformation occurs, the culture of America will also change. A change of this magnitude is always feared by those whose ways of life will be transformed to some unknown degree. Thus, the growth of the Asian and Latino populations will often be seen as threatening not only by whites but perhaps by African Americans as well.

Relative Size of Ethnic Populations

	Percentage of Total Population		
	2008*	2025†	2050†
Non-Hispanic white Americans	68%	62%	46%
Non-Hispanic African Americans	13	13	15
Non-Hispanic Native Americans	0.89	0.7	0.8
Non-Hispanic Asians/Pacific Islanders	5	6	9
Latinos	15	18	30
	100.0‡	100.0‡	100.0‡

*Actual.
†Projection.
Source: U.S. Bureau of the Census (2002, 2009) Population Projections Program, Population Division; U.S. Bureau of the Census, Selected Characteristics of the Total and Native Population, 2004, 2006–2008 American Community Survey.

African Americans began to migrate to the Northeast and Midwest in the early decades of the twentieth century, competing with the white ethnic groups for employment. Puerto Ricans came to the Northeast in large numbers, starting in the 1940s and continuing to the present. Cubans began to come to south Florida in the 1960s and 1970s. Their presence evoked less fear because of their anticommunist views and professed desire to return to Cuba; but their large numbers and Latin culture pinched at Anglo sensibilities. And from the 1960s to

Latino high school and middle school students and young adults march to a park holding signs protesting legislation that increases penalties for illegal immigrants and those who harbor them.

the present, new Asian groups—Koreans, Vietnamese, Taiwanese, Chinese, Filipinos—have migrated to the United States. Each wave of immigration and migration has posed a threat to the integrity of the Anglo-Saxon core.

Although the culture and institution building of each wave of immigrants have broadened the culture and structure of American society beyond the original Anglo-Saxon core, this broadening has always involved the assimilation of immigrant cultures to the Anglo-Saxon core. Even with accommodation, however, the more visible dynamic has been ethnic antagonism—born of and sustained by threat, prejudice, and discrimination—between the new cultures and the older cultural core.

Changes in the relative proportions of subpopulations in a society will almost always generate ethnic antagonism. As the table in Box 3.1 outlines, very large changes in the distribution of ethnic subpopulations are under way, with non-Hispanic whites losing their majority status in 2047, just thirty-seven years into the future. Thus, non-Hispanic whites reading this book are very likely to become just one more minority—albeit the largest minority—in American society. This shift in the relative size of ethnic subpopulations is, however, not new. The United States is indeed a "land of immigrants"; and thus, the process of changing ethnic composition has proceeded since the eighteenth century. Table 3.2 can offer some sense of this longer-term change. The left column lists in order of their respective percentages of the total population the ethnic composition of the United States in 1790. Not surprising, a very large proportion—over

TABLE 3.2 Long-Term Changes in the Distribution and Salience of Ethnic Subpopulations

Ancestry in 1970		Ancestry in 2008	
Ancestry Subpopulation	Percentage of Total Population	Ancestry Subpopulation	Percentage of Total Population
English	47.5%	German	15.2%
African	19.0	African	12.9
Scotch-Irish	8.0	Irish	10.9
German	7.0	English	8.7
Irish (southern)	5.0	Mexican	7.4
Scottish	4.0	Italian	5.6
Welsh	3.0	Hispanic/Latino	4.9
Dutch	2.5	French	3.9
French	2.0	Asian	3.6
Native American	1.0	Polish	3.2
		Scottish	1.7
Spanish	0.5	Dutch	1.6
Swedish/Other	0.5	Norwegian	1.6
British Isle (total)	67.5	Scotch-Irish	1.5
		Native American	1.5
		Swedish	1.4
		Other/Not reported	13.4

Ancestry in 2008
Percentage of Total Population
11.5%
0.9
7.4
6.1
10.1
4.5
15.4
0.51
4.4
2.2
1.2
0.9
1.0
0.9
0.8
0.8
11.5

Source: Social Science Data Analysis Network (SSDAN), 2002; U.S. Census, 1790; 2008 American Community Survey.

77 percent—came from northern European societies, with 67 percent of these from the British Isle—once again signaling the Anglo-Saxon origins of American society. Even at this time, the original immigrants—Native Americans—constituted only about 1 percent of the population—about the same as today, although this figure may represent an undercount. In this sea of white ethnics were African-origin slaves, constituting 19 percent of the population in early American society, although they were confined to the plantation system of the South; and thus, it is not hard to see why an enslaved "black" subpopulation was seen as a threat to the "white" Anglo-Saxon core of America, particularly in the South but eventually in the North as well.

Comparing the left column of Table 3.2 with the right column from the 2008 census is revealing. These figures differ from those in the table in Box 1.4 because the methodologies for their assembly vary, with the right column in Table 3.2 representing a combination of reporting and an actual head count of some ethnic subpopulations, such as African Americans, Asians, and Pacific Islanders, whereas other figures represent reported ancestry, which tends to undercount British Isle–origin persons because this ethnic identity is no longer as salient as it was in 1790. Still, it is interesting that German ancestry and French ancestry remain sufficiently important for individuals who, perhaps, overreport these ancestries. The same may be true for Native Americans. Thus, neither column in the table is wholly accurate, and yet, a rough comparison of the two columns (with a corresponding recognition of methodological problems involved) is revealing, if only to note the changes in the salience of ethnic identity to individuals or to the census takers. Hispanics/Latinos constitute the largest reported ancestry followed by Germans (11.5 percent) and Mexicans (10.1 percent). The British-Isle population has moved down the list, although again, some of this decline is due to underreporting of ancestry. Spanish ancestry in 1790 was near the bottom of the list, constituting 0.5 percent of the population, but with the expansion of American society westward and the eventual Treaty of Guadalupe Hidalgo ending the Mexican-American War, Hispanics (the outcome of mixing of Indian and Spanish genes and cultures) have moved up the list; and as the table in Box 3.1 underscores, they and other Hispanic populations from Central and South America have become the second largest ethnic subpopulation in the United States. European-origin whites (although in a very real sense many Hispanics are at least partly of European origin and, hence, defined as "white" by the Census Bureau) will remain the most numerous subpopulation in America but eventually will lose their majority status by the midpoint of this century.

This long-term pattern of change in the relative salience of ethnicity and the relative size of ethnic subpopulations has consistently generated threats. These threats have been codified into negative ethnic stereotypes and patterns of ethnic discrimination throughout the history of the United States. As emphasized earlier, all of the migrations were threatening to the Anglo-Saxon core, even as people's explicit identification with their European ancestry declined among most whites. Increasingly, with each new generation of descendants, the sense of "being white" has increasingly trumped individuals' identification with their exact ancestry. *White vs. non-white* has increasingly became the focal point of threat, prejudice, and discrimination despite the fact that some of the targets of discrimination—for example, Hispanics, Jews, and Arabs—are themselves defined by the Census Bureau as "white." Whatever the differences in religion and country of origin did to fuel early discrimination lost at least some of its power, while the *perceived* divide between white and non-white gained salience for most of the twentieth century and represented the fuel of threat, prejudice, and discrimination over the last 100 years. Indeed, the increasing portrayal of these differences as "racial" and somehow embodied in significant biological differences only codified the sense of difference of "others" from whites.

Whiteness became the proxy marker of the Anglo-Saxon core, even among descendants of southern European immigrants, while Asian, Latino, Arab, and African-origin ethnics became, to varying degrees, a threat to individuals who, with their white skin color, identified with this core. When people have felt their "American way of life" threatened over the last decades, they are only denoting by another name the cultural and institutional system that was built around the Anglo-Saxon core. Whether these fears had a firm basis in reality could be debated, but the fear and the sense of threat alone—whether real, overblown, or simply a figment of the imagination—was very real in its consequences because it created a system of ethnic stratification that persists to this day. Although there are some modest indications that this system is not as pronounced as it was fifty years ago, it still remains a potential and often an actual source of conflict in American society.

SUMMARY

Ethnic relations in America have been profoundly influenced by the cultural systems and institutional structures of the first colonizers. This is almost always the case when a more powerful population invades the territory of a less powerful population and then seeks to settle there. Throughout world history, this process has occurred again and again, but the New World added a different twist: The settlement and expansion of the conquering population required the accommodation of new waves of immigrants. Some immigrants were imported as slaves, but most came voluntarily from Europe and Asia. As Native Americans were nearly eliminated and isolated on reservations, and Mexicans were conquered and deposed, America became, literally, a land of opportunity for immigrants and migrants. The rapid industrialization of the East and Midwest, along with the expansion of agriculture and ranching in the West, created new opportunities, which stimulated a massive wave of immigration. Among the Europeans, those from northern Europe were the first to come, followed by central and southern Europeans. Most of these Europeans initially settled in the East and emerging Midwest; later, they moved farther west. In addition to these white immigrants, Asian immigrants began to settle on the West Coast; some came before most northern and southern Europeans, but most came at about the same time as these Europeans.

These early immigrants, as well as those who arrived in the latter part of the twentieth century, have had to confront the Anglo-Saxon core, itself an amalgam of cultural and institutional systems of the British Isles, with significant infusions from German, Dutch, Scandinavian, and French cultural traditions. This core consisted of such cultural elements as the English language, English values and beliefs, and English legal tenets, along with mostly northern European institutional structures in economy, government, education, and religion. This core represented the environment to which other ethnic groups would have to adapt and which they would have to adopt, or live with the consequences if they did not. For white ethnic groups, assimilation was easier because of their European heritage and, most important, their skin color; for Asians, physical identifiability and their non-Western culture posed greater problems; for freed slaves, skin color in the face of extreme prejudice and discrimination made it very difficult to adapt to, much less adopt, all the elements of the core; for more recent immigrants—particularly Asians and Latinos—adjustment has not been easy because of the threats that these immigrants pose not only to many members of the Anglo-Saxon core but also to those earlier immigrants who have yet to fully adapt to this core.

Each wave of immigration, as well as each internal wave of migration, has activated the dynamics of discrimination discussed in Chapter 2 and modeled in Figures 2.1 through 2.3. Each ethnic group has altered the Anglo-Saxon core, but only to a point; the persistence of ethnic tension indicates that not all ethnic groups can, are allowed to, or want to assimilate.

POINTS OF DEBATE

Some of the most hotly contested issues in America today revolve around the conflict between subordinate ethnic groups and members of the dominant Anglo-Saxon core. Often as a reaction to discrimination, but also as a matter of preference, ethnic minority groups have sought to cultivate and maintain their distinctive cultural features and patterns of social organization, even if this means that they conflict with the Anglo-Saxon core. The resulting tension and conflict engenders questions such as the following.

1. How flexible can the Anglo-Saxon core be in accommodating the key elements of other cultures and remain the core? Many argue that America must become pluralistic, but to what degree and at what expense? If a society has no clear cultural or institutional core, is such a society viable?
2. Has the existence of blatant and established discrimination in America forced ethnic groups to discard assimilation as an option? If so, has the United States passed the critical point after which accommodation is less likely than ethnic conflict? If this is so, what is to be done? What is the future of the United States if ethnic subpopulations polarize around distinctive cores?

3. Has the Anglo-Saxon core been inflexible, as is often charged by the victims of discrimination? There are clear signs that considerable change has occurred, as reflected in the massive contributions of all ethnic groups to the culture and structure of American society. Even those populations that have experienced severe discrimination have assimilated some elements of their culture. There are two important questions: Can the Anglo-Saxon core absorb more? Are ethnic groups willing to give up more of their own cultural and institutional core in order to decrease the polarization between cores? If the answer is no to both questions, what is America's future?

KEY TERMS

Anglo-Saxon, 61
ascetic Protestantism, 63
Puritanism, 63

states' rights, 65
White Anglo-Saxon Protestant (WASP), 61

Visit our text-specific website at www.mhhe.com/aguirre7e for valuable resources for both students and instructors.

CHAPTER 4

White Ethnic Americans

*I*t is often noted that America is a land of immigrants. The largest waves of immigration occurred in the nineteenth and early twentieth centuries when vast numbers of non-Protestant white Europeans entered the United States. The southern Irish were the first non-Protestants to enter in significant numbers in the early 1800s. In the final decades of the nineteenth century and the first two decades of the twentieth century, additional masses of Catholic Italians and Poles as well as Jews immigrated. This influx posed a threat to the Anglo-Saxon Protestant core, setting in motion the dynamics of discrimination.

These white ethnic populations eventually overcame Anglo-Saxon Protestant discrimination and moved up the socioeconomic ladder. Their success—often used to condemn Native Americans, African Americans, and Latinos for not doing as well—has ironically contributed to present-day negative stereotypes about other ethnic groups and to persistent patterns of discrimination against them. Although the history of these white subpopulations does provide an example of what is possible for other ethnic groups, the greater identifiability of the currently unassimilated makes them targets of prejudice and discrimination that typically inhibit full movement into the American mainstream made up of the Anglos plus the white immigrants who overcame discrimination.

As we emphasized in Chapter 3, the Anglo-Saxon core consists of immigrants from the British Isles (England, Protestant Northern Island, Scotland, and Wales), northern Germany, Denmark, Norway, and Sweden; these populations now inhabit what were historically the regions of the Angles and Saxons. Of course, the early European settlers to North America also included French, Dutch, Portuguese, and Russians. Later, during the nineteenth and early twentieth centuries, other European ethnics, such as Italians, Poles, and Catholic Irish, migrated to the United States and, after a period of intense discrimination against them, were incorporated into the Anglo-Saxon core. Surprisingly, it is difficult to get timely data on these diverse white ethnics of European ancestry; the data are collected during the census and the surveys between the full census every ten years, but they are not always reported. As we saw in Table 3.1 on page 67, 44 percent of Americans who are willing to state their ancestry report that their ancestors were Europeans, with 26 percent of these seeing themselves as descendants of the early European core (or the core of ethnics inhabiting those areas of northern Europe where the Angles and Saxons once lived).

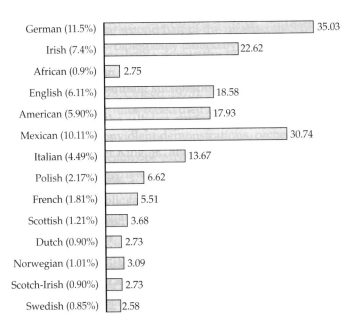

German (11.5%) 35.03
Irish (7.4%) 22.62
African (0.9%) 2.75
English (6.11%) 18.58
American (5.90%) 17.93
Mexican (10.11%) 30.74
Italian (4.49%) 13.67
Polish (2.17%) 6.62
French (1.81%) 5.51
Scottish (1.21%) 3.68
Dutch (0.90%) 2.73
Norwegian (1.01%) 3.09
Scotch-Irish (0.90%) 2.73
Swedish (0.85%) 2.58

(In millions. Percentage of total population in parentheses.)

FIGURE 4.1 Largest reported ancestries in the United States, 2008.
Source: 2008 American Community Survey, People Reporting Ancestry.

Figure 4.1 reports the number (and percentage) of the most frequently stated ancestries. As is evident, the largest reported ancestry is German. If we add up the British Isle ancestries, another 15.6 percent of the population see themselves as coming from northern Europe. (Note: The data in Table 4.1 differ from those in Tables 3.1 and 3.2 because only *stated* ancestry was reported.) Thus, to be a white ethnic means to see one's origins as European. (Of course, in many ways the "other white ethnic groups" reported by the census—for example, white Latinos—also have more indirect European origins, not only linguistically but culturally.) But, despite the fact that the language and other cultural traditions of Latinos have European origins (mixed, obviously, with the indigenous peoples of the Americas), they are still generally viewed as culturally distinct from non-Hispanic whites. Indeed, despite the mixing of indigenous South American and European cultures, white Latinos are threatening to white ethnics. Because non-Hispanic whites have dominated American society, receiving the most resource shares and holding power to sustain the Anglo-Saxon core by forcing all who immigrate to assimilate, larger migrations of Latinos pose a threat to those vested in the Anglo-Saxon core, as we will come to see. Moreover, ethnic subpopulations whose ancestry does not trace back to Europe and who are not defined as "white" have also posed threats to the guardians of the northern European culture and to the institutional systems that dominate the United States. Threat inevitably leads to prejudicial beliefs and discrimination against those who can be identified as "different." As we explore in this chapter, even those who were

TABLE 4.1 Resource Shares of Non-Hispanic Whites Compared to Other Ethnic Subpopulations, 2008

| Ethnic Subpopulation | Educational Attainment | | Median Family Income | Unemployment Rate | Individuals Living in Poverty |
	High School Diploma	College Degree			
Non-Hispanic Whites	87.1%	29.8%	$66.652	5.2%	10.2%
Latinos	62.3	13.3	42,074	7.6	20.7
African Americans	83.0	19.6	40,259	10.1	24.7
Native Americans/ Alaska Natives	76.2	12.7	40,310	12.0*	25.3
Asians	88.7	52.6	77,046	4.0	10.6
Native Hawaiians/ Pacific Islanders	84.2	14.7	58,990	8.0*	15.7

*2006 American Community Survey; 2010 *Statistical Abstract* (U.S. Census Bureau), Tables 224, 225, 609, and 36.

clearly "white" and who came from Europe were also victims of prejudice and discrimination when they first arrived, because they also posed threats to European-origin white ethnics.

RESOURCE SHARES OF WHITE ETHNICS

Table 4.1 assembles data from the 2006 American Community Survey and other sources on the resource shares of non-Hispanic whites, comparing these shares with other ethnic subpopulations. Earlier data that broke out specific white ethnic ancestries are now almost 20 years old, so they are no longer fully reliable. Hence, in the absence of data on the specific ancestry of the European-origin population, we are forced to use as a proxy the category *non-Hispanic whites* and compare their resource shares with those of other ethnic subpopulations. As we emphasized in Chapter 1, resource shares tend to be cumulative. The amount of education that people acquire in a post-industrial society determines the kinds of jobs they can secure, which in turn affects their ability to remain employed and earn incomes that keep them out of poverty.

Thus, reading across Table 4.1, we begin with a simple breakdown of educational attainment: high school and college graduates. As is evident, 62 percent of Latinos have a high school diploma, whereas 87 percent of non-Hispanic whites, 83 percent of African Americans, 76 percent of Native Americans/Alaska Natives, 89 percent of Asians, and 84 percent of Native Hawaiians/Pacific Islanders are high school graduates. Variations across ethnic subpopulations are even greater with respect to college education, with 53 percent of Asians and 30 percent of non-Hispanic whites holding a college degree. Latinos, Native Americans/Alaska Natives, and Native Hawaiians/Pacific Islanders have comparatively low rates of college graduation. African Americans have somewhat higher numbers with college degrees but still considerably less than white ethnics. These educational differences enable white ethnics (and Asians) to secure better-paying managerial and professional jobs that offer more employment security. As Table 1.4 on page 17 reports, close to 37 percent of whites hold such jobs, while 47 percent of Asians do. Only about 18 percent of Latinos and 27 percent of African Americans find themselves in these better-paying and more secure managerial and professional occupations. From older census figures from 1990, it was clear back then and certainly is still the case today that much of this employment advantage among white ethnics remains with the descendants of the original Anglo-Saxon core. For example, 40 percent of British Isle descendants held managerial and professional jobs. The highest percentage is for Russians, but these are mostly Russian Jews who have migrated to the United States to escape persecution, and given the emphasis of Jewish culture on education, it is not surprising that back in 1990 (and no doubt today as well, if data were available), 57 percent of Russian-origin Jews were in managerial and professional occupations.

The advantage of white ethnics from northern Europe is that they came early and could kill off and displace the native populations (onto reservations) and

New York. Ellis Island. reg. No. 3163E

Immigrants walking across a pier toward Ellis Island.

thereby impose the culture that dominates the United States today. Those white Europeans who came during the late nineteenth and early twentieth centuries experienced a great deal of discrimination but had one advantage that many other ethnic populations lacked: They were white and European, and within three generations, they could assimilate into the dominant culture and secure resources. Even darker-skinned southern Europeans were able to do so, and in many ways, Latinos today may be able to take the same path as southern Europeans to full assimilation into the Anglo-Saxon core. There is, however, a major difference between Latino immigrants today and those from southern Europe a century ago: Latinos are coming in far greater numbers and from nations that are much closer to the United States, with the result that they often sustain their culture as they move back and forth between the United States and their country of origin. This combination of mass immigrations and maintenance of cultural traditions poses threats to the Anglo-Saxon core and to those later-arriving European whites who had assimilated into this core.

The history of white ethnics in the United States is thus one of European conquest of Native Americans, importation of Africans as slaves, and intense discrimination against Indian aboriginals and African-origin slaves. But it is also a history of successive waves of white immigrants who posed threats to those who had come earlier. When threatened, earlier white immigrants propagated intensely prejudicial beliefs about new white arrivals and engaged in equally intense discrimination. Let us tell this story before moving on to explore other forms of discrimination against ethnics of non-European origin.

IRISH AMERICANS

Irish Americans constitute approximately 18 percent of the population in the United States, which makes them the third largest ethnic group behind the English and Germans (Lieberson and Waters, 1988:34). The first major wave of Irish immigrants arrived in the 1700s, but the exact national heritage of these immigrants is subject to debate. Most were Protestant Scots-Irish, who had immigrated to northern Ireland after the British conquest of Ireland (Leyburn, 1962), but many southern and Catholic Irish also immigrated—perhaps as many as a third of the total in this first large influx (Dickson, 1966:60–70). Because of prejudice against **papists,** many of these Catholics were forced to convert to some form of Protestantism to avoid persecution. By the end of the Revolutionary War, 10 percent of the colonial population was Irish (signaling that the American legacy of the Irish coincided with American society at its founding).

The next wave of immigration began in the 1830s owing to several factors (Shrier, 1958): the potato famine of the 1840s, persistent British persecution of poor Irish, and British encouragement of emigration as a solution to their "Irish problem." Unlike the earlier wave of immigrants who came in search of more opportunities, many of these southern and Catholic migrants saw themselves as banished to America by the British, which perhaps accounts for their intense loyalty to their homeland (Miller, 1985).

As the first of the non-Protestant white ethnic groups to immigrate to America in large numbers, the Irish were targets of vicious prejudice and sustained discrimination. Two generations later, however, most Irish Americans had overcome these disadvantages.

Identifiability of Irish Americans

As with all white ethnic groups, the Irish could be identified only in terms of distinctive cultural, behavioral, and organizational patterns. In the nineteenth century, very conscious efforts were undertaken to portray mainly southern Catholic Irish as a distinct "race," thereby imputing biological differences where none existed. During this time "Scots-Irish" became a popular label, as Protestant northern Irish sought to distance themselves from southern Catholics. Before the efforts to identify southern Catholics, Scots-Irish simply had considered themselves Irish, but with the emerging hostility toward the southern Irish, these northerners sought to differentiate themselves in order to avoid discrimination.

Underlying prejudicial stereotypes of the southern Irish were objections to their Catholicism, their poverty, and their willingness to work for wages lower than those accepted by earlier immigrants. Prejudicial stereotypes perpetuated the perception of the southern Irish as identifiably different and, hence, legitimate targets of discrimination.

Negative Beliefs about Irish Americans

As early as the eighteenth century, southern Irish were subject to negative stereotyping because of their Catholicism. This religious stereotyping became the basis on which some questioned Irish American political loyalty. Indeed, the suspicion that an Irish American politician would be governed by the pope was articulated when John F. Kennedy—an Irish Catholic—ran for president.

The most vicious stereotypes emerged with the large-scale Irish immigrations of the nineteenth century. Fueled by the threat of so many non-Protestant, low-wage workers, white Protestants stereotyped the Irish as immoral and unintelligent, and Irish Catholics in particular as wicked, ignorant, and temperamental (Knobel, 1986:27). All subsequent waves of Catholic white ethnic groups were similarly stereotyped, especially those, such as the Italians and Poles, who immigrated in large numbers to the United States.

In particular, stereotypes of the Irish were perhaps as vicious as against blacks; that is, they were portrayed as less than human. English prejudice against the Irish was imported to America and intensified; and in the context of evolutionary theories and the plight of African Americans, the English prejudice against the Irish imported to America amplified into vicious stereotypes of the Irish as subhuman, apelike, drunk, hostile, and immoral (Curtis, 1971). The Irish were described as a "missing link" between apes, Africans, and the English. Today these extreme stereotypes have diminished, but at times the Irish are viewed as tending toward drunkenness, pugnaciousness, and corruption. Thus, although the Irish have largely overcome prejudice and discrimination, muted forms of the old stereotypes persist.

The Dynamics of Discrimination against Irish Americans

Economic Discrimination   Like most white non-Protestant ethnic groups who migrated to the United States in the nineteenth century, the Catholic Irish were forced to take low-wage jobs. Earlier Protestant Irish, most of whom were "Scots-Irish," had penetrated business and professional positions, but those who came later were less educated and skilled; as a result, they began their experience in America with jobs in manufacturing, mining, construction (of railroads and canals), textiles, and domestic service. Because many women immigrated alone, domestic service offered these women a place to live. Earlier pre-Revolutionary northern Irish had also done much of the menial and domestic labor, often as indentured servants, but by the 1830s and 1840s, when the southern Irish began to come in large numbers, the Scots-Irish had begun to be economically mobile.

The exclusion of the migrating Catholic Irish workers from anything but unskilled work by Protestant employers was legitimated by beliefs in their "racial" inferiority, low intelligence, general pugnaciousness, and unreliability. Employers used even lower-wage black workers to threaten the job security of Irish workers, generating black–Irish tension that persists to this day in many northeastern cities (Bonacich, 1976; Roediger, 1991). Because Irish children were forced to go to work early in life, the second generation frequently did not acquire the educational credentials necessary for mobility out of low-wage jobs.

By the turn of the twentieth century, however, both the northern and the southern Irish were becoming economically mobile (Dinnerstein and Reimers, 1988).

The industrial expansion in the East and Midwest created new opportunities for more skilled workers, and since the Irish had arrived several decades before the large influx of Italians, Poles, and other white ethnic groups, they were more assimilated and advantaged. Economic mobility also came through political success. In many cities, Irish Americans created and controlled the "big-city political machine." For all their corruption, political machines could provide government jobs to individuals and contracts to Irish-owned businesses. During this time, many Irish American workers overcame discrimination by unionizing; their efforts were so successful that they dominated many local unions, especially in mining, construction, and dock work. Although Irish Americans remained dramatically underrepresented in high-skill and professional jobs, they were establishing a more secure economic base from which subsequent generations could move into higher-skill blue-collar jobs, white- collar positions, and an expanding array of professions. Today most Irish Americans have overcome earlier discrimination, as revealed by their higher incomes, jobs, and educational credentials (Lieberson and Waters, 1988).

Political Discrimination One of the enduring stereotypes about Irish Americans is their involvement in corrupt big-city political machines. Political machines in large cities had, of course, emerged and prospered before the Irish were able to penetrate them, but the massive immigration of southern Catholic Irish to the cities created a new constituency for these corrupt political machines. Large pools of poor, ill-housed, and unemployed individuals sustained the machines, and despite the graft and corruption, the machines provided food, jobs, and housing to people in desperate straits in a national political and economic climate where the role of the federal government in addressing urban problems was minimal.

Not only did the political machines provide needed services, but they became an early path to upward mobility for many Irish Americans as well as for large numbers of Italian, Polish, and Jewish immigrants. The corrupt issuance of city contracts to private businesses created jobs in a government-supported private sector. Moreover, the machines generated networks of ties among political, business, religious, and philanthropic leaders who, in turn, controlled vast arrays of employment opportunities for poor immigrants. Although the machines in Brooklyn, New York, Boston, New Haven, Philadelphia, Chicago, and various smaller cities in the Northeast and upper Midwest often extracted a high price in misuse of tax revenues and in subsidies for unneeded or inefficient workers, early generations of white immigrants would have suffered even more without them.

Big political machines could not endure forever, since their corruption and inefficiency were all too obvious. As white ethnic groups became more secure, the need for these corrupt networks diminished, leading to a series of reform movements that established new structures of city government. However, it was not until the 1970s that the Chicago political machine began to fall apart, which shows how a network of power can exist long after it has ceased to serve useful functions.

Success at the local level of politics did not translate into positions of power for Irish Americans at the national level, however. Prejudicial attitudes toward Catholics in an Anglo-Saxon Protestant society excluded Irish Americans from appointments in the judiciary and executive branches of government and limited their success in statewide and national electoral politics. Only in the 1920s did the Catholic Irish begin to enjoy some success in national politics when Alfred E. Smith became the Democratic candidate for president. It was not until the administration of President Roosevelt in the 1930s that Irish Americans were appointed to visible positions in the judiciary, the White House, and other executive branches of government. President Truman continued Roosevelt's pattern of appointing Irish Americans to powerful government positions. When John F. Kennedy ran for president in the 1960s, many of the old fears about papists were revived, although Kennedy's subsequent election appears to have broken the last discriminatory barriers to full political participation by Irish Americans. Today, the fact that a political candidate is Catholic or Irish is not important unless it influences that candidate's views on such emotionally charged issues as abortion.

Educational Discrimination   Irish Americans have educational achievement scores above the national average. Many Irish American children were educated in Catholic schools, many of which were created to counteract discrimination in the mid-1800s as well as to retain Irish ethnicity in the face of intense efforts of the public schools to "Americanize" Irish Catholics. A vast system of Catholic primary and secondary schools, Catholic universities, hospitals, charities, and community service organizations emerged as a result.

The Catholic school system enabled early generations of Irish (and eventually other Catholic immigrants like Italians and Poles) to overcome discrimination against all non-Protestants in the public schools and to sustain important elements of their ethnicity. As this system of education has evolved, it has provided opportunities for Irish Americans to acquire credentials that have facilitated the movement of the last two generations of Irish Americans into higher economic, political, social, and educational positions. Today the educational component of Catholic parochial schools serves many non-Irish Catholics, such as Mexican Americans, Italian Americans, and significant numbers of African Americans. These schools are no longer sustained by reaction to discrimination in public schools, as in the 1880s, but by the desire to maintain or promote religious affiliation and, simultaneously, to ameliorate the problems of decaying public school systems in many urban areas.

Stratification of Irish Americans

Because the Irish were the first non-Protestant population to immigrate to Protestant America, conflict with the Anglo-Saxon core was inevitable. Large numbers of very poor Catholics, willing to work for low wages and settling in cities where their numbers upset old balances of power and social mores, were threatening to indigenous, Protestant residents. The resulting conflict occurred on several fronts: between higher-wage English workers and lower-wage Irish, between Anglo-Saxon employers in industry who tried to destroy unions and Irish workers who sought the protection of unions, between Anglo-Saxon incumbents in political machines and Irish aspirants to power, and between residents of Anglo-Saxon Protestant neighborhoods and Irish Catholics who desperately needed housing. Conflict led to discrimination; education levels, employment profiles, and residence patterns of the first two generations of Irish Catholics indicate that this discrimination was effective (Lieberson and Waters, 1988). For these early immigrants, poor housing, low-wage employment, and low levels of education were typical.

When Irish Americans gained local political power, as the Catholic system of schools and service organizations developed, and as patronage jobs to workers and contracts to Irish-run businesses increased, Irish Americans began to move forward economically, educationally, and socially by the turn of the century. Today, Irish Americans are highly assimilated, retaining their ethnicity through Saint Patrick's Day celebrations, expressions of loyalty toward their homeland, and vestiges of their old neighborhoods and local political power.

When Irish Americans moved up the socioeconomic ladder, they came into conflict with more recent white immigrants and with African Americans who had migrated northward in the first two decades of this century. These new immigrants began to pose a threat not only to the Anglo-Saxon core but also to the more established Irish Americans. In particular, African Americans were viewed as a threat because industrialists used them as strikebreakers in efforts to destroy the unions of the Irish and other white ethnic groups. Today, African Americans still suffer from the legacy of this hostility (Bonacich, 1976).

Because they are white, the Irish who immigrated to the United States were more easily assimilated into the mainstream of American society than were members of darker-skinned ethnic groups. Today, Irish Americans are almost indistinguishable from the descendants of the Anglo-Saxon core in terms of their place in the American socioeconomic hierarchy.

ITALIAN AMERICANS

In the early decades of the nineteenth century, some northern Italians began to migrate to South and North America in a steady trickle that continued for the rest of the century (Schiavo, 1934; U.S. Bureau of the Census, 1975a). The large-scale immigration of southern Italians began in the 1860s and peaked in the first decade of the twentieth century. In contrast to earlier northern Italians, who tended to be more educated, affluent, and able to enter professions and small businesses, the southern Italians were more likely to be poor, uneducated, and agrarian peasants. Moreover, southern Italians tended to sojourn, staying for short periods, making some money, and returning to Italy. Indeed, perhaps as many as one-third of these later Italian immigrants did return to their homeland, a rate of repatriation far surpassing that of any other ethnic group during this period (Learsi, 1954). In all, some 4 million Italian migrants poured

Immigrant workers laying track.

into the United States between 1880 and 1920, with close to 90 percent coming from southern Italy or the island of Sicily (U.S. Bureau of the Census, 1975a). These peasant immigrants were fleeing poverty, low wages, unemployment, economic and political domination by elites, governmental neglect, and declining agricultural productivity (Lopreato, 1970). Soon after entering the United States, they formed "Little Italys" in various cities, primarily in the Northeast but also in the Midwest and somewhat later in the West. From these locations they sought relatively unskilled jobs in public works projects, such as building of canals, sewer systems, and roadways, and in similar labor-intensive sectors of the economy.

Identifiability of Italian Americans

Like the Irish, southern Europeans were portrayed as a distinct "race" that was inferior intellectually and morally. Both the media and intellectuals depicted Italians as incapable of assimilating into Anglo-Saxon society. Fear of their intermarriage with Anglo-Saxons was expressed routinely. Underlying these attitudes were Protestant prejudices against Catholics, as well as other cultural differences between northern and southern European ethnic groups (Gambino, 1974; Higham, 1963). Moreover, because Mediterranean Italians have somewhat darker skin tones than northern Europeans, their identifiability by skin color made them seem a different "race" to northern Europeans.

Negative Beliefs about Italian Americans

The early use of intelligence tests was particularly harmful to Italian Americans because the tests were highly biased against people who were unacculturated and uneducated (Tomasi and Engel, 1970). Italian American schoolchildren (and other newly arrived white ethnic children as well) and enlisted personnel in the army tended to score poorly on these tests, and these results were used as "scientific proof" of Italians' inferior intellect (Kamin, 1974:1–20). When a group is portrayed as inferior in any way, discrimination follows.

Along with early portrayals of intellectual inferiority came a more persistent "mafia" stereotype portraying Italians as people involved with crime and having little integrity. Up to the prohibition period, Irish and Jewish Americans controlled most organized criminal syndicates. When a number of visible and infamous Italians moved into these criminal syndicates, the Italian gangster stereotype emerged and stuck. For some Italian Americans, crime was a means of upward mobility in a hostile society, but the general crime rates for Italians during this period were actually low (Lopreato, 1970:124–26). The mafia stereotype remains today in American culture—defined, and perhaps perpetuated, by movies such as *The Godfather* trilogy, *The Untouchables, Prizzi's Honor,* and many others, often produced by Italians themselves as if the stereotype were being reversed, glamorized, and exploited for economic gain.

Perhaps even more pernicious are media portrayals of Italian males as somewhat ingratiating but tough, dim-witted, and oversexed womanizers ("The Fonz" in television reruns of *Happy Days*). Italian jokes are still uttered with relative impunity, along with ethnic labels such as "dago" and "wop." Images of Italian Americans as overly emotional, jealous, oversexed when young, as fat mammas when old, and as physical, tough, racist hard hats persist (Gambino, 1974:352). Thus, far more than the Irish and Poles, Italian Americans still suffer from negative stereotyping, despite their success in fighting the effects of economic, political, and educational discrimination for over two generations.

The Dynamics of Discrimination against Italian Americans

Economic Discrimination   Today, Italian Americans have incomes and employment histories approximating those of other whites. Yet, despite the high visibility of a few individuals, Italians are still underrepresented in top administrative positions of government and private industry, even as Italian American workers occupy rank-and-file positions proportionate to their numbers in the general population. Italian Americans are thus just beginning to reach full economic mobility, as their levels of educational attainment and income have surpassed national averages.

The previous 100 years have seen considerable economic discrimination against Italians. From the beginning, many came as indentured workers to bosses who provided low-wage work, overpriced food, and expensive slum housing. Under such a system it was difficult for migrants to escape poverty, but eventually this system began to collapse. Even under less oppressive conditions, early Italian immigrants faced a number of barriers: language, few vocational skills, little education, and isolation in Italian ghettos away from job networks. Blatant discrimination also hindered upward mobility for these immigrants who were paid lower wages and excluded from unions. These practices subsided by the turn of the twentieth century, when Italian Americans became very active in the union movement.

Southern Italian immigrants became upwardly mobile during the first decades of the twentieth century. Union involvement provided jobs of increasing skill; the sons of many unskilled and semiskilled workers moved into higher-skill craft occupations; and entrepreneurial activity among Italian businessmen increased, with many achieving considerable economic success. The Great Depression curtailed some of this progress, but the post–World War II period saw continued Italian American upward mobility into white-collar jobs, professions, and businesses (Greeley, 1977). Some scholars predict that fourth-generation Italians may achieve parity with British and German ethnic groups in levels of education, income, and employment (Alba, 1985).

Political Discrimination   Early Italian immigrants had relatively low voter participation rates, a pattern attributed to the distrust that many southern Italians felt toward government and to the dampening effects of low socio-economic status on political activity (Lopreato, 1970). At the local political level, Italian Americans became allied with the Democratic political machines in northeastern and midwestern cities. Later, anti-Catholic prejudices among the broader population prevented Italian Americans from holding national political office. It was not until 1950 that an Italian American was elected to the Senate. As late as the 1940s, fewer than a dozen Italian Americans served in the House of Representatives. Only in 1962 did an Italian American hold a cabinet post in the federal government. The first Italian American vice presidential candidate was nominated in 1984; two years later the first Italian American was appointed to the Supreme Court.

Although the Protestant reform movements that curtailed the activities of big-city political machines temporarily loosened the Italian American foothold in the halls of local power, upward mobility and a declining distrust of government increased Italian American voter participation to a point where many cities with significant Italian American communities elected Italian mayors and city council members. Thus, even before World War II Italian Americans exhibited a significant presence in local politics, despite the fact that anti-Catholic prejudice prevented Protestant voters from voting for Italian Americans as state and national candidates.

By the 1970s, the political barriers to state and national politics were rapidly coming down. Italian mayors, governors, congressional representatives, and senators became increasingly common. Today, Italian Americans hold office in local, state, and congressional political arenas in numbers approximately proportionate to their numbers in the general population. Third- and fourth-generation Italian Americans have moved rapidly into politics, proving that they have overcome anti-Italian and anti-Catholic prejudice and discrimination.

Educational Discrimination   The first wave of southern Italian migrants to the United States tended to be illiterate and impoverished. Their children went to school for short periods of time to acquire basic skills and then dropped out to help support the family. The high dropout rates were also caused by the pervasive culture in the public schools, which sought to "Americanize" Italians. Children were put under enormous pressure to change their look, their speech, their dress, and their demeanor to conform with a more Anglo-Saxon profile.

The Catholic school system was not a readily available alternative to the first waves of southern Italian immigrants because of conflict with Irish Americans, who dominated this system, and because of their inability to pay for tuition and books. As a consequence, Italian youth either endured the public schools or dropped out. These high dropout rates hindered the second generation's economic mobility.

By the 1920s, Italian Americans had begun to make significant progress in education, a trend that has continued into the present. Today, the average number of years of education completed by Italian Americans surpasses that of many other white ethnic groups and of the white population as a whole. Thus, the third and fourth generations of Italian American immigrants have overcome the effects of discrimination against the first and second generations. As levels of education have increased, upward economic and political mobility has ensued.

Legal Discrimination   The passage of the **Immigration Act of 1924** limited immigration to the United States, especially for eastern and southern Europeans. The quota set for Italians was less than a tenth of the quota for the British and one-fifth the quota for Germans. Clearly the intent was to favor Anglo-Saxons and northern Europeans over all other ethnic groups, with the result that many Italians were prevented from immigrating to the United States. Although the laws were changed several times, only the **Immigration Act of 1965** enabled more Italians to immigrate by using the unfilled quotas of other ethnic groups from northern Europe. However, the earlier restrictions on immigration sent a not-too-subtle message to Italian Americans: You are inferior and undesirable. Such messages supported existing negative beliefs about Italians in the United States and, no doubt, perpetuated discriminatory practices up to World War II.

Stratification of Italian Americans

As the second-largest Catholic population to enter the United States, Italian immigrants threatened the Anglo-Saxon Protestant core. This threat was reinforced by other large influxes of Catholic Poles and of Jews. Nativist sentiments ran high within the Protestant white community. Much like the Irish, Italians were portrayed as an inferior "race" that could potentially "mongrelize" America through intermarriage. Italians constituted the first wave of immigrants from southern Europe to the United States, which made them seem doubly different and, hence, threatening.

In addition to white Protestant hostility, Italians faced, at least initially, Irish fears about the presence of yet another disadvantaged immigrant population. Such fears were aggravated when employers used Italians as strikebreakers against unions heavily populated by Irish workers. The problems that Italians initially had in enrolling their children in Catholic schools attest to the tension between Irish and Italians—a tension that was aggravated by the wave of poor Catholic Polish immigrants.

Their lack of education and job skills, coupled with Protestant and Irish discrimination, ensured that first- and most second-generation Italian Americans would be at the bottom of the socioeconomic ladder. Like all white ethnic groups, however, Italians had some distinct advantages: They were white and possessed organizational resources in family and church; over time these resources could be used to penetrate unions, skilled workplaces, white-collar jobs, professions, and schools. By the third generation, rapid upward mobility was occurring. Today, Italian Americans are above the national average in educational attainment and income. Lingering stereotypes and informal discrimination against Italian Americans persist. The final phase of assimilation is yet to be completed, although it is imminent.

JEWISH AMERICANS

Jews have been the most persistently persecuted minority group in history. Massacres of Jews have occurred since Rome's occupation of present-day Israel in the period before and after the birth of Christ. The intensity of this persecution is etched in the modern conscience by the death camps of Nazi Germany. Indeed, many American Jews are the descendants of those who sought refuge from more recent persecution. The first Jewish immigrants to the United States, the Sephardic Jews, arrived in the 1640s to escape massacres and expulsion from Spain and Portugal; their numbers did not exceed a few thousand. The second group of Jewish immigrants began to enter the United States in the 1840s in an effort to escape widening persecution in Europe. Most of these immigrants came from what is now Germany and settled in the Midwest, causing the Jewish population to grow from 15,000 to more than 250,000 in the early 1880s (Herberg, 1960:176). The third wave of immigration, beginning in the 1880s and lasting until the 1920s, led to the significant presence of Jews in America. Coming from areas of eastern Europe controlled by the Russian czar (and later the communists of the former Soviet Union), some 2 million Jews settled in the United States, primarily in urban areas of the Northeast (Lestschinsky, 1955:56). While many sought refuge from persecution, the vast majority came voluntarily in search of opportunities in a new land (Learsi, 1954; Sklare, 1971). Yet even as the Immigration Act of 1924 curtailed the mass immigration of all ethnic groups to the United States, some 400,000 more Jews immigrated, in most cases to escape Nazi persecution. By the eve of World War II, however, immigration policy had become so strict that many hundreds of thousands of Jews who desperately sought refuge in America were forced to stay in Europe and suffer the consequences of Hitler's death camps. Some 150,000 were able to enter the United States as political refugees; among these were many of the great scientists and intellectuals of modern times—Albert Einstein, Edward Teller, Erich Fromm, Herbert Marcuse, and Bruno Bettelheim.

In more recent decades, immigration statistics for the American Jewish population are inaccurate because the Immigration and Naturalization Service no longer identifies immigrants by religion; estimates run as high as 500,000 recent immigrants. Today, around 6 million Jews live in the United States, a figure that comes close to 50 percent of the world's Jewish population. The rest live primarily in Israel, the recently independent states of the former Soviet Union, and various European and South American countries. The majority of Jewish Americans live in the Northeast, although the number residing in the West and South is increasing rapidly—mirroring the trend in the general population. Jewish Americans represent about 2 percent of the American population; yet their massive immigration in the 1880s activated the same dynamics of discrimination experienced by other white ethnic groups, such as the Irish, Italians, and Poles.

Identifiability of Jewish Americans

Throughout history, Jews have been considered a "race," but the basis for this designation is social and cultural, not biological. Those who have persecuted Jews in the United States and around the world have used the spurious belief that Jews are biologically different as the basis for extreme forms of discrimination. In reality, there is no distinguishing physical trait that makes it easy to designate someone as a "Jew."

Jews are defined by their religious beliefs, which are based on the texts of the Torah, or the first five books of the Bible. **Orthodox Jews** adhere to the Torah in strict terms—ritual, food preparation and consumption, and synagogue attendance. About one-fifth of all American Jews are Orthodox. At the other extreme are **Reform Jews,** who represent perhaps one-third of the American Jewish population and who have modernized and secularized their religious activity. Between these extremes are **Conservative Jews,** who represent from one-third to one-half of all American Jews.

Being Jewish in a Protestant society makes one different, but many Jews are not outwardly religious. Moreover, synagogue attendance rates tend to be low, rendering this particular indicator of religious affiliation relatively useless (except for some Orthodox Jews, who may be easily identified by dress, demeanor, and ritual practices). Thus, religion does not outwardly distinguish Jews from gentiles.

In many respects, the source of Jewish identifiability is the awareness of a shared history of persecution and the sense among Jews that they constitute a community with a unique set of traditions. Because Jews have historically

been treated as a distinct community rather than as a nationality, they have developed organizations, networks, and shared beliefs that have provided them
with a sense of identity and that, during historical episodes of extreme discrimination, have allowed them to survive in hostile environments. Thus, unlike
other white ethnic groups living in the United States whose identity is tied to
their country of origin, Jews have maintained a sense of being a community
that has sustained itself within many countries. Consequently, Jews have been
able to mobilize resources—primarily organizational but also economic and
educational—that make them somewhat distinguishable, *to themselves,* and that
enable them to rank high in terms of education and income in the United States
(Goldschneider, 1986).

Negative Beliefs about Jewish Americans

Because Jews have persisted as a cohesive and successful community within
hostile societies, negative beliefs about them have evolved over time and, under
conditions of extreme persecution, have intensified. These beliefs have been reinforced by the **middleman minority** positions Jews have historically occupied;
as we noted in Chapter 2, middleman minority groups are traditionally targets
of hostility.

From the Middle Ages to the present, Jews have been the subjects of persistent prejudicial beliefs and stereotypes. Although Christ was crucified by
the Romans, some people believe that Jews were the culprits. In a Christian
society like the United States, this belief undergirds hostility toward Jews. In
fact, some Catholic and Protestant ministers have in the past promoted this
idea, conveniently ignoring all the pertinent historical facts. Jews are also
stereotyped as shrewd, crafty, cheap, money-grubbing, materialistic, and sly
(Glock and Stark, 1966; Gordon, 1988). Another set of beliefs is based on the
"Jewish conspiracy." In the 1920s and 1930s in the United States, people such
as Henry Ford actively promulgated the idea that Jews were involved in an
international conspiracy to control all governments. The Ku Klux Klan, the
German-American Bund, media personalities such as the Catholic priest
Charles E. Coughlin, and even Charles Lindbergh saw Jews as conspiring to
control the world. Even as late as the 1970s, a member of the Joint Chiefs of
Staff could be heard arguing that Jews "own, you know, the banks in the
country, the newspapers" (Selzer, 1972). More recent debates over the threat
of Zionism and the **Jewish lobby** in Congress have revived elements of the
Jewish conspiracy prejudice.

Most surveys and polls report dramatic drops in negative stereotypes about
Jews over the last sixty years (Lipset, 1987). Many Americans hold very positive
views of Jews as intelligent, educated, and industrious. Yet often lurking beneath
the surface are subtle condemnations of Jews as being *too* bright, hardworking,
and ambitious. Many of the older stereotypes—from "Christ killers" to "money
grubbers"—still prevail. People know that it is unacceptable in most public situations, including surveys and polls, to utter these negative beliefs, but the recent
increase in acts of vandalism at Jewish cemeteries and synagogues indicates that

below the polite surface lurk powerful prejudices against Jews. These beliefs often legitimize discriminatory practices against Jews in the United States.

The Dynamics of Discrimination against Jewish Americans

The comparatively high incomes and levels of education among Jewish Americans are a tribute to their ability to overcome open discrimination in jobs, politics, housing, and education, as well as more covert discrimination in clubs, fraternal organizations, and other social groups. Yet, despite a record of economic and academic success, Jews are underrepresented in many occupations, professions, and high-level positions of power.

Economic Discrimination Early Jewish immigrants assumed middleman minority positions. Although most Jews of German origin arrived with little money, they had entrepreneurial skills that enabled them to start small businesses (primarily in the garment, jewelry, meat, and leather trades) as well as trading and financial positions. By the 1890s, census data report that almost 60 percent of Jews were in trade and finance, 20 percent were in office work, and only 6 percent were in the professions. With centuries of experience in finding economic niches in the hostile environments of Europe, Jews were able to find such niches in the United States (Glazer, 1957).

The eastern European Jews who began to immigrate to the United States in the 1880s tended to be less educated and skilled than earlier German immigrants; as a result, they established an economic foothold in unskilled manufacturing jobs, as did other white immigrants. Men and women worked long hours for low wages in sweatshops; many women did sewing and laundry in the home to help make ends meet. Those eastern European immigrants who had small-business experience were able to find middleman minority niches, as had earlier German migrants. Because education and study have always been highly valued in the Jewish community, considerable upward mobility was possible for the sons and daughters of these Jewish immigrants. For example, by the early 1900s, Jews in the Northeast were moving into law, medicine, and other professions and assuming middle-level clerical positions in businesses and government.

Immigration was cut off in the 1920s, and those who had made it to the United States continued their economic mobility. When the Great Depression hit in the 1930s, however, this mobility was curtailed by economic discrimination. The success of Jewish Americans was now intensely resented in a tightening job market; signs reading "No Jews need apply" were common. Jews were excluded from many professional positions in banking, teaching, medicine, law, and engineering, as well as more skilled blue-collar and clerical jobs. Jews began to experience systematic, institutionalized discrimination, which forced them to find economic opportunities in risky sectors such as media and small business, and in professional and clerical jobs for which they were overqualified. The legacy of economic discrimination remains today, for Jews are underrepresented in high-level positions in banking, in management positions at savings and loans, utilities, and insurance companies, and the top levels of management in almost all industries. The two exceptions to this pattern are the media and plastics, in which Jews took the early risks.

On average, Jewish Americans are wealthier than non-Jews. This wealth is the result of taking risks in a narrow range of businesses such as clothing, mass communications, jewelry, and merchandising, while overcoming quotas and outright bans in professions such as law and medicine. Jewish Americans exist in what is termed a "golden ghetto," but it is nonetheless a ghetto. In the present, however, the pattern of informal exclusion appears to be diminishing; it is likely that Jewish Americans will move into a broader range of management positions commensurate with their education and skill.

Open exclusion (or token representation) of Jews in country clubs, some fraternal and community organizations, and many elite social circles indicates that informal discrimination and quotas persist even today in the second decade of the new millennium. Because these organizational affiliations are often crucial to the development of informal contacts and networks necessary for economic success and mobility, Jewish Americans will continue to feel the effects of this form of exclusion.

Political Discrimination   Unlike many minority groups who have established themselves in economic middleman positions, Jewish Americans have been politically active, voting in large numbers and engaging in volunteer political activity. Yet, despite their economic and academic success, this involvement has not translated into significant political power until recent decades. Jews have become governors of a few northeastern states over the years, and they have been successful in local politics where there is a substantial community of Jewish Americans. Yet Jewish Americans did not gain access to higher-level administrative positions in the federal government until the 1930s; they have had only a handful of Supreme Court appointments, despite the fact that a high proportion of lawyers and law professors are Jewish Americans; and they reached proportionate representation in Congress only in the 1970s. Jewish Americans are now overrepresented in Congress, holding 8 percent of Senate seats and constituting 7 percent of the House membership.

Although Jewish Americans have become increasingly prominent in politics, their underrepresentation in top management positions in industry and manufacturing limits their ability to use informal economic power to secure top-level appointments in those governmental posts where experience as a corporate manager is considered important (Alba and Moore, 1982; Zweigenhaft and Domhoff, 1982). Yet 90 percent of Americans say that they would vote for a qualified Jewish presidential candidate, whereas less than 50 percent would have done so five decades ago (Marger, 2000:211). Such shifts in attitudes indicate that Jewish Americans will become increasingly assimilated in the political arena.

Legal Discrimination   Unlike many other societies, the United States never legally institutionalized **anti-Semitism.** Before the signing of the Constitution, most states had established "Christian-only" restrictions for public office. Indeed, it is possible that some signatories to the Constitution were anti-Semitic (or anti-non-Christian); yet these prejudices are not reflected in law or in government policy. The closest instances approaching legal discrimination against Jews have been the **blue laws** of many communities that require businesses to close on Sunday—a day when many Jewish businesses could remain open.

Discrimination against Jewish Americans has been largely informal. Jews have had to overcome informal restrictive quotas in jobs and education, informal restrictive housing practices, and informal restrictive memberships in clubs and social organizations. The law has rarely supported these practices, except in the area of housing, where written restrictive covenants were enforced until the 1960s. Yet legal tolerance of informal discrimination is, in fact, a form of legalized discrimination. Indeed, until passage of the various civil rights acts in the 1960s, the legal system did not attack the injustices of such informal practices of discrimination.

Educational Discrimination It may seem absurd, on the surface, to consider educational discrimination against the most educated ethnic subpopulation in the United States. The long tradition of respect for learning and education in the Jewish community is so powerful that it has been possible to overcome clear patterns of discrimination. One of these patterns was established at the turn of the century, when Jewish American children were segregated in many of the public schools in the Northeast. Despite this segregation, however, Jewish students completed high school in much higher numbers than did non-Jews. Another discriminatory pattern was the informal, but often articulated, quota system for Jewish American high school graduates in American colleges and universities. Particularly in private schools, this system of limiting Jewish enrollment existed well into the 1960s. Also, on college campuses, discrimination in membership within fraternities and sororities was, and is, rampant. Jewish students have responded by forming their own fraternities and sororities. In private elite schools, the informal contacts and networks formed socially can be crucial to future occupational placement in mainstream corporate America; in this respect, many Jewish Americans are at a disadvantage. However, the magnitude of Jewish academic achievement in a society valuing educational credentials has enabled Jewish Americans to find business and professional niches and, increasingly in recent decades, to penetrate large, elite corporations. Despite their obvious economic success, though, Jewish graduates still encounter invisible barriers and must endure the subtle favoritism given to less educated and skilled non-Jews.

Stratification of Jewish Americans

Because many Jewish Americans have been enormously successful, the fact that many Jews live below the poverty line (but in low percentages compared to the rest of the population) is often overlooked. In spite of their qualifications and credentials and because of language and professional barriers, many recently arrived Russian Jews make their livings as cab drivers, cooks, and food servers. Success has come for Jews despite sometimes intense informal discrimination, legitimized by prejudicial beliefs. Such discrimination has been fueled by perceptions of threat in the minds of non-Jews, perceptions that have by no means disappeared. All immigrants once competed for industrial jobs, especially when the depression diminished the job market. Jewish American skill in running small businesses, in education, and in the professions posed a threat to gentiles. Coupled with long-standing and inaccurate European beliefs (imported to America) that Jews are shrewd and conspiratorial, this sense of threat increased and, in turn, intensified informal discrimination.

Jewish Americans are concentrated in the middle and upper middle socio-economic strata but still remain underrepresented in elite political and economic spheres. However, because movement into more highly elite positions has become increasingly possible, Jewish Americans are likely to penetrate and achieve parity in this sphere.

SUMMARY

The 100 years from the early nineteenth century to the first decades of the twentieth century was the first mass immigration of non-Protestant Europeans to America. Their religion and eagerness to work threatened the existing Anglo-Saxon core. The non-Protestant southern Irish arrived in the early years of the nineteenth century, followed in the second half of the century by large influxes of Italians, Poles, and Jews. Because these migrants were white and European, their early experiences with discrimination were more readily overcome than the experiences of those who are more readily identified by surface biological features.

The advantages of white skin in overcoming discrimination in America are revealed in the resource shares of white ethnics today. They secure better jobs, earn more money, attain more education, and live in less segregated neighborhoods than most non-European ethnics. Thus, while the legacy of negative stereotyping persists and discrimination is still evident, these forces have not prevented white ethnic groups from gaining their share of the resources available in America.

The Irish, who today represent the third-largest ethnic population after those from the British Isles and Germany, were the first of the white ethnics to come to America after the Anglo-Saxon core. The Protestant Irish had arrived in the 1700s, but it was the Catholic Irish immigration beginning in the 1830s that escalated discrimination against the Irish. These non-Protestant migrants came from the heart of rural poverty and were desperate for any work—thereby representing a threat not only to Protestantism as the dominant religion but to the wages and economic security of those already settled in America. These perceived threats fueled prejudicial stereotypes of Irish Catholics as a distinct "race" who were wicked, ignorant, and less than human. Efforts to exclude them from better jobs, centers of political power, public schools, and adequate housing were, in the long run, unsuccessful as the Catholic Irish worked their way up the occupational system. They captured or created the big-city political machines, utilized the Catholic school system to overcome discrimination in public schools, and used their financial and political clout to move into better neighborhoods. This mobility threatened other whites, but it also led to considerable assimilation of the Catholic Irish into the societal mainstream, which reduced the threat experienced by the descendants of earlier immigrants. Indeed, the more successful Catholic Irish became, the more they began to fear the new waves of European immigrants who would threaten their hard-won gains.

Small numbers of northern Italians immigrated to the United States during the early decades of the nineteenth century, but beginning in 1860 large numbers of poor, less educated, rural southern Italians entered the country. As with the Irish, systematic efforts were made to identify these Italians as a separate "race" because of their Catholicism, southern European ways, and Mediterranean skin tones. These characteristics made them different from the Anglo-Saxon core and subject to prejudicial beliefs and blatant discrimination. Initial negative stereotypes of Italian Americans branded them as lacking intelligence and, somewhat later, as having loose morals and a propensity toward violence as well as crime. More recent stereotyping focuses on the presumed emotionality, sexuality, bigotry, and hotheadedness of Italian Americans. Such negative stereotyping was initially used to bolster discrimination in jobs, schools, and politics. Laws were passed to restrict immigration from southern Europe. Yet, as with other white ethnics, Italians' white skin, strong family structures, commitment to church, and effective use of unions enabled second- and third-generation Italians to move up the stratification system so that today they are above most other ethnics in the shares of resources. Still, there are lingering stereotypes about Italians, often highlighted in the media. These may still serve to support informal patterns of discrimination.

Jews have been persecuted all over the world. As their numbers increased during the 1840s in the United States and especially when immigration accelerated in the 1880s, discrimination against Jews became as obvious here as elsewhere in the world. Later, in the years preceding and during World War II, more Jews came to escape the ravages of Nazism. Today, a steady stream of Jews still migrates to America, making the United States the place of residence for almost half of the world's Jewish population. Like other white ethnic minorities, Jews were distinguished as a peculiar "race," which made them just "different" enough to justify discrimination. Negative stereotypes could be brutal, such as those portraying Jews as "Christ killers" (an erroneous charge since the Romans performed the execution). More subtle and age-old stereotypes of Jews as cheap, sly, and clannish, coupled with more blatant and paranoid visions of a world Jewish conspiracy, still haunt Jewish Americans, as well as Jews all over the world. Out of necessity, Jews have had to sustain a strong sense of ethnic identity, hence their need to establish a viable set of institutions in a discriminating world. As they have done so, they developed the organizational and financial resources to succeed in educational attainment, business, and professional activity. Yet this success is circumscribed by exclusionary practices in almost all spheres of American life. Ordinary jobs, many professions, business opportunities, and top management positions still remain somewhat closed to the Jewish population. Significant inroads into politics and government jobs have been made by Jews only in recent decades, but informal discrimination persists in housing, social clubs, and non-Jewish businesses.

For all white ethnics—Jews, Italians, Irish, and many others—white skin has made a big difference in their overcoming discrimination. By simply adopting the culture, speech, values, and other characteristics of the Anglo-Saxon core, white ethnics could blend with the general population and move up the educational and occupational ladder. They have realized the "American dream." Many of the descendants of the white ethnic immigrants who blazed an upwardly mobile trail have forgotten—perhaps gratefully—the legacy of discrimination in words like "wop," "Paddy," or "Polack." The descendants of the white ethnic immigrants are often the perpetuators of bigotry and discrimination against people of color.

Their own tenuous economic standing has contributed to the tradition of racism among white ethnics. Discrimination against African Americans emerged full-blown in the early decades of the twentieth century when black workers were used as strikebreakers (Bonacich, 1976; Olzak, 1992). Early Asian immigrants experienced considerable resistance when they were perceived as a threat to the hard-won gains of white ethnics. And Latinos were also viewed as a potential labor pool that would take away the jobs of white ethnic laborers. Recent patterns of increased immigration by Latinos and Asians, coupled with old prejudices against African Americans, sustain the sense of threat among white ethnics over their jobs and culture. Such threats are magnified by global corporate systems that pull jobs overseas. As we have seen, threat is the fuel behind prejudice and discrimination. Competition with empowered people of color makes the success of some white ethnics seem uncertain. The movement of manual labor into the world economy, coupled with the proportional decline of members of the original Anglo-Saxon core and their white converts, has increased ethnic tensions in America and now represents a major obstacle to peaceful ethnic relations in the twenty-first century.

POINTS OF DEBATE

Caucasians or people with European-looking features are at an advantage in American society. They are able to overcome discrimination by simply assimilating into the Anglo-Saxon core, while retaining a few of their old ethnic traditions that do not threaten this core. By contrast, people of color and those with non-European features must face constant reminders from others about their "distinctiveness." Even with social assimilation into much of the core, they still stand out physically. The unwillingness of white ethnics to accept the efforts at social mobility of members of other ethnic groups toward realizing the American dream makes for many points of debate.

1. Given their different history in the United States, is it possible for white people to understand what it is like to "stand out" and to be vulnerable to the prejudicial beliefs and acts of discrimination nonwhites encounter? Can whites recognize the enormous psychic costs for members of readily identifiable minority populations? What can be done about this situation? Should current efforts to impose a "political correctness" ideology on all others be allowed to continue? If so, who is to decide what is correct? Or, alternatively, is the introduction of sensitivity training in the workplace, school, or community a better path? If so, who decides what will be taught, from what perspective, and *by* whom *to* whom? Or is it best to let the forces involved take a natural course? If so, should a society that values equal opportunity permit the continued existence of discrimination that results from a "hands-off" policy toward assimilation?

2. Can white Americans fully understand that the playing field has not been, and is not today, level in a society that values equality of opportunity? The legacy of slavery, Jim Crow, conquest and annexation, reservation life, and many other patterns of discrimination makes it difficult for many, though not all, nonwhites to have the same chance in the society as whites. White Americans tend to be fixated on, and angry over, the reverse discrimination that inevitably accompanies efforts at inclusive affirmative action. Must white Americans suffer the same frustration and anger that many members of minorities have endured over the decades? Is it the same? Or is it possible for white Americans to accept a certain amount of reverse discrimination in order to compensate for past discrimination against specific ethnics? If not, then what is to be done by white America to curb the pathologies inherent in decades, if not centuries, of discrimination—the pathologies of racism, violence, crime, drug use, welfare dependency, and other problems that accompany long-term discrimination?

KEY TERMS/KEY LEGISLATION

anti-Semitism, 95
blue laws, 96
Conservative Jews, 92
Immigration Act of 1924, 90
Immigration Act of 1965, 90

Jewish lobby, 93
middleman minority, 93
Orthodox Jews, 92
papists, 82
Reform Jews, 92

 Visit our text-specific website at www.mhhe.com/aguirre7e for valuable resources for both students and instructors.

CHAPTER 5

African Americans

*I*mported as slaves, treated as property to be bought and sold, denied citizenship rights, and considered less than human for much of American history, most African Americans have not been able to enjoy the benefits that come with living in the United States. The legacy of two hundred years of slavery, thirty years of post–Civil War oppression, and another century of systematic discrimination in housing, employment, education, and nearly every social sphere persists. Even as many of the old forms of discrimination have been dismantled since the mid-1960s, discrimination remains a central part of the African American experience (Farley and Allen, 1987; Jaynes and Williams, 1989; Schafer, 1993).

The effects of 350 years of oppression are not suddenly undone, for the weight of the past stands as a barrier in the present (Pinkney, 1984). How does one overcome, for example, the effects of residing in inner-city slums and public housing projects, growing up in single-parent households, living in a social climate in which most young men have lost hope of finding employment and women are overburdened, attending crowded and often dangerous schools, and walking down crime-ridden streets (Bullard, 1991; Caputo, 1993)? These conditions did not suddenly emerge; rather, they are the product of past discrimination, and now they operate as a new kind of discriminatory barrier. White Americans often fail to recognize this fact. Indeed, African Americans are frequently condemned for not overcoming these barriers, as if centuries of massive oppression could be quickly eradicated by individual initiative and drive (Blauner, 1989; Farley, 1987; Hughes and Madden, 1991). So even now, when institutionalized discrimination has been greatly reduced, the damage of the past remains, and few in the United States are seriously addressing this damage. Moreover, even as formal discrimination has decreased, subtle patterns of informal discrimination persist. As a result, today many African Americans are still denied equal access to the valued resources of society.

RESOURCE SHARES OF AFRICAN AMERICANS

The Impoverishment of African Americans

One very good indicator of how well, or badly, a subpopulation is doing in the United States is the rate of poverty. According to the U.S. Bureau of the Census,

TABLE 5.1 Percentage of African Americans and Non-Latino White Americans Living in Poverty

Year	Black	White
2008	24.7%	8.6%
2000	22.7	7.4
1990	30.7	10.0
1980	31.0	9.0
1970	33.5	9.9
1960	55.1	18.1

Sources: U.S. Bureau of the Census, 1979a, 1983c, 1989a, 1991c, 1999a, 2002b, 2003c, 2005c, 2009.

TABLE 5.2 African American Household Median Income as a Percentage of White Median Income

Year	Ratio of Black to White Income
2008	0.63
2000	0.68
1990	0.59
1980	0.56
1970	0.64
1960	0.55
1950	0.54

Sources: U.S. Bureau of the Census, 1979a, 1983c, 1989a, 1991c, 1999a, 2002b, 2005c, 2009.

approximately 12 percent of the population is defined as "poor," meaning, in essence, people's incomes do not meet government-established standards for adequate food, housing, clothing, and other necessary resources. These standards have varied over the last fifty years, as have the income levels necessary to meet them, but they have remained constant in the last decade. African Americans are disproportionately poor, as Table 5.1 documents. As of 2008, close to 25 percent of African Americans were living in poverty, and this figure might be higher if the government's outmoded method for calculating poverty reflected more accurately the actual costs for many necessities of living (see Turner, 1992, for a review).

The Income of African Americans

In absolute terms, the income of African Americans has increased, even taking inflation into consideration; and relative to whites, blacks have made some gains, although they still lag behind whites.

Table 5.2 shows the ratio between black and white median family income from 1950 to 2008. With the exception of 2000, and 2008 as well, the ratio of black to white income remained relatively the same between 1950 and 1990. The 1980s saw a drop in the ratio to the levels of the 1950s and 1960s. The decrease between 1970 and 1990 was the result of (1) cutbacks in government job programs for the poor in general and African Americans living in the inner city in particular, (2) dramatic decreases in the number of relatively unskilled jobs in the economy, and, most important, (3) the rapid rise in female-headed single-parent families in the black population over the last three decades, at a time when white families increasingly became dual-income families (Jackson, 1993).

But despite these problems, median family income of blacks relative to that of whites increased between 1990 and 2006, but dropping by 2008. The reason for this improvement is that nearly one in seven black families earns over $50,000, compared to one in seventeen in 1967. Since the ratio of black to white income includes the incomes of this higher-income black middle class, poor blacks are much worse off relative to whites. Thus, the figures in Table 5.2 combine incomes of both African Americans who escaped poverty and those who did not; and since the figures extend to the 1950s, when there were very few middle-class blacks, these statistics show that more African Americans are poor now than in the past. Moreover, among these poor, a significant amount of income is derived from welfare and other government programs and, hence, does not signal participation in the job market, the occupational system, and the mainstream of American society. This lack of participation results in a pattern of marginalization among many in the African American community—a pattern that is difficult to change.

A long-term study funded by the Pew Charitable Trust and executed by the Brookings Foundation (Isaacs, 2007) has examined the economic mobility of black and white families over several decades. This study followed 2,300 families over thirty years and recorded the income differences between black and white families, with particular attention to the fate of children in the family. The key question was: Do white and black children realize the "American Dream" of earning more money (in inflation-adjusted dollars) than their parents? Several dramatic findings emerged from this study.

Using income figures from the sample of 2,300 families, black incomes had fallen over the last decades to 58 percent of white income in 2004 (this figure varies from that in Table 5.2 because the data source is different from that reported by the Census Bureau). Indeed, despite the optimism in the wake of the civil rights movement of the 1960s, many of the hopes of those African American families who were upwardly mobile have not been realized. While there has been a considerable amount of mobility of African American families to the middle classes, the disparity between white and black incomes has not decreased; indeed, it has moved back close to the level of twenty-five years ago. Part of the explanation for this growing disparity is that incomes among black males have declined (in inflation-adjusted or constant dollars), with much of this decline made up by increases in black women's income. Yet, since white male income has remained relatively stable while white female income has increased, the gap between African American and white families has widened. Thus, black children grow up in families with a much lower income than white families, and this fact reduces their chances of mobility.

The data, however, reveal an even more surprising fact: African American adult children are less likely than their white counterparts to have higher incomes than their parents. Of special note is that children of middle- and upper-middle-class black families are far more likely than white children to be *downwardly* mobile, earning less than their parents. A startling 45 percent of black children whose parents are clearly in the middle classes end up in the bottom 20 percent of income earners—a dramatic move downward. Thus, many of the gains of parents *are not transferred* to their children; and while some white children are downwardly mobile, the differences between African American and white children are dramatic. If we turn the issue around and ask what percentage of children are upwardly mobile, 37 percent of white children in the middle income groups end up earning more than their parents, whereas only 17 percent of African American children from middle-class families do so.

Turning to children born into families at the bottom of the income distribution in the United States, poor African American children are more likely to remain poor than are their white counterparts. Fully 54 percent of black children stay poor, whereas 31 percent of whites do so. Thus, the "American Dream" that people can pull themselves up the stratification ladder and pass on their success to their children does not appear to apply to African American families. And, though the dream is perhaps not always true for white families, it is far more likely to be realized, whether a white child starts at the bottom or at the midpoint of the class system in the United States.

The Occupational Distribution of African Americans

There have been dramatic changes in the distribution of jobs among African Americans. In 1960, only 13 percent of blacks could be labeled "white-collar workers," whereas in 2008, 53 percent held white-collar jobs. This improvement, while significant, needs to be qualified by the kinds of white-collar jobs African Americans have been able to find. Many of these jobs are not high-paying because they are clerical and service jobs. Table 5.3 compares whites and blacks across the five major categories that the U.S. Bureau of the Census uses to classify occupations. In the higher-paying white-collar occupations categorized as "managerial and professional," whites are much more likely to hold these better-paying jobs, while in the higher-paying blue-collar categories, such as "construction and maintenance," only 6.7 percent of blacks have these jobs. Indeed, the occupations most likely to be held by African Americans are in

TABLE 5.3 Distribution of African Americans and Whites in Various Occupations, 2008

Occupation	Whites	African Americans
Managerial and professional	40.1%	29.7%
Sales and office	23.5	23.4
Service occupations	13.4	23.4
Construction and maintenance	11.0	6.7
Production, transportation, and material moving	12.0	16.8

Source: U.S. Bureau of the Census, 2010 *Statistical Abstract*, Table 606.

Black men and women are underrepresented in managerial and professional occupations as compared with non-Latino whites.

lower-paying blue-collar labor, service labor, and clerical white-collar work. Thus, although considerable progress has been made in opening up the occupational system to African Americans, they are still underrepresented in the high-end blue- and white-collar occupations, as was the case two decades ago (Bates, 1995; Darity and Myers, 2001; Farley and Allen, 1987; Swinton, 1989). The situation for African Americans becomes even more clouded when unemployment rates for whites and blacks are compared (see Table 5.4). For many decades, African Americans have been twice as likely to be unemployed than whites.

TABLE 5.4 Unemployment Rates for African American Workers Compared with White Workers

Year	Percentage of Black Unemployed	Percentage of White Unemployed	Ratio of Black to White Unemployment
2008	7.9%	4.1%	1.9%
2006	12.6	5.2	2.4
1998	9.6	4.0	2.4
1994	11.5	5.3	2.2
1990	11.3	4.7	2.4
1980	13.2	6.3	2.1
1970	8.2	4.5	1.8
1960	10.2	4.9	2.1
1950	9.0	4.9	1.8

Sources: U.S. Bureau of the Census, 1991c, 1993b, 1995, 1999a, 2001a; U.S. Bureau of the Census, 2010 *Statistical Abstract*, Table 614; Webster and Bishaw, 2007.

Part of the explanation for the higher unemployment rate for African Americans is the greater percentage of black workers in service jobs, where employment is less secure, and in blue-collar jobs, which have been decreasing over the last forty years. Some unemployment can be attributed to discrimination: More black workers are laid off than white workers.

Unemployment denies people access to resources such as money and dignity. The unemployed often turn to the welfare system, which further erodes their dignity and which, in light of Congress's effort to "reform" welfare in 1996, forces many onto the streets. Moreover, unemployment makes it difficult, if not impossible, to build a stable life around home, family, and hope for the future (Caputo, 1993; Eggers and Massey, 1992; Schneider and Phelan, 1990).

Educational Attainment of African Americans

Today, access to good jobs, income, and other resources depends on a person's educational credentials. African American attendance in schools has, of course, been a hotly contested issue—from the early efforts at desegregation in the 1950s and 1960s to the controversy over forced busing in the 1970s and 1980s (Boozer, Krueger, and Wolkon, 1992). This situation alone signals the institutional inequities that have prevented blacks from attaining educational credentials equivalent to white Americans. Despite the desegregation controversy, which still rages on today, African Americans have made significant gains over the last decades in securing credentials that have increased their access to valued resources. As Table 5.5 shows, the gap between blacks and whites with high school diplomas has been closing over the last forty years. Moreover, for most of this period, the percentage of African Americans who have completed four years of college increased, and despite a dip in 2008 for whites, a wide gap remains between blacks and whites.

TABLE 5.5 Educational Attainment Levels of African Americans and Non-Latino Whites

Year	High School*		College†	
	Blacks, %	Whites, %	Blacks, %	Whites, %
2008	83.0%	87.1%	19.6%	29.8%
2006	81.1	90.1	17.6‡	30.6‡
1994	73	82	13	23
1990	66	79	11	22
1980	51	69	8	17
1970	31	55	4	11
1960	20	43	3	8

Note: Persons 25 years old and over.
*Four years of high school.
†Four years or more of college.
‡Data for 2006 denote receipt of college degree.
Sources: U.S. Bureau of the Census, 1995, 1999a, 2001b, 2003b; U.S. Bureau of the Census, 2010 *Statistical Abstract,* Table 224; Webster and Bishaw, 2007.

Housing of African Americans

Housing is a valued resource. Where one lives determines access to other resources—jobs, good schools, clean air, peace and quiet, lack of crime, and so on (Bullard, 1993; Whetstone, 1993). African Americans have endured a tremendous amount of discrimination in housing, and, as a consequence, they are disproportionately confined to the inner cities (Farley, 1995; Jaynes and Williams, 1989; Wildavsky, 1990). Furthermore, they are segregated more than any other large ethnic population in the United States. Table 5.6 shows the residential segregation index for blacks in representative metropolitan areas: A low number indicates mild levels of segregation, whereas a high score represents high levels (a score of 100 would signal complete segregation of blacks). Among the sixteen metropolitan areas with the largest black population, however, the index score rises considerably to about 80 (Jaynes and Williams, 1989:27). As the black population increases in a metropolitan area, the level of segregation increases dramatically. Yet, as the most recent analysis of segregation between blacks and whites indicates, the peak period of segregation may now have passed (Farley and Frey, 1994), although Table 5.6 reveals that considerable segregation persists. Table 5.7 underscores the fact that the degree of segregation is very high in the most segregated metropolitan areas. Even in the least segregated metropolitan areas, the index scores are still rather high. However, the recent reductions in white–black segregation can be accounted for by increases in the Latino population. Census data classify Latinos as white, and this ethnic group has nearly the same levels of poverty as blacks (McKinney and Schnare, 1989). Hence, these poor Latinos have become integrated with blacks in urban poverty; thus reducing statistically white-black segregation.

Segregation of African Americans means that this minority is concentrated in inner cities and in city public housing. The result is that African Americans have (1) reduced access to jobs (because many companies have moved to the suburbs), (2) reduced capacity to go to good schools (because many inner-city schools are underfunded, overcrowded, and plagued with problems ranging from drugs and crime to high dropout rates), and (3) reduced ability to live and grow up outside the sphere of rampant crime, drug use, and gang activity (Calmore, 1993).

TABLE 5.6 Trends in Residential Segregation of African Americans

Year	Degree of Segregation, %
2001	59%
1990	58
1980	53
1970	59
1960	56

Sources: Frey and Myers, 2002; Harrison and Weinberg, 1992; McKinney and Schnare, 1989; U.S. Department of Housing and Urban Development, 1991.

TABLE 5.7 Segregation Indexes for Most and Least Segregated Metropolitan Areas, 2000

	Most Segregated			Least Segregated	
Rank	Metropolitan Area	Index	Rank	Metropolitan Area	Index
1	Gary, IN PMSA*	88	1	Jacksonville, NC MSA	32
2	Detroit, MI PMSA	87	2	Yolo, CA PMSA	32
3	Milwaukee-Waukesha, WI PMSA	84	3	Lawrence, KS MSA	34
4	New York, NY PMSA	84	4	Santa Cruz-Watsonville, CA PSMA	34
5	Chicago, IL PMSA	84	5	Lawton, OK MSA	35
6	Newark, NJ PMSA	83	6	Boulder-Longmont, CO PSMA	37
7	Flint, MI PMSA	81	7	Redding, CA MSA	37
8	Buffalo-Niagara Falls, NY MSA†	80	8	Boise City, ID MSA	37
9	Cleveland-Lorain-Elyria, OH PMSA	80	9	Fayetteville, NC MSA	38
10	Saginaw-Bay City-Midland, MI MSA	79	10	Eugene-Springfield, OR MSA	38

*PSMA: Primary Metropolitan Statistical Area.
†MSA: Metropolitan Statistical Area.
Source: Frey and Myers, 2002.

Life Span of African Americans

The ultimate resource is life and health. How long will you live? Figure 5.1 documents the life expectancy of whites and blacks in America over the last thirty years (National Vital Statistics Reports, 2002, 2004, 2007). While all Americans are living longer, the gap between whites and blacks remains rather high. An African American male will live, on average, to be 69.5 years old, while his white counterpart will live six years longer at 75.7 years. A black female will live about as long as a white male, 76.3 years, but still four years less than her white counterpart, who can expect to live until she is 80 years old. Another way to examine inequalities in life expectancy is to compare infant mortality rates. White babies die at the rate of about 5.7 babies per 1,000 births, whereas black infants die at well over twice this rate, at 14.0 deaths per 1,000 births. These high infant mortality rates indicate that African Americans do not have full access to the medical care system in the United States (see Table 5.8). As we noted in Chapter 1, some of the causes of death of African Americans are also revealing. African Americans are more than twice as likely as whites to die from diabetes, kidney disease, bacterial infections, and hypertension. More dramatically, they are almost six times more likely to die from homicide than are whites.

Thus, African Americans do not have the same level of access to money, jobs, education, housing, and health care as do white Americans and, as we will see, other ethnic groups (Wallace, 1990). Our goal is to understand how and why this inequity exists. In seeking an explanation, we will use our discussion in Chapter 2; in fact, the reader may want to review Figures 2.1, 2.2, and 2.3 on pages 47, 52, and 53 before proceeding. As the model in Figure 2.3 predicts, the explanation for the plight of African Americans resides in easy identifiability

FIGURE 5.1 Life expectancy by race and sex: United States, 1970–2004.
Source: National Vital Statistics Reports, 2002, 2004, 2007.

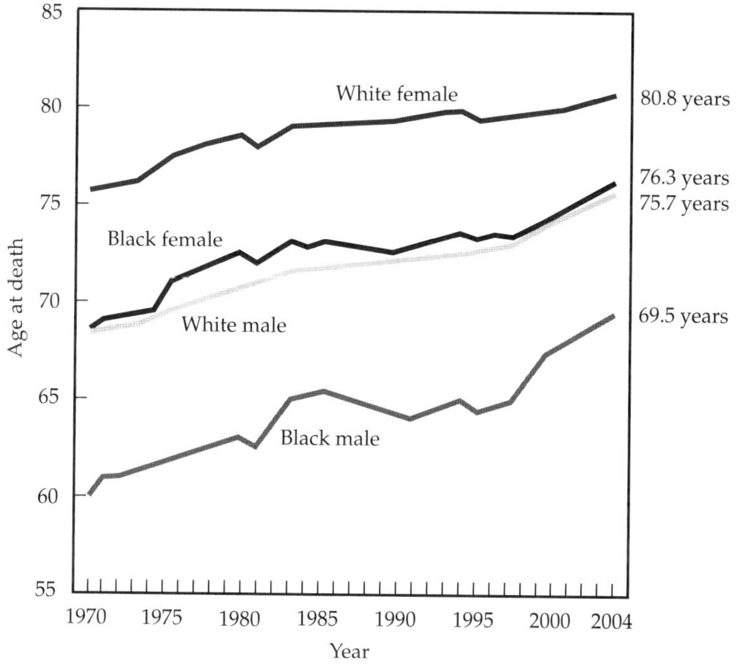

TABLE 5.8 Infant Mortality Rates by Race: United States, Selected Years, 1990–2005

	1990	2000	2003	2005
White	7.6	5.7	5.7	5.7
Black	18.0	14.1	14.0	14.0

Source: National Center for Health Statistics, Health: United States, 2008.

as targets of discrimination, large numbers, lack of entrepreneurial skills, negative stereotyping and prejudice by members of the dominant society, and victimization through both institutionalized and informal discrimination.

THE DYNAMICS OF DISCRIMINATION AGAINST AFRICAN AMERICANS

Identifiability of African Americans

Being black poses a problem in a white world: You stand out, and dramatically so. Black and white are perceived as opposite colors; a black person cannot easily "blend" into a predominantly white America. Skin color is, in the biological sense, a minor genetic trait, but in the sociological sense it is anything but minor. Identifiability makes people easy targets of discrimination. Most members of white ethnic groups look like the dominant population, and most Latinos are not physically identifiable as members of an ethnic group. Black people cannot shed their color, but co-mingling has occurred since the Africans were pressed into slavery, resulting in generations of individuals with various degrees of dark-skin pigmentation. Interethnic marriages have increased somewhat in recent decades, further influencing the color balance of the American population. Yet skin color, no matter what the permutation, continues to identify some as targets of discrimination.

Sociocultural traits also contribute to discrimination. Poverty and unemployment statistics for African Americans reflect their disproportionate representation in the lower classes; demeanor, speech, and dress further distinguish many members of the African American community. These characteristics are reinforced by black culture, which has evolved in reaction to slavery and the discrimination that blacks have endured since "emancipation."

Even when socioeconomic standing and/or culture are not obvious, skin color alone remains as a basis of discrimination. For example, Joe Feagin (1991) conducted in-depth interviews with black middle-class persons and found that they experienced discrimination in public places, such as restaurants, stores, swimming pools, and parking areas. Thus, to be denied service, to be told to go, or to suffer epithets are still very common experiences for blacks in America. The prejudice and discrimination that middle-class African Americans live with cannot be attributed to class or culture, but simply to skin color.

Negative Beliefs about African Americans

More than any other ethnic population in the United States, and perhaps in the world, African Americans have been the victims of negative beliefs and stereotypes. Negative beliefs have also reinforced the identifiability of blacks, making them unique in a negative way. Such stereotypes have then been used to legitimize discrimination in a society whose core values are based on liberty, freedom, and equality (Andrews, 1994; Staples, 1975).

In the early period of slavery, from 1650 to 1820, whites viewed Africans as "uncivilized heathens," "bestial," "sexually aggressive," and as suffering the "curse of God" who made them black (Jordan, 1968; Turner and Singleton, 1978). Although there is some debate as to whether all white southerners held such hard views (Roediger, 1991:24), these beliefs changed somewhat when abolitionists in the North challenged them. Slavery became a "positive good," protecting Africans from their "savage impulses" and responding to their "childlike dependency." Yet, even in the abolitionist North, stereotypes portrayed Africans as ignorant, lazy, and immoral (Fredrickson, 1971:51). During this period the **"black Sambo" stereotype** evolved (Boskin, 1986), which portrayed black people as childlike, helpless, shuffling, and fumbling (but with potentially aggressive tendencies) (see Box 5.1).

Box 5.1
The First "R"

Debra Van Ausdale and Joe R. Feagin conducted a study of children at a day care center. They observed how these young children interacted during the course of their play activities. What immediately became evident to the investigators is that children are very well aware of "race." Unlike much of the literature, which simply assumes that children pay little attention to markers of various ethnic groups, these investigators found that the opposite was the case. Very young children have rather sophisticated cognitive conceptions of "race"; moreover, they act on these conceptions. At times they reveal behaviors that can only be described as "racist." Thus, the broader cultural stereotypes of various ethnic groups are picked up rather early in children's lives; they learn from their parents, peers, media, and other sources a great deal of information about the first "R" long before they can read, write, and do arithmetic. For example, one three-year-old child picked up her cot and moved to the other side of the classroom during nap time. When the teacher asked why she did this, she replied that "I can't sleep next to a nigger." She then pointed to a four-year-old African American girl and uttered that "Niggers are stinky. I can't sleep next to one."

When young minority children are asked about their experiences with racism, they almost always report reactions like that of the little three-year-old girl. Imagine a legacy of such reactions, beginning at an early age, and perhaps we can get a sense of why minority children often feel uncomfortable around whites. What is interesting is that both professionals and the lay public simply fail to perceive that these kinds of reactions of the young to ethnic differences occur. There is, in a sense, a collective denial that young children, presumed to be so innocent, can also be racists.

Source: Van Ausdale and Feagin, 2001.

After the Civil War, when the short-lived but significant gains of radical Reconstruction were undone, African Americans were portrayed as inferior because they had not been able to take advantage of the "equal opportunities" offered by Reconstruction. Even in enlightened circles, blacks were often portrayed as not having progressed as far as whites on the evolutionary scale; so, without segregation as well as supervision and control, African Americans would revert to their more primitive state. In the South, this state was perceived to be one of laziness, criminality, and lustfulness (especially for white women, a belief that conveniently overlooked some slaveholders' lust for black women); in the North, this state was viewed as one of childlike docility and kindness that needed to be channeled (by whites). Whether vicious or benign, treatment of African Americans was based on the belief that black people are biologically inferior and must be segregated (Fredrickson, 1971).

Between the world wars, from 1914 to 1941, evolutionary theory and results on intelligence tests were interpreted to confirm as "scientific fact" the inferiority of blacks, although social scientists began to attack this position and to argue that the differences between black people and white people (as well as all "races") were the result of environmental rather than biological differences. Yet the prevailing belief continued to advocate segregation as necessary and desirable in order to prevent "black inferiority" from diminishing the white biological stock.

The post–World War II period saw a dramatic shift in beliefs about African Americans. A consensus slowly emerged in more progressive circles that segregation was harmful, that blacks were not innately inferior, that the appearance of inferiority reflected cultural deprivation stemming from undesirable environments, and that improvements in schooling, job opportunities, and neighborhoods were the key to making life better for African Americans. Such progressive beliefs began to shape broad public perceptions (though not universally), and perhaps more significantly, they began to affect federal governmental policies, at least to a degree. Yet many still believed that integration was unnecessary and undesirable.

More recently, beliefs about African Americans have been mixed. Three decades ago, 65 percent of Americans believed that blacks were unmotivated, and only a decade ago almost 50 percent thought that blacks were lazy (see Turner and Payne, 2002, for a summary of the most recent poll results summarized in the following). These attitudes have softened somewhat, but not as much as one might think. In 2000, half of Americans still believed that African Americans lacked motivation, and one-third saw blacks as lazy. Moreover, public sentiment for government assistance for African Americans had turned much more harsh than it was at the peak of the civil rights movement in the 1960s. Only 40 percent of Americans thought that government should aid blacks; and only 30 percent believed that government should ensure fair treatment in jobs. And between 30 percent and 40 percent believed just a decade ago that blacks "should not go where they are not wanted" and that it is acceptable to "keep blacks out of the neighborhood." These kinds of attitudes have made it extremely difficult for African Americans to feel comfortable in so many contexts critical to their well-being, because a significant proportion of the population holds negative beliefs about their motives and their rights to fair treatment.

Indeed, beliefs have hardened against help for African Americans over the last decade (for example, see Box 5.2). Some people think that liberal policies have gone too far: "Affirmative action," or measures designed to rectify past patterns of discrimination, is often seen to discriminate against white people; busing destroys neighborhood schools; and integration forces people to live near those whom they would rather avoid. Others believe that liberal policies have encouraged African Americans to depend on government for welfare, jobs, and education, thereby preventing many blacks from improving their lives. Many others, fearing the emergence of an urban underclass of angry, unemployed youth, have called for more government spending on programs to provide opportunities for African Americans. Some have urged the government and the private sector to provide real rather than illusory opportunities. Others feel that individuals and communities must develop their own resources to break the cycle of poverty and government dependency. This last outlook has gained some currency over the last few years and has been used to cut back

---

Box 5.2
White Backlash?

There is no question that California has been undergoing a demographic transformation over the past two decades that has altered the *complexion* of the state's population. In 2000, the representation of whites in the state's population dropped below 50 percent. One result is that racial and ethnic minorities became noticeably visible and increased their *identifiability* for whites in the state's population. Given the theoretical framework for ethnic relations outlined in Chapter 2, another result from the increased *identifiability* of racial and ethnic minorities in California's population is white backlash against their transformation of the state's population. We use the following example to show the potential emergence of white backlash against racial and ethnic minorities in California.

During Black History Month 2010, the Pi Kappa Alpha fraternity at the University of California–San Diego sponsored a ghetto-themed party, *Compton Cookout*. The party invitation posted on Facebook promised to provide guests with "a taste of life in the ghetto." Male guests were encouraged to dress in baggy athletic wear in the style of rappers from the Los Angeles suburb of Compton. Female guests were encouraged to dress as "ghetto chicks" who have fake gold teeth, start fights, and wear cheap clothes. According to the Facebook invitation, the menu would include chicken and watermelon.

A few days after the *Compton Cookout*, the editor of *Koala*, a campus publication, appeared on the university's student-run television station to defend the party. Commenting on the African American students who protested and demanded that the university administration sanction those responsible for sponsoring the party, the editor referred to them as "ungrateful niggers." Two days after the television show, a noose was hung in the campus library. The next day, a white pillowcase fashioned into a KKK-style hood was found on campus.

One could consider the events at the University of California–San Diego as isolated and not reflective of a campus climate that is welcoming to racial and ethnic minorities. However, to do so disregards the use of racial stereotypes and racist symbols that show the presence of a campus climate that is intolerant of minorities. While the campus administration did endorse a plan to increase the number of African American students and faculty on campus, as well as offering more multicultural classes, the question remains—do the events at UC–San Diego signal the emergence of a white backlash against minorities?

Sources: Archibold, 2010; Gordon, 2010.

---

federal aid programs for the poor in general and African Americans in particular. Some believe that "minorities are getting too much" at the expense of whites (Kluegel and Bobo, 1993). The passage of Proposition 209 (California Civil Rights Initiative) by the majority of California voters in the 1996 November election was fueled by the belief that "minorities had received more than their share" at the expense of white persons. And, in response to these sentiments, the welfare reform of 1996 ensured that the poor would get less, and for a shorter period of time.

Box 5.3
An Obama Effect on Prejudicial Beliefs?

In 1998, the "Implicit Association Test" was developed to measure "implicit" biases that people may not recognize in themselves. The test tries to get at subconscious cognitions, emotions, and beliefs. The methodology revolves around having people rapidly categorize words and images, and critics naturally would contend that such a test cannot accurately measure complex cognitions. You can take a demonstration of the test and see for yourself by visiting https://implicit.harvard.edu/implicit/.

Before the election of Barack Obama to the presidency, the test revealed that about 75 percent of individuals who had taken the test showed some implicit anti-black bias. The lead researcher gave the test to seventy-four college students in the spring of 2008, as the campaign for president increased in intensity. The results were rather surprising because it showed almost no anti-black bias, and in fact, about 45 percent of the test-takers appeared to favor blacks over whites. Of course, these were college students, highly involved emotionally in the 2008 presidential election, but the finding is significant in at least this respect. High visibility and demonstrable competence of an African American can, if only briefly, change perceptions about members of the larger ethnic subpopulation. Even after his first year in office, President Obama's policies were under constant attack, and a majority of Americans in early 2010 did not favor many of these policies. And yet, the President himself was more positively evaluated than his policy initiatives.

It could be that the general observations we offered in Chapter 2 that macro-level visibility and power of a leader of an ethnic minority can cause micro-level personal perceptions of a the entire minority subpopulation to improve. The positive characteristics of Barack Obama that led to his election can, for a time at least, translate to a change in ethnic stereotypes as the fuel ethnic prejudices that, especially in the case of African Americans, legitimate ethnic discrimination and stratification.

What people say on a survey is often very different from what they really feel, and as a result, African Americans must constantly be aware that people will express in words or deeds their negative attitudes. White Americans cannot imagine what it is like to confront uncertainty in almost every situation about how one will be treated. This diffuse anxiety takes a heavy toll on African Americans, who must constantly monitor others to see if negative attitudes toward them will become manifest, and few whites are willing to even consider the psychological costs to African Americans, to say nothing of the sociological costs of experiencing subtle forms of discrimination in jobs, schools, public places, and neighborhoods.

Many studies document that when blacks and whites have opportunities to interact and associate, prejudicial attitudes decline. But this is at the interpersonal level; at a community level, a different picture emerges. Ironically, negative beliefs about African Americans tend to increase as their percentage of the local population increases. Marylee Taylor (1998), for example, found that whites' prejudices toward blacks increased as the percentage of blacks in a community rose. Even when blacks were highly segregated and, hence, not in contact with whites, prejudice increased. In contrast, prejudice did not increase significantly when the proportion of other minorities, such as Latinos, increased in a community. Thus, African Americans' presence escalates fears and prejudice in ways not typical of other minorities, and these prejudices represent an enormous burden to African Americans.

Institutionalized Discrimination against African Americans

Legal Discrimination   Dominant beliefs usually become codified into laws; in turn, these laws sanction certain types of behavior. So it was with beliefs about blacks in America, against whom it was once legal to discriminate. Moreover, undermining and, often, defying the law are informal discriminatory practices that are not codified but are deemed appropriate in a climate in which the law makes discrimination acceptable.

Legal Discrimination under Slavery and in Slavery's Aftermath   It is difficult to determine whether the first Africans in America were slaves or indentured servants; the historical record is not clear on this point (Jordan, 1962). By the 1650s, however, there is evidence that some colonies had laws distinguishing between white and black servants, with black servants and their children consigned to servitude for life. By the early eighteenth century, the broad legal framework of slavery in the South had become clearly codified (Stampp, 1956; Starobin, 1970:7):

1. Blacks were to be slaves for life.
2. Slaves were *both* property and persons; owners held title to blacks as property and had some responsibilities to blacks as persons.
3. Children would inherit their mother's status as a slave.
4. Christian baptism did not automatically lead to freedom.
5. Marriages between blacks and whites were prohibited.
6. Blacks could not acquire or inherit property.
7. Blacks could not engage in litigation or enter into civil contracts; they could not testify against whites in court, nor could they sit on juries.

Such codes reaffirmed beliefs about the "bestiality" of slaves and legitimized slavery by making it acceptable for white Americans to buy slave labor. In the North, the laws were considerably more benign, but few questioned the biological inferiority of blacks or the norm of economic, educational, and political discrimination (Fredrickson, 1971:1–43, 1981, 1988; Litwack, 1961:30–38). With the admission of border and southern states to the Union in the early 1800s, a considerable amount of debate in Congress ensued over the legal rights of African-origin people. The coexistence of free blacks in the North and slaves in southern and border states made it difficult to define the constitutional rights of slaves in the growing Union. The issue was effectively avoided in 1821 when Missouri was admitted to the Union, for Congress enacted a loosely worded law that allowed the states to legislate as they pleased, with the proviso that no

Box 5.4
Changes in African American Beliefs about African Americans

Two new analyses of survey data show that beliefs of African Americans about themselves are changing. Mathew Hunt (2007) analyzed data from the General Social Survey from 1977 to 2004 regarding beliefs about the reasons for blacks' current disadvantages. Blacks are now less likely to use structural explanations about discrimination than they were two decades ago; they are likely to emphasize motivational deficiencies of individuals when explaining disadvantages of African Americans. A related study released by the Pew Research Center (2007) also shows a dramatic change in blacks' beliefs. In 1994, 60 percent of blacks believed that racial prejudice and discrimination were keeping blacks from succeeding economically, with only 33 percent blaming the individual; in 2007, however, 53 percent of African Americans saw individuals as responsible for their own condition, with only 33 percent emphasizing prejudice and discrimination. Still, around 60 percent of African Americans surveyed felt that blacks often face discrimination when searching for jobs and housing, whereas less than 30 percent of whites saw discrimination in employment and housing. Thus, even as blacks' beliefs have shifted toward explanations emphasizing individuals and, in so doing, have converged with those of whites, there remain very large differences in whites' and blacks' perceptions of the prevalence of prejudice and discrimination.

Another interesting finding from the Pew data is that class more often than race is seen as explaining the black condition. For example, in 1986, 44 percent of African Americans saw differences in respective fates of whites and blacks as related to life chances stemming from a person's class position, whereas in 2007, 61 percent emphasized class as explaining life chances. Moreover, there is considerable divergence *within* the black population in beliefs about what accounts for blacks' disadvantages. Middle-class blacks have beliefs that converge with those of whites blaming lack of individual motivation for lack of success.

Despite this new conservative turn among black viewpoints, especially those of the middle class, there has also been a considerable shift in the level of optimism among blacks about their economic prospects. Fewer than half of those polled said that they expect life to get better, whereas twenty years ago 57 percent said that they thought that life would improve. This growing pessimism is, no doubt, related to other data from the Pew study cited earlier indicating that 45 percent of children from middle-class black families fail to carry on their parents' success and remain in the middle class. Their pessimism thus has a clear basis in reality.

citizens "shall be excluded from the enjoyment of any of the privileges and immunities to which such citizen is entitled under the Constitution of the United States." Thereafter, until the Civil War, northern laws were increasingly relaxed, while southern legislatures passed ever more restrictive laws.

Abolitionist pleas for at least "humane treatment" of the "inferior race" were beginning to have a small impact on public opinion, and those states with few black residents began to accord them broader citizenship rights. However, these formal laws contradicted informal **Jim Crow practices** of the North, which, despite the lofty tenets of formal laws, excluded most African Americans from access to jobs, education, and housing (Woodward, 1966).

It appears likely that the abolitionist ideology was used retroactively to justify a massive northern invasion of the South for economic and political reasons. Nevertheless, the war abolished forever the institution of slavery, and, hence, the economic base of the South. In 1866, the abolition of slavery was formally ratified in the **Thirteenth Amendment.**

In reaction, southern states began to enact **black codes** restricting the rights of freed slaves. These codes were enforced through violence, which, for the remainder of the century, was to become the key to maintaining black subordination to whites. The details of these codes varied, but several restrictions were

---

Box 5.5
The Execution of Black Slaves

The following table provides some descriptive statistics for black slave executions in the United States between 1641 and 1865. Most black slave executions occurred in Deep South states. While black slaves were more likely to be executed for theft in Deep South states, they were just as likely to be executed for murder and rape regardless of geographical region. In general, black slaves were most often executed for murder, followed by participation in a slave revolt, rape, theft, arson, and poisoning. The most common form of execution was hanging, and most executed black slaves were males.

Selected Characteristics of Black Slave Executions in the United States, 1641–1865

	Deep South States*		Border States[†]		Northern States[‡]		Total	
	N	%	N	%	N	%	N	%
Criminal offense								
Murder	566	78%	105	15%	52	7%	723	100%
Rape	110	77	22	15	11	8	143	100
Theft	115	92	7	6	3	2	125	100
Slave revolt	207	84	8	3	31	13	246	100
Arson	45	67	7	10	15	23	67	100
Poisoning	51	88	2	3	5	9	58	100
Method of execution								
Hanging	1,351	85%	158	10%	87	5%	1,596	100%
Breaking on the wheel	31	47	3	5	32	48	66	100
Gibbeted	20	95	0	0	1	5	21	
Gender								
Male	1,179	83%	136	10%	106	7%	1,421	100%
Female	119	79	19	13	13	8	1,551	100

*Alabama, Arkansas, Florida, Georgia, Louisiana, Mississippi, North Carolina, South Carolina, Texas, and Virginia.
[†]Kentucky, Maryland, Tennessee, and West Virginia.
[‡]Illinois, Massachusetts, Missouri, New Jersey, New York, and Pennsylvania.
Source: Aguirre and Baker, 1999.

common to all of them. Blacks could not (1) vote, (2) serve on juries, (3) testify against whites, (4) carry arms, and (5) enter certain occupations (depending on the state). The codes also stated that black vagrants could be consigned to forced labor. Thus, after the Civil War, the free South was unified in its attempts to impose new legal restrictions on African Americans.

In reaction to these codes, the violence used to enforce them, and perceptions that President Andrew Johnson was being too conciliatory toward the South, radical Republicans in Congress began to assume control of Reconstruction. The radicals in Congress mounted a two-front legal attack on discrimination in the South by advocating (1) the division of the South into military districts and the enforcement of new constitutional conventions on each southern state and (2) the passage of the Fourteenth and Fifteenth Amendments, which were ratified by northern and reconstituted southern states in 1868 and 1870, respectively. The **Fourteenth Amendment** was an extension of an earlier civil rights act (vetoed by Johnson and then overridden by Congress) that was designed to overrule the emerging black codes. The **Fifteenth Amendment** extended suffrage to African Americans. Reforms in the South were soon followed by the **Civil Rights Act of 1875,** which outlawed northern Jim Crow practices. In this way, Congress forced the South and, to a lesser extent, the North to accept black participation in mainstream American life.

Had radical Reconstruction continued over several generations, institutionalized discrimination in America would have been markedly reduced. However, by 1880, the radical Republicans had lost control of Congress and the presidency. Almost immediately, new exclusionary laws were passed at local and state levels. These laws were, in essence, a codification of informal practices of segregation and exclusion, reinforced by the ever-present threat of white violence (Williamson, 1984:229). In turn, the Supreme Court began to legitimize the reemergence of Jim Crow practices in the 1890s. First, the Court declared unconstitutional the Civil Rights Act of 1875, thus denying African Americans access to public conveyances and amusement facilities used by white Americans. Then, in 1896, the Court ruled in *Plessy v. Ferguson* that segregated facilities for blacks and whites were not in violation of the Thirteenth and Fourteenth Amendments to the Constitution, since, as the Court declared: "If one race be inferior to the other socially, the Constitution cannot put them on the same plane" (Pinkney, 1969:28).

Codifying exclusionary and segregationist practices in the highest laws of the land firmly established the culture and structure of discrimination in America, in both institutional and informal practice (Cella, 1982; Horowitz and Karst, 1969). It was with this national legal legacy that blacks entered the twentieth century (Steele, 1990). During this period, African Americans became increasingly urban. In the North, however, a myriad of discriminatory laws prevented black integration into white institutions and black participation in the world of white American affluence. Many did not consider such laws illegal or immoral; they were legitimized by the highest court in the land and reflected the post–Civil War belief that blacks had been given a chance and had demonstrated their inferiority. These court decisions were subsequently reversed, but great damage had been done and informal discrimination in housing, jobs, education, and other spheres persists to this day. Such formal legal barriers and the informal climate of discrimination they created made up the legacy which African Americans sought to overturn in the civil rights movement of the twentieth century (see Box 5.6).

Legal Discrimination in the Twentieth Century   Through the first half of the twentieth century, state and local codes discriminated against blacks in many vital areas of life. In education, African Americans in the South attended

---

Box 5.6
Over a Century after *Plessy v. Ferguson*

On June 7, 1892, Homer Plessy became part of an incident that would shape the entire twentieth century in America. Plessy was self-described as one-eighth "colored," and on this day he refused to move out of the "whites only" railroad car on the East Louisiana Railroad traveling between New Orleans and Covington. Plessy was seen to violate a two-year-old state law in Louisiana that required "separate but equal" facilities for blacks and whites. Plessy's refusal was staged to test the state law, but the Louisiana decision went against him.

The issue was important because throughout the South, except for South and North Carolina as well as Virginia, segregation laws had been rapidly emerging for intrastate travel on the railroads, which, at this time, provided the major means of long-distance travel. In the 1890s, it was not inevitable that black–white segregation would occur; it was, instead, entirely possible that these emerging state laws could be struck down and the process of integration—however slow and difficult—could have proceeded. The case went to the Supreme Court, and the history of black–white relations in America was forever changed in 1890. Justice Henry Billings Brown—a man who had grown up in the North—wrote for the majority opinion and argued that facilities need not be identical to be equal, and if blacks see their segregation as inferior, "it is not by reason of anything found in the act, but solely because the colored race chooses to put that construction on it." Thus, if blacks saw their segregation as a signal of inferiority, it was in their minds, not in the legal mandate. Writing a strong dissent was Justice John Marshall Harlan, a Kentuckian who had even been a Confederate officer, who predicted just what happened: The *Plessy v. Ferguson* decision would become the legal mantle for creating segregated facilities in all spheres, not just public transport.

It was not until the early 1950s that the *Plessy v. Ferguson* decision was overturned, and by then much of the damage had been done. White America had begun to move: up the occupational ladder, into the suburbs, into better schools, into colleges and universities, and into post–World War II prosperity. Blacks had been shut out during these critical decades between the *Plessy* decision and the *Brown v. Board of Education* decision in 1954, which declared segregated schools to be inherently unequal.

Source: Adapted from a syndicated column by Edwin M. Yoder, Jr., and from C. Vann Woodward's *The Strange Career of Jim Crow,* 1966.

segregated and inferior schools, a circumstance supported by state and local codes and enforced with threats of and actual violence from the white community. In housing, Federal Housing Authority (FHA) codes prevented integration of housing subsidized by the FHA, which confirmed and reaffirmed restrictive covenants in trust deeds (that certain ethnic groups could not own property in an area) and discriminatory lending practices of bankers. In the job market, most craft unions and many industrial unions established rules that either restricted or forbade black membership or created separate black auxiliary (and less powerful and effective) unions; in both cases, these practices prevented African Americans from moving beyond a narrow range of lower-paying jobs. In politics, especially in the South, state and local governments enacted voting laws that were differentially enforced for blacks and whites, a practice that kept African Americans disenfranchised. For example, in the 1890s and after, Alabama, Georgia, Louisiana, Mississippi, North Carolina, South Carolina, and Virginia all enforced literacy tests for blacks but not for whites (Bell, 1973). Since two-thirds of the black population in these states was illiterate at that time, the vast majority of African Americans were disenfranchised. Such literacy tests, often loaded with trick questions, were common well into the twentieth century. In contrast, illiterate whites could have the literacy requirement waived if they owned property or if they revealed a "good character" or could understand English. Across all sectors of society, then, African Americans confronted laws and rules that excluded them into the 1960s.

From this blatant legal discrimination—which reinforced and encouraged informal discrimination in housing, schools, jobs, and politics—the civil rights movement was born. For two decades, in the 1950s and 1960s, blacks and sympathetic whites organized to eliminate the legal basis of discrimination. They employed a broad array of tactics—lawsuits culminating in Supreme Court decisions, mass protests, boycotts, sit-ins, and lobbying in Congress. The first big legal victory was the 1954 Supreme Court decision in *Brown v. Board of Education of Topeka, Kansas,* which declared segregated schooling inherently inferior and, hence, discriminatory (Kluger, 1975). By the 1960s, public opinion outside the South had become sympathetic to the black struggle. The result was the enactment of a series of significant laws—the **Voting Rights Act of 1965** and the **Civil Rights Acts of 1964 and 1968.** Congress passed these laws to eliminate legal and informal discrimination in employment, unions, housing, voting booths, and schools.

These laws were not enacted until 100 years after the Civil War. Although they have helped African Americans enormously, these relatively recent laws cannot reverse the damage done by a long history of legal discrimination. Indeed, it was during the hundred years after the Civil War that the United States was transformed into an affluent, industrial society; yet, many African Americans were not allowed to be beneficiaries of this national success.

Undoing the legacy of legal discrimination is a formidable challenge to American society in the present century. Unfortunately, the 1980s and early 1990s did not evidence a strong commitment to meeting the challenge. In fact, there even were efforts to weaken some laws; for example, the Reagan and first

Bush administrations sought to soften the Voting Rights Act by limiting funding for its enforcement by the Justice Department, and by supporting a civil rights law that practically eliminated the Voting Rights Act. Moreover, attempts to reinterpret other laws in the courts, especially with respect to the affirmative action policies stemming from the Civil Rights Act, and to enforce laws selectively, particularly with respect to job and housing discrimination, were made by Congress and the presidents of the 1980s and 1990s. Most important is the near absence of political will to create laws to help African Americans overcome the cumulative effects of legal exclusion from the American mainstream. This lack of political will exists because the majority of Americans believe that today the inequities African Americans experience are the result of their lack of motivation and individual effort (Kluegel and Bobo, 1993; Kluegel and Smith, 1986). When a voting majority does not see the present problem, it is difficult to redress past discrimination. It is not surprising, then, that many African Americans continue to meet obstacles in their efforts to participate fully in the institutional structure—economy, education, politics, and housing—of the society.

Nowhere is the lack of knowledge about the cumulative effects of discrimination more evident than in the area of **affirmative action.** The civil rights laws of the 1960s, as interpreted by Executive Order 11246, required organizations doing business with, or receiving funds from, the government to increase minority representation in those organizations (Jaynes and Williams, 1989:316). In practice, these government mandates applied primarily to businesses receiving (directly or indirectly) government contracts, and to education, especially higher education. As affirmative action policies were more rigorously enforced in the 1970s and early 1980s, they became increasingly unpopular. Charges (both legal and informal) of **reverse discrimination** could be heard from some white employees and students. Moreover, one effect of affirmative action was the creation of informal quotas favoring members of minority groups and, to a lesser extent, women in male-dominated occupations and in the sphere of education; this public perception that quotas do indeed exist is then used to validate the charge that some whites are the victims of discrimination. This charge has led many people to believe that affirmative action no longer is about equality of opportunities but is about group preferences. Yet, without affirmative action, or a similar policy, how are the effects of past discrimination to be overcome? Without some degree of preference afforded African Americans affected by past discrimination, many will have difficulty achieving equality with white Americans in school and in the workplace.

In recent decades, the courts have issued somewhat contradictory decisions (Jaynes and Williams, 1989; Marger, 2000), perhaps reflecting the public's ambivalence over affirmative action. In some cases, such as *Weber v. Kaiser Aluminum* in 1979, the Supreme Court ruled that employers could use "race" as a criterion for hiring and could employ quotas. A year earlier, however, in *Regents of the University of California v. Bakke,* the Supreme Court ruled in favor of Bakke, a white male who had been denied entrance into medical school because of quotas for minority students. During the Reagan and first Bush administrations, the Supreme Court, which had been generally supportive of affirmative action, began to shift as new appointees to the Court began to influence decisions. Recent decisions not only have weakened the impact of affirmative action but have also made it more difficult for members of minority groups to prove in court that they have been victims of discrimination. As the Court's composition shifted again in the 1990s, it became difficult to predict the fate of affirmative action programs, but it is unlikely that any new laws will be enacted to bolster affirmative action programs in light of the general public's hostility to such programs (Kluegel and Bobo, 1993; Takaki, 1987:223–32). Indeed in 1996, the *Hopwood v. Texas* decision, the first major decision since *Bakke,* went against the University of Texas, which had sought to use "race" as a criterion for special admission policies; and in a highly controversial decision in 1996, the Board of Regents of the University of California eliminated race and ethnicity as criteria for special admission to the university, a decision that was challenged in the courts but that, like the *Hopwood* ruling, worked against affirmative action as it was practiced in the 1970s and 1980s.

Despite gains in treatment by the legal system, the most volatile point of contact between African Americans and the legal system is the police. In a 1999 Gallup poll of blacks and whites on the question of whether or not the police profile blacks for questioning, 77 percent of African Americans say they believe that such targeting of blacks occurs, and four out of ten say that they have been stopped for no reason other than the color of their skin (Jet, 2000). This figure increases dramatically among young black men, 72 percent of whom indicate that they have been stopped, some many times. Despite these figures, it is rather surprising that a majority of African Americans have a positive opinion of their local police, but still over one-third do not. And a clear majority of African American men between the ages of eighteen and twenty-four have highly negative views about the police—not surprising, since this is the targeted group. A somewhat surprising finding from the poll is that a majority of white Americans—some 56 percent—believe that police profiling of blacks is widespread. Thus, it is clear that negative stereotypes of young black males have worked against the black population, who are much more likely to be stopped routinely and questioned by the police than are their white counterparts. Like all Americans, African Americans want to be treated fairly by the police, since this is the portion of the legal system that directly touches their lives. It is not clear that they get the same treatment, and indeed the opposite appears to be the case. Most of the various mass "riots" and "revolts" of the last half of the twentieth century began with a "routine" police arrest; anger against not only the police but the larger white society often then led to violence that escalated until the military was called in to restore order. In the twenty-first century, there is still anger at the police, and it may have the same disruptive potential that it has had in the past (see Box 5.7).

Economic Discrimination

Slavery and Its Aftermath   Prior to the Civil War, the economic organization of the South became heavily dependent on a large slave population. While the historical record does not mark precisely when slavery was first

Box 5.7
When Whites Riot and Cover Up

Tulsa was a rapidly growing oil city in 1921. Oklahoma was producing over a third of the country's oil, with Tulsa producing about 90 percent of the state's total oil production. Oil production was driving Tulsa's economy and expanding job opportunities for black workers. However, there was an increasing sense of white nativism in Oklahoma that was being fueled by the Ku Klux Klan. Some portions of the white population began to resent the increasing social and occupational mobility of blacks in Tulsa.

On the morning of May 31, 1921, police arrested a black shoeshine man named Dick Rowland for allegedly assaulting a 17-year-old white female elevator operator. The arrest was the springboard for what became known as the Tulsa Race War. Despite the fact that the white female did not file charges against Rowland, rumors of his arrest caused 2,000 white persons to demonstrate outside the courthouse demanding that Rowland be lynched.

A confrontation between the white demonstrators and about 75 armed black war veterans who had approached the police offering to help defend the courthouse resulted in an outbreak of violence. According to witnesses, a shot was fired by someone. The white demonstrators assumed it was fired by one of the black war veterans. The black war veterans assumed it was fired by one of the white demonstrators. The clash between the two groups resulted in an invasion of as many as 10,000 whites, creating havoc and destruction in a predominantly black neighborhood, Greenwood, home to Tulsa's black teachers, doctors, and laborers.

By the time the governor called in the National Guard on June 1 to bring things under control, about 700 African American families had fled the city looking for safety, and about 4,000 African Americans were forced into internment camps guarded by armed whites. The estimated death count was fewer than 10 whites and about 250 blacks. More than 30 blocks in Greenwood had been destroyed, and more than 10,000 blacks were left homeless.

As tragic as the riot was for the black community in Tulsa, one of the saddest aspects of it became hidden in Tulsa's past. A lingering rumor about the Tulsa Race War was that many blacks, far more than the estimates of white city officials, had been killed and buried in mass graves. The rumor led Don Ross, a state legislator, in 1996 to push through a bill forming the Tulsa Race Riot Commission. The Commission's mandate was to locate survivors of the riot in order to document its history, to determine if survivors were entitled to reparations, and to investigate the rumor about the mass graves.

The Commission's initial findings confirmed the rumor of mass graves. Testifying before the Commission in September 1999, an 88-year-old man told the commissioners of seeing huge crates standing by unmarked pits in the paupers' section of the city's cemetery. Before he was told to move away from the crates, he admitted, he saw the bodies of four black men in one crate. State archaeologists have been charged with testing the ground in the city's cemetery with radar in order to see if such bodies lie underneath. According to the Commission's chairman, Bob Blackburn, recovering any remains will be the first step toward reconciliation between blacks and whites in Tulsa, and the breaking of a seventy-eight-year-old silence.

On February 2001, the Tulsa Race Riot Commission issued a final report recommending that direct payments be made to survivors and descendants of riot victims.

(continued)

The commission also called for a memorial to the dead, scholarships and a tax check-off program to fund economic development in the Greenwood district, where the race riot took place. The commission decided not to excavate for human remains because of rumors that babies were buried in the mass graves and of fears that the possible excavation of babies would result in bad publicity. In February 2003, a legal tem led by Johnnie Cochran and Harvard law professor Charles Ogletree Jr. filed a reparations lawsuit on behalf of the survivors and descendants of victims and survivors of the race riot, based on the findings of the Tulsa Race Riot Commission's report. In September 2004, the U.S. Court of Appeals ruled against the victims of the Tulsa Race Riot. The Tulsa Race Riot Commission's final report is available at: www.okhistory.org.

Source: This account of the Tulsa Race Riot was drawn from the following sources: Scott Ellsworth, *Death in a Promised Land: The Tulsa Race Riot of 1921* (Baton Rouge: Louisiana State University Press, 1982); R. Halliburton, "The Tulsa Race War of 1921," *Journal of Black Studies* 2 (1972): 333–57; "The Riot That Never Was," *The Economist,* April 24, 1999, p. 29; "Panel Seeks Clearer View of 1921 Tulsa Race Riot," *New York Times,* Feb. 21, 1999, p. 28; "Searching for Graves—and Justice—in Tulsa," *New York Times,* March 20, 1999, p. A14; "A City's Buried Shame," *Los Angeles Times,* Oct. 23, 1999, pp. A1, A16.

institutionalized, it is clear that by 1670 most black people in America, adults and children, had been forced into lifelong servitude. Slavery became rapidly institutionalized because of the agricultural economy emerging in the South. In contrast to the North, which was beginning to industrialize and urbanize by the time of the American Revolution, the South remained heavily agricultural, relying on the export of cotton, tobacco, hemp, rice, wheat, and sugar. Different states tended to specialize in only some of these crops, but all states had one feature in common: the reliance on an inexpensive and relatively large labor pool to cultivate large tracts of land. It is not clear whether slavery was the most efficient form of agricultural organization (see Fogel and Engerman, 1974; Genovese, 1965; Williamson, 1984:12–14), but the shortage of labor and the abundance of land in the southern colonies placed a high value on involuntary labor. As a result, slaves were used to initiate the plantation system, and once initiated, the system was operated to "keep in line" a large and potentially volatile population. The initial importation and enslavement of blacks in the seventeenth century was facilitated by the early settlers' cultural beliefs about the "bestial" nature and less-than-human status of Africans (Jordan, 1968). Such negative beliefs accelerated the pace of enslavement, a process that violated the official core values of American society.

The distribution of slaves in the South reflected the economic priorities and power relations within that part of the country (Stampp, 1956; Starobin, 1970:5). By 1860 there were about 4 million slaves in the South. Over 50 percent were owned by only 12 percent, who held the large tracts of fertile land that formed the basis of the southern economy. Slavery emerged and persisted largely because a small group of politically powerful landowners required cheap labor and made slavery acceptable in the agricultural sector of the economy and then, to a very limited extent, in mining, iron production, textile manufacturing, and small industry (Lander, 1969; Lewis, 1979, 1989). Thus, by the dawn of the Civil War, most agriculture in the southern economy and a few industrial and craft sectors (Newton and Lewis, 1978) relied on slave labor. The institutionalization of slavery in the southern economy, plus the fear of retaliatory violence by slaves, partially accounts for the resistance of this "peculiar institution" to change (Stampp, 1956).

White violence against African Americans has historically been a means of control and domination. Here, in the twentieth century, two blacks were hanged without trial or due process for supposed crimes against whites.

The South countered abolitionist attacks on slavery by further codifying beliefs based on the "Sambo" stereotype (Boskin, 1986; Turner and Singleton, 1978). Although most abolitionists did not hold the Sambo stereotype, even the most radical abolitionists believed in the intellectual inferiority of blacks (Fredrickson, 1971). Differences in the northern and southern belief systems no doubt reflected the respective economic dependency of the northern and southern economies on slave labor. Because few blacks lived in the North, its economy remained unaffected by abolition or the colonization of the black population. In the South, however, the loss of slave labor threatened widespread disruption of the southern economy and lifestyle.

Only a war between the states could break the culturally legitimized institution of slavery in the South. During the brief period of radical Reconstruction afterward, large numbers of blacks gained access to many skilled trades and began to assume ownership of farms. But as noted earlier, Congress in 1877 changed its legislative mind toward ethnic relations. For thirty years thereafter

African Americans were systematically excluded from skilled nonfarm occupations and thrust into tenant farming or low-wage labor for white landowners or into menial labor and domestic work in both rural and urban areas. Such a dramatic reversal of the economic policies of radical Reconstruction was legitimized by the limited conception of "equality" of the then-dominant laissez-faire ideology (economic and individual activity should go unregulated) and by the Social Darwinism ("survival of the fittest") of the late nineteenth century.

By the turn of the century, 90 percent of all African Americans remained in the South, 75 percent living under oppressive conditions in rural areas. For a number of reasons, the quality of life for African Americans, especially those in rural areas, worsened dramatically during the early years of the twentieth century (Hamilton, 1964): (1) The high birthrates of rural families began to exceed their ability to secure sufficient income in the depressed economy of the South; (2) the nature of agriculture changed dramatically with mechanization and the consequent displacement of black labor; (3) the cotton industry, on which many blacks depended for survival, began to move to the Southwest and then was devastated by the boll weevil; and (4) many whites used violence—beatings, burnings, and lynchings—to maintain black subordination (see Box 5.8) (Aguirre and Baker, 1991; Rable 1984; Tolnay and Beck, 1992; Williamson, 1984:180–223). These and other "push factors" led blacks to migrate from the South into the urban areas of the North. By 1914, these "push factors" were combined with "pull factors" from northern cities: The onset of World War I had cut off European migration while rapidly expanding the very industrial production that had for decades drawn

---

Box 5.8
The Long Legacy of Lynching in the South

A recent study on present-day homicide rates in the South began with an interesting hypothesis: Past frequency of lynching of African Americans by whites in the South would still exert effects on violence and homicide in those counties and places where the rate of lynching had once been high. Lynching involved brutalization of blacks by whites and generated a culture supporting violence. On the other side, the victims of lynching developed self-help adaptations that also led to a culture of violence. This culture of violence has been passed down from generation to generation, right up to the present, and leads to higher rates of homicide in the areas where lynching was common. At least, this is what the authors of the study hypothesized. The data on homicide rates showed a consistent positive effect of lynching in the past on homicide rates in the present. The effects on blacks and whites were somewhat different, however. Lynching had an effect on homicide in general among blacks, but for whites, lynching appears to have an effect only on a particular kind of homicide: interracial homicides arising out of interpersonal conflict between blacks and whites. Lynching thus created a culture of violence that still influences homicide rates for whites on blacks when interracial conflict occurs.

Source: Messner, Baller, and Zevenbergen, 2005.

European migrants to American cities. Suddenly, there were economic opportunities for African Americans in northern cities, with the result that between 1914 and 1920, nearly a million blacks migrated to urban areas in the industrial North. This migration was to be the first of a series of large-scale shifts in the black population; by 1960 over three-fourths of that population resided in cities, with only one-half remaining in the South. Patterns of economic discrimination became urban as opposed to rural, and national in contrast to regional.

Many of the early migrants to northern cities initially found jobs during the peak of wartime production, but they also encountered white discrimination and violence (Bonacich, 1976). African Americans tended to live in segregated tenements that early European migrants had abandoned because of their dilapidated and unsafe condition; when blacks ventured into white neighborhoods and into certain occupations, acts or threats of violence frequently occurred. For example, twenty-five "race riots" broke out between June and October of 1919 (Turner, Singleton, and Musick, 1984). This violence was intensified as black laborers were used as strikebreakers in corporate America's effort to stifle the union movement. Whites attacked blacks, then black workers retaliated, bringing a counterattack by whites. The resulting violence forced police to quell such riots. The hostility toward blacks; based on the threat of job displacement, persists today in many urban areas of the Northeast and Midwest.

With the end of wartime production and the onset of the Great Depression of the 1930s, the economic situation of African Americans worsened once again. Unemployment and hunger increased, and even welfare allocations were differentially distributed among blacks and whites (Pinkney, 1969:33–34). The New Deal ushered in some changes, but the capacity of nascent civil rights groups to generate change was limited. Wage and job discrimination and exclusion from unions continued until well after World War II.

World War II, like World War I, caused a massive black migration to urban areas in both the North and South. As African Americans became concentrated in key wartime industries in urban areas, they began to exert political pressure, forcing President Roosevelt to ban discrimination in wartime industries and pressuring the Congress of Industrial Organizations (CIO) to allow some black workers into the unions' ranks (although most unions, especially craft unions, used informal means to keep black workers out, or in low-paying positions).

Patterns of Present-Day Discrimination   The effects of slavery and established patterns of discrimination persist today. Black workers are overrepresented in menial service jobs; they are underrepresented in professional and managerial occupations; they are twice as likely to be unemployed; they earn slightly less than two-thirds the wages of white workers; and they are twice as likely to be poor. This legacy of slavery costs all Americans a great deal in (1) lost productivity among the large pool of potential black workers; (2) lost consumption of gainfully employed African Americans, which could, in turn, encourage production for all workers; (3) lost tax revenues from African Americans who lack a steady job; and (4) lost federal, state, and local revenues allocated to social welfare programs in order to maintain black households.

The legacy of economic discrimination has been compounded by other conditions over the last two decades:

1. The decrease in skilled and semiskilled blue-collar jobs in the economy at a
    time when most employment barriers have been eliminated.
2. The movement of employment opportunities to the suburbs, making em-
    ployment difficult for inner-city blacks to secure because of past housing
    discrimination (see the section on this topic later in this chapter).
3. The decline in industrial union power and membership at a time when they
    have become fully open to blacks.
4. The increase in low-paying service jobs relative to the higher-paying and
    skilled blue-collar jobs that historically allowed many white immigrant
    ethnic groups to assimilate and become upwardly mobile.
5. The influx of new immigrants who compete with black workers and small-
    business owners for jobs.
6. The national fiscal crisis, which has reduced the amount of money available
    for social programs in general and poverty programs in particular.
7. The resurgence of conservative beliefs that government cannot and should not
    try to solve the economic problems of African Americans (indeed, government
    is now seen as part of the problem in that it supports welfare dependency).

Thus, the economic plight of today's African Americans is difficult to address,
even though many of the legal barriers to discrimination have been removed.
Even though legal and institutionalized discrimination have receded, more
subtle patterns of informal discrimination persist.

Many African Americans today continue to pay a penalty for their skin color
when seeking jobs—assuming that they live in an area where they have access to
jobs. For example, the Urban Institute in Washington, DC, sent teams of black
and white men as job seekers to over four hundred interviews for jobs advertised
in the newspapers of Washington and Chicago. The workers were matched with
identical qualifications. The results showed that 15 percent of the white applicants received job offers compared to 5 percent of the African Americans. During
the job selection process, white men advanced to the next round of interviews
20 percent of the time, whereas black men did so only 7 percent of the time.
White men reported rude or otherwise unfavorable treatment during the job-
seeking process 27 percent of the time, while the corresponding figure for black
men was 50 percent. These findings were confirmed in a landmark study by the
Russell Sage Foundation (1999). Employers still hold many negative stereotypes
about African Americans, and these prejudices influence their hiring decisions.
In Detroit, for example, it took unskilled and unemployed whites 91 hours to
generate a job offer, whereas it required 167 hours for a black to receive an offer.
Beliefs that blacks are welfare dependent, that they are more likely to commit
crimes, and that they are difficult to get along with all work to bias the hiring
practices of employers against African Americans. These stereotypes are particularly pernicious because they place blacks at a disadvantage in job competition
with recent immigrants who are not subject to these negative beliefs and who, as
a result, are more likely to get jobs than blacks. Thus, despite Americans' beliefs

that affirmative action guarantees African Americans favorable treatment, this study indicates that African Americans still experience discrimination.

Once employed, African Americans often are not promoted because of informal discriminatory practices, especially in white-collar corporate jobs. In a pioneering study on women and minorities in nine of the Fortune 500 corporations, the U.S. Department of Labor (1991) found a "glass ceiling" blocking these groups from access to "corporate pipelines" leading to managerial and executive positions. African Americans, in particular, experience this subtle, almost invisible barrier in a variety of ways. First, blacks and other minority groups are more likely than whites to be placed in human resources and public relations positions, which, unlike sales and production jobs, are off the "fast track" to management. Second, blacks are more likely than whites to be excluded from networks, mentor programs, and policy-making committees; as a result, they do not acquire the contacts, information, and experience necessary for movement up the corporate ladder. Third, hiring at the executive level is typically conducted outside the human resources and personnel departments, without concern about affirmative action and without systematic efforts by corporate executives or their "head hunter" search firms to create a diverse pool of applicants. Instead, informal networks and discussions usually influence hiring at the higher levels of a corporation, the kind of contact from which African Americans are routinely excluded.

African Americans often encounter another pattern of informal, and perhaps at times inadvertent, discrimination when attempting to set up a business. For many white Americans, owning and running a business has been one path to affluence. For African Americans, however, this path is strewn with obstacles. African American–owned businesses tend to be economically marginal, labor-intensive proprietorships that must withstand heavy competition from entrepreneurial immigrants vying for the same clientele. Also, it is more difficult for black Americans to secure credit than it is for white Americans, since lending agencies use criteria that favor those with "white credentials" (such as higher education, current collateral, and high credit ratings) and those who intend to service white shopping-center clientele. However, while all small businesses are high-risk ventures, there is no evidence that black businesses in ghetto neighborhoods are any more risky than white ventures in white neighborhoods. For example, in the 1960s the Small Business Administration began extending loans according to criteria other than credit history and collateral. In 1964, 98 of 219 special loans went to African Americans; and only 8 of the 219 loans became delinquent and none were liquidated (Turner and Singleton, 1978). For a while the Minority Business Development Agency helped expand minority-owned businesses, but in the 1980s its resources and programs were cut back. Such cutbacks are a form of discrimination, especially when it is recognized that African Americans do not receive Small Business Administration loans proportionate to their numbers in society. Almost thirty years later, the Federal Reserve Board of Boston issued a report showing that blacks were 60 percent more likely than whites to be rejected for bank loans (Smith, 1992). Thus, the public's perceptions of "preferences" for blacks are inaccurate.

Part of the informal process of discrimination are the criteria defining a good worker—criteria that are biased against African Americans in favor of white Americans. For instance, employers look at formal education credentials, which white Americans are more likely to have, even for jobs that do not require them. Or, to take another example, white speech styles and personal demeanor associated with middle-class subculture (which, in reality, are seldom related to actual job performance) are preferred in certain jobs (Jaynes and Williams, 1989:321). Invidious discrimination is thus built into the hiring practices of many of America's businesses—a discrimination that perpetuates the disadvantaged position of African Americans.

Political Discrimination Without political power, it is difficult for those who experience discrimination to diminish it. Until recent decades, African Americans have been almost completely disenfranchised, with little or no political power. Today, even with the historic election of an African American for president, blacks' participation in the political arena is not proportionate to their numbers because of the long-established pattern of exclusion. Several historical facts explain the low level of political participation in the black community today:

1. Prior to the Civil War, blacks held the right to vote or hold office in only five states (all northern with very small black populations).
2. In the nineteenth century, blacks voted and held office in significant numbers only during the brief period of radical Reconstruction following the Civil War.
3. In the 1870s, congressional commitment to Reconstruction had waned; and when the presidential election of 1876 became deadlocked in the Electoral College and was thrown into Congress, Republicans abandoned the principles of Reconstruction in order to "buy" southern votes. The result was that blacks were systematically excluded from the polls, with almost complete disenfranchisement in the South by 1895 (Kousser, 1974; Williamson, 1984:224–84).
4. Through a variety of tactics—from poll taxes through "literacy tests" to threats of violence—blacks living in the South remained politically excluded from the 1890s until well into the 1960s (Daniel, 1973). Urban blacks who lived in the North and South had somewhat more voting power, but a broad array of tactics kept many African Americans disenfranchised and diminished the power of those who participated in local and national elections.

Thus, the relative lack of black political power is largely a result of the long history of intended and deliberate political exclusion, especially in the South. The patterns of political discrimination have continued well into this century with strategies such as the poll tax, the "literacy test," and the "Constitution test," which were differentially enforced for African Americans and poor whites. When these measures were declared illegal, administrative obstruction—long lines, much paperwork, elaborate documentation of residence, and so forth—effectively prevented most African Americans from registering to vote. Underlying these obstructions was the frequently implemented threat of white violence visited on the homes of those blacks who sought to register to vote or who actually voted.

It was not until the mid-1960s that many of these exclusionary tactics were declared unconstitutional. With the Voting Rights Act of 1965, political participation among blacks increased. However, the removal of these roadblocks and a growing political consciousness among African Americans caused discriminatory political strategies to shift from denying the vote to diluting the impact of black voting power by gerrymandering congressional districts in order to "break up" the ghetto as a voting bloc and spread its votes among two or more districts where whites outnumbered the now-divided African American vote.

In the decades following the civil rights movement and the Voting Rights Act of 1965, African Americans have made significant political gains, especially at the state and local levels (Jaynes and Williams, 1989:208–9; Turner and Payne, 2002; Welch, 1990). Although black voter participation still lags behind that of whites, the elimination of most barriers to black electoral participation has led to significant changes. For example, approximately 300 mayors are African American; many of the largest cities in the United States are governed by black mayors. Many city, county, and state legislators, municipal judges, constables, and sheriffs, and some standing and select committee chairs in Congress are black. Yet, even with this kind of political representation, African Americans still constitute considerably less than 2 percent of all elected offices and officials in the United States (Joint Center for Political Studies, 1977, 1996; Turner and Payne, 2002). Moreover, at the national level, where important policy decisions affecting blacks will be made, African Americans are not proportionately represented: Less than 10 percent of Congress is black; and aside from some high-profile cabinet members there are very few African Americans in top-level positions in the executive branch of government (Pohlmann, 1990; Turner and Payne, 2002; White, 1985).

Even in areas where African Americans have made real gains—political influence and control of large cities—they have come at a time when political and economic power has shifted to the suburbs and, because of the fiscal problems of most large cities, to state and federal government. Black political control of the large cities really means that black officials must deal with the financial, educational, and social problems that were created by past discrimination and that caused many whites to move to the suburbs. "Control" over cities marked by poverty, gangs, deteriorating schools, high levels of crime, deficit budgets, slums, empty industrial buildings, and expensive social services is not likely to improve the political power base of African Americans. City politics does not greatly influence national politics, which is where most important political decisions affecting the welfare of African Americans are ultimately made.

African American candidates are almost always elected in locations where they are the majority—with only a few exceptions. Significant numbers of white Americans tend not to vote for black candidates, and so African Americans usually have power only where there is an overwhelming black constituency. Thus, while significant gains in political power are evident, African Americans remain underrepresented in the political system, a system that often fails to address their problems and needs.

Educational Discrimination

Educational Discrimination before and Immediately after the Civil War
By the dawn of the Civil War, all southern states had enacted compulsory ignorance laws for slaves. These laws, which some slaveholders chose to violate,
prohibited whites from teaching slaves to read, write, and calculate. Moreover,
clandestine schools for slaves operated everywhere in the South, and many
freed slaves received education in segregated public facilities (Turner, Singleton,
and Musick, 1984). In some states, such as North Carolina, literacy among
blacks was as high as 43 percent, but in the Deep South literacy was probably no
more than 10 percent.

In the North, educational opportunities were much better for African
Americans in the decades before the Civil War. Religious groups, some munici-
palities, and a number of philanthropists created educational opportunities for
blacks. Yet these opportunities were not universally available. At the higher-
education level, the first black university—Lincoln University in Pennsylvania—
opened its doors to a few students. In 1833, Oberlin College became the first
mainstream college to admit African Americans in significant numbers.

After the Civil War, the establishment of free public schools in both the
North and South was initiated (Cash, 1941:3–102). Yet, much of the education of
African Americans occurred in private schools sponsored by religious societies
and philanthropists. By the 1870s, state legislatures had mandated free public
education for all citizens, and by 1880, one-third of all black children were

Photograph shows African American students walking through a crowd of white
students during early school integration.

registered in school (Weinberg, 1977:45–54). But during the 1880s, the tide turned against black education. Public funding at the local level slowed considerably, although African Americans were required to pay taxes for all schools, both white and black. In some southern states, government spending on African American schools became voluntary. Between 1870 and 1905, the sixteen southern states in which 90 percent of all African Americans lived spent one-fourth as much on black schools as they spent on white schools. Most of these black schools were vocational, providing literacy and teaching the rudiments of a trade.

By the dawn of the twentieth century, literacy among African Americans had increased to as much as 40 percent (Turner, Singleton, and Musick, 1984), but still, a system of dual education was firmly in place. This system of separate and decidedly unequal schools became more pronounced as blacks began to move to urban centers in the North and South.

Educational Discrimination in the Twentieth Century   In the urban areas of the North and South, school attendance and literacy increased, but in a segregated school system. In this system, the South spent two to three times as much on white students as on black students, assuring that the latter would receive an inferior education (Bullock, 1967). Moreover, despite gains in literacy within this unequal system, illiteracy among African Americans was six times that among whites, and as late as 1969, it was still four times that of whites. It was not until 1975 that black enrollment in schools reached parity with white enrollment (Turner, Singleton, and Musick, 1984:123). But the quality of education for African Americans was consistently inferior for the simple reason that schools were segregated. Between 1920 and 1940, the pattern of segregated schools spread throughout the United States. In the South, state legislators, local political figures, school boards, and courts all worked to create a segregated educational system; in the North, housing discrimination and threats of white violence produced residential segregation, which led to separate school systems.

As this dual system was established, blacks and their white supporters began to raise questions (Kluger, 1975). In the late 1940s and early 1950s, the National Association for the Advancement of Colored People (NAACP) and the Urban League began to push not only for African American voting rights but also for equality in education. This effort culminated in the NAACP's successful appeal in 1954 before the Supreme Court stating that separate schools are unequal and, therefore, are in contradiction to the Fourteenth Amendment to the Constitution *(Brown v. Board of Education of Topeka)*. In rendering this landmark decision, however, the Supreme Court did not set a timetable for its implementation. Hence, local school boards dragged their feet, citing complexities and the need for additional time. Indeed, local officials routinely ignored court orders for desegregation. During the 1960s, however, black and white activism increased and led to the passage of the Civil Rights Act of 1964, which strengthened the federal government's hand in forcing the states to comply with desegregation orders; and hence, under the threat of withholding federal funds and military coercion, the states increased school integration, especially in the South.

A series of court decisions in the 1970s reinforced the push for school integration. In 1971 *(Swann v. Charlotte-Mecklenburg Board of Education)*, the Supreme Court ruled that busing was an appropriate tool for achieving integration; in 1973 *(Keyes v. Denver School District No. 1)*, the Court ruled that evidence of government actions to maintain segregation, such as site selection for schools or manipulation of attendance zones, was sufficient to require desegregation using busing and other means. Yet, in another series of decisions in the 1970s, the Court rejected the regionalization strategy, which would require suburban districts to be part of the desegregation effort in large cities. This latter set of decisions, coupled with white protests and violence over busing, has made the desegregation of the inner city a difficult process. And so, in the 2000s, over half of all black students continued to attend schools in which minority students are the majority of the students enrolled (National Center for Education Statistics, 2007).

In the period between 1920 and 1960, most black students in the South attended black colleges. In the 1950s, however, forced desegregation of state universities in the South began; today, there is little evidence of discrimination in admissions to public universities in either the South or North. At private colleges and universities, the picture is more complicated. A combination of sincere efforts to comply with affirmative action and fear of losing federal funds has led most private colleges and universities, especially those heavily involved in government-funded research, to recruit and assist members of minority groups, especially African Americans. For some institutions less dependent on federal monies, both explicit and covert discrimination in admittance procedures continues. Yet efforts by colleges and universities to recruit and assist African Americans have not succeeded in stemming the decrease in African American enrollment, particularly among males (Cuyjet, 2006; Maxwell, 2004).

African Americans have endured a long history of exclusion from the educational system; even today they are overrepresented in poor, minority-filled schools. While the data are inconclusive, some findings show that blacks who attend integrated schools are more likely to graduate, attend college, and live in integrated neighborhoods (Feagin, 1989:242). Thus, to the degree that African Americans continue to cluster in the inner city, they are more likely to attend segregated schools and less likely to attend college. In addition, housing segregation remains an important cause of discrimination in education.

As part of the general debate on school vouchers, proponents of using government money to finance private schools often point to the desire of minority populations, particularly African Americans, to have options besides the public schools. This sentiment is understandable because the public schools in ghetto neighborhoods are notoriously bad, in just about every sense: state of repair of the buildings, equipment and books, teacher qualifications, crowding of classrooms, drugs, and danger. Yet if school vouchers were allowed, it is not clear that African Americans would be better off. If there were good private schools in their neighborhoods, such a program might work. Otherwise, it would be difficult for poor families to transport their children to private schools. Moreover, once public school monies go to private schools as vouchers, the already underfinanced public schools would decline even further, giving those who cannot attend private schools an even worse public school environment. True, in a voucher program, public schools could receive vouchers, but these would not be sufficient to maintain old and decaying facilities, nor would they be sufficient to improve the quality of the curriculum and, at the same time, maintain security. Thus, vouchers are unlikely to help the very poor improve their level of access to quality education.

Housing Discrimination   One's place of residence determines access to other valued resources—jobs, schools, public facilities, health care, and social services. When African Americans experience discrimination in housing, they become isolated from the mainstream and are, in effect, excluded from other social arenas, even if there is no intent to discriminate in these arenas. Housing discrimination has confined many African Americans to inner cities at a time when jobs have moved to the suburbs and transportation systems to the suburbs have decayed. Housing discrimination thus works against African Americans not only in their efforts to find work but also in their capacity to gain access to decent schools, public facilities, and services.

The first black migrants to northern cities were forced—not only by their meager resources but also by threats of white violence and discriminatory landlord policies—into the decaying cores of the cities. While the wartime industries of World War I provided many jobs, and while the geographical concentration of cities allowed easy access from the ghetto to work, a *pattern* of African American residential isolation in urban areas had been initiated. This pattern was often formalized in communities by restrictive covenants that forbade integrated neighborhoods. During the Great Depression of the 1930s, when economic opportunities vanished in the North and elsewhere, black migration to the cities waned. During this period the federal government enacted highly discriminatory legislation that forged the current profile of urban America.

The most significant piece of legislation was the federal act creating the Federal Housing Authority and the FHA mortgage loan guarantee program, which subsidized home mortgages for whites. In the post–World War II period, the FHA and the related Veterans Administration (VA) mortgage guarantee programs stimulated the rapid flight of white Americans from the cities to the suburbs. African Americans were prevented from joining this flight because of discriminatory administrative rules of law that stated that neighborhoods of "mixed races" could not be subsidized by the government. From 1950 to 1962, the year when President Kennedy finally issued an executive order to the contrary, the practice of providing FHA and VA loan guarantees primarily to white neighborhoods continued. Even after 1962, FHA policy was "ineffectively integrationist."

Industry and commerce began to follow the white population to the suburbs, and eventually, as assembly-line production with its need for large tracts of land came to dominate sectors of the economy, industry began to pull residents out of the cities. As industry and workers moved out of the city, commerce and service industries followed. Some African Americans were able to commute to these jobs, but as mass transit services began to deteriorate in the post–World War II period, commuting became difficult. At the same time, as the tax base that financed city schools diminished, schools with heavy concentrations of black students languished for lack of financial resources. Furthermore, large suburban communities began to exert enormous political power in metropolitan and statewide government. Thus, urban–suburban segregation, largely created by FHA law, has profoundly limited African Americans' access to jobs, quality schools, and political power.

To cope with the consequences of this segregation, other federal laws have been enacted, but they have not eliminated slum conditions, and, more important, some have exacerbated patterns of segregation. One of the key legislative acts of the New Deal initiated public housing, which, by 1937, had acquired the social purpose of eliminating substandard housing. Unfortunately, changes in the law in the late 1930s turned administration of the public housing projects over to the cities, resulting in housing projects that were built in existing slum areas, which, in turn, perpetuated black confinement to the inner city. Urban renewal in the decades since the 1950s has been another major attempt to revitalize slum areas and to restore the decaying downtown commercial areas in order to attract middle-class suburbanites back to the city. The result of the program has been the destruction of slum housing, which forced the poor into public housing projects where few wished to live. Model cities programs, introduced in the 1950s through the 1960s, have not done much better because they did not attack the basic problem—urban–suburban segregation.

A crucial Supreme Court decision made even more difficult the breakdown of urban–suburban inequities. In 1973 the Court ruled that suburban communities do have zoning control over patterns of land use in their communities. This ruling allowed local suburban governments to alter the zoning of land tracts to keep public housing and federally subsidized home-ownership programs for African Americans out of the suburbs.

Important civil rights legislation passed in the 1960s has been ineffective in counteracting discrimination because (1) it has often gone unenforced because the civil rights division of the Justice Department is understaffed, underfinanced, and overtly unsympathetic and (2) it has placed the burden of litigation on the *individual* against whom discrimination has occurred—a personally and financially arduous process. More important, this legislation does not address the fundamental need for a *mass* migration of African Americans to the suburbs (or a mass white migration to the cities). Of course, any such policy would encounter resistance in local communities, which, under the 1973 Supreme Court ruling, can "zone out" government-sponsored housing for African Americans. One of the ironies of housing laws is that from the mid-1930s until the mid-1960s, whites were given mortgage subsidies by the FHA and VA to move into the suburbs en masse, whereas current laws prevent a similar mass exodus of blacks. Moreover, current Supreme Court rulings prevent the implementation of massive federal programs to integrate the suburbs. Thus, suburban integration must happen slowly, on an individual-by-individual basis. These laws reinforce the discriminatory belief that the absence of African Americans from the suburbs is a result of their failure to avail themselves of "equal" educational and economic opportunities that would allow them to buy a house there.

Throughout the period of suburbanization of whites and confinement of blacks to the cities, informal practices of **redlining** have persisted whereby residents of integrated neighborhoods or residents of less affluent neighborhoods with large numbers of African Americans have difficulty securing home mortgages. These practices are now so well documented that special enforcement of antiredlining laws now occurs, but because of the subtlety of the practice, it is often difficult to catch and prosecute the offenders. And even if one could assume that all redlining could be stopped, much of the damage has already been done: African Americans have been denied home ownership because banks would not lend them the money, while equivalently positioned whites have received mortgages and have been able to enjoy the benefits of home ownership (Huskisson, 1988; Minerbrook, 1993; U.S. Commission on Civil Rights, 1996).

STRATIFICATION OF AFRICAN AMERICANS

Affluent and Poor African Americans: The Widening Gap

As a result of legal, economic, political, educational, and housing discrimination, significant numbers of black Americans have been pushed to the bottom rungs of the stratification system. Indeed, African American families were the only ethnic group to see poverty rates increase in the first years of the new century (U.S. Bureau of the Census, 2002b). They tend to have few resources, as was documented at the outset of this chapter, and even fewer prospects for the future. Some African Americans have "made it" out of poverty and the lower socioeconomic stratum. Indeed, the percentage of black families that earn more than the national median family income—around $61,355 per year in 2007—has increased dramatically over the last decade. African Americans are thus divided by social class, and although many middle-class African Americans still encounter discrimination in public places, in jobs, in housing, and in education, they no longer live in poverty.

Many of those outside the middle class live in slums or, even worse, public housing projects in the inner city; they live in crime-ridden and dangerous neighborhoods; they send their children to inferior schools; they work—if they can find work—for low wages in jobs with little security, few benefits, and an uncertain future; they seek help from the welfare system, which erodes their self-respect and which, with new "reforms," is even less helpful; and if they are women, they are often raising their children alone. Indeed, a majority of black children are now raised by single parents, most of whom are women living in poverty. Thus, the situation for poor blacks has been made worse by the disruption to the family structure.

The African American Underclass: Myth or Reality?

Many white Americans are concerned—indeed, even fearful—of perceived trends in the urban minority population, especially urban African Americans: more babies born out of wedlock; more unmarried women on welfare; more violent crime; more drug use and related crime; more school dropouts and illiteracy; and more unemployed males. Some believe that these social and economic ills are concentrated in the "American underclass," which is presumed to be mostly black (Auletta, 1982). Currently, debate rages in the media, public, and academia over what this underclass is, who belongs to it, how big it is, and how fast it is growing (Baca-Zinn, 1989; Fainstein, 1993). Definitions vary, but a reasonable one is the convergence of "a number of social ills including poverty, joblessness, crime, welfare dependency, fatherless families, and low levels of education or work-related skills" (Ricketts and Sawhill, 1988:316). Some sociologists are convinced that the black underclass represents a major problem in America (Wilson, 1987).

Documentation of this underclass among African Americans reveals, however, a somewhat different picture (Jencks, 1991:28–102): The proportion of black single mothers collecting welfare has declined since 1974; violent crimes rates among blacks have declined; black dropout rates from schools declined in the 1980s; the gap in secondary school graduation rates has closed; and the percentage of 17-year-olds with basic reading skills steadily rose in the 1980s. However, some problems have grown worse: Joblessness for males has risen, and the number of babies born out of wedlock has increased to over 65 percent among African Americans, resulting in an increase in single mothers. These data, then, do not support the existence of an African American underclass. The minority of African Americans who do meet the criteria for membership in an underclass receive much publicity, and the much larger African American population is further stigmatized by their activities.

Threats and Hostility toward African Americans

White hostility toward African Americans and the resulting discrimination has been fueled by a sense of threat. During slavery, many working-class whites, encouraged by slaveholders, feared the release of large numbers of blacks into the labor market and society in general (thereby destroying the "southern way of life"). When northern industries used African Americans as strikebreakers in the first decades of the twentieth century, white workers feared the loss of their jobs. Today, many white Americans fear "black violence" (fostered by the riots of the 1960s and 1990s, the increase in gang activities, the high crime rates, and the perception of a growing "underclass"). Moreover, specific fears about the "costs" of welfare as well as the "taking" of jobs through affirmative action have added to white fears.

These fears have translated into negative stereotypes of African Americans as prone to crime and violence, as morally and sexually promiscuous, as unwilling to work, and as draining the white taxpayer through welfare dependency. In turn, these stereotypes have been used to justify informal discrimination, the dismantling or underfunding of programs to help the urban poor, negligence in enforcing laws or policies prohibiting discriminatory practices against black workers, and, most important, hesitancy in mounting a serious effort at job creation for African Americans. The result is that African Americans' share of valued resources has not increased appreciably over the last three decades, even as formal discrimination has been greatly mitigated. This fact is used to further the negative belief that African Americans have "not taken advantage of their equal opportunities." For example, most media portrayals of black youth revolve around gangs and criminal activity in an attempt to symbolize their purported unwillingness to "take advantage of opportunity" in U.S. society (Gomes and Williams, 1990; Lyman, 1990; Reed, 1993).

RESPONDING TO DISCRIMINATION

Protest during Slavery

During slavery, African Americans were severely limited in what they could do to protest their situation. White violence and the plantation system, coupled with easy physical identification of black-skinned individuals, were extremely effective in maintaining oppressive social control. Music represented one form of protest; **Negro spirituals** depicted the troubles and dissatisfaction of African slaves. Sabotage, such as the burning of barns and destruction of farm tools, was another form of protest. Slaves also practiced quiet resistance by faking illness and working slowly. Suicide and infanticide (to keep children from being enslaved) were other forms of protest. Running away was perhaps the most effective protest, although being caught meant severe punishment. The **Underground Railroad** to the North for freed slaves, created by northern abolitionists and humanitarians, made this form of protest somewhat successful. Open, and frequently violent, revolt was not uncommon throughout the slave era; Nat Turner's revolt in 1831 was the most famous because sixty whites were killed.

Protest after Slavery

The problem for freed slaves was to build institutions that could, in turn, become resources in their fight for greater equality. After the fall of radical Reconstruction, this became extremely difficult because of the imposition of Jim Crow laws and white violence. Yet institutions were being built. The church became perhaps the most important and effective institution because it was difficult for whites to deny African Americans the right to worship; indeed, white Americans tended to see the church as pacifying the African American community. In reality, church leaders were the most effective protest organizers in the twentieth century.

Education represented another institution that was slowly built. Historically, gaining access to public schools had been difficult; yet, black attendance, even in segregated schools, increased dramatically from the end of the Civil War until today. In the 1990s, black high school graduation rates were on a par with those of whites, although new problems in dropout rates began to emerge in the late 1990s. A system of private **Negro colleges** emerged in the late 1800s as a means to circumvent the exclusion of African Americans from private and state colleges in the South. Over time, a public African American college network was created. Today, the challenge in higher education is to increase enrollment of black students in formerly exclusionary universities and, simultaneously, to sustain the black colleges, which were once the main source of higher education for African Americans in the South.

African Americans began to vote in large numbers during Reconstruction, but political organization was difficult in the post-Reconstruction South because of intense efforts to disenfranchise blacks (McAdam, 1982:65–67, 1988; Williamson, 1984:224–58). Indeed, only with the massive migration out of the South from 1910 to 1930 did African Americans gain political clout, albeit only in their new northern location; and even there, white violence and other tactics kept black voters from gaining political access. In 1940 in the South, no more than 10 percent of the eligible black voters were registered in any state; in most southern states the registration was under 5 percent, and for four states it was under 1 percent (McAdam, 1982:79). Yet the existence of the NAACP and its frontal attack on Jim Crow during the 1930s led to a series of favorable Supreme Court decisions that reenfranchised African Americans in enough numbers to form an important voting bloc. During and after World War II, the black migration continued to the North and West, where the climate of political oppression was less severe. The stage was then set for the political mobilization of the 1960s. (For a review of the NAACP and the career of Thurgood Marshall, see Rowan, 1993; see also Box 5.9.)

Box 5.9
African American Women in the Civil Rights Movement

The most famous leaders of the civil rights movement are men, Dr. Martin Luther King, Jr., being the most famous of all. But women were also leaders, playing key roles in initiating protests, mapping out strategies, and mobilizing necessary resources. Here are some of the most prominent and important black women in the civil rights movement:

Ella Baker: She was an officer of the National Association for the Advancement of Colored People, a founder of the Southern Christian Leadership Conference, and a supporter of the Student Nonviolent Coordinating Committee.

Daisy Bates: With the support of the NAACP, she played a major role in the integration of the Little Rock, Arkansas, public schools. Single-handedly she spearheaded a grassroots community campaign to enroll black children in all-white public schools.

Mary McLeod Bethune: She was president of the National Association of Colored Women from 1924 to 1928. She established the National Council of Negro Women in 1935, and President Franklin D. Roosevelt appointed her director of the Division of Negro Affairs in 1936.

Mary Burks: As founder and first president of the Women's Political Council (WPC) of Montgomery, Alabama, she led the WPC in the Montgomery bus boycott of 1955–1956.

Septima Poinsette Clark: She established "citizenship schools," which combined the teaching of literacy with protection of voting rights. The schools spread throughout the southeastern United States and were, in large part, responsible for voter registration of thousands of African American southerners.

Autherine Foster: She was the first black student at the University of Alabama (1956).

Fannie Lou Hamer: She founded the Freedom Farm Cooperative, which made it possible for 5,000 people to grow their own food and own 680 acres of land. In 1972 she helped found the National Women's Political Caucus.

Juanita Mitchell: In April 1942, she directed a citizens' march of 2,000 people on Maryland's capitol in Annapolis that resulted in the appointment of the Governor's Interracial Commission, the appointment of black police officers, and an investigation into charges of police brutality in the black community.

Constance Motley: Serving as an associate counsel for the NAACP Legal Defense Fund over a period of twenty years, she prepared legal briefs for *Brown v. Board of Education* (1954).

Diane Nash: While a student at Fisk University, she was a key figure in the sit-in movement of the 1960s to end segregation at restaurants, lunch counters, and theaters in Nashville, Tennessee.

Rosa Parks: Known for her December 1, 1955, refusal to surrender her seat to a white passenger in a crowded Montgomery, Alabama, bus, she was the spark for the Montgomery bus boycott.

Ida Wells: She was a newspaper columnist, writing for the *Conservator,* an African American newspaper in Chicago, and for the *Chicago Tribune.* Wells published a book in 1901, *Lynching and the Excuse for It,* in which she argued that lynching was used by whites to intimidate blacks from becoming involved in politics in order to maintain white power in the South. Wells was one of the founders of the NAACP in 1909.

Margaret Wilson: She became the first black woman to serve as chair of the board of directors for the NAACP.

Sources: Bernice M. Barnett, "Invisible Southern Black Women Leaders in the Civil Rights Movement: The Triple Constraints of Gender, Race, and Class," *Gender & Society* 7(2): 162–82 (1993); Jessie C. Smith (ed.), *Notable Black American Women* (Detroit, MI: Gale Research, 1992); Darlene C. Hine (ed.), *Black Women in America: An Historical Encyclopedia* (Brooklyn, NY: Carlson Publishing, 1993).

Violence was a common occurrence in the post-Reconstruction era, right up through the interwar years. Until the 1940s, most violence by African Americans was in reaction to the violence initiated by whites, but from the 1940s on, and particularly in the 1960s, black rioting emerged as an effective form of protest, calling attention to problems and, at the same time, prodding fearful white Americans into limited responses to alleviate these problems.

The Last Sixty Years

Beginning in the 1940s and escalating during the 1950s and 1960s, black protest against continued subjugation took an array of forms: The NAACP continued to press its case in the courts, winning such important decisions as *Brown v. Board of Education of Topeka*; individual protests, such as Rosa Parks's refusal to go to the back of the bus, became the rallying cry for boycotts and other forms of collective protest; organized, nonviolent demonstrations, orchestrated by religious leaders such as Martin Luther King, Jr., and by civil rights organizations such as the Student Nonviolent Coordinating Committee, became an extremely effective tool in calling attention to and mobilizing broader sentiments against the continued segregation of public facilities (from lunch counters to schools); voter registration drives, especially after the Voting Rights Act of 1965, dramatically increased the voting power of African Americans; urban violence in the form of riots escalated in the 1960s, calling attention to and forcing a response from government; militant black political organizations and leaders, Malcolm X, the Black Panther party, the Black Muslims, and some members, such as Stokely Carmichael, of the Student Nonviolent Coordinating Committee, began to advocate that acts of white violence and oppression should be met with equal force (for a history of the Black Panther party, see Hilliard and Cole, 1993).

These protests created a climate in the 1960s for the passage of a series of civil rights laws, which, in turn, facilitated more protest, more voter registration, more

Nationally, colleges and universities are becoming increasingly female. African American women lead African American men in college and university enrollment.

legal redress of grievances, more individual actions against acts of discrimination, more awareness among the general public about the plight of African Americans, and, for a time, more militancy in "black power" parties and organizations. For the first and only time since radical Reconstruction, the federal government, under Lyndon Johnson's Great Society initiative, seriously addressed the problems of the poor in general and African Americans in particular with a broad array of programs. During this period African Americans made significant gains in income and educational attainment, in assistance in housing and medical care, and in job training. Many of these gains have been undone over the last four decades; others have remained static. Despite the Los Angeles riots of 1992—the most costly in the city's history—violent protest was less effective in the 1990s than in the 1960s. More effective is the growing voting power that has come with increased voter registration among African Americans.

Protest has been, at best, only partially effective in combating discrimination. Protest has brought improvement in the economic, political, and social positions of African Americans, but the continued existence of poverty, segregation, and subtly institutionalized discrimination emphasizes that the descendants of the slaves must live under conditions that no other minority group in American history has had to endure. These conditions will, in the future, be the driving force behind further protests—from the violence of alienated gang members, to the retreat of separatist groups, to the legal assault on the more subtle forms of discrimination, and perhaps a new wave of mass protests.

THE NEW AFRICAN AMERICANS

Over the last four decades, African-born individuals and families have increasingly immigrated to the United States. In the 1970s and 1980s, many Africans came to America to enhance their education, with a clear desire to return home and help rebuild their postcolonial nations. By the 1990s, however, Africans began to immigrate with the intent of establishing permanent residency and even citizenship in the United States. There was a series of push factors in this new wave of immigration: salaries for professionals were exceedingly low in most African countries; authoritarian states had emerged in many African nations; corruption at all levels of these nations was rampant; and the unfavorable position of most African nations in world-system trade tended to keep nations poor, even those with valuable resources to export. There were the obvious pull factors to America—education, jobs, political freedoms, and comparative affluence.

The 1986 Immigration Reform and Control Act and the 1990 Immigration Act suddenly increased opportunities for the African-born who wanted to become permanent residents. Without these changes in laws regulating immigration from Africa, neither push nor pull factors could be put into play, but once the gates were opened, if only slightly, Africans began to immigrate to the United States. The Immigration Reform and Control Act made it easier for all undocumented immigrants to secure resident status, while the Diversity Visa

TABLE 5.8 Foreign-Born African Population, 1960–2007

Year	Foreign-Born (in millions)	African-Born	African-Born as % of Foreign-Born
1960	9.7	35,355	0.4%
1970	9.6	80,143	0.8
1980	14.1	199,723	1.4
1990	19.8	363,819	1.8
2000	31.1	881,300	2.8
2007	38.05	1,419,317	3.7

Sources: Data for 2000 to 2007 from U.S. Census Bureau, 2000 Census, 2007 American Community Survey. Data for earlier years from U.S. Census Bureau Working Paper 29: C. Bibson and E. Elnnon, "Historical Census Statistics on Foreign-Born Population of the United States: 1850–1990," U.S. Government Printing Office, Washington, DC. Available online.

Program of the 1990 Immigration Act promoted immigration from hitherto underrepresented countries and regions of the world for as many as 50,000 qualified Africans to immigrate annually into the United States (Takougang, 2010). Table 5.8 documents the increasing size of the African-born population in the United States. In 1960, this population represented only 0.4 percent of the total foreign-born population, but by 2007, 3.7 percent of the foreign-born population had immigrated from Africa, with well over a half million establishing permanent resident status, and with still more to come in the next decade. (Note: Figures in Table 5.8 are slightly different from those in other tables, due to somewhat different data sources and analyses.) While the percentage of African-born is still small, it can still be seen as a new wave of African-origin residents to America, coming this time not as slaves but as comparatively well educated individuals seeking new opportunities.

These new immigrants often migrate to where they have friends and relatives—as is the case with most migrants. They tend to concentrate in urban areas and, over time, migrate to more suburban communities, often in response to difficult conditions in America's urban slums. Table 5.9 lists the metropolitan

TABLE 5.9 Metropolitan Areas with Largest African-Born Population

Metropolitan Area	% of Black Population	% of Total Metro Population
Washington, D.	6.1%	1.6%
New York City	3.4	0.8
Atlanta	2.9	0.8
Minneapolis/St. Paul	15.4	0.9
Los Angeles	2.7	0.3
Detroit	2.1	0.6
Houston	3.1	0.5
Chicago	2.4	0.7
Dallas	3.6	0.5
Boston/New Hampshire	9.8	0.7

Source: U.S. Bureau of the Census, 2000 Census.

TABLE 5.10 English Proficiency and Educational Attainment of Recent Immigrant Populations

	Total U.S. Population	Immigrant Populations*				
		All Immigrants	**African**	Asian	Europe, Russia, Canada	Latin America, Caribbean
Not fluent in English	0.6%	30.5%	**7.6%**	23.4%	11.5%	44.0%
Less than high school education	17.1	39.1	**10.6**	21.2	23.5	57.4
College degree	23.1	23.3	**51.1**	42.5	28.9	9.1
Advanced degree	2.6	4.2	**10.2**	7.8	5.8	1.9

*Data are for both single and "mixed race" ethnics.
Source: U.S. Bureau of the Census, 2000 U.S. Census.

areas receiving the most African-born immigrants. As a proportion of the total population in these metropolitan areas, these new African Americans represent less than 1 percent of the total, except in Washington, DC, and the surrounding areas in Maryland and Virginia. But, in some areas, they constitute a significant percentage of the black population of African Americans whose ancestors came to America as slaves. For example, African-born individuals and families constitute 15 percent of the black population in Minneapolis/St. Paul, 9 percent in the Boston area, and 6 percent in Washington, DC (where a very high percentage of the population is black).

This new wave of African immigration is composed of well-educated Africans; in fact, they are more educated than the U.S. population as a whole and all other immigrant populations, even Asians who are also highly educated. Table 5.10 documents that only 7.6 percent of African-born compared to over 30 percent of all immigrants are not fluent in English, with only 11 percent having less than a high school education, compared to almost 40 percent of all other immigrants. Fifty-one percent of African-born immigrants have a college degree compared to 23 percent of the total U.S. population; this percentage is even higher than for Asian immigrants, among whom 42.5 percent have college degrees. Moreover, these African-born immigrants have advanced degrees at a much higher rate than the general population (10.2 percent vs. 2.6 percent), and again, this percentage is several points higher than that among Asian immigrants.

Some of these well-educated African immigrants cannot, however, secure jobs commensurate with their education. They often seek quick employment or suffer from discrimination, with the result that some are employed in relatively low-skill jobs, such as cab drivers, parking lot attendants, airport workers, and servers or cooks in restaurants. Others become entrepreneurial, owning restaurants, specialty stores catering to the needs of African immigrants, health care agencies, and other service companies (Takougang, 2007). Interestingly, many wives and children who have stayed in Africa and who were receiving support from their working husband are now joining them in the United States because

TABLE 5.11 Percentage of African-Born Employed Workers Compared to All Foreign-Born Workers in Various Occupations

Occupation	African-Born		All Foreign-Born	
	Male	Female	Male	Female
Management, business, finance	12.6%	9.2%	10.2%	10.2%
Information technology	3.9	2.0	3.8	1.9
Other sciences and engineering	4.9	2.1	3.9	2.1
Social services and legal	2.6	3.3	1.1	2.0
Education/training and media/entertainment	5.2	7.2	3.3	7.0
Physicians	2.3	1.7	1.2	1.0
Registered nurses	1.0	7.3	0.3	3.4
Health care support	3.8	12.7	0.6	5.2
Services and support	25.9	28.4	25.0	36.3
Administrative support	8.6	13.4	5.3	14.8
Construction, extraction, and transportation	16.4	1.9	26.9	3.2
Manufacturing, installation, repair	10.0	4.6	14.8	8.9

Source: U.S. Census Bureau, 2006 American Community Survey.

job opportunities are so much greater for women in the United States than in Africa. Table 5.11 summarizes the occupations employing men and women from Africa compared to all foreign-born residents in the United States. As is evident, both African-born males and females are involved in management/ business/finance, services/support, with men highly visible in information technology/science/engineering, as well as construction, extraction, and transportation; with women prominent in administrative support and health care support.

It is difficult to know how many of these jobs fall below the education and skill levels of African-born workers, but beyond employment difficulties, there are other problems that these immigrants face. As they pursue the "American Dream," like all other immigrants before them they must often deal with the highly negative stereotypes imposed upon blacks in general in the United States. They can be perceived as criminals, drug dealers, welfare cheats, and lazy individuals—indictments that are unfair to both the descendents of slaves and the well-educated and ambitious African immigrants today. African-born immigrants generally do not feel as accepted as immigrants from Cuba, Europe, and Asia who possess credentials that are even less impressive than those of the new African immigrants. The only answer for this lack of perceived acceptance is that they are simply defined as "black" and thereby subject to many of the subtle but still very powerful prejudices of non-black members of the population and to the discrimination that is fed by these widespread prejudices.

At the same time, African immigrants are often not accepted by the descendents of the first Africans to come to the United States. The latter often portray the new Africans as seeing themselves as superior. At times, this hostility can go so far as first Africans blaming present-day African immigrants' ancestors for slavery, arguing that these ancestors did not fight hard enough to prevent the capture and enslavement people in Africa hundreds of years ago. Such an extreme belief only underscores the tension that can exist between the new and older African American community.

Thus, with a president who is the son of a person born in Africa and, moreover, with a general decline in the intensity of prejudicial beliefs about African Americans in the United States, the color of skin still makes people targets of prejudice and discrimination. Well-educated and articulate Africans can be lumped into the general category of "black" and have the same problems as other African Americans in finding work, schools, and housing, although it is clear that many African immigrants of today move to the suburbs to escape the worst of the difficulties of slums and ghettos in America's urban areas. Another decade, perhaps, will give a better indication of how the sons and daughters of these immigrants from Africa have faired in American society. Some may have realized their parents' hopes; others may have become caught in the vortex of urban slums in American society.

SUMMARY

African Americans were brought to the United States as slaves and were denied access to the most basic resources, even after slavery ended. Blacks have thus experienced higher rates of poverty, lower incomes, more segregation in housing, higher rates of unemployment, less access to higher education, and shorter life spans than nearly all other groups of Americans. Discrimination is relatively easy to practice against African Americans because their black skin makes them easy to identify. Historically, African Americans have had to endure some of the most vicious negative beliefs, which have been used to justify discrimination in jobs, housing, education, and all institutional spheres in American society. These beliefs and patterns of discrimination have been fueled by the white perception of a "black threat." Such forces have combined to institutionalize discrimination against black Americans.

In the legal arena, in pre–Civil War days, both free and enslaved blacks were denied all rights of citizenship. In the Jim Crow period after slavery and up to the 1960s, African Americans had to overcome a combination of laws, court decisions, and enforcement practices that sought to deny them access to the resources enjoyed by white Americans. In the economic sphere, black workers have been denied access to all categories of jobs, although in recent decades many African Americans have made dramatic progress in securing good jobs. As slaves, blacks were simply excluded from the political process. Their manumission followed by the rapid collapse of radical Reconstruction introduced the Jim Crow practices that kept blacks from registering to vote through the first half of the twentieth century. The civil rights movement begun in the late 1950s opened the door for large numbers of African Americans to participate in the American political process. In the educational arena, black slaves were deliberately kept illiterate; after slavery their exclusion from the educational system was maintained as long as possible, especially in the South. Separate schools for blacks and whites, as well as black colleges, represented the fall-back position during most of the twentieth century. Only over the past few decades has any significant school integration occurred, and such integration is still hampered by white resistance and the segregation of blacks from white neighborhoods.

In housing, African Americans are the most segregated minority in America, save for those Native Americans confined to reservations. Such segregation was created and maintained by white violence against blacks who ventured into white neighborhoods, by lending policies of banks, and by governmental housing programs.

This system of institutionalized discrimination has confined African Americans to the lowest strata of the class system in America, although in recent decades a significant proportion of the black population has been able to overcome discrimination and move into the middle classes. This movement has only highlighted the fate of those who have not been mobile.

POINTS OF DEBATE

African Americans are the only members of a minority in America that were imported against their will as slaves. Slavery existed until 1865, ending with the Civil War. Except during the brief period of radical Reconstruction, new forms of vicious discrimination ensued. For most of the twentieth century, blacks were systematically denied access to jobs, housing, politics, and education, while being subjected to white violence and negative stereotypes. The legacy of these forces haunts America today, posing what we earlier termed the "second American dilemma": How is this legacy to be undone? In answering this question, some hotly debated issues emerge.

1. Does white America owe black America compensation for past acts of discrimination? If so, how much? Most Americans are now against forced busing to integrate schools. Many are antiwelfare, believing that welfare mothers have babies in order to increase their allotments; some are against higher taxes to support any social action programs. Some white Americans want to build more prisons to house those they fear. Many are more willing than in the past to live in integrated neighborhoods but worry (needlessly) about loss of property values. At the same time they complain about reverse discrimination when confronted with affirmative action programs that may limit their employment prospects. In light of these beliefs and attitudes, it will be difficult to address the legacy of the past, even if white America is sympathetic in the abstract. But are white Americans willing to live with the consequences of these attitudes? This poses another point of debate.

2. The legacy of discrimination against black Americans is manifest in two directions: One is the hard work and effort by many to overcome discrimination; the other is the entrapment of millions of African Americans in the pathologies of decaying urban areas. These pathologies revolve around drug use, violent crime, gang activity, high dropout rates from schools, very high rates of out-of-wedlock births, and an increasing number of single-parent households. Can America allow this to continue and not experience

the consequences of these pathologies? Are Americans willing to allow them to fester, thereby putting an even harder and potentially more volatile edge on black–white relations in America?

3. Even in the wake of the most expensive riot in American history, which took place in Los Angeles, Americans in the 1990s remained remarkably insensitive to the depth of the problems. Indeed, they continued to visualize the plight of African Americans in very individualistic terms, as a character flaw of blacks and not a structural flaw of society. Can white Americans continue to blame only the victims of discrimination and not also their own white ancestors, if not themselves? Anglo-Saxons tend to assume that they are a rational people who pragmatically assess costs and benefits. If blacks are not wise enough to realize the consequences of crime, drug use, out-of-wedlock babies, and unstable families, then they must accept the costs. But the costs will not be only on the victims; they will continue to spill over into the whole society in the form of the enormous expense of building more prisons, health care costs brought about by violence and drugs and despair, the loss of productive activity with so many alienated youth in gangs and the corresponding welfare burden, all costs that will burden many mainstream aspects of American society. Thus, can white Americans afford to continue to hold such a narrow view of human behavior as expresses itself in their attitudes toward blacks without addressing the more deep-seated forces behind these social problems?

KEY TERMS/KEY LEGISLATION

affirmative action, 121
black codes, 117
"black Sambo" stereotype, 110
Brown v. Board of Education of Topeka, Kansas (1954), 120
Civil Rights Act of 1875, 118
Civil Rights Acts of 1964 and 1968, 120
Fifteenth Amendment (1870), 118
Fourteenth Amendment (1868), 118
Hopwood v. Texas (1996), 122
Jim Crow practices, 116
Keyes v. Denver School District No. 1 (1973), 134

Negro colleges, 139
Negro spirituals, 139
Plessy v. Ferguson (1896), 118
redlining, 137
Regents of the University of California v. Bakke (1978), 121
reverse discrimination, 121
Swann v. Charlotte-Mecklenburg Board of Education (1971), 134
Thirteenth Amendment (1866), 117
Underground Railroad, 139
Voting Rights Act of 1965, 120
Weber v. Kaiser Aluminum (1979), 121

 Visit our text-specific website at www.mhhe.com/aguirre7e for valuable resources for both students and instructors.

CHAPTER 6

Native Americans

Leif Ericson and Christopher Columbus were comparative newcomers to the Americas. Long before their "discoveries," people began to cross the land bridge connecting Alaska with the Asian continent, perhaps as long ago as 40,000 years. They came in search of food, hunting wild game and gathering indigenous plant life, and they settled the entire face of North, Central, and South America. As they settled in distinctive niches, they evolved diverse cultures. Some, such as those among the Maya, Incas, and Aztecs, developed cultures and organizational structures as sophisticated as those in other parts of the world. In what was to become the United States, however, the several hundred societies and perhaps as many as 300 language groups of the native people were comparatively simple, making them highly vulnerable to conquest by white Europeans. Some were hunters and gatherers, others focused on fishing, a few on herding, and some on horticulture. All constituted viable societies, but on contact with Europeans, they would be wholly or partially destroyed. The history of Native Americans[1] after European contact is thus one of conquest and domination.

ON THE VERGE OF EXTINCTION

We can only estimate how large the Native American population was prior to its contact with the Europeans. In 1860, Emmanuel Domenech (1860) estimated that the precontact population was between 16 and 17 million. One of the limitations of early estimates, however, is that they represent subjective impressions and extrapolations based on early contacts with villages and settlements (Snipp, 1989:6). The first generally accepted scientific estimate of the sixteenth-century Native American population was produced by James Mooney (1928), who

---

[1]*A note on terminology:* Our use of the term "Native American" is intentional. First, we use it to emphasize the presence of the population prior to the arrival of European explorers. Implicit is the observation that Native Americans were not "discovered." Second, the term "Native American" encompasses a number of indigenous nations. Jaimes (1992:113) has noted, "American Indian Peoples whose territory lies within the borders of the United States hold compelling legal and moral rights to be treated as fully sovereign nations."

150

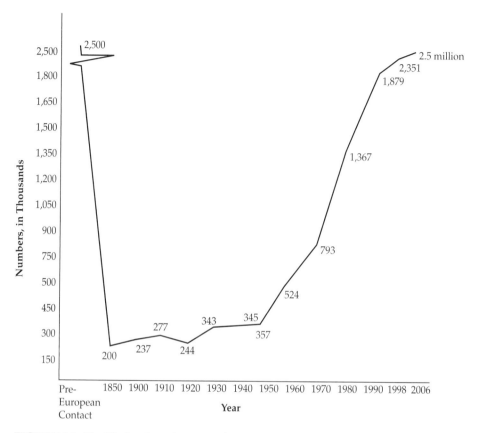

FIGURE 6.1 The Native American population, 1850–2006.

estimated the North American aboriginal population to be about 1.2 million persons at the time of European contact. A more recent estimate puts the precontact population between 2 and 5 million (Snipp, 1989), although some still argue that the number was in fact much larger.

Figure 6.1 illustrates the decrease in the Native American population between 1600 and 1850, from around 2.5 million (a conservative estimate) to only around 200,000 (Spinden, 1928). This decline can be viewed only as genocide, or the near elimination of a population. Lack of immunity to European diseases, or what some have called "ecological warfare"; displacement from lands and consequent starvation; widespread killing in "war"; and cold-blooded murder all account for this sudden drop (Crosby, 1976; Merrell, 1984). Thus, if we needed an indicator of discrimination against Native Americans, a tenfold drop in the size of the population is as good as any. But this figure does not tell the whole story, for even as the population has replenished itself over the last 150 years, it has done so amid the residue of those conditions that led to attempted genocide.

Over the last century, with the exception of the 1920s, the Native American population has grown for each census period. Part of the decrease in population during the 1920s has been attributed to an influenza epidemic. By 1930, however, the population was again growing, and by 1950, this growth began to accelerate, a trend that Snipp (1989) suggested constituted a Native American "baby boom" equivalent to the postwar boom among white Europeans. The result was that between 1950 and 2004, the Native American population grew by over 600 percent. This increase was caused by changes in public policy toward Native Americans in 1950, and attitudes shifting from fear and hate to sympathy and guilt. Improved health care resulted in lowered infant mortality rates and increased life expectancy for adults.

Another factor in this growth has been the willingness of Native Americans to be identified as such, resulting in the increased capability of government agencies, such as the U.S. Bureau of the Census, to identify them. The "self-pride" movements among disadvantaged ethnic groups in the 1960s, for example, increased the ethnic awareness of Native Americans; it became a matter of pride to identify oneself as an "Indian" because the term no longer carried such negative connotations and stereotypes. Indeed, some researchers have suggested that the increase in the Native American population between 1960 and 1980 is not solely the product of health programs (Clifton, 1989; Passel, 1976; Passel and Berman, 1986) but, rather, is a marker of increased ethnic pride as more and more people were willing to proclaim themselves as "American Indian" on U.S. census forms. However, increased ethnic pride may result in a high "overcount" of the American Indian population. According to Passel (1993), while 54 percent of the growth in the American Indian population between 1960 and 1990 could be attributed to demographic factors, 46 percent of the growth resulted from nondemographic factors. One of the most salient nondemographic factors is enhanced self-identification as an American Indian. Thus, there may be as many persons that perceive themselves as American Indians as there are "real" American Indians.

In an effort to sort out the actual numbers of Native Americans, the U.S. Bureau of the Census now asks questions about "mixed" ancestry (in their terms, "mixed races"). The count in Figure 6.1 is for those reporting *only* Native American, and in 2006, this number was 2.5 million individuals. If, however, people reported that they were Native American and members of another ethnic group, the number jumps to 4.1 million reporting some Native American ancestry. Table 6.1 summarizes the numbers of individuals reporting mixed ancestry with whites and blacks. Table 6.2 summarizes the respective counts

TABLE 6.1 Reports on Native American Ancestry, Alone and in Combination with Other Ethnic Groups, 2000

Native Americans alone	2,475,956
In combination with other ethnics	4,119,301
With whites	1,082,683
With blacks	182,494
With whites and blacks	112,207
With other combinations	265,961

Source: U.S. Bureau of the Census, 2001b.

TABLE 6.2 Size of Tribal Groupings of Native Americans, 2000

Tribal Grouping	One Tribal Grouping Reported	American Indian and Alaska Native Tribal Grouping Alone or in Any Combination*
Total	**2,423,531**	**4,119,310**
Apache	57,060	96,833
Blackfeet	27,104	85,750
Cherokee	281,069	729,533
Cheyenne	11,191	18,204
Chickasaw	20,887	38,351
Chippewa	105,907	149,669
Choctaw	87,349	158,774
Colville	7,833	9,393
Comanche	10,120	19,376
Cree	2,488	7,734
Creek	40,223	71,310
Crow	9,117	13,394
Delaware	8,304	16,341
Houma	6,798	8,713
Iroquois	45,212	80,822
Kiowa	8,559	12,242
Latin American Indian	104,354	180,940
Lumbee	51,913	57,868
Menominee	7,883	9,840
Navajo	269,202	298,197
Osage	7,658	15,897
Ottawa	6,432	10,677
Paiute	9,705	13,532
Pima	8,519	11,493
Potawatomi	15,817	25,595
Pueblo	59,533	74,085
Puget Sound Salish	11,034	14,631
Seminole	12,431	27,431
Shoshone	7,739	12,026
Sioux	108,272	153,360
Tohono O'odham	17,466	20,087
Ute	7,309	10,385
Yakama	8,481	10,851
Yaqui	15,224	22,412
Yuman	7,295	8,976
Other specified American Indian tribes	240,521	357,658
American Indian tribe, not specified[†]	109,644	195,902
Alaska Athabascan	14,520	18,838
Aleut	11,941	16,978
Eskimo	45,919	54,761
Tlingit-Haida	14,825	22,365
Other specified Alaska Native tribes	2,552	3,973
Alaska Native tribe, not specified	6,161	8,702
American Indian or Alaska Native tribes, not specified	511,960	1,056,457

*The numbers by American Indian and Alaska Native tribal grouping do not add to the total population. This is because the American Indian and Alaska Native tribal groupings are tallies of the number of American Indian and Alaska Native *responses* rather than the number of American Indian and Alaska Native *respondents*. Respondents reporting several American Indian and Alaska Native tribes are counted several times. For example, a respondent reporting "Apache and Blackfeet" would be included in the Apache as well as Blackfeet numbers.

[†]Includes respondents who checked the "American Indian or Alaska Native" response category on the census questionnaire or wrote in a tribe not specified in the American Indian and Alaska Native Tribal Detailed Classification List for Census 2000.

Source: U.S. Bureau of the Census, 2002e.

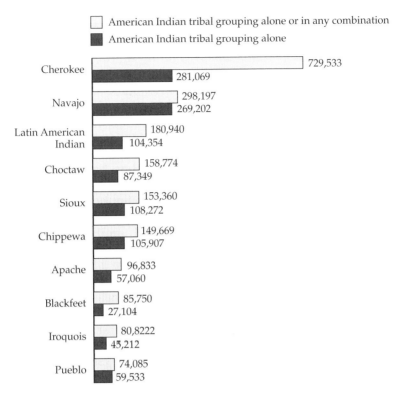

□ American Indian tribal grouping alone or in any combination
■ American Indian tribal grouping alone

Cherokee — 729,533 / 281,069

Navajo — 298,197 / 269,202

Latin American Indian — 180,940 / 104,354

Choctaw — 158,774 / 87,349

Sioux — 153,360 / 108,272

Chippewa — 149,669 / 105,907

Apache — 96,833 / 57,060

Blackfeet — 85,750 / 27,104

Iroquois — 80,8222 / 45,212

Pueblo — 74,085 / 59,533

FIGURE 6.2 Ten largest American Indian tribal groupings, 2000.
Source: U.S. Bureau of the Census, 2002e.

for tribal groupings for those reporting only Native American ancestry and for those reporting mixed ancestry. Figure 6.2 reports the count for the ten largest tribal groupings.

Native Americans represent less than 1 percent of the total population, slightly more if we count those of mixed ancestry. In only one state, Alaska, do Native Americans constitute more than 10 percent of the total population. Table 6.3 lists in rank order those states that had at least 1 percent of Native Americans in 2004. In Alaska, with the largest Native American population, the four largest tribal groupings are the Eskimo, Tlingit-Haida, Athabascan, and Aleut, as is reported in Figure 6.3. Only ten cities with 100,000 in population have over 1 percent of their population who are Native Americans, as is reported in Figure 6.4. Thus, although Native Americans constitute just a small percentage of the total population in the United States, they represent a significant subpopulation because they were here first. Since having contact with whites, they have been subject to especially brutal patterns of discrimination. Along with African Americans, who were imported as slaves, the aboriginals of the North American continent represent a special case because of the long history of discrimination that has denied them access to valued resources.

TABLE 6.3 States Where Native Americans
Constitute at Least 1 Percent of Population

State	Percentage of State's Population
Alaska	15.6%
New Mexico	8.9
Oklahoma	8.0
South Dakota	7.3
Montana	6.0
Arizona	5.6
North Dakota	4.1
Wyoming	2.1
Washington	1.7
Utah	1.4
Oregon	1.4
Idaho	1.4
Minnesota	1.1

Source: U.S. Bureau of the Census, 2002e.

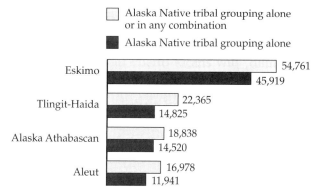

FIGURE 6.3 Largest Alaska Native tribal groupings, 2000.
Source: U.S. Bureau of the Census, 2002e.

RESOURCE SHARES OF NATIVE AMERICANS

Compared with other ethnic populations in the United States, Native Americans have been severely constrained in their interaction with mainstream society. This isolation is the result of the numerous treaties between the U.S. government and the Native American tribes that marginalized and subordinated them, thereby limiting their opportunities to secure valued resources (Deloria, 1976).

Income of Native Americans

Historically, Native Americans have had very low incomes, the lowest on average of any ethnic group. Over the last decade, however, the incomes of

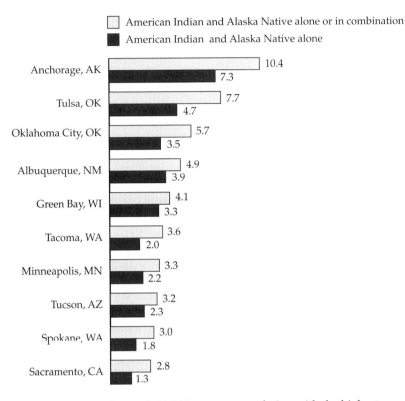

FIGURE 6.4 Ten places of 100,000 or more population with the highest percentage of Native Americans, 2000.
Source: U.S. Bureau of the Census, 2002e.

TABLE 6.4 Median Family Income of Native Americans Compared to Non-Latino Whites and General Population, 2007

Native Americans/Alaska Native	$40,310
Non-Latino whites	65,652
Total U.S. population	**$61,173**

Source: 2010 *Statistical Abstract*, Table 36.

Native Americans have risen somewhat and are now a bit higher than those for African Americans but still lower than those for Latinos, non-Latino whites, and Asian/Pacific Islanders. Table 6.4 reports average median household incomes. These data may overrepresent the income of Native Americans compared with other ethnic groups because households are often much larger, being composed of several generations. Even without this qualification, $40,000 is a very low income for an entire household; and when compared with non-Latino whites, Native American income is only 61 percent of white income.

TABLE 6.5 Occupational Distribution of Native Americans, 2007

Ethnic Subpopulation	Percentage of Adults Employed in:					
	Management/ Professional	Service	Sales/ Office	Construction/ Extraction/ Maintenance	Production/ Transport/ Materials Moving	Fishing/ Farming/ Forestry
Native American/ Alaska Native	25.3%	22.4%	22.9%	13.5%	14.3%	1.6%
Non-Latino white	36.6	15.0	25.9	10.0	11.9	0.7
Total U.S. labor force	**34.6%**	**16.7%**	**25.6%**	**9.7%**	**12.7%**	**0.7%**

Source: 2010 *Statistical Abstract,* Table 36.

Occupational Distribution of Native Americans

As reported in Table 6.5, Native Americans are underrepresented in white-collar occupations, particularly management and professional jobs, and over-represented in low-paying service occupations and, to a lesser extent, sales and office jobs. Occupational distributions for Native Americans are also based on their patterns of residence. In general, Native Americans living on the reservation are more likely to be employed in blue-collar occupations, whereas off-reservation Native Americans are more likely to be employed in white-collar occupations. Moreover, according to Snipp (1989:239), "About 32 percent of Indian men and 37 percent of Indian women living on or near a reservation are employed by federal and local government authorities, compared with 16 percent of men and 17 percent of women residing in nonreservation areas." Many of the government-created jobs for Native Americans living on reservations have been low-paying ones, particularly during the 1970s. Although federal programs have been instrumental in providing an array of public works jobs in trades and construction, like all such "make-work" it is subject to political more than economic forces and does not, therefore, lead to steady employment patterns (see Box 6.1). The large percentage of Native Americans in service occupations on reservations may not, according to Snipp (1989:241), "constitute a major source of employment for the American Indian labor force. . . . It is most likely that many traditional occupations for American Indians, such as traditional crafts (especially those purchased mainly by other Indians), provide a livelihood insufficient for survival and consequently may be practiced as an avocation and not as a principal source of income."

Educational Attainment of Native Americans

As Table 6.6 reveals, the educational outcomes of the Native American/Alaska Native population lag behind those of the non-Latino white population and the total U.S. population. The most noticeable differences in educational outcomes for the Native American/Alaska Native population, when compared to other populations, are at the post secondary level, especially for those with college

Box 6.1
The Economic Well-Being of Native American Women

There is wide variability in economic situations among Native American and Alaska Native women. Incomes across the board are lower than the average among all Native Americans. When compared to non-Hispanic white male incomes, even more dramatic evidence on the plight of Native American and Alaska Native women's situation emerges. The figures below document the ratio of women's earnings to those of non-Latino white males and the percentage of women who are in poverty as a result of these lower incomes. As is evident, incomes of Native American women are low compared to those of white males, whereas among Alaska Natives, women's incomes approach those of women in the general population, although poverty rates remain high because of the cost of living in Alaska.

	Ratio of Earnings to Those of Non-Latino White Males	Percentage of Women in Poverty
All Native American Women	57.8	25.0%
American Indians		
Apache	53.3	35.0%
Blackfeet	69.0	24.4
Cherokee	66.3	19.2
Cheyenne	No data available	
Chickasaw	66.3	14.1
Chippewa	63.3	22.0
Choctaw	68.0	19.1
Comanche	71.8	14.6
Creek	66.3	19.6
Iroquois	74.5	19.1
Lumbee	60.8	20.3
Navajo	58.0	64.0
Potawatomi	69.0	14.4
Pueblo	56.3	16.1
Puget Sound Salish	74.5	20.2
Seminole	55.3	25.3
Sioux	66.3	36.5
Tohono O'odham	55.3	40.8
Yaqui	52.5	42.6
Alaska Natives		
Athabaskan	77.3	19.3%
Aleut	71.8	14.7
Eskimo	81.5	20.5
Tlingit	71.8	14.3

Sources: Institute for Women's Policy Research, 2007; Urban Institute, 2004.

degrees. To put these outcomes in perspective, Native Americans/Alaska Natives generally earn less than 1 percent of the undergraduate and graduate/professional degrees awarded in the United States annually (Chronicle of Higher Education, 2005). Given that education is essential to success in the job market

TABLE 6.6 Educational Attainment of Native American Adults 25 Years Old and Older, 2007

Ethnic Subpopulation	Percentage with:		
	High School Diploma	College Degree	Graduate Degree
Native American/Alaska Native	76.2%	12.7%	4.3%
Non-Latino white	87.0	29.1	10.7
Total U.S. population	**84.5%**	**17.3%**	**10.1%**

Source: 2010 *Statistical Abstract,* Table 36.

and the income that such success brings, it should not be surprising that much of the shortfall in the income of Native Americans is related to their lack of the necessary educational credentials for well-paying jobs.

Life Span of Native Americans

Once Europeans came to North America, Native Americans lived very dangerous lives. Early on, the lack of immunity of Native Americans to European diseases, coupled with landgrabs, killings, and forced resettlement on reservations, led to the dramatic decimation of the Native American population, as Figure 6.1 documents. It is safer today to be a Native American, and in fact, Native Americans are far less likely to die of certain diseases than whites, African Americans, and Latinos. For example, Native Americans are slightly less likely than African Americans and Latinos to die from heart disease and cancers. Yet Native Americans do not live as long as non-Latino whites—dying, on average, almost four years earlier. Part of the explanation for this early mortality resides in lack of access to health care. As Table 1.7 on page 20 documents, 31 percent of Native Americans do not have health insurance, a figure that is almost three times that of whites, 10 percent higher than for African Americans, 15 percent higher than for Asians, and in general, double that of the total population. This lack of access to health care helps explain not only the shorter life spans of Native Americans compared to non-Latino whites, but it also accounts for the higher infant mortality rates of Native Americans, which are around 3.5 percent higher than for non-Latino whites and, in fact, are only exceeded by the rate for African Americans (Spalter-Roth, Lowenthal, and Rubio, 2005). Another factor in the shorter life spans of Native Americans is violence. Native Americans are almost twice as likely as whites to die from homicide. And finally, Native Americans are again almost twice as likely as whites to die from an automobile accident.

Housing of Native Americans

Native Americans tend to have lower-quality housing than whites. They are less likely to live in owner-occupied housing, more likely to live in a mobile home, more likely to live in a smaller (that is, lower number of rooms) home, and more likely to have extra persons per room in each household (U.S. Bureau of the Census, 1973b, 1983a, 1993a). Also, the quality of domestic life for many Native Americans is very different from that of most white Americans. For example, fewer Native American households have complete bathrooms, and fewer have access to public water, public sewers, complete kitchens, and telephones (Rumbelow, 2002). In 1990, 5 percent of the Native American population lived in housing units that lacked complete plumbing facilities, compared to 1 percent of the U.S. population as a whole. In addition, Native Americans tend to live in households that lack complete kitchen facilities (5 percent), depend on well water (17 percent), and are not connected to a public sewer system (67 percent). Comparable figures for the U.S. population are 1 percent, 14 percent, and 1 percent, respectively.

In the twenty-first century, housing still remains a serious social problem for Native Americans. While the development of public housing on Indian reservations in the 1960s was intended to alleviate overcrowding, more than 40 percent of Native Americans live in overcrowded or substandard housing (Biles, 2000). In testimony before the Senate Committee on Housing and Urban Affairs (2002), Franklin Raines, chairman and CEO of Fannie Mae, noted that low incomes and high poverty rates prevented Native Americans from qualifying for conventional mortgages. He noted in his testimony that in 1999 there were only 471 home mortgages on Indian lands. As a result, less than 33 percent

Photograph of John Lane's Navajo Family Posing for Norman Rockwell.

of the Native American population owns homes compared with 67 percent of the U.S. population (U.S. General Accounting Office, 2002).

Aside from the quality of life in most Native American dwellings is the issue of where these dwellings are located. Some 25 percent of the native population lives on government-regulated reservations, separated and isolated from the general population, and another 15 percent lives near the reservations. Thus, around 40 percent of the Native American population is dramatically segregated, not only by neighborhood but by territory. This situation, the legacy of past discrimination, forces a significant percentage of Native Americans to be dependent on economic opportunities on and around the reservation, which, typically, is isolated from mainstream society. Most Native Americans view this isolation in a positive light, as a way to recapture their quickly vanishing culture (Ambler, 1990). On the negative side, however, this segregation increases their dependency on the federal government, which in the past has not demonstrated great sympathy for maintaining Native American cultures.

Aside from isolation on reservations, Native Americans are segregated from non-Latino whites in metropolitan areas. Overall, Native Americans record a dissimilarity index of 33, which means that 33 percent of whites would have to move to new cities and neighborhoods within cities to achieve full integration (Massey and Denton, 1988). Table 6.7 summarizes the indexes of dissimilarity (segregation) for the highest- and lowest-ranked metropolitan areas.

Poverty of Native Americans

In the 1970s, the U.S. government officially acknowledged that Native Americans were the most impoverished group in the United States and that this population lived in conditions rivaling those found in the Third World (U.S. Department of Health, Education and Welfare, 1976). For example, at that time,

TABLE 6.7 Metropolitan Areas with Highest and Lowest Dissimilarity Indexes for Non-Latino Whites and Native Americans

	Highest			Lowest	
Rank	Metropolitan Area	Index	Rank	Metropolitan Area	Index
1	Flagstaff, AZ-UT MSA	75	1	Panama City, FL MSA	20
2	New York, NY PMSA	75	2	Enid, OK MSA	22
3	Bergen-Passaic, NJ PMSA	72	3	Medford-Ashland, OR MSA	23
4	Yakima, WA MSA	72	4	Pedding, CA MSA	24
5	Nassau-Suffolk, NY PMSA	72	5	Eugene-Springfield, OR MSA	25
6	Newark, NJ PMSA	72	6	Pensacola, FL MSA	25
7	Tucson, AZ MSA	68	7	Yuba City, CA MSA	25
8	Pittsburgh, PA MSA	67	8	Atascadero-Paso Robles, CA MSA	27
9	Middlesex-Somerset-Hunterdon, NJ PMSA	64	9	Modesto, CA MSA	27
10	Chicago, IL PMSA	64	10	Oklahoma City, OK MSA	28

Source: Frey and Myers, 2002.

TABLE 6.8 Percentage of Native Americans Who Are Poor, 2007

Ethnic Subpopulation	Percentage Who Are Poor
Native American/Alaska Native	25.3%
Non-Latino white	10.2
Total U.S. population	**13.0%**

Sources: 2010 *Statistical Abstract,* Table 36.

14 percent of Native Americans lived in crowded housing, 67 percent lived in houses without running water, 48 percent lived in houses without toilets, and 32 percent had no means of transportation. Thirty-three percent of Native American families were living below the poverty line compared to 8.6 percent of white families. Ten years later, 24 percent of Native American families were living below the poverty line compared to 7 percent of white families (Aguirre, 1990), but by 1990, conditions had worsened, with almost 36 percent of Native American families living below the poverty line.

Today, the poverty rate for Native Americans has declined to about what it was in 1980. As Table 6.8 summarizes, over 25 percent of Native Americans live below the official poverty threshold, compared to 10 percent of non-Latino whites and 13.0 percent of the total population. By comparing these figures with those for other ethnic groups (see Table 1.1 on page 15), Native Americans continue to be one of the most impoverished ethnic subpopulation in the United States. African Americans and Latinos are not far behind—at 25 percent and 23 percent, respectively—but stereotypes that Native Americans are *all* getting affluent off Indian gaming are clearly contradicted by the facts: high rates of poverty and, as Table 1.2 on page 17 documents, a median household income lower than that of any other ethnic subpopulation in America, except African Americans.

THE DYNAMICS OF DISCRIMINATION AGAINST NATIVE AMERICANS

Identifiability of Native Americans

Movie stereotypes aside, it is not so easy to identify Native Americans physically, for such characteristics as high cheekbones, reddish complexion, straight black hair, almond-shaped eyes, and very little male facial hair are not universal among Native Americans, and any of these characteristics can be found among other populations (Snipp, 1989:26). In contrast to these popular notions of "Indians," there are more explicit biological definitions that highlight the five genetic features unique to Native Americans: earwax texture, organic compounds in urine, blood types and Rh factor, fingerprint patterns, and the ability to taste the test chemical phenylthiocar bamide (Snipp, 1989). Although trivial in any genetic sense, some of these characteristics, especially those related to "blood quantum," were to become the bases for constructing a social definition of who is "Indian." The need to define an Indian based on blood quantum became important at the turn of the nineteenth century when the U.S. government took an active role in determining land rights for Indians and non-Indians in the western United States (Harmon, 1990; Meyer, 1991; Smits, 1991).

In the late nineteenth century, the U.S. government made a systematic attempt to identify Native Americans. Jaimes (1992) suggests that this effort stemmed more from an interest in limiting treaty obligations than in promoting collective identity among native peoples. The vehicle for doing so was a **blood quantum measure,** or the degree of "Indian blood" an individual possessed. The **Dawes Act of 1887,** also known as the General Allotment Act, empowered the government to "test" blood levels to identify someone as an "Indian" and thereby entitled to government treatment under treaty obligations. If this degree was below certain levels, then treaty obligations could be ignored.

To this day **percentage of Indian blood** is an important bureaucratic marker for determining who is entitled to government assistance and who qualifies for special programs, such as affirmative action. For example, in 1986 the Department of Health and Human Services proposed that one-fourth blood quantum be a requirement for receiving medical services at Indian Health Service clinics (Snipp, 1989). In adopting this approach—which no other ethnic population must submit to—the government presumes that blood makes "Indians" a distinct race with certain behavioral propensities (Bieder, 1980). More materially, the earlier Dawes Act used "blood" to determine who was eligible for land or, more important, who was not entitled to land because of insufficient "Indian blood." As a consequence, between 1887 and 1934, the land base to which Native Americans were entitled was reduced from 138 million acres to 48 million acres (House Committee on Indian Affairs, 1934). For those Native Americans who did qualify to receive land, most found that the allocated land was arid or semiarid, almost useless for agriculture. In contrast, the most attractive and fertile native-occupied land was reserved for nonnative populations (Deloria and Lytle, 1983).

Negative Beliefs about Native Americans

Despite their visibility in U.S. popular culture, Native Americans did not earlier occupy a meaningful place in the sociohistorical fabric of U.S. society (Churchill, 1993). In the past, Native Americans often were portrayed as either "noble savages" or "savage redmen" in movies and on television. Native Americans were stigmatized as pastoral relics in an industrial society: the cigar store Indian and the Indian face engraved on the nickel (see Box 6.2 and Box 6.3). Moreover, Native Americans often are portrayed as partially mute in popular culture. In American literature, "the Indian" tends to be a passive witness to others' actions. For example, Queequeg in *Moby Dick,* Tonto in *The Lone Ranger,* and Chief Broom in Ken Kesey's *One Flew Over the Cuckoo's Nest* do not speak. The same may be rightly said of most other Native American characters inhabiting the pages of Euroamerican fiction (Durham, 1992:428). And even the depiction of Native Americans as silent has resulted in a set of negative beliefs (Churchill, 1992; Jones, 1988; Osborne, 1989).

Box 6.2
What's in a Team Name?

The use of an ethnic label as a mascot is perhaps one of the most degrading things that can happen to a population. It is a sign of disrespect and low regard. If one doubts this conclusion, let us rename some prominent teams: the Washington Negroes, the Florida State Jews, the Cleveland Italians, or the Atlanta WASPs. Or let's construct some new names that reflect the ethnicity of an area: The Los Angeles Dodgers can become Los Angeles Mexicans; the San Francisco 49ers can become the San Francisco Chinamen; the Los Angeles Angels of Anaheim can become the Anaheim Viets; the Chicago Bears can become the Chicago Polacks; the New York Giants can become the New York Spics.

In the United States, no ethnic group other than Native Americans is used as a mascot. Yet, when efforts are made to change the name of a sports team on the basis of this inappropriate usage, there is often resistance. Some teams, such as the Stanford Cardinals (formerly the Indians), have changed their names, but most have not.

Recently, the National Collegiate Athletic Association (NCAA) adopted a resolution that, in essence, forces colleges and universities to abandon mascots of ethnic subpopulations, particularly Native Americans. If they do not, they will not be eligible for postseason play and will suffer other costly penalties. Thus far, several exemptions have been given to teams, such as the Florida State Seminoles; and it

Atlanta Braves mascot, Homer the Brave.

will be interesting to see if this resolution is enforced. See the following readings for a discussion of the issue:

Anil Adyanthaya, "Sports, Mascots, and Native Americans," *Boston Globe* (June 5, 2005): p. D11.

L. R. Baca, "Native Images in Schools and the Racially Hostile Environment," *Journal of Sport and Social Issues* 28: 71–78 (2004).

C. Richard King and Charles F. Springwood, "Fighting Spirits: The Racial Politics of Sports Mascots," *Journal of Sport and Social Issues* 24: 282–304 (2000).

Leslie Linthicum, "Some Welcome NCAA Ban on Native Mascots, Others Say Nicknames Are OK If They Are Respectful of Indians," *Albuquerque Journal* (August 6, 2005): p. D1.

Pauline T. Strong, "The Mascot Slot: Cultural Citizenship, Political Correctness, and Pseudo–Indian Sports Symbols," *Journal of Sport and Social Issues* 28: 79–87 (2004).

Box 6.3
"Whites" as Team Mascots

In Box 6.2 we asked the question "What's in a team name?" The focus is on the use of Native Americans as mascots for team sports. While most white persons may not see a problem with sports teams using Indians as mascots, how would white people respond if they were used as a sport team mascot?

An intramural basketball team organized by Native American students at the University of Northern Colorado adopted "Fightin' Whites" as their team mascot. The team is made up of Anglo, Native American, and Hispanic players. The team T-shirt symbolizes the "Fightin' White" as a 1950s-style white man with dimples and shiny, tidy hair. The T-shirt bears the slogan "Every thang's gonna be all white!" According to the students, they adopted "Fightin' Whites" as their mascot because they wanted to raise awareness about culturally insensitive mascots in a community (Eaton, Colorado) debate regarding a local high school's use of an Indian mascot. The high school's mascot is a caricature of a hook-nosed Indian brave wearing a loincloth, a feather sticking out of his braid, and arms crossed over a bare chest.

Ray White, a Mohawk on the college basketball team, said about the team mascot, "It's not meant to be vicious; it is meant to be humorous. It puts people in our shoes, and then we can say, 'Now you know how it is, and now you can make a judgment.'"

White persons in Eaton have expressed their disappointment with the basketball team's "Fightin' Whites" mascot, especially because it has caused Native Americans to become more vocal about their opposition to the high school's mascot. A white resident in the community reflects its sentiments: "It's gone on for years. Why are they just now bringing it up? If they are offended, sorry, but, I mean, why? How is this offending you? They say, 'The big nose, the potbelly,' but those are little things. There are other issues in the world to be worried about."

(continued)

How would most whites respond to seeing a Native American sports team adopt "Fightin' White" as their team mascot?

What do you think? Should Native Americans adopt mascots based on white cultural stereotypes as a strategy for convincing sports teams to remove mascots based on Native American cultural stereotypes?

Source: Julie Cart, "Irked by Mascot, Team Retaliates," *Los Angeles Times* (March 15, 2002): p. A12.

Savage Redmen   The portrayal of the Native American as a ruthless killer of white settlers in movies and television can be traced to the early stages of European contact (Stedman, 1982). As Europeans moved westward, they discovered that they would have to either remove the Native Americans from their lands or learn to share the land. Rather than attempt to live alongside the natives, European settlers decided to take the land. When the natives resisted, European settlers produced the ruthless savage stereotype (Brown, 1970; Shively, 1992). The death of European settlers was seen as a savage act imposed on innocent people. Such stereotypes became common in the media of the time, which tended to sensationalize and caricature, and promoted a tidal wave of anti–Native American sentiment (O'Connor, 1980).

"Fat Cat" Capitalists   Land has always been a pivotal feature in conflicts between Native and white Americans. One of the more recent negative beliefs is that Native Americans have become "fat cats" from the minerals and resources on their land—a belief that is empirically wrong in light of their poverty rates (Anderson, 1992). At issue is the potential wealth in Indian lands—oil, natural gas, uranium, or other resources. Churchill and LaDuke (1992:241) note that "approximately one-third of all western U.S. low-sulphur coal, 20 percent of known U.S. reserves of oil and natural gas, and over one-half of all U.S. uranium deposits lie under the reservations."

The stereotype of Native Americans as "fat cats" is negative in that it implies that Native Americans are undeserving of these resources. Similar to the early stereotype of Native Americans as "unwanted land occupants," the negative portrayal of Native Americans as "fat cats" reinforces their perceived threat to white society and its control of resources. This stereotype has facilitated the federal government's transfer of mineral-rich Native American lands to U.S. control (LaDuke, 1981) and has limited the amount of opposition in the appropriation of these mineral-rich lands. For example, the bulk of the ore-bearing portion of the copper belt found on the Papago reservation during the 1920s was removed from the Papago domain by the U.S. Congress.

The expansion of casinos on Indian reservations has created a new version of the "fat cat" capitalist stereotype. The "casino fat cat capitalist" depicts Indians as millionaires with luxury homes and automobiles, and an unlimited source of money from Indian casinos. According to Barlett and Steele (2002), the "new" fat cats in Indian casinos are non-Indians who serve as investors and consultants and who pocket as much as 40 percent of the total revenue generated by Indian casinos. However, the reality for Native Americans is that while a few tribes have made their members wealthy, the vast majority of Native Americans do not benefit from Indian casinos (Safire, 2002). For example, twenty-three tribes with casinos earning more than $100 million a year accounted for 56 percent of the $8.2 billion in total Indian gaming revenues in 1998—yet the tribes' members comprise about 5 percent of the total Native American population (Pace, 2001). One can observe in Table 6.9 that Indian gaming benefits the smaller tribes, while the larger tribes, such as the Navajo

TABLE 6.9 Annual Casino Revenue for Select Indian Tribes

Tribe	Population	Casino Revenue per Member*	Federal Aid per Member
Navajo	260,010	$ 0	$ 912
Hopi	11,267	0	2,006
Mississippi Choctaw	8,823	25,048	5,717
Seminole	2,817	87,682	8,540
Mashantucket Pequot	677	1,624,815	2,304
Miccosukee	400	250,000	20,560
Santa Ynez	159	1,257,862	8,360

*Based on annual casino revenue divided by the number of tribal members. Of course, if the actual "profits" that go to the tribes were divided by the number of tribal members, the per-member amounts would be dramatically lower.
Source: Barlett et al., 2002.

and Zuni, do not receive any gaming revenue—revenue that could significantly improve the quality of life for the Navajo and Zuni by improving housing conditions and reducing poverty.

More recent data reveal that of the 561 federally recognized tribes, less than half (201) have some form of gaming operation. Total revenue in 2001 was up to $12.7 billion, but this revenue was very unevenly distributed and did not usher in dramatic economic changes across Native American tribes. Many of the tribal nations did enjoy considerable economic benefit, but these same nations were among those *already* with high levels of economic development, business activity, and full employment. Many of the poorest tribes received no benefits at all, but a few such as the Gila River and Cheyenne River Sioux did undergo significant economic transformation with gaming facilities. Still, a good many gaming operations are only marginally profitable, and some have not been profitable (Hillabrant, Earp, Rhoades, and Pindus, 2004). Thus, common perceptions that gaming has made Native Americans "fat cats" are severely overdrawn, misrepresenting the reality. Indeed, the median family income figures (Table 6.4) and the very high poverty rate (Table 6.8) document that Native Americans are still not doing as well as mainstream Americans.

Institutionalized Discrimination against Native Americans

Legal Discrimination   The early European explorers and settlers described the Native Americans as innocent, ingenuous, friendly, and naked. In a sense, the Native Americans were seen as childish—one of the early stereotypes about them (Jarvenpa, 1985). As more European settlers arrived, English concepts of property—land transfer, titles, deeds—were inserted into the relations between the settlers and the natives (Delgado and Stefancic, 1992). It is not surprising to find, then, that much of the discrimination against Native Americans was tied very closely to the legalistic legitimation of landgrabs by European settlers. The bulk of this discrimination is found in legal documents, especially treaties, that defined the nature of Native Americans' presence and residence on their own land (see Box 6.4).

The taking of Native American land by whites was philosophically legitimized by the principle of **Manifest Destiny,** the belief of European Americans that "through divine ordination and the natural superiority of the white race, they had a right (and indeed an obligation) to seize and occupy all of North America. . . . During the nineteenth and twentieth centuries, the philosophy of Manifest Destiny was accompanied by several pieces of legislation that accomplished under . . . law that which would not have been legally justifiable through military force" (Morris, 1992:67). Central pieces of legislation that defined the U.S. government's relationship with Native Americans include the following (Churchill and Morris, 1992):

- **Indian Removal Act (1830).** Andrew Jackson used this act to force the mass relocation of the Creek, Cherokee, Choctaw, Seminole, and other Indian nations during the 1830s. The intent was to open up the territory east of the Mississippi for settlement by white Americans and their African slaves.

Box 6.4
The Cost of Indian Identifiability: The Passage of The Indian–White Miscegenation Laws

The Disney studios made a lot of money bringing the story of Pocahontas to the movie public. The image of Pocahontas was romanticized in popular thinking to show the "noble" character of Indian and white relations. The reality, however, is that the marriage between Pocahontas and John Rolfe in Virginia in 1614 was hardly representative of the times, let alone a catalyst for other Indian–white marriages.

The English colonists were surely not very interested in promoting marriages between whites and Indians, but instead were more interested in promoting their "racial purity" by controlling such interracial marriages. For one thing, the English colonists were unwilling to accept Indians, even Christianized ones, as equals. As Karen Woods notes (1999:51), the passage of **Indian–white miscegenation laws** was a means for white men to assert "power over people of color and over white women."

According to Woods, the English colonists' fears of blood mixture between Indians and whites resulted in the passage of these laws that prohibited marriage between Indians and whites and that outlined harsh punishments for white women giving birth to "interracial bastards." Indian–white miscegenation laws were passed in Virginia (1691), North Carolina (1715), Massachusetts (1786), Rhode Island (1798), and Maine (1821). Most of the other colonies and surrounding territories avoided the existence of Indian–white miscegenation laws by enacting laws prohibiting the "entry" or "settlement" of Indians.

Source: Karen Woods, "Law Making: A 'Wicked and Mischievous Connection': The Origins of Indian–White Miscegenation Law," *Legal Studies Forum* 23:37–70 (1999).

- **Major Crimes Act (1885).** This act allowed the United States to extend its jurisdiction into Native American territories. Since the sovereignty of Native American territories was defined by treaty, this act nullified the treaty's purpose, which had permitted Native Americans to exercise their own jurisdiction within their own territories.
- **General Allotment Act (1887).** Also known as the "Dawes Act," this act was designed to break up the collective ownership of Indian lands by requiring Indians to identify themselves by means of a "blood quantum" code. Under the act, "full-blood Indians" received the deeds to land parcels over which the U.S. government exercised control for twenty-five years, and "mixed-blood Indians" received "patents in fee simple"—basically land rental agreements—and were forced to accept U.S. citizenship. As a result of the act's implementation, the United States acquired over 100 million acres of Native American land between 1887 and 1934.
- **Indian Citizenship Act (1924).** This act conferred U.S. citizenship on all Native Americans born within the territorial limits of the United States. The act's purpose was to curtail the demand for indigenous identity among Native Americans. To protest, the Hopi and Onondaga refuse to acknowledge the act by issuing their own tribal passports.

- **Indian Claims Commission Act (1946).** There is some speculation that this act originated, in part, as a response to the role the United States played at the Nuremberg trials. The act was designed to provide legal recourse to those Native Americans who felt that their land was unjustly taken away from them. The act established the Claims Commission, which was responsible for hearing cases brought forward by Native Americans. The commission, however, was not empowered to return land to any Native American; rather, it was required to assign a monetary value to the land in question— "at the time it was taken." As a result, awards given out by the commission tended to be very small. In general, the act gave the United States the tool with which to legitimize its claim to Native American lands.
- **Relocation Act (1956).** This act created job training centers in urban areas for Native Americans. The purpose of the act was to force Native Americans off the reservation by offering job training opportunities only in urban areas. Native Americans participating in the job training programs were required to sign formal agreements that they would not return to their reservations.
- **Alaska Native Claims Settlement Act (1971).** The act removed the sovereign status of the Indian nations in Alaska by incorporating them into the United States. Approximately 44 million acres of Native American lands were turned into U.S. assets. The importance of this act is that the incorporation of Native American lands included the oil beneath and the timber on top.

Treaties were the first step in the colonization of Native Americans. Most of the legal concepts—such as land deeds and land tenure—were foreign to natives, but they accepted treaties as a "good-faith" attempt at coexistence with the whites. Native Americans perceived treaties as a recognition of their sovereignty as Indian nations and assumed that they were on an equal legal footing with the United States. The second step in the colonization of Native Americans was congressional legislation, such as the acts reviewed above, which became a tool for displacing Native Americans from their lands (McDonnell, 1991; Parker, 1989). Congress's efforts to alter the original treaties with Native American nations were motivated by the white settlers' demands for yet more land. Without their land, Native Americans lost their sovereign status and became a fully colonized population (see Box 6.5).

All these manipulations of the law increasingly undermined the promises of the 1787 Northwest Ordinance:

> The utmost faith shall always be observed towards the Indians; their land and property shall never be taken from them without their consent; and in their property . . . they shall never be invaded or disturbed . . . ; but laws founded in justice and humanity shall from time to time be made, for preventing wrongs being done to them, and for preserving peace and friendship with them.

Such laws, as it turns out, were used as a tool for doing great wrong.

Political Discrimination   Native Americans were squeezed politically both ways: The treaties defined each native nation as a "foreign" government, albeit

Box 6.5
Who Were the Real "Savages"?

Historical analyses dispute the stereotype of the wagon train of white settlers being attacked by hordes of "screaming Indians" (Hurtado and Iverson, 1994). Between 1840 and 1860, when the Plains migrations occurred, some 250,000 white settlers crossed the Great Plains on their way farther west. During this period 362 white Americans and 426 Native Americans died in all the recorded battles. Cooperation was much more common between migrants and natives. For example, regarding Indian and white relations on the California frontier, Hurtado (1982:245) has noted that "instead of resisting the whites, restricting settlement, and impeding development, California's Indians worked obediently in the whites' fields and homes in return for food and shelter."

The real savagery came from federal troops and federal agents who sought to pacify the Native Americans, killing them arbitrarily and making their lands available to the white settlers. Although the Native Americans certainly defended themselves, most of the massacres were committed against Native Americans. In the early 1800s, Governor William Henry Harrison of Indiana expressed concern that "a great many of the Inhabitants of the Fronteers [*sic*] consider the murdering of the Indians in the highest degree meritorius" (quoted in Edmunds, 1983:262). As Figure 6.1 demonstrates, the vast majority of Native Americans were killed by 1850.

heavily regulated by the U.S. Congress. Hence, the members of these "Indian nations" could vote and exercise their political rights only within their "tribe" and "tribal council." Not until 1924 with passage of the Indian Citizenship Act could they vote outside their reservation. Even after 1924, when Native Americans could vote, discriminatory practices—literacy tests, poll taxes, informal discrimination, gerrymandering of districts—were used to discourage their voting. Thus, Native Americans were excluded from full political participation and of course from assuming local, state, and national political offices. At the same time, regulation by the **Bureau of Indian Affairs (BIA),** whose key administrators have traditionally been whites, limited Native Americans in their ability to determine their fate on the reservations where they could vote. John Collier, for example, Commissioner of Indian Affairs from 1933 to 1945, accused the Bureau of Indian Affairs of despotism rooted in rules and regulations that sought to dispossess Indians from their lands and increase the Indians' impoverishment (Kelly, 1975; Kunitz, 1971) (see Box 6.6).

In recent years, Native Americans have gained more political power. They have increased their numbers at the voting booths and, consequently, in political office—particularly at local levels. Also, the BIA has become less restrictive and more sensitive to the needs and interests of its clients. Yet the legacy of past discrimination remains today, and its consequences for Native Americans need to be discussed.

Box 6.6
What's in a Gravesite?

Obviously, dead bodies are in a gravesite. Only Native Americans, as a conquered people, have had to endure the desecration of their gravesites and the religious-cultural significance of these sites. Let us propose an alternative scenario: A crew of Native American archaeologists arrives at a cemetery in which members of an ethnic group are buried. They lay a grid over the site, and with careful picking, dusting, sorting, and recording, they then empty the gravesite of its bones. These are then carted back to a reservation, where they are stored in large drawers, labeled and numbered, and used for research by Native American scholars who want to know about a particular ethnic group. Perhaps some of the bones are reassembled and put on display; maybe some are dressed up in native costumes and put on display in a reservation museum.

Few non–Native Americans would tolerate such treatment of their ancestors. Yet many Americans cannot understand why Native Americans are upset at the desecration of their ancestral burial grounds.

In an attempt to prevent further removal of artifacts from Indian burial grounds, the U.S. Congress approved the Native American Graves Protection and Repatriation Act of 1990 (Coughlin, 1994; Tsosie, 1999). Two important provisions in the act are (1) museums are required to notify tribal groups of remains for which the tribes may have a claim or cultural link and (2) goods excavated on federal or tribal land belong to the Indian tribal group that claims the goods.

The Political Consequences of Being Conquered "Nations" As we have noted, treaties were utilized to subdue and then dislocate Native Americans from their land—thereby opening up the land to white settlers. By dislocating them from their lands, the federal government removed the basis—land—on which Native Americans could demand political sovereignty (Brown, 1970; Deloria, 1969); with a reduced territorial land base over which they could exercise political power, Native Americans lost power vis-à-vis white Americans. According to Deloria (1992) the concepts embedded in the treaty agreements between Native Americans and the federal government were rooted in the idea of the European mini-state. European states would utilize diplomatic relationships, such as treaties, to coexist with other populations within a territory. However, such relationships enabled the stronger, more powerful participant to dominate the weaker, less powerful participant. As a result, the door was open to take land from or to colonize the land of the weaker participant, and as colonization proceeded, less care and concern were exercised in negotiations with Native Americans.

Native Americans entered treaty agreements with the belief that they would be accorded equal political status with the United States and did not perceive treaty agreements as the basis by which an expanding nation, the United States, would usurp their lands. For Deloria (1992:269), it was Native

Americans' misperception of treaty agreements that resulted in their being regarded as "suspect" in the political infrastructure of U.S. society:

> Formal diplomatic relations were established with the various indigenous peoples and international political status was accorded them. The difficulty, however, was one of perception. European mini-states had family relationships with the rulers of larger nations, they were contiguous to the powerful countries of Europe, and they represented long-standing historical traditions going back to the time of original settlement when the barbaric tribes had divided the Roman Empire. Indians could not claim this history and since they were of a different "race," and had different religions, languages, and cultures altogether, their political rights, even when phrased in European terms, were always considered to be intellectually suspect.

Treaties were a blatant expression of political discrimination by the United States against Native Americans. To enhance the political colonization of Native Americans established by treaty, the federal government utilized legislation such as the Major Crimes Act (1885), General Allotment Act (1887), Indian Citizenship Act (1924), and Indian Reorganization Act (1934) to extend its jurisdiction over Native American lands (Williams, 1990). This legislation gave the federal government absolute control over land tenure and the political governance of "Indian nations." Indeed, the federal government increased the role of nonnatives in tribal decision making, and according to Robbins (1992:90), this colonial administration of natives often operates under the guise and illusion of self-determination by tribal councils:

> The current reality is that American Indian governance within the United States has been converted into something very different from that which traditionally prevailed, or anything remotely resembling the exercise of national self-determination. Through the unilateral assertion of U.S. "plenary power" over Indian affairs, a doctrine forcefully articulated in the 1885 *United States v. Kagama* case, the status of indigenous national governments has been subordinated to that of the federal government. . . . Under legislation such as Public Law 280, which emerged during the 1950s, the status of Indian nations has been in many cases again unilaterally lowered by the United States, this time to a level below that of the states, placing the indigenous governments affected by the change in approximately the same postures as counties. . . . In sum, it is accurate to observe, as has been noted elsewhere, that American Indian nations within the geography presently claimed by the United States exist in a condition of "internal colonization."

Political Control by the BIA   The BIA was originally housed in the War Department (the precursor to the current Department of Defense), a clear signal that the bureau was designed to control a conquered people. Later, the BIA was moved to the Department of the Interior, but a bureaucratic pattern had already been set. Because Native Americans were a conquered enemy, tight regulation of their internal political affairs could be justified. Only federal prison inmates, and perhaps the Confederacy in the brief period of radical Reconstruction after the Civil War, have experienced this degree of external control by government.

Some kind of protective agency like the BIA was perhaps necessary when it was established in 1825, the period when genocide was at its peak. But the consequence of bureaucratic regulation has been much like that of contemporary welfare programs: It created dependency; it undermined Native American culture; it denied its clients self-respect; and it most significantly undermined the capacity for self-governance. Even today, as greater efforts are being made at encouraging self-governance, the colonized status of Native Americans on their reservations thwarts such efforts. In turn, the lack of self-governance and the dependence on the federal government is used to justify continued government intrusion, thereby perpetuating the colonized and dependent status of many Native Americans.

Much of the problem resides in the structure of the BIA itself. As a highly centralized bureaucracy with its central offices located in Washington, DC, the bureau is too removed from its clients. From this central office, the bureau fans out into area administrative offices, then to around sixty field installations, such as boarding schools and irrigation projects, and finally into several hundred minor installations. Until recently (and even today but less so than in the past) too much authority has resided in Washington and the area offices, which are staffed primarily by nonnatives. The result is that those closest to the problems of Native Americans in the field installations have the least authority and must constantly seek higher approval by nonnative administrators.

In addition to this source of inefficiency and insensitivity to the needs and problems of its clients, the BIA bureaucracy must cope with myriad tribal rules, archaic legislative acts, recent legislation, and judicial precedents when seeking to make important decisions. For example, there are close to 400 treaties, well over 5,000 legislative statutes, hundreds upon hundreds of Interior Department and solicitor rulings, over 600 opinions submitted by the attorney general, around 100 tribal constitutions, almost that many tribal charters, and vast numbers of BIA administrative procedures. With this complex load, decisions are made slowly and given unnecessarily detailed review. Administrators become ritualists who lose sight of the goal of the BIA—to assist Native Americans—and, instead, often view the interests of the BIA and its clients as opposed. The conflict between Native Americans and the BIA is most evident in the area of economic discrimination. The BIA administered treaties bureaucratically, and efforts to thwart Native American self-determination have inhibited economic development on the reservations.

A report from the National Academy of Public Administration (1999) drew further attention to the mismanagement of the BIA, noting that "the lack of credible management of BIA appears to impair its capacity to represent Indians within the administration and before Congress." The report noted that record keeping is so incomplete and chaotic that internal auditing arms of the BIA cannot monitor the $1.7 billion budget. Indeed, the report concluded that management is so lax in the BIA that the agency violates federal laws governing finances. Even the current head of the BIA acknowledges that the criticisms of the report are justified. Thus, the BIA continues to be a serious problem in lives of Native Americans.

The BIA is not the only governmental agency abusing Native Americans. In 1999, government lawyers for the Treasury Department, which manages trust fund accounts worth some $500 million for 300,000 Native Americans, were found to have given false testimony to the federal judge overseeing lawsuits against the Treasury for mismanagement of the fund. In a shocking report, the Treasury Department was found to have shredded 162 boxes of documents related to the case and then lied to the judge about its actions. These actions occurred while the judge was hearing testimony that the Treasury Department had also destroyed microfilm potentially pertinent to the case. Thus, other governmental agencies have conspired against the interests of Native Americans, the very group that they are supposed to be serving. It is not surprising, therefore, that the government is viewed suspiciously by Native Americans, since the same old patterns of deceit and obfuscation have persisted into the twenty-first century.

Economic Discrimination One reason European explorers ventured to the New World was to find lands that they could exploit. These European explorers assumed that by conquering as many "foreign" lands as possible, they would increase the economic power of their country. The settlers who came to what is now the United States also saw land as necessary for establishing their own economic base in their new surroundings. The treaties between the federal government and the Native American nations were a crucial step in colonizing the natives; these treaties, and later acts of Congress, displaced natives from their lands, making these lands accessible to white settlers. As a result, Native Americans became economically colonized—their lands were not under their control to use as an economic tool. Jaimes (1992:127) notes that the manner in which the federal government robbed Native Americans of their economic power could be highly devious:

> In constricting the acknowledged size of Indian populations, the government could technically meet its obligations to receive "first rights" to water usage for Indians while simultaneously siphoning off artificial "surpluses" to non-Indian agricultural, ranching, municipal, and industrial use in the arid west. The same principle pertains to the assignment of fishing quotas in the Pacific Northwest, a matter directly related to the development of a lucrative non-Indian fishing industry there.

The loss of their lands and resources undercut Native Americans' economic infrastructure; they were unable to derive a livelihood from stock raising, herding, and agriculture. For example, in 1940, 58 percent of the Navajo reservation derived a livelihood from raising sheep and farming, but by 1958 the number had dropped to below 10 percent. Speaking for the Native Americans, Winona LaDuke (as quoted in Jaimes, 1992:128–29) states that the denial of livelihood has produced poverty and hopelessness:

> [We] have the lowest per capita income of any population group in the U.S. We have the highest rate of unemployment and the lowest level of educational attainment. We have the highest rates of malnutrition, plague disease, death by exposure and infant mortality. On the other hand, we have the shortest

life-span. Now, I think this says it all. Indian wealth is going somewhere, and that somewhere is definitely not to Indians. I don't know your definition of colonialism, but this certainly fits into mine.

Unemployment and dependency on welfare are the results of economic discrimination (Ainsworth, 1989; Tinker and Bush, 1991). Morris (1992:70) emphasizes that what makes the economic condition of Native Americans unique is the amount of political and economic control as well as manipulation exercised by the BIA. The BIA often creates employment opportunities for Native Americans that keep them tied to governments. According to a report prepared by the U.S. Commission on Civil Rights in 1975, on the Navajo reservation, for example, 35 percent of the working-age population was employed year-round, leaving 65 percent of the working-age population unemployed; of the 35 percent, the majority (over 60 percent) was employed in government programs. The unemployed are likely to depend on federal subsidies (e.g., welfare) for their livelihood, and federal programs employing only a small proportion of Navajo people ensure the dependence of a larger proportion on the welfare system. Churchill and LaDuke (1992) argue that this pattern of maintaining Native Americans at a subsistence level continued through the 1980s and into the 1990s. Indeed, the budgetary cutbacks in social services during the Reagan and first Bush administrations threatened even the base subsistence of many Native Americans.

One effort to increase the resources available to Native Americans, and in turn to increase their degree of independence, has been to seek agreements with corporations to extract resources from reservation lands in exchange for rents

Casinos offer some hope for economic viability on Indian reservations. However, it will take more than casino revenue to offset the cumulative effects of past economic, political, and legal discrimination.

and profit shares. Although the BIA has led the way in this effort, the economic condition of Native Americans (largely created by past BIA actions) places them in a poor bargaining position. Moreover, the corporations often gain a low-wage labor force and a nonregulated work environment, especially with respect to safety and health codes for workers.

The economic dependence of Native Americans on federal employment programs and social services increases their colonized status in the United States, even when negotiating with private corporations. Native Americans thus experience economic discrimination that prevents them from utilizing their central asset—land—to become economically self-sufficient. As a consequence, they remain economically dependent on government, on the one side, and potential victims of predatory practices of economic enterprises, on the other.

The proliferation of casino-style gambling on some Indian reservations is often seen as a potential way to overcome the cumulative effects of past economic discrimination. One hundred sixty-six of the 550 tribes had casinos in 1996; twenty-eight tribes were losing money; and fifty-four were making only enough money to offer $10,000 per tribal member. A report written in 1999 by the BIA concludes that "the results of shifting federal Indian policies, coupled with limited resources and investments in Indian communities and Indian people, cannot quickly be reversed by a few good years of casino revenues"(quoted in Barlett and Steele, 2002). Moreover, even with casino revenues, the BIA calculated that in 1998, tribes received only about one-third of what they needed for basic problems, such as child welfare, courts, land management, and assistance to the elderly. Funding fell short by at least $1.2 billion in meeting the needs of Native Americans. In asking for the BIA report, Congress wanted to consider shifting the allocation of federal monies to the poorest tribes, because some smaller and more affluent tribes get much more funding per person than larger, poorer tribes. Yet the report cautioned against this policy, and Native American leaders are adamantly against reallocation. Their reasoning is that all Native American tribes are underfunded and that to take from one tribe to give to another is simply a way "to equalize poverty."

More recent data from the Urban Institute indicate that in 2001 this mixed picture of the economic effects of gaming operations persists. Many nations continue to lose money. Most make only small profits and, hence, can offer only modest salaries, stipends, and basic services to their members; and most nations do not receive any benefit from gaming operations (Hillabrant, Earp, Rhoades, and Pindus, 2004; Zelio, 2005).

Educational Discrimination   Education was a key element in efforts to colonize Native Americans. In general, formal education was designed to facilitate submission; it is not surprising, therefore, that the "education" of the Native American population began very early after the arrival of the Europeans (Cross, 1999). For example, as early as 1611, French Jesuit missionaries established schools along the St. Lawrence River to educate Indians in the French manner (Mulvey, 1936). During the early 1600s, Spanish Jesuits in California developed a system of mission schools that focused on teaching Indians in Spanish as required by the Spanish government (Bishop, 1917). These early educational efforts emphasized "conversion" of the native to European culture and language, with the result that Native American languages and cultures were suppressed. Noriega (1992:373–74) has noted:

> In effect, the system by which Native Americans are purportedly "educated" by Euroamerica has from the onset been little more than a means by which to supplant indigenous cultures. This has had, or at least has been intended to have, the predictable effect of demolishing the internal cohesion of native societies, thereby destroying the ability of these societies to resist conquest and colonization.

The Educational Model   The educational model imposed on Native Americans by Europeans was rooted in the boarding school. Children were required to attend schools away from their homes, and they were rarely permitted to visit their families. The Bureau of Indian Affairs promoted the boarding schools as the best vehicle for assimilating Indian youths into American society (Trennert, 1982). As a result, Indian youths were often removed from their homes at the age of 6 and were not returned to their homes until their schooling was completed around the age of 18. When "educated" Native American children returned home, they had often lost much of their own culture and their place in this culture. As Noriega (1992:381) notes, "Altogether, the whole procedure conforms to one of the criteria—the forced transfer of children from a targeted racial, ethnic, national, or religious group to be reared and absorbed by a physically dominating group—specified as a Crime Against Humanity under the United Nations 1948 Convention on Punishment and Prevention of the Crime of Genocide."

Native American families attempted to prevent the dislocation of their children by hiding them from education authorities. Lummins (1968) documents efforts by the Hopi to prevent Mormon missionaries from sending their children to the Intermountain School in Utah. After Hopi parents refused to hand their children over to the Mormon missionaries, federal troops were called in to round up the children. The Hopi greeted the troops by showering them with rocks. The troops subdued the Hopi, rounded up the majority of their children, and sent them to a boarding school in Utah. One result of the Mormon missionaries' involvement in Indian education was the fracturing of the Hopi into two factions—Mormon Hopi and traditional Hopi (Thompson and Joseph, 1944; Titiev, 1944).

Higher Education   While boarding schools were designed to dislocate native youths from their tribes and families, higher education focused on two concerns: (1) vocational training rather than advanced academic studies and (2) the mainstreaming of Native Americans into white society (Wright and Tierney, 1991). Despite the efforts of Dartmouth and Harvard to educate select Native American students, tribal resistance to higher education was widespread. Historically, Native American tribes have regarded the higher education of their youths as a last step in their isolation from the tribe. For example, the Six Nations' response to an invitation from the College of William and Mary in 1744 to send their sons to the college was (as quoted in Wright and Tierney, 1991:13) the following:

> We love our children too well to send them so great a Way, and the Indians are not inclined to give their children learning. We allow it to be good, and we thank you for your Invitation; but our customs differing from yours, you will be so good as to excuse us.

The **Indian Reorganization Act of 1934** was the U.S. government's first step in shaping higher education policy for Native Americans. Until then, religious missionaries and charities had initiated efforts in this area. The Indian Reorganization Act of 1934 attempted to increase Indian participation in higher education by establishing loan and scholarship programs, but students remained reluctant to pursue a higher education because they regarded college as a hostile and alienating environment.

It was not until the 1970s that Native Americans were able to address the issue of tribal colleges. The **Indian Self-Determination and Education Assistance Act of 1975** and the Tribally Controlled Community College Assistance Act of 1978 were instrumental in shifting control of higher education from the federal government to the tribes. Native Americans could now develop a higher education system that was neither paternalistic nor assimilationist in its goals. As a result, there are now thirty-two tribally controlled colleges in twelve western and midwestern states (American Indian Higher Education Consortium, 1999). Together, these institutions service about 11,000 students and enroll about 9,200 students on a full-time basis. However, these colleges are dependent on the U.S. federal government for their financial existence. It may be that higher education for Native Americans may not survive as long as it is dependent on a government that has a history of ignoring the cultural and social rights of the tribes. As Wright and Tierney (1991:17) have observed:

> Because Indian students most often live in economically poor communities, tuition is low and local tax dollars do not offer much assistance. Congress has authorized up to $6,000 per student, but, in reality, the amount released to the colleges decreased throughout the Reagan era so that by 1989 the amount generated for each student was only $1,900. . . . One would think that if the government was serious about increasing opportunities for Indian youth, then colleges would be provided the funds necessary to aid those youth.

The history of formal education for Native Americans has been marked by repression of their cultural, linguistic, and social identity (Davis, 1998; Deloria and Laurence, 1991). Boarding schools were developed with a paternalistic goal—to civilize the "savages" by having them trade in their moccasins for shoes, their language for English, and their cultural beliefs for traditional western religion (Bartelt, 1992). Overall, higher education has not created the same opportunities for self-fulfillment and advancement available to white Americans or other minority groups.

STRATIFICATION OF NATIVE AMERICANS

By almost any indicator—median income, years of schooling, job classification, housing, medical care, life expectancy—Native Americans are at or near the bottom of the resource-distribution ladder. Their socioeconomic position is perpetuated by the reservation system: Native Americans are isolated from the broader society in the government's effort to maintain bureaucratic control and in their own attempt to preserve what is left of their indigenous cultures. Coupled with the fact that much of their land (which could serve as an economic base for mobility within and between Native American and non–Native American class systems) has been lost, the prospect for economic development on reservations is uncertain. Those nations located on land rich in natural resources have some hope if they can secure capital and avoid nonexploitative relations with both the government and the private sector.

The impoverishment of the Native American population emerged and persisted because of the dynamic processes outlined in Chapter 2 (see especially Figure 2.3 on page 53). Native Americans were readily identifiable because of their cultural and organizational distinctiveness, and they have historically posed threats to white Americans, many of whom saw them as potentially inhibiting the growth and expansion of society (Russell, 1994). As a result, a range of negative stereotypes—from "the savage" to "the fat cat"—has legitimized discriminatory practices: attempted genocide under the guise of war, continued acts of violence and murder, isolation on reservations, land-grabbing, denial of voting rights, removal from traditional lands to new and unfamiliar reservations, efforts to force Native Americans to conform to European culture, stealing of mineral and resource rights, and rigid bureaucratic control by agencies of the federal government. All these forces sustained the identifiability of Native Americans while denying them resources. The result was the creation of not only a colonized population but also an ethnic caste.

To break this cycle of discrimination, individual Native Americans face difficult choices: to stay on impoverished reservations and try to preserve what is left of their culture or to enter a Eurocentric society that is not prepared to facilitate their upward mobility. In either case, the majority of Native Americans will remain isolated either in the lower socioeconomic stratum of mainstream society or in the impoverished reservation system (see Box 6.7).

RESPONDING TO DISCRIMINATION

War as a Nonviable Response

The initial response of Native Americans to the European invasion of their homelands appears, on balance, to have been one of cooperation and accommodation, punctuated by acts of violence. As it became evident to Native Americans that their territories were to be occupied and that they were to be displaced, more conflict occurred. Given their numerical and technological

Box 6.7
Problems Faced by Indian Youth

While Indian casinos attract a lot of public attention, other aspects of the American Indian community are ignored. It is often assumed by the American public that Indian gaming provides Indian communities with financial resources that allow them to live better than most Americans. It is also believed that Indian gaming results in financial gains that enable Indian communities to rid themselves of social problems.

One social problem that has been increasing in Indian communities is violent crime, especially among Indian youth. Indian youth are facing challenges that often result in violence as well as drug and alcohol abuse. Senator Ben Nighthorse Campbell has stated, "The greatest challenges facing American Indian youth are overcoming the obstacles to living a normal childhood, receiving a sound education, and being equipped to compete for jobs in the modern economy. Obstacles such as violence, drug and alcohol abuse, poorly funded schools, discrimination, and racism place incredible burdens on American Indian youth." Senator Campbell has identified social forces—normal childhood, a sound education, and job skills—that are important to altering the life experiences of Indian youth away from negative social outcomes. Accordingly, Senator Campbell identifies some of the social correlates that are associated with negative social outcomes for Indian youth—violence, drugs, and alcohol abuse.

VIOLENCE

There is no question that one outcome of participation in gang activities is violence. The number of Indian youth involved in gangs became more noticeable after 1990. Before 1990, less than 10 percent of Indian communities reported gang problems among youth. The Bureau of Indian Affairs noted in 1997 that 132 tribes reported 375 gangs with almost 5,000 members operating on or near Indian reservations. In 2000, 23 percent of sixty-nine Indian communities reported active youth gangs, with the majority (59 percent) of Indian communities reporting the presence of between one and five gangs. The offenses that Indian youth gang members are most often involved in (by order of decreasing frequency) are: graffiti, vandalism, drug sales, aggravated assault, burglary, theft, and robbery.

DRUG AND ALCOHOL ABUSE

The alcoholism death rate for Indian youth between the ages of 15 and 24 is 5.5 deaths per 100,000 compared with 0.3 for other minorities and whites. Indian youth are arrested at twice the national average for alcohol-related crimes. The drug-related death rate for Indian youth is 3.3 deaths per 100,000 compared with a death rate of 3.0 for other minorities and 2.3 for whites.

DEATH

Indian youth are 58 percent more likely than either black or white youth to become crime victims. Indian youth account for 13 percent of all Indian deaths, compared to 4 percent for other minorities and 3 percent for whites. The suicide rate among

(continued)

Indian youth is 2.7 times the rates for other minorities and whites. Indian youth under the age of 15 are murdered at a rate of 2.6 per 100,000 compared with a rate of 1.8 for other minorities and 1.2 for whites.

There is increasing concern in Indian communities that the needs of Indian youth are being ignored. The preceding statistics suggest that Indian youth are at risk in American society, probably more than other minority or white youth. Tribal leaders are concerned that the increasing participation of Indian youth in criminal and deviant activities puts the Indian community at risk. In particular, the participation of Indian youth in criminal activities challenges Indian community notions of collectivism and sharing. Indian youth are vital to the continuity and strength of the Indian community. As such, American society must not lose sight of what needs to be done to help Indian youth meet the challenges they face.

Sources: Arrillaga, 2001; Campbell, 2000: 1–5; Major and Egley, 2002; Wound, 2000.

disadvantage, however, war was not a viable response for the Native Americans. Indeed, war led to near extinction. By 1871, the remaining Native Americans and their nations had been conquered, moved to reservations, and made wards of the federal government.

Retreatism as Another Nonviable Response

One response of colonized populations is to mount retreatist social movements in the belief that supernatural powers will intervene and return the people to some idealized era. Among Native Americans such **millenarian movements** occurred frequently in the latter part of the nineteenth century and remain in some form to this day.

The most famous millenarian movement occurred in the 1870s among the Great Plains natives in **Ghost Dance groups** who were responding to a vision that Native Americans would return on a train in great numbers just as the earth swallowed up all white people. When this did not occur, the movement died down, but a decade later, a new Ghost Dance vision stimulated another movement. Although these movements did not persist, they initiated some cooperation among tribes, an initiative that would have increasing significance.

As the Ghost Dance movement receded, **peyotism** spread through the Great Plains. A mild hallucinogen, peyote, gave religious ceremonies a new power because of the experiences induced. This movement sought to develop an intertribal religion, mixing some elements of Christianity and Mormonism that had been forced on them with holdovers from their own religions. This movement was assailed, especially because drugs were involved; nonetheless, under the constitutional protection of religious freedom, it became organized as the Native American Church in 1918 and affiliated with Christian groups (Price, 1978). Over the decades, Native American criticism of Christianity has mounted, but membership continues to increase. The Native American Church was the first successful effort at **pan-Indianism,** the unification of Native American nations for explicitly political purposes (Stewart, 1987).

One of the more radical movements seeking to rally Native Americans in pursuit of political goals, the American Indian Movement is known for its confrontations with the federal government and the Bureau of Indian Affairs. In 2003, a crowd gathered to mark the thirtieth anniversary of AIM's standoff against the government at Wounded Knee, South Dakota.

Pan-Indianism and Ethnogenesis

In a sense, the Ghost Dance groups represented pan-Indianism; the peyote sacrament evolved into the Native American Church, which has taken on explicitly political goals. The Iroquois Confederation represented an earlier version of pan-Indianism but was confined to the Iroquois, as were a number of similar confederations dating back to the time of the first contact with Europeans. In many ways, pan-Indianism is a form of **ethnogenesis** whereby subgroups who have certain common traditions and have experienced similar patterns of discrimination seek to form a new kind of ethnic identity. Historically, Native American populations were very different in language, culture, and social structure, but they all experienced similar patterns of discrimination, which have given them a basis for forming a new ethnicity that mixes elements of their traditional cultures with new beliefs about how they have been treated by the institutional systems of "white America."

It was only after decades of BIA domination that Native Americans began to unite in significant numbers (Snipp, 1986). The **National Congress of American Indians (NCAI)** was the first truly nationwide organization to represent Native Americans and to engage in active lobbying in Washington (much as the NAACP and Urban League have done for African Americans). This organization has had numerous successes in overcoming restrictive laws and abusive bureaucratic practices by the BIA. Perhaps its greatest accomplishment was to establish the Indians Claims Commission, which has been active and successful in returning land to Native Americans and in remunerating Native Americans for past abuses.

The **American Indian Movement (AIM)** represents a more radical movement to organize Native American nations to pursue political goals, a movement dominated by Plains tribes. The founders, Clyde Bellecourt and Dennis Banks, began by using both confrontational tactics—such as patrols to monitor the police—and more subtle strategies such as alcohol rehabilitation and school reform. The AIM is best known for its confrontations with the federal government and the BIA. **Fish-ins** to protest government interference with traditional Native American fishing areas, seizing Alcatraz Island in the San Francisco Bay in 1969, and the Wounded Knee confrontation brought considerable media notoriety to the AIM and, perhaps even more important, sensitized many white Americans to the plight of the descendants of the first Americans (Eagle, 1992).

Under President Nixon in the 1970s, some progress was made in addressing Native American grievances. But the intensity of confrontation has not diminished; indeed, it has intensified because of the accurate perception that the progress of the 1970s waned in the 1990s and that the government relies on conservative tribal leaders' judgments in making policies. Moreover, infighting among factions of Native American militants has escalated the violence, as has the perception that a civil rights movement much like that among African Americans could be more successful (Schaefer, 1990:196). Yet the influence of the AIM appears to be waning, and a new point of conflict has emerged: control and development of the resources on and under Native American land.

The Economic Battle

In 1975, the **Council of Energy Resource Tribes (CERT)** was formed, with the goal of forming an OPEC-like cartel to coordinate the development of, and perhaps manipulate the market for, the resources on reservation land. Vast reserves of oil and other key resources are located on Native American lands. Yet the effort to develop and control these resources has not been highly successful. A few notable exceptions can be found, but CERT has threatened many people and mobilized large mineral and energy companies in ways that may be counterproductive to Native American economic advancement, although the long-term efforts of CERT may prove otherwise.

Other economic development programs are based on the special status of reservation lands as sovereign nations—albeit easily invaded and highly regulated nations. The use of reservations for gambling has increased over the last decade; the shift from bingo and card parlors to much more sophisticated gaming resorts has been financed and managed by hotel and gambling interests from nonreservation locations, such as Las Vegas and Atlantic City. These new kinds of enterprises provide employment and cash flow for tribes, but they rarely lead to independence from outside economic interests, who take the lion's share of profits and who maintain management control of the hotels and casinos. Moreover, gambling invites further government regulation in an effort to avoid the infiltration of organized crime and other illegal activities.

Box 6.8
Facts Quiz on Native Americans/Alaska Natives

See how you do. Answers are at the bottom of the page (don't peek).

1. What percentage of Native American tribes have gambling operations: (a) over 75 percent, (b) over 50 percent, (c) less than 50 percent, (d) less than 25 percent?
2. Which state has the largest number (not percentage of population, but actual numbers) of Native Americans: (a) Alaska, (b) North Dakota, (c) New Mexico, (d) California?
3. Which city/county has the largest number of Native Americans and Alaska Natives: (a) Los Angeles, (b) Fairbanks, (c) Oklahoma City, (d) Maricopa County, AZ?
4. Which region has the largest number of Native American/Alaska Native businesses: (a) Los Angeles-Long Beach-Riverside, CA, (b) Cook County, IL, (c) Maricopa County, AZ, (d) Fairbanks Metropolitan Area?
5. If those who report only their Native American/Alaska Native ancestry are added to those who report an additional ancestry to their Native American ancestry, how large would the Native American/Alaska Native population be: (a) 3 million, (b) 3.5 million, (c) 4.0 million, (d) 4.5 million?
6. At current rates of growth, can you guess how large the Native American/Alaska Native population will be in 2050: (a) at least 5 million, (b) more than 6 million, (c) more than 7 million, (d) more than 8 million?

Answers: 1. c, 2. d, 3. a, 4. a, 5. d, 6. d.

Thus, through organized protest, punctuated by sporadic violence, Native Americans have significantly reduced the government's abusive practices. But a basic dilemma remains: Much of Native American culture is gone, yet assimilation into the Eurocentric mainstream is difficult and, for many, undesirable. If economic development, self-governance, and increased prosperity are to be achieved on the reservation, then new cultural traditions, new sources of start-up capital, and new relations with government and industry will have to be created. Pan-Indian organization, effective lobbying, and strategic protests offer the best hope for the future.

SUMMARY

Long before Europeans discovered the Americas, earlier immigrants from Asia had settled and established viable societies. These societies were, however, comparatively simple; though they had existed for thousands of years, they were no match for the Europeans, who by 1850 had nearly eliminated the native populations of the Americas. The conquest of "American Indians" and their subsequent confinement to reservations has left a legacy of discrimination rivaled only by the treatment of African Americans, who were imported as slaves. In income, access to jobs, educational attainment, rates of poverty, standards of housing, and life span, the original Americans rank at the bottom on almost all shares of valued resources in the society.

This condition has been sustained by the identifiability of Native Americans and by the embellishment of "distinctiveness" by the government's emphasis on "blood" and other biological features (rather minor ones). Such identifiability has been accompanied by derogatory stereotyping of Native Americans as savages, cigar store Indians, fodder for killing by "noble" cowboys, reservation drunks, fat cat capitalists, and many other vicious stereotypes. Only recently have these stereotypes been mitigated by some superficially more favorable portrayals of Native Americans. They still must endure the humiliation of being used as athletic team mascots and disrespect to their burial grounds via archaeological assaults. Identifiability of Native Americans has been encouraged by a system of government categories and policies, which, along with negative stereotyping, has legitimized discrimination via treaty agreements that have been routinely violated by Anglos, forced transfers of populations, mendacious practices by the Bureau of Indian Affairs, bans on voting, diminution of citizenship rights of the first Americans even on their reservations, loss of landownership and the economic potential of these lands, bias in hiring, and inferior schools on and off the reservation. By any indicator of well-being, Native Americans are worse off than any other ethnic population in America because of discrimination.

Native Americans have fought this discrimination, first by unsuccessful wars, then by retreatism in the face of their conquest, and recently by active movements to foster a pan-Indian culture. The call of pan-Indianism engages Native Americans in political and legal protest and, most important, develops administrative expertise which can, perhaps, enhance the potential wealth of the remaining native lands.

POINTS OF DEBATE

Many Americans see the conquest of the native population as an outcome of war fought fair and square. Yet no other population conquered by the Anglo-Saxon core has had to endure the discrimination experienced by Native Americans. Indeed, in the twentieth century, efforts were made to help rebuild the conquered nations around the world and to establish friendly and mutually beneficial relations with their inhabitants. Such has not been the case for American Indians, who were displaced from their land, confined to reservations, regulated by government, and cheated at almost every turn by both government and large-scale economic enterprises. The legacy of this treatment of America's true natives now raises important points of debate.

1. Should the lands, or at least portions of them, that were taken in violation of treaties be given back to the Native Americans, or should they be compensated for the loss of their most valuable asset? Most white Americans are against any such effort; but in a society that values the principle of justice within the rule of law and order, should not past violations of the law be redressed in some way?

2. Should Native Americans be encouraged to enter the mainstream of society or stay somewhat isolated on the reservations, preserving what is left of their cultures? To do the former would require enormous expenditures in creating new educational and job opportunities, whereas the latter, without subsidizing the economic development of the reservations, would perpetuate the current situation. How can either policy mitigate white Americans' resistance to public expenditures for welfare or their increasing fear of the development of Native American lands? Even more recent use of lands for gambling, which whites and other ethnics use and enjoy, generates protest from adjacent communities who fear a change in their lifestyle. Is such protest legitimate in light of the lifestyle adjustments forced on the first Americans over the last two centuries?

3. Is it time to dismantle the Bureau of Indian Affairs and allow Native Americans to go their own way? Or is the bureau necessary to protect Native Americans from predatory practices and to facilitate economic development? Or is some other form of government assistance needed, a form not so rooted in past patterns of exploitation?

KEY TERMS/KEY LEGISLATION

Alaska Native Claims Settlement Act (1971), 170
American Indian Movement (AIM), 184
blood quantum measure, 163
Bureau of Indian Affairs (BIA), 171
Council of Energy Resource Tribes (CERT), 184
Dawes Act of 1887 (General Allotment Act), 163
ethnogenesis, 183
fish-ins, 184
General Allotment Act (1887), 169
Ghost Dance groups, 182
Indian Citizenship Act (1924), 169
Indian Claims Commission Act (1946), 170

Indian Removal Act (1830), 168
Indian Reorganization Act of 1934, 179
Indian Self-Determination and Education Assistance Act of 1975, 179
Indian–white miscegenation laws, 169
Major Crimes Act (1885), 169
Manifest Destiny, 168
millenarian movements, 182
National Congress of American Indians (NCAI), 183
pan-Indianism, 182
percentage of Indian blood, 163
peyotism, 182
Relocation Act (1956), 170

 Visit our text-specific website at www.mhhe.com/aguirre7e for valuable resources for both students and instructors.

CHAPTER 7

Latinos

*B*y the midpoint of the nineteenth century, the existence of Spanish-speaking populations posed a new front for ethnic conflict—adding to the ethnic tensions arising from the persistence of slavery and the "wars" with Native American nations. The Spanish had exerted their influence on the southern portions of the Northern Hemisphere, Central and South America, as well as the island populations off the shores of Florida and the Deep South. Inevitably the uneasy relations between the two cultures, the Anglo-Saxon core and various white ethnic groups from other European societies on one side, and Latinos on the other, would culminate in a clash.

The term **Latino** does not denote a unified ethnic population (Jones-Correa and Leal, 1996; Portes and MacLeod, 1996; Saenz, 2004). Although the Latino population in the United States consists of three major groups—Mexicans, Puerto Ricans, and Cubans—it also incorporates immigrants from Central and South America who immigrated in noticeable numbers during the past two decades (Jaffe, Cullen, and Boswell, 1980; Johnson, Johnson-Webb, and Farrell, 1999; Lopez-Garza and Diaz, 2001; Munoz, 1989).

Today, there are over 40 million Latinos living in the United States. As Table 7.1 documents, this population constitutes 15.4 percent of the total population in the United States, which is almost double its percentage of three decades ago. Sixty-six percent of the Latino population is of Mexican origin and ancestry; 9 percent is from Puerto Rico; and 3.5 percent is from Cuba. In this chapter we focus on these three Latino populations because they represent the most coherent subsets of Latinos living in the United States. But, as Table 7.1 shows, the numbers of Central and South Americans together constitute a larger group than Cubans and Puerto Ricans. However, because they originate from a diverse set of nations, they do not form a coherent ethnic subpopulation—other than their status as Latino immigrants.

What concerns non-Latinos, of course, is the rapid influx of immigrants from Spanish-speaking nations into the United States and their comparatively high birthrates. The result is that between 1990 and 2008, the Mexican-origin population increased their representation in the Latino population by 6.4 percent, the Puerto Rican population decreased by 0.8 percent, and the Cuban population remained at 3.5 percent. Factoring in all Latinos from other nations, the growth rate of Latinos between 2000 and 2008 was about 3 percent. Thus, the

TABLE 7.1 Latino Population by Origin/Ancestry, 2000 and 2008

	Percentage of U.S. Population		Percentage of Latino Population	
	2000	2008	2000	2008
All Latinos	12.5%	15.4%		
Mexicans	7.4%	10.1%	59.3%	65.7%
Puerto Ricans	1.2	1.4	9.7	8.9
Cubans	0.4	0.5	3.5	3.5
Central Americans	0.6	1.3	5.1	8.7
South Americans	0.5	1.3	4.0	9.1
Dominicans	0.3	0.4	2.0	2.8

Sources: U.S. Bureau of the Census, 2004b, Table 1, p. 1; U.S. Bureau of the Census, American Community Survey, 2008.

number of Latinos in the United States is increasing. Anytime a population's numbers increase relative to those of another population, the sense of threat increases, inevitably giving rise to ethnic tension and the potential for conflict.

These differential rates of population growth are especially dramatic because Latinos are concentrated in comparatively few states, although the spread of Latinos throughout the United States has escalated over the last decade. In 2008, Latinos constituted over 35 percent of the total population in California, Arizona, New Mexico, and Texas; they represented 10 to 25 percent of the population in Nevada, Colorado, Illinois, New York, and Florida; and 5 to 10 percent of the population in other states. Table 7.2 provides a statistical portrait of the Latino population's distribution across states for 2000 and 2008. If we break down the United States by regions, Latinos were 11.3 percent of the population in the Northeast, 5.3 percent of the population in the Midwest, 14.5 percent in the South, and 26.6 percent in the West (U.S. Bureau of the Census, 2002d; U.S. Statistical Abstract 2008, Table 18; 2008 American Community

TABLE 7.2 Distribution of Latino Population across States: 2000 and 2008

State	% in 2000	% in 2008	% Change, 2000–2008
California	31.0%	28.7%	−2.3%
Texas	18.9	18.8	−0.1
Florida	7.6	8.2	0.6
New York	8.1	6.9	−1.2
Arizona	3.7	4.2	0.5
Illinois	4.3	4.2	−0.1
New Jersey	3.2	3.0	−0.1
Colorado	2.1	2.1	0.0
New Mexico	2.2	1.9	−0.2
Georgia	1.2	1.7	0.4
Other states	17.7	20.2	2.5
Total	100.0%	100.0%	

Sources: Pew Hispanic Center tabulations of 2000 Census (5% IPUMS) and 2008 American Community Survey (1% IPUMS).

Survey 2008). Thus, it is the West that is undergoing rapid change, and within thirty years, half of the population of the western United States will be Latinos, and by 2050, 31 percent of the total population in the United States will be of Latino ancestry. Demographic change of this magnitude ensures ethnic tension.

Non-Latino Americans are concerned not only with the rapid growth of the Latino population but also with the immigrant status of Latinos, many of whom enter the country as undocumented aliens. Indeed, getting an accurate count of the Latino population is difficult because many individuals understandably do not want to talk to census takers. The official figures released by the U.S. Census Bureau show that 62 percent of all Latinos were born in the United States and 38 percent are foreign-born. That latter category fuels the sense of threat—that undocumented immigrants are overwhelming the culture and institutions of the Anglo-Saxon core. The 38 percent figure is probably low because so many immigrants go unreported—a fact that is not lost on non-Latino Americans and stokes the fires of fear and political hyperbole. Among the foreign-born who are not citizens, there is considerable variability by nation of origin. For example, because they have started to come to the United States in large numbers only recently, 56 percent of Central Americans and 43 percent of South Americans in the United States are foreign-born and not citizens. Other countries of origin for immigrant subpopulations who have been in the United States for longer periods reveal lower percentages who are foreign-born: 32 percent of Mexican-origin immigrants, 0.6 percent of Puerto Ricans (who have rights to citizenship), 27 percent of Cubans, 43 percent of Dominicans, and 18.6 percent of all other Latinos are foreign-born and not citizens. These numbers naturally pose threats, especially since initial immigration is concentrated in relatively few states and communities within these states (U.S. Bureau of the Census, 2004b:8; see Figure 7.1). Box 7.1 provides a descriptive profile of the Latino population.

RESOURCE SHARES OF LATINOS

Poverty Levels of Latinos

As can be seen in Table 7.3, the poverty rate for Mexican Americans and Puerto Ricans is more than two times that of non-Latinos, while the poverty rate for Cuban Americans is more than the rate for non-Latinos. Most Mexican American and Puerto Rican households headed by females are in poverty, and the head of household is likely to be a non–high school graduate (Aguirre, 1990; Baca-Zinn, 1995; Enchautegui, 1997). The limited success of government-sponsored antipoverty programs in Latino communities caused policy makers to argue that poverty had become a persistent and severe social problem in the 1990s for the Latino population (Krueger and Orszag, 2002; Miranda, 1991; Perez and Martinez, 1993; Zambrana and Dorrington, 1998). However, the economic policies implemented by President Clinton in the 1990s had some effect on reducing poverty among all Americans, Latinos in particular (Pear, 1998).

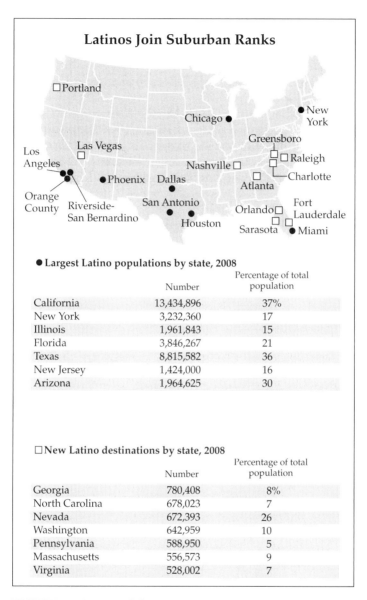

Latinos Join Suburban Ranks

● Largest Latino populations by state, 2008

	Number	Percentage of total population
California	13,434,896	37%
New York	3,232,360	17
Illinois	1,961,843	15
Florida	3,846,267	21
Texas	8,815,582	36
New Jersey	1,424,000	16
Arizona	1,964,625	30

□ New Latino destinations by state, 2008

	Number	Percentage of total population
Georgia	780,408	8%
North Carolina	678,023	7
Nevada	672,393	26
Washington	642,959	10
Pennsylvania	588,950	5
Massachusetts	556,573	9
Virginia	528,002	7

FIGURE 7.1 Areas with largest Latino populations and new Latino destinations.
Source: 2008 American Community Survey; Pew Hispanic Center, Latinos by Geography 2008.

In 2008, the total population had a poverty rate of 19.5 percent, while non-Latino whites had a poverty rate of 8.2 percent (2008 American Community Survey). Among other Latinos besides Mexican-origin, Puerto Ricans, and Cubans, poverty rates varied from 15 percent for those of South American ancestry to a high of over 27 percent for Dominicans. To the extent that persistent poverty is a marker of ethnic stratification, the Latino population is indeed stratified.

Box 7.1

The Latino Population in the United States, 2008

POPULATION

- With 47 million persons in the Latino population, it constitutes 15 percent of the U.S. population. Between 2007 and 2008, about 1.5 million Latinos were added to the population, resulting in a percentage increase of 3.2 and, thus, making Latinos the fastest growing ethnic group in the United States.
- Between 1990 and 2008, the Latino population in the United States increased from 22.4 million to 46.9 million.
- Sixty-four percent of the Latino population is comprised of Mexican-origin persons, 9 percent Puerto Rican, 3.5 percent Cuban, 3.1 percent Salvadoran, 2.7 percent Dominican, and 17.7 percent other Latino. Almost half of the Dominicans living in the United States reside in New York City, and about half of the Cuban population resides in Miami-Dade County, Florida.

DISTRIBUTION OF THE POPULATION

- Forty-eight percent of the Latino population lives in California or Texas; 13.5 million Latinos reside in California and 8.9 million reside in Texas. There are 16 states with at least a half-million Latino residents—Arizona, California, Colorado, Florida, Georgia, Illinois, Massachusetts, Nevada, New Jersey, New Mexico, New York, North Carolina, Pennsylvania, Texas, Virginia, and Washington. The state with the highest percentage of Latinos in its population is New Mexico (45 percent).
- Los Angeles County contains the largest number of Latinos (4.7 million) than any other county in the United States. Starr County (Texas) claims the greatest proportion of Latinos (97 percent) in its population of any other county in the United States. Forty-eight of the 3,142 counties in the United States are majority-Latino.

FAMILIES AND CHILDREN

- There are about 11 million Latino households in the United States; of these, 62 percent include children younger than 18.
- Latinos comprise 25 percent of children younger than 5, and 22 percent of children younger than 18 in the United States. The median age of the Latino population is 27.7 years, in contrast to 36.8 years for the U.S. population.
- The median income of Latino households is $38,679. The poverty rate among Latino households is 22 percent. Almost one-third of Latinos lack health insurance.
- Seventy-eight percent of Latinos 5 years and older speak Spanish at home.

EDUCATION

- Sixty-two percent of Latinos 25 years and older had at least a high school education, and 13 percent had a bachelor's degree or higher.
- Almost four million Latinos 18 years and older have at least a bachelor's degree. Latinos comprise 12 percent of the undergraduate and graduate student populations in the United States.

OCCUPATIONS

- Of Latinos 16 years and older, 18 percent work in management, professional, and related occupations; 18 percent work in production, transportation, and material moving; 24 percent work in service occupation; 20 percent work in sales and office; and 20 percent work in farming, fishing, and forestry.

BUSINESSES

- There are almost two million Latino-owned businesses in the United States. Nearly 43 percent of Latino-owned businesses are in construction, administrative and support, waste management and remediation services, repair and maintenance; and 36 percent are in retail and wholesale trade.
- The counties in the United States with the highest number of Latino-owned businesses are: Los Angeles County (188,422); Miami-Dade County (163,187); and Harris County, Texas (61,934).
- Latino-owned businesses generate $222 billion in revenue, with 29,168 of them generating $1 million or more.
- Forty-five percent of Latino-owned businesses are owned by Mexicans, Mexican Americans, and Chicanos.

Sources: U.S. Census Bureau, 2008 American Community Survey.

Income of Latinos

In Figure 7.2, the median incomes of non-Hispanic whites and Latinos are compared from 1967 to 2007. As is evident, the gap between their respective incomes has remained fairly constant over the last forty years, with Latino incomes over the last two decades averaging a bit less than 70 percent of non-Latino income, although the most recent data report an increase in this percentage up to 70 percent (as can be seen by the figures in Table 7.4). Many

TABLE 7.3 Poverty Rates for Selected Latino Subpopulations

| Year | Population Living in Poverty, % | | | | |
	Non-Latino White	Mexican American	Puerto Rican	Cuban American	Central/South American
2008	9.5%	22.9%	24.8%	14.6%	16.8%
2006	8.5	22.0	25.3	16.3	
2002	8.0	22.8	26.1	16.5	
2000	7.5	24.1	25.8	17.3	
1998	8.2	27.7	33.1	12.5	
1994	9.4	31.8	38.7	19.9	
1990	8.8	27.7	30.4	12.5	
1980	9.1	21.4	33.4	11.2	
1970	7.8	26.8	28.2	13.1	

Sources: U.S. Bureau of the Census, 1973a, 1983a, 1991b; Current Population Survey: 1994 Annual Demographic Survey (March Supplement); Proctor and Dalaker, 2002, 2003; Ramirez and de la Cruz, 2003; www.census.gov/ hhes/www/poverty/detailedpovtabs.html; 2010 *Statistical Abstract*, Table 39.

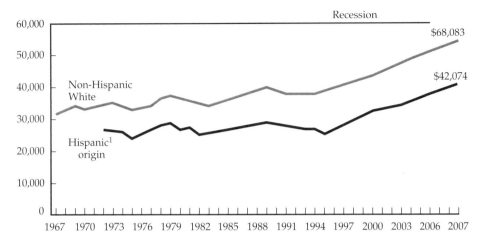

FIGURE 7.2 Median household income by race and Hispanic origin, 1967–2007.

[1]Hispanic may be any race. Data not available prior to 1972.

Sources: 2008 American Community Survey; U.S. Bureau of the Census, Current Population Survey, March 1968 to 2001; U.S. Bureau of the Census, 2005c; Webster and Bishaw, 2007, Table 1, p. 3. 2010 *Statistical Abstract,* Table 36.

more Latinos, compared to non-Hispanic whites, find themselves in jobs that offer few opportunities for advancement (Hortenstine, 2005), and this fact accounts for the persistence of this differentiation between non-Hispanic white and Latino incomes. While some Latinos have been upwardly mobile, their places in the bottom rungs of the stratification system have been replaced by newer immigrants or by the high birthrates among those who cannot be mobile for lack of education. The end result is persistence of income differentiations. Among Latinos, Mexican Americans had the lowest proportion (23.6 percent)

TABLE 7.4 Latino Income Differentials Relative to Non-Latino White Income

	Latinos		
Year	Total Latino Population*	Males[†]	Females[‡]
2007	0.69	0.64	0.77
2006	0.70	0.62	0.77
2002	0.68	0.63	0.73
2000	0.67	0.62	0.73
1998	0.63	0.58	0.71
1993	0.62	0.63	0.77
1988	0.64	0.61	0.80
1983	0.67	0.67	0.91

*Latino income as a proportion of non-Latino income.

[†]Latino male income as a proportion of non-Latino *male* income.

[‡]Latino female income as a proportion of non-Latino *female* income.

Sources: U.S. Bureau of the Census, 1994a; March 1998 CPS (Internet release date: August 7, 1998); Current Population Survey 2000 (Internet release date: December 10, 2001); Current Population Survey, 2002 (Internet release date; June 18, 2003); U.S. Census Bureau, Current Population Survey, 2006 Annual Social and Economic Supplement; 2010 *Statistical Abstract,* Table 227.

earning $35,000 or more in annual income compared to Puerto Ricans (34.8 percent) and Cuban Americans (34.3 percent).

The median household income in 2002 for Mexican Americans was $33,574, for Puerto Ricans $31,752, and for Cuban Americans $35,831 (Ramirez and de la Cruz, 2003). From another perspective, Mexican American median household income in 2002 was 73 percent, Puerto Rican median household income was 69 percent, and Cuban American median household income was 77 percent of the non-Latino white median household income. The income gap between Cuban Americans and non-Latino whites is smaller than for either Mexican Americans or Puerto Ricans. In addition, the median household income of Mexican Americans in 2002 was 94 percent and Puerto Rican median household income was 89 percent of the Cuban American median household income. Interestingly, one can observe in Table 7.4 that the incomes of Latinos and Latinas are below those of non-Latino whites.

Occupational Distribution of Latinos

Table 7.5 shows that relatively more persons in the non-Latino white population (43.7 percent) and in the Cuban American population (32.3 percent) work in managerial and professional occupations, whereas 17 percent of Mexican Americans and 28 percent of Puerto Ricans have these jobs. A noticeable number of Mexican American workers (27.8 percent) are farmers and laborers; 12.2 percent of Puerto Ricans hold such positions; and 14.7 percent of Cuban Americans have these jobs—a figure that approaches the 11.4 percent for all non-Latinos. This occupational distribution offers some insight into the reasons for differences in median earnings among the three Latino groups. The concentration of Cuban American persons in managerial, professional, technical, and sales occupations versus the percentage of Mexican Americans and Puerto Ricans in service, production, and labor occupations accounts for the disparity in earnings among Latino subpopulations. Managerial, professional, and technical occupations are associated with higher pay, more job security, and better fringe benefits than are service, production, and labor occupations.

Educational Attainment of Latinos

Table 7.6 shows the educational attainment of Latinos. In general, the levels of education attained by Latinos are below those of non-Latinos. The educational attainment of Mexican Americans at both the high school and college levels are lower than those of Puerto Ricans, Cubans, and Central/South Americans. Comparatively speaking, Puerto Ricans and Cubans made larger educational gains between 1970 and 2008 than Mexican Americans. The availability of U.S. Census data on the Central and South American population in the United States suggests that despite the population's emergence in the United States over the last ten years the educational attainment of Central and South Americans surpasses that of Mexican Americans.

TABLE 7.5 Occupational Distribution among the Latino Population, 1970–2006

Occupation	Non-Latino White, %						Mexican American, %						Puerto Rican, %						Cuban American, %					
	2006	2002	2000	1990	1980	1970	2006	2002	2000	1990	1980	1970	2006	2002	2000	1990	1980	1970	2006	2002	2000	1990	1980	1970
Professionals, managers	43.7%	35.1%	33.2%	27.3%	26.4%	25.4%	17.2%	11.9%	11.9%	11.3%	14.2%	10.2%	28.2%	19.5%	17.1%	17.1%	16.6%	15.6%	32.3%	24.3%	23.5%	24.0%	22.6%	23.4%
Clerical workers, salespeople, craftspeople	29.4	29.2	30.3	33.2	39.7	40.2	24.7	22.6	22.4	25.3	36.9	30.4	30.8	35.8	34.9	31.4	45.3	47.8	33.8	35.1	34.0	33.9	45.3	45.2
Operatives, service workers	15.5	22.4	22.6	23.8	27.2	28.5	30.3	34.3	34.8	31.7	37.7	42.2	28.8	29.1	28.2	31.8	32.2	30.3	19.2	25.1	24.6	25.8	25.7	24.3
Farmers, laborers	11.4	13.3	13.9	15.7	6.7	5.9	27.8	31.2	30.9	31.7	11.2	17.2	12.2	15.6	19.8	19.7	5.9	6.3	14.7	15.5	17.9	16.3	6.4	7.1

Sources: U.S. Bureau of the Census, 1973a, 1983a, 1983b, 1991b; March 1994 CPS; March 1998 CPS; March 1998 CPS Supplement (Internet release date: August 7, 1998); March 2000 Current Population Survey (Internet release date: March 6, 2001); U.S. Bureau of the Census, Current Population Survey 2002 (Internet release date: June 18, 2003); U.S. Census Bureau, Current Population Survey, Annual Social and Economic Supplement 2006.

TABLE 7.6 Levels of Education Attained by Latinos and Non-Latinos, Persons 25 Years Old and Older

	High School Graduate or More, %					College Degree or More, %				
Year	Non-Latino	Mexican American	Puerto Rican	Cuban American	Central/South American	Non-Latino	Mexican American	Puerto Rican	Cuban American	Central/South American
2008	87.1%	55.2%	76.4%	80.0%	69.1%	29.8%	9.1%	15.5%	28.1%	20.3%
2005	86.0	52.2	72.4	73.4		37.8	8.2	13.8	24.6	
2002	87.4	50.6	66.8	70.8		28.6	7.6	14.0	18.6	
1990	79.6	44.1	55.5	63.5		22.2	5.4	9.7	20.2	
1980	69.6	38.1	45.9	34.6		17.4	4.9	5.6	12.2	
1970	62.6	33.3	43.8	33.4		14.1	4.3	3.4	12.6	

Sources: U.S. Bureau of the Census, 1973a, 1983a, 1983b, 1991b; March 1994 CPS; March 1998 CPS Supplement (Internet release date: July 29, 1999); March 2000 Current Population Survey (Internet release date: March 6, 2001); March 2002 Current Population Survey (Internet release date: June 18, 2003); U.S. Census Bureau, Annual Social and Economic *Supplement* (Internet release date: October 2007); 2010 *Statistical Abstract*, Table 39.

Life Span of Latinos

Life expectancy statistics show large differences between the Latino and non-Latino populations. The Centers for Disease Control and Prevention (2002) reports that Latina mothers are less likely to receive prenatal care than non-Latina mothers. The reason given by Latina mothers for their decision not to pursue prenatal care is that they do not have the money or health insurance to pay for a doctor's visit (see Box 7.2). Latina mothers are also more likely than non-Latino mothers to give birth to infants with low birth weight.

Death rates for the Latino population are little studied because death certificates identify "race" rather than ethnicity (Becerra et al., 1991). Still, an analysis of Latino death rates by the National Center for Health Statistics (2002) found the following: (1) The leading cause of death for both Latino and white American children 1 to 14 years of age was unintentional injury (e.g., fires, drowning, motor vehicle injury); however, approximately 21 percent of Latino children ages 1 to 14 were the victims of homicide, compared to 13 percent of white children. (2) The leading cause of death for Latino and white young adults ages 15 to 24 was unintentional injury, but homicide accounted for 47 percent of Latino deaths, compared to 10 percent of deaths among white Americans. In contrast, suicide accounted for 31 percent of deaths among young white adults and 10 percent among Latinos in this age category. (3) In Latino and white cohorts ages 25 and older, heart disease was the leading cause of death.

Another reason for the discrepancies in life expectancy between non-Latinos and Latinos is Latinos' limited access to health care. The higher incidence of low birth weight among newborn Latino children reflects two aspects of the health care delivery system: the limited availability of affordable health care in general and prenatal care in particular (Ginzberg, 1991; Granados et al., 2001; LeClere, Rogers, and Peters, 1997; Zambrana and Logie, 2000) and the lack of affordable health care coverage for the Latino population (Granados et al., 2001; Treviño et al., 1991; Vitucci, 1999). These limitations prevent most Latina mothers from obtaining neonatal services until the eighth or ninth month of pregnancy, when they can then utilize health care services available through social welfare programs. Less neonatal care translates into greater risks for infants.

Another reason for shorter life expectancy is violence (Martinez, 1996). The large proportion of deaths caused by homicide among Latinos in the 1 to 14 and 14 to 25 age ranges reflects the risk of living in areas with high crime rates and the presence of gang violence. For example, Latino youth are four times more likely than white youth to be the victims of gang violence (U.S. Department of Justice, 1991b, 1991c, 2002). Latino youth are also more likely than white youth to feel unsafe or threatened while attending school (U.S. Department of Justice, 1995).

Housing of Latinos

Housing segregation limits opportunities by confining an ethnic group to areas where jobs, education, health care, and security are less available (Freeman,

Box 7.2
Latino Children at Risk

The Latino population will continue to grow during the twenty-first century, and, as a result, its **identifiability** will be ever more evident. For example, between July 2003 and July 2004, the U.S. Latino population grew from 39.9 million to 41 million, or 14 percent of the U.S. population, compared with 37 million African Americans (12 percent of the U.S. population); thus, Latinos recently became the largest minority group in the United States. However, as we have observed in this chapter, despite its growth, Latinos have yet to achieve significant gains in access to valued resource shares. One of those resource shares is health care. With a large proportion of its population consisting of young children and adults, it is not surprising to find Chicano children and their families at risk in their health care status. Highly salient features of the health care condition of Latino children and their families are outlined here:

- One-third (34.7 percent) of all children under age 18 in the United States without health insurance are Latino. However, Latino children comprise only 18 percent of all children under age 18 in the United States. From another perspective, there are 2.9 million Latino children under age 18 in the United States without health insurance, so about one out of every five Latino children under age 18 is without health insurance.
- Twenty percent of Latino children under age 18 are uninsured, compared to 9 percent of African American children and 6 percent of white children.
- The health insurance rate for Latino children under age 18 fell from 26 percent in 1998 to 20 percent in 2003. Between 1998 and 2003, the health insurance rate for Latino parents dropped 3 percent, resulting in almost 2 million uninsured parents.
- More than 7 in 10 Latino children without health insurance are eligible for coverage through Medicaid or SCHIP (State Children's Health Insurance Program), but they are not enrolled.
- More than 40 percent (41.4 percent) of Latino children without health insurance did not receive any medical care during 2003, compared with 18 percent (17.6 percent) of insured Latino children.
- Latino children without health insurance are 10 times more likely not to receive needed medical care than Latino children with insurance (6.1 percent vs. 0.6 percent).
- Three-fourths (74.7 percent) of Latino families with insured children report that their children have someone they think of as their personal doctor or nurse, compared with less than half (41 percent) of Latino families with uninsured children.

Sources: U.S. Bureau of the Census, Current Population Survey (September 2004); Centers for Disease Control and Prevention, 2003 National Health Interview Survey, and 2003 National Survey of Children's Health; Kaiser Family Foundation, "Key Facts: Race, Ethnicity and Medical Care" (June 2003); The Commonwealth Fund, "Hispanic Patients' Double Burden: Lack of Health Insurance and Limited English" (February 2003).

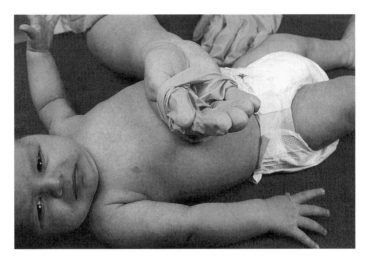

Many Latinos have limited access to health care because they lack
the money or the insurance to pay for it.

2000; Santiago and Wilder, 1991; Wood, 2001). Thus, minority ethnics not living
among the dominant groups in a society will have reduced access to resources
(Flippen, 2001; Lopez, 1986; Palm, 1985; Williams and Collins, 2001). Accordingly, a report on neighborhood segregation in the United States for 2000 shows
that Latinos in general live in neighborhoods where they comprise almost half
of the residents (Frey and Myers, 2002). In their study of the Latino population
in the United States, Bean and Tienda (1987) recorded the following patterns of
residential segregation: (1) Puerto Ricans living in the New York City area are
highly segregated residentially. This segregation pattern is based largely on
racism. Since some Puerto Ricans are of African heritage, they are more likely to
be relegated close to African American neighborhoods, which tend to be isolated from white American neighborhoods. (2) Mexican Americans in the Los
Angeles area experience less residential segregation than Puerto Ricans in New
York City. Since Mexican Americans constitute 22 percent of the Los Angeles
area's population (and Latinos, in general, an even greater percentage), their
large numbers increase the probability of contact in diverse residential areas.
(3) Compared with Puerto Ricans and Mexican Americans, Cuban Americans in
the Miami area reveal the lowest level of residential segregation and the highest
rate of contact with the white population. Bean and Tienda (1987:177) concluded that the consequences of Latino segregation

> are uncertain, but probably depend on the extent to which it is voluntary or
> involuntary. In this regard, Puerto Ricans are clearly at greatest risk of being
> denied equal access to spatially determined resources like education, health,
> security, and employment.

Although Latinos as a whole are not as segregated as African Americans
from other ethnic populations, their level of segregation has actually increased

slightly since 1980. Latinos showed a dissimilarity index of .502 in 1980 (meaning over 50 percent would have to move to another neighborhood to gain equal representation in all neighborhoods in a city). In 2000, this index had risen to .509, the increase probably representing the tendency of new immigrants— particularly undocumented immigrants—to stay within Latino neighborhoods where they would not stand out and be easy targets for law enforcement agencies. By way of comparison, African American segregation, while much higher than that evident for Latinos, declined somewhat from a dissimilarity index of .727 in 1980 down to .640 in 2000 (U.S. Bureau of the Census, 2002c). Thus, due to ghettoization of undocumented immigrants, very little progress in reducing Latino segregation from the general population has been made over the last twenty years.

In sum, then, Latinos have less access to valued resources—income, education, health care, and housing—than white Americans, although degrees of access to these resources vary among the three Latino groups (Aponte, 1991). Cuban Americans clearly have more access than either Puerto Ricans or Mexican Americans; and Mexican Americans have the least access of the three groups, despite the fact that they are less residentially segregated than Puerto Ricans. Let us now examine in more detail each of these three populations, in order to understand the specific forces that have determined their respective resource shares.

MEXICAN AMERICANS

Identifiability of Chicanos

Language and culture have set people of Mexican origin apart from mainstream society (see Box 7.3). The proximity of Mexico to the United States, coupled with frequent contact cross the 2,000-mile border, has preserved the Spanish language as a prominent feature of social intercourse between the two cultures (Aguirre, 1980, 1984, 1988). Unlike many European immigrants who cut their ties with their homelands, Mexican Americans, or Chicanos, have had less incentive to abandon their native culture (Langley, 1988). Indeed, early Mexican American settlers regarded the Southwest as *their* homeland until the Anglo-Saxons invaded and made it part of the United States.

The maintenance of language and other features of Mexican culture have served to segregate Mexican Americans, perpetuating incentives to marry within the Latino population and to sustain traditional behavioral and social patterns (such as birthrates and family structure). Many Mexican Americans speak Spanish or speak English with an accent, have slightly darker skin than most Americans of European descent, and are overrepresented in certain occupations (see Table 7.5). Taken together, these differences create a relatively high degree of **identifiability,** which, historically and currently, is the basis for discrimination. To understand the dynamics of this discrimination, as well as the sense of threat and prejudicial beliefs that sustain such discrimination, we need to review briefly the history of the Mexican American

---

Box 7.3
"English Only!" Not a Problem for Latinos

A recent study by the Pew Trust on language documents that the children and grandchildren of Latino immigrants acquire facility with English at about the same rate as previous generations of non-Latino immigrants. This finding calls into question the sometime shrill rhetoric that English as the national language is being threatened by Hispanic immigration. The study found that, while many immigrants spoke little or no English upon their arrival, the next two generations had learned English and, indeed, their use and even ability to speak Spanish had declined dramatically. As the figures below document, Mexican immigrants are the least likely to speak English upon arrival in the United States, whereas Puerto Ricans are the most likely to speak English, but as the figures on the second and third generation for all Latinos clearly document, 94 percent of third-generation descendants of immigrants speak English very well and, equally significant, the increasing fluency in English is accompanied by a sharp decline in the ability to speak Spanish by the third generation. Indeed, only 29 percent of the third generation can speak Spanish very well.

Foreign-born Latinos who speak "little or no English" (by country/area of origin):

Mexico	71%
Dominican Republic	64%
Central America	62%
Cuba	57%
South America	44%
Puerto Rico	35%

Language use across generations:

Generation	Percentage Who Speak English "Very Well"
First	23%
Second	88
Third	94

Thus, the data indicate that language acquisition among Latinos is very much like that of earlier European immigrants: by the third generation, they speak English fluently and lose much of their ability to speak the language of their grandparents. Data such as these can, perhaps, quell the concern of the broader American public about whether or not Latinos will become "assimilated" into the Anglo-Saxon core. They will speak the language of the core and, as have other ethnic subpopulations, they will probably integrate into the core, while at the same time retaining elements of their distinctive ethnic heritage.

---

population. This overview tells the story of a population of conquered people (similar to Native Americans), imported menial labor (similar to African Americans, but without the extremes of slavery), and generally unwanted and illegal immigrants.

The History of Mexican Americans: Conquest, Displacement, and Exploitation

Early History: The Conquest   By 1602, a handful of Spaniards had explored most of the southwest borderlands—from Galveston to San Diego, from Sonora to Santa Fe, and from the west coast of Mexico to Monterey. In time, the Spanish settlements in the Southwest came to consist of a fairly rooted colony in New Mexico, an easily held and fairly prosperous chain of missions in coastal California, and a number of imperiled settlements in Texas and Arizona. By 1790, the population of the Southwest, estimated at 23,000, was almost entirely Spanish speaking (American Council of Learned Societies, 1932).

The presence of a large Spanish-speaking population in the Southwest facilitated, to a degree, the adjustment of the incoming Anglo-Saxons because they could adopt much of what was useful. For example, Spanish and Native American words were incorporated into the English vocabulary, and styles of architecture found in the Southwest—the one-story ranch house and buildings with tiled roofs, adobe walls, patios, and verandas—were adopted (Hernandez-Chavez et al., 1975).

Between the Battle of San Jacinto in 1836 and the Gadsen Purchase of 1853, the United States came to acquire most of the Southwest. A significant event in Mexican American history was the **Treaty of Guadalupe Hidalgo** in 1848, which concluded the war between the United States and Mexico (Estrada et al., 1988; Hietala, 1985). This treaty guaranteed to all Mexicans living in the "new" American territory a number of basic rights: full American citizenship, retention of Spanish as a recognized and legitimate language, political liberty, and ownership of property. The treaty was rarely enforced, however, which opened the door to social and political exploitation.

Despite the guarantees of the Treaty of Guadalupe Hidalgo, the Anglo-Saxons assumed the right to impose the English language on all the inhabitants of the Southwest (Villareal, 1988). Laws were written in English, leaving Spanish speakers ignorant of the law, especially laws protecting their property; Spanish was not used in the courts; and school instruction in Spanish was forbidden. As a result, Mexicans were at a disadvantage in protecting their property, in seeking redress through the courts, and in acquiring an equal education. Mexicans living in the Southwest soon became the objects of prejudice (Pitt, 1966).

For Mexican Americans, the period leading into the early nineteenth century involved loss of land, social status, culture, and language. This group became a minority in the United States by being conquered (Acuña, 1981), and as the Anglo-Saxon population settled in the Southwest and control of the Southwest borderlands passed into their hands, Mexican Americans became an ever more subordinate ethnic minority.

After 1848, when the Anglo-Saxon population opened the Southwest for expansion, major economic transformations ensued. The loss of social, political, and economic status relegated Mexican Americans to a source of cheap labor. Hence, the major thrust of Anglo-Saxon economic development of the Southwest was in labor-intensive industries—agriculture, mining, and railroads (Barrera, 1979). As this development increased, more people from south of the border immigrated to U.S. territory. For example, between 1890 and 1900 the Mexican-origin population in the Southwest grew from about 75,000 to over half a million (McWilliams, 1968).

The arrival of large numbers of Mexican immigrants threatened the precarious socioeconomic status of those already living in the Southwest. Since the majority of immigrants from Mexico were illiterate and poor, they were willing to accept the lowest wages; as a consequence, the white American population tended to regard all Mexicans, including descendants of the original landholders in the Southwest, as "cheap labor." Indigenous Mexican Americans were perceived by the Anglo core as no different from poor Mexican immigrants—a perception that pushed almost all those of Mexican extraction to the bottom rungs of the stratification system (Murguia, 1975).

Mexican Americans in the First Half of the Twentieth Century　Immigration of Mexicans into the Southwest was closely linked to the economy. On the U.S. side of the border, as labor-intensive industry expanded, the demand for cheap labor served as a "pull" factor for Mexican immigrants. On the Mexican side of the border, the revolution of 1910 to 1917 operated as a "push" factor for Mexicans seeking refuge and employment. The push out of Mexico was reinforced by the fact that employers in the United States were looking for a source of inexpensive labor to compensate for the shortage of American workers created by World War I. Soon, Mexicans became a subordinate labor force: paid less than white American laborers for the same work, concentrated in the low-paying occupations, and often indebted to their employers for food and shelter.

As the southwestern economy fluctuated, employers often had too many workers and not enough work. Ironically, the need for cheap labor to run the labor-intensive industries of the Southwest also created the need to eliminate the presence of surplus labor during economic downturns. For example, between 1870 and 1930 immigration policy was relatively unrestricted for Mexican immigrants, who were allowed to enter the United States on an open-door policy to fill the need for labor. But the Great Depression of the 1930s changed immigration policy dramatically. As white Americans lost jobs and homes, anti-Mexican feelings emerged; and as whites increasingly competed with those of Mexican origin for low-wage jobs and welfare benefits, white resentment toward "Mexicans" grew. The result was a repatriation movement for Mexicans, a movement that included both indigenous Mexican Americans and those who had more recently immigrated. Between 1929 and 1935 over a half million Mexicans were repatriated (Chavira, 1977; Hoffman, 1974; Humphrey, 1941).

While immigration initiatives such as Operation Wetback were deterrents to illegal immigration, they were not effective in stemming the demand for inexpensive labor. An interesting feature of immigration reform in the 1980s was its focus on employers; rather than continuing to fixate on the number of Mexicans crossing the border, the U.S. Congress placed the burden on employers (Bean, Edmonston, and Passel, 1990; Bean, Vernez, and Keeley, 1989). For example, in 1986 Congress implemented the **Immigration Reform and Control Act (IRCA)** to prohibit employers from hiring illegal immigrants and to establish a monitoring system for employer compliance. Yet a study to examine the progress of the IRCA found that the enforcement of employer sanctions is weak, that few criminal and civil fines have been assessed against employers, and that a low degree of cooperation between employers and the Immigration and Naturalization Service prevails (Fix and Hill, 1990) (see Box 7.4).

Negative Beliefs about Chicanos

As the process of subordinating the indigenous Mexican population in the Southwest began, Mexicans were portrayed in highly negative and stereotyped terms (Reisler, 1996). Many slaveholders, and former slaveholders, who had

---

Box 7.4
Chicano Farmworkers and Pesticides

Chicano farmworkers who pick and harvest America's agricultural crops face tremendous risks from the pesticides sprayed on the crops. In particular, since children make up a large share of the farmworker pool, the risks of cancer and/or learning disability from exposure to pesticides for them are of national concern (Benavides, 1981; Moses, 1993; Taylor, 1973). In an attempt to discuss the health danger of pesticide exposure to farmworkers, the House of Representatives Select Committee on Aging held a series of hearings. Maria Gomez spoke before the Select Committee on Aging (1992:10–11) regarding her experience as a farmworker:

> My name is Maria Gomez. I live in Pharr, Texas. I have been a worker in the field for twenty years.
> First of all, I would like to talk about pesticides in work. Little by little they have been killing us because there is no regulation for these pesticides. Back in 1985, they were already using planes to spray the fields, and I was in my home asleep when one of these planes flew over my home and sprayed, and the spray came into my house.
> The doctors are not trained as to what reaction the pesticide has on the body and what other complications you could have with the medication. The medication that was given to me produced high blood pressure. This was also complicated by the fact that I was picking cantaloupe melon in the field; it is in the heat of the day and the sun also caused some of these side-effects.

The occupational health of Chicano farmworkers is an important concern in large agriculture-producing states like California and Texas. Various resources on the Internet can inform interested students about legislation at the state and federal levels regarding farmworker safety, and about organizations that focus on the health issues of Chicano farmworkers. For example,

- Occupational health issues of farmworkers: www.lib.berkeley.edu/PUBL/guide13.html
- News stories on farmworkers: http://news.pacificnews.org
- Organizations focused on farmworker issues: www.americaspolicy.org/borderlines; and www.sfsu.edu/~cecipp/chavez&farmworkers.htm

settled in the Southwest in the second half of the nineteenth century, portrayed Mexicans as an inferior "race," biologically tainted by Indian blood. The early perception of Mexicans as "greasers" (presumably because some once greased wagon wheels) and as cowardly originated after the defeats of the Mexican Army in the 1880s (Keller, 1985; Meyer, 1978; Ortego, 1973). Those who insisted that Mexicans constituted a distinctive "race" thus based their negative stereotypes on perceived biological traits. As a result, during the first decades of the twentieth century, fear was expressed in Congress and in diatribes by white nativists that the "white race" would be "mongrelized" because of excessive contact with Mexicans, whom many regarded as lazy, shiftless, lawless, and potentially violent (Almaguer, 1994; Stoddard, 1973).

These stereotypes persisted in the second half of the twentieth century (Duran and Bernard, 1973) and still exist today. Males of Mexican origin have been portrayed as "banditos" (fat, lazy, thieving, and immoral) or as overly "macho" and violent street criminals. Mexican American women have been viewed as young seductresses or as passive mothers of violent gang youth and wives of lazy husbands (Mazon, 1984; Paredes, 1977; Simmons, 1973). Consequently, "Mexican-looking" people, Spanish-speaking people, or individuals who speak English with a Spanish accent must endure prejudice about their character, honesty, work ethic, and reliability (Martinez, 1969). These beliefs have justified past discrimination; now they legitimize current treatment of Mexican Americans. Negative beliefs about Mexican-origin persons in the United States are reinforced by the depiction of Mexicans as deviants—especially as criminals or drug dealers—in the mass media (Keller, 1985; Robinson, 1963). The focus by the television and newspaper media, for example, on Mexican Americans and Mexicans carrying the Mexican flag in protests against Proposition 187 in California fueled nativist sentiments in the Anglo population, sentiments that supported the discrimination against Mexican Americans (Aguirre, 1995a).

The Dynamics of Discrimination against Mexican Americans

Economic Discrimination Despite the anti-Mexican sentiment of the 1930s and the resulting repatriation movement, the United States sought assistance from Mexico during the 1940s to fill labor shortages in agriculture created by World War II. In 1942 the United States and Mexico established a labor contract system known as the "Bracero Program." Participating Mexican workers were granted temporary visas and labeled **braceros** (hired hands). The **Bracero Program** operated from 1942 to 1964. During its existence about 5 million Mexican workers entered the U.S. labor force as legal seasonal workers (Garcia, 1980).

The U.S. Congress used the Bracero Program as a way of reducing the number of illegal immigrants from Mexico. By extending the Bracero Program beyond World War II, Congress sought to provide some relief for the struggling U.S. Border Patrol, which had been relatively ineffective in its control of illegal immigration. In 1954, for example, Congress allowed the Border Patrol to launch **Operation Wetback,** which targeted Mexican immigrants who did not have papers identifying them as braceros. Congress gave the Border Patrol blanket authority to stop and search any "Mexican-looking" person. Between 1954 and 1959, the patrol returned 3.8 million people to Mexico (Grebler, Moore, and Guzman, 1970). Operation Wetback reinforced the perception among Mexican Americans that their presence in the United States would always be marginal and tenuous.

Mexican Americans in the Second Half of the Twentieth Century   Comparatively speaking, Mexican immigration between 1970 and 1990 was overshadowed by immigration from Central and South American countries. In contrast, most of the growth of the Mexican American population between 1970 and 1990 was the result of high birthrates of those already living in the United States (McCarthy and Valdez, 1986).

The identification of Mexican Americans as a colonized people has perpetuated discriminatory economic practices. One source of discrimination was built into the wage structure of the Southwest. The availability of Mexican workers created a depressed labor market, providing only limited menial jobs with very few economic rewards and benefits (Romo, 1989).

Economic discrimination against Mexican Americans has been aggravated by a number of circumstances. First, until the 1960s, many labor unions actively discriminated against Mexican Americans (Grebler, Moore, and Guzman, 1970). As a consequence, Mexican American workers were prevented from moving to higher-wage and -skill positions which, in turn, could serve as the springboard for further mobility by subsequent generations—much as union jobs had done for white European immigrants. Today, although institutionalized discrimination has declined, the economy has shifted away from industrial work, thereby reducing the number of better-paying jobs and forcing many Mexican Americans onto the welfare rolls or into service, agriculture, and light-industrial jobs with low wages, little security, and no benefits. Second, the existence of a large unemployed Mexican American labor pool, either just across the border or in urban areas, has depressed wages and kept workers from demanding new benefits—lest they be fired and replaced by more eager and pliant workers. Third, the undocumented citizenship status of many Mexicans has driven down wages because undocumented aliens will rarely protest wages and working conditions—unless they are willing to run the risk of being deported.

The imposition of the English language on Mexican Americans not only contradicted the intent of the Treaty of Guadalupe Hidalgo but also caused a form of economic discrimination (Falcon and Campbell, 1991): Because laws were changed from Spanish to English and court proceedings were conducted only in English, land grants written in Spanish were deemed worthless, and Mexican Americans were forced to rent their own land (Aguirre, 1982). In the Southwest, where landownership became a measure of power, Mexican Americans soon became second-class citizens, displaced from their land and forced into the low-wage labor market.

Chicanos, however, did not always accept economic domination passively. "Social banditry" emerged, a phenomenon that reinforced prejudicial beliefs. For example, Las Gorras Blancas (the White Caps) was a group of Mexican American social bandits around 1887 who protested their loss of land by cutting down fences and burning property acquired by white ranchers—especially those who had obtained land through manipulation of the English-speaking court system (Barrera, 1985). Las Gorras Blancas received widespread support in the Mexican-origin community, but this support was not strong enough to sustain a major challenge to the erosion of Mexican American land rights. Today, protest has diminished with the waves of undocumented workers and illegal aliens. Indeed, all protest invites harsh response in a political climate that is highly receptive to mass deportation of Mexicans who have recently come to the United States.

Some Mexican American protests against economic discrimination have been remarkably effective, however. In the 1960s, Cesar Chavez unionized the farmworkers. Through the use of media, personal charisma, and well-organized boycotts and strikes, Chavez and his followers greatly improved the working conditions and wages of agricultural workers. To this day, United Farm Workers of America operates effectively to improve wages and working conditions—most recently extending its lines of battle to include the dangers of chemical pesticides to both workers and consumers. Yet the limited success of the Mexican American farmworkers has not been matched by Mexican Americans living in cities. Urban Chicanos remain vulnerable to an oversupply of undocumented labor and the actions of law enforcement agencies.

Legal Discrimination   The use of English by the Anglo core as the language of the courts, despite guarantees to the contrary in the Treaty of Guadalupe Hidalgo, has been a crucial step in depriving Chicanos of justice. For example, in an analysis of Mexican American prisoners who had been executed between 1890 and 1986, Aguirre and Baker (1989) note that Mexican American prisoners given capital sentences had lower rates of appeal than either white American or African American prisoners because either they did not understand the legal rights communicated to them in English or they were unable to communicate in English with the court. The inadequate defense of Mexican American prisoners increases their number in the prison population, thus reinforcing prejudicial beliefs that they are criminally prone, or natural "hardcore criminals."

Perhaps more significantly, because many Mexican Americans are subjected constantly to questions about their citizenship, they have been abused by those enforcement agencies—first the **Texas Rangers** and later the **Immigration and Naturalization Service (INS), U.S. Border Patrol,** and state highway police—designed to detect, capture, and deport "Mexicans." Special law enforcement agencies charged with the task of targeting a particular ethnic subpopulation often become vehicles for discriminatory abuse.

The strain between the Mexican American population and the mainstream legal system was established early with the creation of the Texas Rangers. According to Grebler, Moore, and Guzman (1970), the Texas Rangers were created in 1835 as a symbol of white American control over the social progress of the

Texas Rangers drag the dead bodies of Mexican "banditos."

Mexican American. Though their primary purpose was to protect the Texas Republic from the Mexicans, the Texas Rangers spread their law enforcement presence throughout the Southwest. The rangers were given wide latitude in their treatment of Mexicans and Mexican Americans; and, as a consequence, beatings, lynchings, firing squads, and dismemberment were common (McWilliams, 1968). In fact, the general view of many Chicanos and Mexicans is that "every Texas Ranger has some Mexican blood. He has it on his boots" (Murguia, 1975).

Historically, the Texas Rangers in particular were highly abusive of the rights of Mexican-origin families in Texas. As the photograph depicting Texas Rangers dragging the dead bodies of Mexican "banditos" reveals, the response of the Rangers was often severe. Indeed, a common practice was to declare that land-holding Mexican-origin individuals and families were "banditos," leading to their arrest and, equally often, their flight back to Mexico. Since those who fled were afraid to return to their lands, they became delinquent in their taxes with the result that their land was seized for failure to pay taxes. Even if a particular family was not designated as bandits, the indiscriminate violence meted out by the Rangers led many to flee. Moreover, the designation of individuals or families as criminal was often rather arbitrary, and the punishment as depicted in the photograph hardly ever fit the crime (usually quite minor), if there actually had been criminal activity. This combination of actual violence and threats of violence by law enforcement agencies allowed whites to grab the lands of many ranching and farming Mexicans while creating a climate of fear about what law enforcement agents would do next.

Similar to the Texas Rangers, the U.S. Border Patrol was created in 1924 to protect the United States from Mexican infiltration. Congress gave the patrol the authority to apprehend those suspected of illegal entry into the United States and to search persons and property within 25 miles of the U.S.–Mexico border (Grebler, Moore, and Guzman, 1970). The primary target of the Border Patrol became the "wetbacks"—Mexicans who crossed over to the United States by swimming across the Rio Grande. The patrol became ever more oppressive in its efforts to apprehend illegal aliens, cruising the streets in Mexican American neighborhoods and stopping any "Mexican-looking" person who acted in a suspicious manner (McWilliams, 1968). Through its actions the Border Patrol communicated to the Mexican American community their tenuous place in American society.

Two major efforts of the Border Patrol had a significant impact on the Mexican American population. First, the Border Patrol deployed enforcement procedures during the Great Depression of the 1930s to deport Mexicans who were identified as burdens to U.S. society. Second, as noted earlier, it initiated Operation Wetback in 1954 to combat the "wetback invasion" of illegal aliens, allowing as many as 3.8 million Mexicans to be deported without due legal process (Grebler, Moore, and Guzman, 1970). These two efforts by the Border Patrol resulted in the deportation of longtime Mexican American residents of the United States—Mexican American parents and their children born in the United States—along with immigrant Mexicans. These massive efforts served to brand the remaining Chicanos wrongfully as second-class citizens.

Studies of police tactics in small communities have shown that Mexican Americans are victims of prejudicial attitudes, indiscriminate searches and detentions, and high arrest and conviction rates (Aguirre and Baker, 1994; Morales, 1972, 1973; Welch, Gruhl, and Spohn, 1984). The 1970 report of the U.S. Commission on Civil Rights, *Mexican Americans and the Administration of Justice in the Southwest*, identified several discriminatory police actions: use of excessive force, verbal abuse, discriminatory treatment of juveniles arising from the nonnotification of parents, and random stops and searches. A decade later, the papers presented at the National Latino Conference on Law Enforcement and Criminal Justice documented similar patterns of police abuse in the Chicano community (U.S. Department of Justice, 1980). This same pattern of abuse persists today.

Fears about the enforcement of laws regarding citizenship status were demonstrated dramatically in the response to the amnesty provision of the 1986 Immigration Reform and Control Act (IRCA). This provision allowed many undocumented immigrants to apply for legal residence. While over 1.7 million undocumented aliens did apply, this figure was far below the estimated 3 million who were eligible for amnesty. At the same time that amnesty was offered, new restrictions on immigration were imposed, including penalties (not strictly enforced thus far) on employers who give jobs to undocumented workers and screening of welfare applicants for migration and citizenship status. The effectiveness of the IRCA now seems questionable; undocumented Mexicans continue to enter the Southwest, and documented workers and legal citizens are subject to abuse by law enforcement agencies targeting "Mexican-looking" people.

Educational Discrimination   When the Mexican American population was employed primarily as agricultural workers in the early 1900s, practically no formal education was offered to children, and it was well into the 1930s before the lack of schools for Mexican American children was considered a problem. As schools were built, educational segregation prevailed as a result of housing segregation, local ordinances, and gerrymandering of school and district lines. Even as integration increased in the 1970s and 1980s, Mexican American teachers, administrators, and counselors were dramatically underrepresented in school systems.

This near absence of Mexican American school personnel, coupled with powerful local pressure exerted by white Americans, sustained the Anglo-Saxon American school culture, even in predominantly Mexican American neighborhoods and districts. Mexican American children were thus placed in a school system that was alien to their culture. Although children in European ethnic groups often had the same experience in school, they did not have to experience the constant conflict between the Anglo culture of schools and the culture of their homeland just across the border. Chicano children sometimes experience ambivalence at home because of their parents' close ties to their Mexican homeland and customs. They are torn between two cultures—the Mexican culture of their family and the American culture of the school and broader society. Moreover, because the school system has always been designed to "Americanize" immigrants, students living in the two cultures—that of the Mexican homeland across the border and that of their new or temporary place of residence—have often become alienated from schools. Because many Mexican American schoolchildren resisted heavy-handed efforts at Americanization, they were placed in segregated schools, under constant pressure to become "American" (Grebler, Moore, and Guzman, 1970; Rubel, 1966; Sanchez, 1951; San Miguel, 1987). For example, Mexican American children who spoke Spanish in school were often the victims of corporal punishment from teachers (for example, spanking with a paddle); Mexican American children were ridiculed by teachers if they brought burritos or tacos to school for their lunch. In the end, "good" American citizens were those Mexican American children who rejected their ethnic identity and culture.

In the only other major study conducted on the education of Mexican Americans in the Southwest, the U.S. Commission on Civil Rights (1972) found that teachers tended to ridicule Mexican American students who spoke English with an accent, exclude them from classroom discussion, refrain from asking them questions during classroom lessons, and punish them corporally for speaking Spanish in the classroom or on the school playground. The commission (1972:48) concluded its report by stating:

> The basic finding of the Commission's study is that school systems of the
> southwest have not recognized the rich culture and tradition of the Mexican

American students and have not adopted policies and programs which would enable the students to participate fully in the benefits of the educational process.

Contributing to the sense of alienation in the school was the belief that Mexican American children needed only a rudimentary education before they dropped out and entered the low-wage labor pool. This belief, in turn, became a self-fulfilling prophecy: Schools imposing mainstream American culture on Mexican American children, with little sensitivity to or appreciation of their place in two active cultures, caused children to become unhappy in school, which led them to drop out.

The Elementary and Secondary Education Act passed by Congress in 1968 allocated some funds for bilingual education. The hope was that, if Spanish-speaking children could be sensitively introduced to English and the dominant Anglo-Saxon-European culture, their education would prove more effective, thereby reducing dropout rates. Yet very little bilingual education actually ensued in the early 1970s, and only with a 1974 Supreme Court decision *(Lau v. Nichols)* prohibiting schools from ignoring the language difficulties of national-origin minority groups did bilingual education increase. Currently, bilingualism in schools is not universal (Aguirre, 1995b; Macias, 1993). More recent political movements for "English only" as the official language of all Americans, culminating in the passing of formal laws in several states, have slowed the progress of bilingual education (Adams and Brink, 1990; Califa, 1989; Juarez, 1995). For example, in November 1986, voters in California approved Proposition 63 declaring English the official language of the state. The importance of Proposition 63 is that it was approved by the voters in a state with a sizable population of non-English speakers. Other states that have approved English-only amendments and that have large numbers of non-English speakers in the state's population are Arizona, Colorado, and Florida. Moreover, the effectiveness of bilingual education in helping Mexican American children is the subject of intense debate (Imhoff, 1990; Padilla and Benavides, 1992).

As a result of these discriminatory factors, many Mexican American children leave school early. Today only about 50 percent graduate from high school (Aguirre and Martinez, 1993). Without an education in a society that values it, the economic prospects of Mexican American youth are indeed dim (Aguirre and Martinez, 1984).

Political Discrimination   With the signing of the Treaty of Guadalupe Hidalgo in 1848, Mexicans living in the Southwest became citizens of the United States. However, the disregard for the rights granted to Mexicans in the treaty placed the latter in a relatively powerless position. At times, Mexicans responded to their colonization—for example, the mobilization of Las Gorras Blancas, mentioned earlier—but the majority of the Mexican population did not develop a cohesive political identity with which to challenge the Anglo population. By the 1920s, however, Mexican Americans were awakening to the reality that they would be politically powerless as long as the mainstream white population perceived them as foreigners. Thus, first attempts to create a political identity focused on integration into mainstream American society (Garcia and de la

Garza, 1977). For example, in 1921 in San Antonio, Texas, middle-class Mexican Americans formed the **Orden Hijos de America** as a signal to the white population that they were interested in participating in U.S. society—even at the expense of accepting negative stereotypes for their behavior. In 1929, the **League of United Latin American Citizens (LULAC)** was founded in Corpus Christi, Texas, by Mexican Americans who chose to refer to themselves as "Latins" in order to reinforce their loyalty, in the eyes of white Americans, to the United States (Marquez, 1993).

Later, Mexican American veterans returning from World War II encouraged increased political activity in their communities. These war veterans saw that they were returning to a country in which they were regarded as second-class citizens. Two of the most significant political organizations arising out of the efforts of these war veterans during the 1940s and 1950s were the **G.I. Forum** and the **Community Service Organization** (Hero, 1992). The G.I. Forum advocated the rights of Mexican American war veterans, sought representation in Congress, encouraged voter registration, and focused attention on the segregation of schoolchildren. The Community Service Organization was formed in Los Angeles as a community-based organization to encourage Mexican American participation in local, state, and national elections.

Despite these efforts to increase political participation, Mexican Americans remained politically underrepresented in the 1960s. Yet this was a period of awakening in the Mexican American community, as political events stimulated political awareness. For example, the "Viva Kennedy" movement in the 1960 presidential campaign, the land rights movement led by Reyes Tijerina to reclaim land in northern New Mexico, the farmworkers' movement led by Cesar Chavez, and the rise of **La Raza Unida** as a political party in Texas were all manifestations of a newfound political awareness.

The post-1970s signaled a period of political decline among Chicanos, although various radical political parties, such as the La Raza Unida in Texas, formed to wage local political campaigns. As Hero (1992) has noted, most of the political organizations formed before 1970 became involved in moderate political activities—voter registration, legal challenges to redistricting, and lobbying efforts at the local and state levels. As a result, political efforts within the Chicano population have shifted to the development of traditional political techniques with which to forge a unified social, economic, and political identity.

In the 1990s, Mexican Americans were politically underrepresented at all levels of political life: at the local level (mayors, city council members, school board members, county supervisors, sheriffs), at the state level (state legislators, court judges and justices, and governors), and at the national level (congressional representatives, senators, federal judges, and high-level executive appointees) (Hero, 1990). During the 1980s and early 1990s, the Republican White House had little incentive to initiate efforts to redress this imbalance of power because Mexican Americans traditionally vote overwhelmingly for the Democratic party. Some progress has since been made at the local and state levels in those cities and districts where Mexican Americans outnumber non-Latinos, but even here progress is slow. For example, Los Angeles, which is now close to 50 percent Latino, elected its first Chicano representative, Gloria Molina, to the Los Angeles Board of Supervisors in only 1991. Without political power proportionate to their numbers or their needs, Mexican Americans have found it difficult to address other forms of discrimination (Garcia, 1996).

Stratification of the Mexican-Origin Population

As a consequence of the long history of economic, legal, educational, and political discrimination against individuals of Mexican origin, Chicanos are disproportionately overrepresented in lower socioeconomic positions in American society. As a population, they tend to be more successful than African Americans and Native Americans, but they remain disproportionately locked into agricultural labor, urban barrios with high crime and little hope, and jobs that have few benefits and no future.

The negative beliefs about Mexican Americans—prone to criminality, lazy, un-American, uneducable, overly macho or seductive, welfare dependent, gang oriented, and violent—have legitimized discrimination and aroused fears among non-Latinos. Like all institutionalized patterns of discrimination, Mexican Americans are seen as a threat. At one time Europeans saw Mexicans as a military enemy. More recently, those of Mexican origin have posed a series of threats: as a low-wage labor pool that could potentially undercut higher-wage labor, as a political threat to European American ways of speaking and thinking; as a threat to social order arising from criminality and gang activity; and, most recently, as a numerical threat in the Southwest, where they are rapidly becoming a numerical majority. In turn, as the number of Mexican Americans has increased, new threats have emerged and old ones have been intensified. For example, fears about the schools' being overrun, about loss of white control of local politics, about burdens on the welfare and health care systems, about lost jobs for non-Latinos, and about the loss of white mainstream cultural hegemony have all escalated. These fears fuel discrimination, even in an age when antidiscrimination laws are well established. This discrimination can be subtle—housing discrimination, low educational expectations, biased hiring practices—or it can be blatant—English-only political movements and attacks on bilingualism. The result is a population disproportionately stuck in the lower stratum of American society.

PUERTO RICANS

The forces that created the minority population of Puerto Ricans stand in marked contrast to those that forged the Mexican American community. Puerto Ricans became U.S. citizens in 1898, when the United States annexed Puerto Rico, and the **Jones Act of 1917** allowed Puerto Ricans free access to the U.S. mainland long before the island became a commonwealth in 1952. By the 1940s, the U.S. Census indicated that 70,000 Puerto Ricans had settled

Hispanic female in traditional dress dancing in a Puerto Rican Parade in New York City.

on the mainland, but during the 1950s, almost 20 percent of the island's population migrated to the United States (Fitzpatrick, 1987). By 1970, over 800,000 Puerto Ricans were living on the U.S. mainland, 57 percent of whom were island-born. In 1993, the Puerto Rican population on the U.S. mainland was estimated at 2.4 million (U.S. Bureau of the Census, 1994a) and, today, it continues to grow.

Both "push" and "pull" factors have affected the Puerto Rican migration. First, the island's size, 35 miles wide by 100 miles long, has generated problems of overpopulation; many island residents view the United States as a place to improve their living standard—especially with regard to adequate housing and employment (Maldonado-Denis, 1972). Second, conferring full U.S. citizenship rights on island residents meant that Puerto Ricans could enter the United States without having to confront restrictive immigration quotas and harassment by enforcement agencies such as the Border Patrol and the INS. Third, lowered costs for air travel between San Juan and New York City have encouraged movement to and from Puerto Rico.

Identifiability of Puerto Ricans

Like other Latinos, Puerto Ricans are identifiable by their language, although they are far more likely to be bilingual than Mexican Americans. Puerto Ricans are also frequently visible owing to their skin color, categorized by some as "black" if they are particularly dark or as Latino if they have a lighter skin tone.

In fact, because the island of Puerto Rico has been a U.S. colony since the late 1800s, the cultural differences between Puerto Ricans and white Europeans are less critical than are perceived biological differences—a situation that is the reverse for Mexican Americans. Because some perceive Puerto Ricans as members of a distinct "race," discrimination can become intense.

Negative Beliefs about Puerto Ricans

Like Mexican Americans, Puerto Ricans are at times considered lazy, submissive, and immoral, and to have propensities for crime and gang violence (Díaz-Cotto, 1996; Lopez, 1973; Wagenheim, 1973). Because poor Puerto Ricans are concentrated in a few cities, and mostly in the New York City area, they are viewed as a drain on the welfare system and social services. Much like African Americans, they are stigmatized on the basis of their welfare dependency, large families, and lack of stable employment. These beliefs create a sense of threat among some in the white population and legitimize the resulting patterns of discrimination.

The Dynamics of Discrimination against Puerto Ricans

Economic Discrimination   As is the case with Mexican migrants, the timing of Puerto Rican migration to the United States is related to cycles in the U.S. economy. During the 1950s job recruiters would go to the island of Puerto Rico to recruit workers for the increasing number of sweatshops in the garment industry (Morales, 1986). The targets of these recruiting efforts were farmworkers in the sugar cane industry. The inability of Puerto Rico to offer these farmworkers urban jobs caused many to migrate to the United States in hopes of increasing their economic well-being (Ayala, 1996). Despite increased industrialization in Puerto Rico during the 1960s, people continued to leave the island because the Puerto Rican economy failed to absorb the growing population of unemployed farmworkers (Maldonado, 1976; U.S. Commission on Civil Rights, 1976).

Increasing unemployment and factory closings in the United States during the 1970s did not stem the tide of migration from Puerto Rico. At the same time, however, a pattern of return migration from the United States emerged, despite an unemployment rate of 20 percent in Puerto Rico (Morales, 1986). As Bean and Tienda (1987:25) summarize:

> The persistent inability of many island migrants to secure steady employment on the mainland, coupled with the displacement of Puerto Rican workers from declining textile and garment industries in the northeast during the decade of the 1970s, set in motion a return migration process whose scale and duration cannot be predicted.

Puerto Ricans have experienced job discrimination in much the same form as both Mexican Americans and African Americans. Those who lack fluency in English have not performed well on occupational screening tests, even for menial manual jobs. Those with darker skin color have often been excluded from skilled trade and craft unions, which today remain predominantly white. Specifically in New York City, Puerto Ricans have been negatively affected by structural changes in the city's economy away from the kinds of blue-collar jobs that provided an economic and social springboard for white ethnic groups. Similarly, Puerto Ricans who have moved to other northeastern cities have experienced the same shift in occupational structure, resulting in limited job opportunities. Unlike Mexican Americans, who are widely dispersed across urban and rural areas of the Southwest, Puerto Ricans, like urban African Americans, are concentrated in cities with a declining industrial and union base, forcing them to take temporary and low-wage jobs. Moreover, informal discrimination operates, much as it does for urban African Americans, to block Puerto Ricans from higher-wage occupations and to keep them in a large, over-supplied labor pool sustained by the welfare system. Housing discrimination almost equal to that experienced by African Americans (indeed, African American and Puerto Rican neighborhoods are often contiguous or overlapping) and inadequate public transportation limit access to jobs far from their neighborhoods (Mendoza Report, 1978).

Poverty rates for Puerto Ricans exceed those for Mexican Americans; many return to Puerto Rico, even though job prospects are dim there. This mobility creates the same problem for Puerto Ricans as it does for Mexican migrants: Movement back and forth disrupts family life, reduces the chances for building a stable employment history, and inhibits full integration into mainstream American culture, all of which further limit economic opportunities for Puerto Ricans.

Legal Discrimination Puerto Ricans face a U.S. criminal justice system in which "the police are often seen as oppressors who do not speak the language, do not understand the culture, and lack empathy and sensitivity when acting in what otherwise would be a minor or routine situation" (Carro, 1980:369). In 1965, Chicago's Puerto Rican community rioted for three days to protest police brutality (Cruz, 1995). Members of the Puerto Rican community felt that they had been the victims of police brutality since their arrival in Chicago in the 1950s (Padilla, 1987). A detailed study (Sissons, 1979) of how U.S. criminal justice organizations treat Puerto Ricans found the following: Puerto Ricans are victims of language discrimination in the courts; Puerto Ricans are prosecuted for some activities that are legal in Puerto Rico, such as playing the numbers and cockfighting; Puerto Ricans are more likely to be institutionalized than placed on probation; and, compared with white Americans, Puerto Ricans receive longer sentences for the same criminal acts.

Educational Discrimination The relegation of Puerto Ricans to low-wage occupations, along with rampant housing discrimination, has limited their ability to move both within and out of urban environments, especially in New York City. Consequently, many Puerto Rican children attend schools in which they are the majority; this de facto segregation limits educational opportunity (Fitzpatrick, 1987).

The concentration of a large portion of the Puerto Rican population in low-wage seasonal jobs, along with movement to and from the island of Puerto Rico, creates waves of unemployment, thereby increasing the chances that Puerto

Rican youth will drop out of school in order to help the family by obtaining a job in the low-wage seasonal sector. As a consequence, only about 65 percent of Puerto Ricans have completed high school, and only about 13 percent have completed college.

Within the schools, language skills are an issue for many Puerto Rican children. Relatively few teachers and administrators are Latino, so the culture of the school system is unfamiliar. Spanish speakers often are labeled as "learning disabled" on account of limitations in their English-speaking skills and understanding of Euro-American cultural traditions. Language barriers, movement to and from the island, and the need to help support the family in temporary jobs all contribute to a high dropout rate among Puerto Rican youth, and to marginal career opportunities for many.

Political Discrimination   Puerto Ricans are underrepresented in local, state, and national politics. Even in New York City, where it could be expected that their numbers would translate into political power, Puerto Ricans are not prominent in city government, the judicial system, state legislatures, or Congress (Falcon, 1984, 1988). Part of the problem is that only about 20 percent of registered Puerto Ricans vote, a pattern that reflects deeper problems.

One reason for political disempowerment, as Hero (1992:40) notes, is that "Puerto Ricans often do not see themselves as permanent residents on the U.S. mainland—that is, they feel that they will someday return to the island—they do not develop deep political attachments on the mainland." As a consequence, they do not mobilize effective and stable bases of power, despite their large numbers in key cities. A second source of apparent political apathy is that big-city **political machines** traditionally have paid little attention to the Puerto Rican population. Early on these machines tended to be dominated by white Americans of European origin who saw little need to respond to a sojourning ethnic group. Moreover, Puerto Ricans traditionally have been more politically radical and left-wing than politicians in entrenched city machines find acceptable; these politicians typically do not feel the need to respond to extremist political voices. Consequently, as networks of power were being constructed in large cities during the 1930s and 1940s, Puerto Ricans were excluded, and the legacy of this exclusion persists today, even as many political machines are being dismantled (Hardy-Fanta, 1993). Without an established network of patronage appointments and informal ties, it is difficult for Puerto Ricans to exert power proportionate to their numbers. Without political power, it is almost impossible to attack other forms of discrimination in housing, schools, the workplace, and the courts.

Puerto Ricans have reacted to their relative powerlessness on both the island and the mainland. A nationalist movement on the island seeks separation from the United States, but the majority want statehood or the current status quo. While the platforms of the Republican and Democratic parties advocate statehood for Puerto Rico, the fact that it has not been achieved says a great deal about the reluctance of Congress to incorporate formally a Spanish-speaking population into the Union. On the mainland, a number of community service organizations has sought to organize legal services, family counseling, voter registration, political debate, and women's consciousness within the Puerto Rican community. Efforts have also been made to increase attendance in the city school systems (Fitzpatrick, 1987).

In contrast to these quiet organizational efforts, some strategies have been more aggressive. Perhaps fueled by President Johnson's effort in the 1960s to reduce poverty, political militancy grew among Puerto Ricans. One manifestation of this militancy was the emergence of the **Young Lords,** who used community services such as providing hot lunches and patrolling schools for drug dealers to focus attention on the plight of the Puerto Ricans in New York City (Baver, 1984; National Puerto Rican Coalition, 1985). The Young Lords also became involved in nationalist politics that advocated the severing of ties with the island of Puerto Rico.

Despite some of the strides Puerto Ricans have made, they remain politically isolated, even in areas where their numbers are great. Without political power, the ability to overcome social and economic stratification is limited.

Stratification of Puerto Ricans

Discriminatory practices against Puerto Ricans are legitimized by highly prejudicial beliefs. These practices and beliefs are ultimately fueled by a sense of threat among non-Latinos in the cities where Puerto Ricans are concentrated. Some white Americans fear that Puerto Ricans will "dilute" white European culture, that they will have to pay for increased social services to Puerto Ricans who are unemployed and have too many babies, that they will lose their jobs to Puerto Ricans who will work for less, that they will have to share local political power, that they will lose control over the Eurocentric curriculum in schools, and that they will become the victims of gang violence and crime.

Aside from the barriers created by prejudice, Puerto Ricans must battle an economic system that fails to accommodate them. They cannot easily move into middleman minority niches; their numbers are too large in key cities and their entrepreneurial skills are lacking. Without a firm foothold in the economy, the educational system, or the political arena, most Puerto Ricans living in the United States have fallen to the lower stratum of American society, although a sizable minority has moved into the middle and upper-middle classes.

CUBAN AMERICANS

Fewer than 50,000 Cubans lived in the United States before Fidel Castro overthrew the regime of Fulgencio Batista in 1959 (Perez, 1980). This coup led to an exodus of Cubans seeking political asylum during the 1960s. By 1970, over a half million Cubans resided in the United States (Massey, 1983), and by the end of the 1970s, Cuban American communities were firmly established in south Florida. Although the Cuban population grew to slightly over 1 million persons by 1993, it is the smallest segment of the Latino population compared to the Mexican American and Puerto Rican segments. Its relatively small size and concentration in Florida, especially Miami, have created a Cuban American ethnic enclave with an economic base in small business (Wilson and Portes, 1980).

Several factors differentiate the arrival of Cubans in the United States from that of Mexicans and Puerto Ricans. First, the Cubans came to the United States as political refugees from communism; hence, they were perceived as desirable in light of the politics of the cold war. Their arrival stimulated the U.S. Congress to enact legislation creating for Cubans a resettlement program that provided job training, employment assistance, small-business loans, mortgage assistance for home purchases, educational services (such as bilingual instruction), and reimbursement for school districts educating Cuban children (Rogg, 1974).

Second, the majority of early Cuban refugees were from the upper and middle classes, with professional and technical training as well as entrepreneurial skills and resources; these attributes could shield them from menial work and low-status occupations. Although many Cuban refugees did have to accept low-paying jobs on their arrival, the legislation approved by Congress allowed them to retrain so that they could pursue business and professional options. This opportunity enabled many refugees to transport their occupations and professions in Cuba to the United States.

The opportunity for Cuban Americans to gain upward mobility has had visible results: Cuban-owned enterprises in Miami increased from 919 in 1967 to more than 8,000 in 1980; close to one-third of all businesses in Miami are Cuban owned; 75 percent of the workforce in construction is Cuban, and 40 percent of the industry is Cuban owned; Cubans control 20 percent of the banks in Miami, accounting for 16 out of 62 bank presidents and 250 vice presidents (Bach, 1980; Wilson and Portes, 1980). In 1988, five of the ten largest Latino businesses were located in Dade County, Florida (Shorris, 1992).

In 1980, Fidel Castro emptied Cuban prisons and mental hospitals, declaring that "all" who wished to leave Cuba could do so. Thus began the **Mariel boatlifts** from the Cuban port of Mariel to south Florida. An entirely different population of Cubans now entered the United States, a predominantly darker-skinned, poorer, and often unemployable population. The composition of the Cuban population in the United States thus began to shift. Many of these more recent refugees created problems for the U.S. government and for the Cuban community in south Florida in the areas of employment, crime, housing, and welfare services (Boswell, 1985).

Negative Beliefs about Cuban Americans

Cubans were not faced with the level or kind of stereotyping and discrimination that Mexican Americans in the Southwest or Puerto Ricans in the cities of the Northeast encountered. For example, the appropriation of funds by Congress to create bilingual multicultural public instruction in Dade County, Florida, guaranteed that Spanish-speaking Cuban children could maintain their Spanish-language skills while acquiring English-language facility (Pedraza-Bailey and Sullivan, 1979). As a result, Cuban children were not perceived as foreigners in public instruction, as Mexican Americans were in the Southwest.

Cubans were welcome in the United States because they were anti-Castro and anticommunist. Whereas Mexican Americans and Puerto Ricans were treated as territorial minority groups, Cubans were regarded as refugees waiting for the removal of Castro from power. Although many Americans did not initially expect Cubans to remain in the United States, as Cubans assimilated into American society, they were perceived as industrious, intelligent, and law-abiding (Bryce-Laporte, 1982).

The Mariel boatlift in 1980, along with growing recognition that most Cubans are here to stay, has altered many Americans' perceptions of Cubans. Hostility toward Cubans has escalated (Portes and Rumbaut, 1990). Moreover, African Americans in south Florida have begun to discriminate against Cubans as a reaction to their own increasingly subordinate economic status. Many African Americans living in this region are now competing with low-wage labor from Cuba. As the welfare and social services burden of the Mariel boatlifts has reduced benefits for African Americans, the latter's intolerance has increased, culminating in a series of riots in Liberty City and Overtown, Florida.

The Mariel experience may have triggered latent white and manifest African American resentment toward Cubans. Then, as Miami has expanded its image as a bilingual–bicultural community, resentment from the non-Latino community has increased. In November 1980 voters in Dade County approved an English-only ordinance that reversed the policy of official bilingualism established by the Board of County Commissioners in 1973 with the official support of Congress. An analysis of the voting patterns showed that non-Latino white citizens voted overwhelmingly for the English-only ordinance because they wanted to limit the increasing Latinoization of south Florida. Positive perceptions of Cubans as anticommunist refugees have shifted to a more negative belief based on their language as well as their Latino cultural roots, their more recent criminality and violence, and their success in "Latinoizing" south Florida.

The Dynamics of Discrimination against Cuban Americans

Economic Discrimination   The arrival of Cubans as political refugees triggered a response from the federal government that insulated them from many of the economic obstacles faced by Mexican Americans and Puerto Ricans. To the government, the comparatively small numbers of Cubans meant that social and educational programs could focus on mainstreaming Cuban refugees into the U.S. economy. As a result, the Cuban American population has been over-represented in white-collar professions and businesses, while being underrepresented in agricultural and blue-collar occupations (Boswell, 1985).

The entrepreneurial skills of many Cuban refugees allowed for the creation of an ethnic enclave—"Little Havana" in Florida—that facilitated the economic transition of newly arrived Cuban refugees (Wilson and Portes, 1980). The emergence of Cuban-owned firms, especially in Dade County, Florida, provided employment opportunities for other Cuban refugees. These opportunities made it possible to stratify Cuban refugees as employers or low-wage earners, with the result that Cuban-owned firms reproduced in microcosm the stratification evident in pre-Castro Cuba. Indeed, as in the pre-Castro era, Cubans in lower-paying jobs have been subject to the exploitive economic practices of entrepreneurial Cuban business owners.

The arrival of the **Marielitos** in the United States in 1980 added a new stratum to the socioeconomic structure of the Cuban American population. The majority of the Marielitos were single, black, adult males with a criminal background. The arrival of the Marielitos in Dade County was so dramatic that the county's unemployment rate jumped from 5 percent to 13 percent (Boswell, 1985). The unwelcome reception given to the Marielitos by the American public was reinforced by the Cuban American community in Miami as well. Like other dark-skinned minority groups in the United States, the Marielitos were exploited as a cheap-labor pool that could be hired and fired at will.

Legal Discrimination   The comparatively high socioeconomic status of the early Cuban migrants, the relative recency of their arrival in the United States, and their image as anti-Castro, anticommunist political refugees have limited their involvement with the U.S. legal system. The majority of the Cuban American population resides in an economic and social niche that insulates them from unnecessary contact with law enforcement agencies. There are, however, two exceptions to this situation, both centering on the Marielitos.

First, the 1980 Mariel boatlifts created a logistical problem: Where were an estimated 125,000 Cuban refugees to be housed? The Carter administration responded by using Eglin Air Force Base as a processing center for the Marielitos (Boswell, 1985). The majority of the Marielitos regarded their move to Eglin as an attempt by the president to institutionalize them, a reminder of their status as prisoners in Cuba. As a result, soon after their arrival in Eglin, the Marielitos rioted and federal troops were called in. The Marielitos were the first segment of the Cuban American population to come into conflict with U.S. law enforcement agents in much the same way as the unwanted Mexican immigrants.

Second, the arrival of the Marielitos in Miami brought unexpected social problems to the Cuban community. A large number of the Marielitos had been Cuban prisoners because they were drug addicts (Page, 1980). Not surprisingly, their arrival increased the incidence of drug use in Miami's Cuban population. Since the majority of the Marielitos were black, the African American community in Miami perceived them as a threat to the positive relationship it had forged with law enforcement agencies; if crime-prone and drug-using Marielitos were mistaken for African Americans, the latter would suffer at the hands of law enforcement agencies. As a result, African Americans pushed for a distinction between Marielitos and themselves in treatment by the law—a pressure that only increased discrimination against newly arrived Marielitos.

Educational Discrimination   In contrast to the prejudice and discrimination experienced by Mexican Americans and Puerto Ricans in the educational system,

Cubans were offered educational programs as a vehicle for assimilation into U.S. society. Hence, the education of Cubans in the United States has not been associated with the production and perpetuation of inequality. Indeed, the average level of education attained by the Cuban American population is closer to that of the non-Latino white population.

The recent **"English as the official language" movement** has been particularly strong in south Florida, changing the receptiveness of schools to bilingual and special programs for Cubans at the very time that the most needy members of this population—the Marielitos—entered the educational system (Castro, Haun, and Roca, 1990). Consequently, more recent, poor, and black Cuban immigrants are likely to experience the same types of educational discrimination as other Latino migrants.

Political Discrimination   People in the initial waves of Cuban refugees to the United States were members of the professional, entrepreneurial, and/or upper classes in Cuba, who, like most people in affluent social strata, were politically conservative. Their self-perception as "exiles" and their commitment to preserving the class distinctions eliminated by Fidel Castro caused a majority to align themselves with the conservative politics of the Republican party (Torres, 1988). According to Hero (1992), the Reagan administration was instrumental in promoting conservative politics in the Cuban American population. For example, the Cuban community lobbied for the creation of Radio Jose Marti and for aid to the Nicaraguan contras. The Cuban community has also exhibited its ability to serve as a voting bloc for Republican party candidates to the Florida state legislature. Moreover, in local community politics, Cubans have been highly successful in securing seats on city councils and school boards. Such success, however, has caused political backlash from African Americans, who overwhelmingly vote against Cuban candidates, and, increasingly, from white Americans who are also threatened by Cuban political success.

With the fall of communism as a cold war threat, and with the social and economic problems associated with more recent Cuban immigrants, the success of Cuban Americans in politics may begin to level off. Also, African and white Americans may feel threatened by Cuban politicians as national politics moves away from its fifty-year obsession with containing communism. Thus, despite the success of Cubans in the political arena, political discrimination against them may well increase over the next decade.

Stratification of Cuban Americans

If there is a success story among the Latino population, it is Cuban Americans. Their entry into this country was a positive one. The U.S. government created social, educational, and occupational programs that allowed them to transfer their social and economic positions in Cuba to the United States. They lead other Latinos in educational, economic, and occupational attainment. In some cases, the Cuban American population has outpaced the non-Latino white population. Despite the recency of their arrival in the United States, most Cuban

Americans enjoy a privileged position in U.S. society relative to other Latinos (Nelson and Tienda, 1985; Rodriguez, 1992). Stratification is more evident *within* the Cuban community, however. Recent immigrants are more likely to be black, less skilled, poor, unemployable, drug addicted, and criminal; like their counterparts within the African American community, they may eventually constitute a volatile subpopulation. Those who are willing and able to work may be exploited by their employers, as is the case with many other Latinos and African Americans. Thus, although Cubans as an aggregate are highly successful, considerable inequality and stratification exist within the Cuban population (Perez, 1986).

As African Americans and white Americans feel more threatened by the Cuban American presence, discrimination against, and stratification of, Cubans are likely to increase. The English-only movement in Dade County, Florida, is perhaps a harbinger of a new, more intense wave of institutionalized discrimination.

SUMMARY

With the Spanish conquest of Mexico, Central and South America, and parts of the Caribbean islands, Spanish-speaking populations surrounded the English-speaking Anglo-Saxon core in the United States. Inevitably they were to come into conflict, with the Anglo-Saxon core winning all of the important confrontations. The consolidation of formerly Spanish territories as part of the United States (or at least as part of its sphere of influence), coupled with subsequent patterns of immigration and settlement from formerly Spanish-controlled areas, has created a highly dynamic and fluid situation as the Latino population has become America's largest minority. Most of this large Latino minority is of Mexican origin, with significant numbers of Puerto Ricans, Cubans, and both Central and South Americans.

The largest group in the Latino population, Mexican Americans, lags behind Puerto Ricans and Cuban Americans in educational attainment, income, and occupational status. Chicanos are thus at the bottom of the Latino population, whereas Cubans are at the top and Puerto Ricans somewhere in between. Rank in resource distribution and stratification is the result of intense and institutionalized discrimination against those of Mexican origin, somewhat less severe discrimination against those from the island of Puerto Rico, and more favorable treatment of early anti-Castro Cuban refugees, with growing discrimination against those who have immigrated recently.

Among Mexican Americans, retention of the Spanish language, as well as other cultural traits, sustains their identifiability, making them easy targets of discrimination since the Mexican-American War. Continued immigration, both legal and illegal, from Mexico has maintained this identifiability, which has been codified into negative stereotypes ranging from portrayals of males as "banditos" and, later, as macho and violent street criminals to images of young women as seductresses and of mature women as overbreeding, passive mothers of street gang members, and the accepting wives of lazy husbands or macho men. These beliefs help sustain discrimination in jobs and wages in both rural and urban settings as well as in every facet of life. They have legitimated mal-treatment by the legal system since the early betrayals of the Treaty of Guadalupe Hidalgo by Anglos. The educational system fails to recognize the special learning problems of Spanish-speaking youths who are members of a culture that has not fully abandoned its original home or accepted its new home. In politics a wide variety of tactics, from gerrymandering to intimidation by the Immigration and Naturalization Service and the Border Patrol, have kept Mexican Americans disenfranchised relative to their numbers in the popula-tion. Such patterns of discrimination are sustained by widespread fears among non-Latinos about the rapidly growing size of the Spanish-speaking population and what this will mean for Anglo culture and institutions.

For Puerto Ricans, who became U.S. citizens through the annexation of Puerto Rico and the Jones Act, which gave them free access to the mainland, dis-crimination has taken a pattern somewhat different from the discrimination against the Mexican-origin population. Puerto Ricans are visible not only be-cause of their language and culture but also because a significant portion of the population bears the dark skin of their African origins. For both segments of the Puerto Rican population, negative stereotypes of them as lazy, sneaky, clan-nish, crime-prone, violent, and welfare dependent have been used to justify discrimination in jobs, in treatment by law enforcement, and in schools. At least 35 percent of the over-25 age groups have not completed high school. In politics they are underrepresented even in those areas with very high numbers and con-centrations of Puerto Ricans. In housing they are victimized by high segregation. Because Puerto Ricans continue to be concentrated in the urban Northeast, they are perceived as a threat to non-Latino whites in this region of the country, thereby guaranteeing continued patterns of discrimination.

For Cuban Americans, who have been treated as desirable anticommu-nist refugees of the Castro regime in Cuba rather than as undesirable immi-grants, discrimination has been much less intense. Since the early waves of Cubans were upper and middle class with technical, professional, and busi-ness skills, they were not subjected to the same intense stereotypes as were other Latinos. However, the more recent arrival of waves of poor and often criminal Cubans, many of whom are black, to the mainland has escalated the level of discrimination. With the recognition by many, especially those in south Florida, that Cubans are here to stay, negative stereotyping much like that experienced by Puerto Ricans is beginning to accelerate, foretelling fu-ture discrimination.

Until the last decade, Cubans were able to prosper economically, often with the help of programs sponsored by the federal government, and to become politically successful and powerful in south Florida. Their success and refugee status shielded them from entanglement in the legal or law enforcement sys-tem. Educationally they achieve at a rate higher than non-Latino whites. But as poorer Cubans have entered the country, they have brought many of the prob-lems of the poor—from crime to drug abuse—and this shift has changed the perception of Cubans in the present and, perhaps, in the future.

Increasingly, all Latinos are seen as a threat because their numbers are increasing relative to the European-American stock. This threat has reinvigorated old prejudicial beliefs against Latinos and legitimated new patterns of discrimination in schools, in the activities of law enforcement agencies, in politics, and in the job markets for low-skilled workers. Mexican-origin people suffer the most discrimination and prejudice because they are the largest, fastest-growing, and, hence, the most threatening of the Latino ethnic groups. But recent Cuban refugees still suffer a great deal of discrimination and prejudice within and outside the Cuban community, and unskilled Puerto Ricans have a difficult struggle in the financially burdened cities of the Northeast. In the near future, then, Latinos will come to rival African Americans for the dilemma they pose to the Anglo-Saxon core in a free and democratic society that values equality of opportunity.

POINTS OF DEBATE

As the size of the Latino population grows and as white ethnic Americans approach being a bare majority of the total population, the sense of threat among non-Latino Americans will increase, potentially setting into motion new and intense forms of discrimination. On the other hand, the very size of the Latino population by the midpoint of the twenty-first century will serve the Latinos as a resource for economic and political power against the discrimination that ensues from the threat. In any case, the next fifty years will pose a number of volatile points of debate.

1. Can English be maintained as the ascendant language, or are parts of the country to become bilingual? Non-Latino Americans feel intensely that all immigrants must learn English, but because Latino immigrants remain close to their country of origin, Spanish remains the language of everyday use among large numbers of Latinos. Should this use of language and other non-Anglo cultural traits be suppressed? Or are Americans going to have to change their views about bilingualism in America? In either case, debate and action will be intense.

2. Because the Latino population will be so large and, eventually, a clear majority of the population in the Southwest, the patterns of assimilation evident for other minority populations may not occur. Latinos may be able to carve out a social niche within the Anglo-Saxon core, maintaining their own economic, cultural, educational, and religious institutions. The intensity of feeling in the Southwest about language will thus be magnified many times over, as Anglos seek to stop this potential subsociety in America. What will happen? Violence? Mass exodus of non-Latinos? Adjustment and accommodation of non-Latinos to a dual culture and society? Or will this confrontation of lifestyle and culture be avoided? There are no clear answers to these questions, indicating that ferment and debate will be intense—as is already evident.

3. Americans do not feel that they "owe" Latinos compensation for past acts of discrimination in the same way that they owe African and Native Americans. This lack of "collective guilt," coupled with rising fears about the Latinoization of American culture, will pose a real problem for non-Latino Americans who resent with ever greater intensity the invasion of their territory, institutions, and cultural patterns. How is this resentment to be mitigated? Can it be reduced? Or are non-Latino Americans and Latinos on a collision course? And what will be the outcome of this collision as it intensifies from the political posturing of today to the dramatically escalated rhetoric and potential Latino political empowerment of tomorrow?

KEY TERMS/KEY LEGISLATION

Bracero Program, 206
braceros, 206
Community Service Organization, 213
"English as the official language"
   movement, 223
G.I. Forum, 213
identifiability, 201
Immigration and Naturalization
   Service (INS), 208
Immigration Reform and Control
   Act (IRCA), 204
Jones Act of 1917, 214
La Raza Unida, 213

Latino, 188
League of United Latin American
   Citizens (LULAC), 213
Mariel boatlifts/Marielitos,
   220, 222
Operation Wetback, 207
Orden Hijos de America, 213
political machines, 218
Texas Rangers, 208
Treaty of Guadalupe Hidalgo
   (1848), 203
U.S. Border Patrol, 208
Young Lords, 219

 Visit our text-specific website at www.mhhe.com/aguirre7e for valuable resources for both students and instructors.

CHAPTER 8

Asian and Pacific
Island Americans

Early immigrations to the United States came from the east across the Atlantic Ocean, mostly from northern Europe. As the European-origin population spread across the continent in the eighteenth and early nineteenth centuries, the remaining indigenous populations of Native Americans in the Midwest and West were displaced and confined to reservations. Conflict with Spanish-speaking populations soon ensued, culminating in the Treaty of Guadalupe Hidalgo and the eventual annexation of states in the Southwest and West into the territorial borders of the United States. Events in the eastern and southern portions of the emerging nation, however, dominated ethnic dynamics in America during the nineteenth century, as new waves of European immigrants came to America and as tensions over slavery and the growing North–South split led to the Civil War and its aftermath.

With the discovery of gold in California and the ensuing gold rush, people from lands west of the Pacific Ocean side of the North American continent began to immigrate to America in significant numbers. The first new immigrants came from China and Japan in the late nineteenth and early twentieth centuries, and because of their distinctive eye fold and unique non-European culture, they were easily identified as "different" and subject to discrimination. Somewhat later, Filipinos and Koreans also began to immigrate. The former often came through Hawaii, where they had performed agricultural labor. These Asian "hordes," as they were often perceived, posed threats that fueled prejudice and discrimination.

Despite the fact that these Asian immigrants came from widely different cultures, they first were lumped together as "Asians" and later, by the U.S. Census Bureau, as "Asian/Pacific Islanders," with the result that data on diverse subpopulations of Asians and Pacific Islanders cannot always be broken down by more specific ethnicities. Today, the U.S. Census Bureau distinguishes between Asians and Pacific Islanders, but even with this needed separation, it must be remembered that these two categories encompass very diverse subpopulations that have distinctive histories and cultures. And, with more recent immigrations from Asia and the Pacific Islands over the last decades, this diversity of cultures has only increased. Still, because Asians and Pacific Islanders are often treated by the majority population *as if* they come from two cultures, the new distinction between Asians and Pacific Islanders is not wholly arbitrary. However, some subpopulations that are counted as Asian, such as those from India and Pakistan, do not have the eye fold distinguishing other Asian subpopulations; and indeed, these two ethnic groups are more likely to experience discrimination typical of Arab Americans, as is explored in Chapter 9. Thus, problems remain in the current Census Bureau categories, but we have to work with them.

Since the Pacific Islander population in the United States is very small and only recently broken out from the larger "Asian" category, we have more data on the dynamics of discrimination against Asian Americans. Thus, we devote most of this chapter to Asians, especially the largest subpopulations, but we conclude with a short section on Pacific Islanders that, as more data become available, we will be able to expand on in the years to come.

ASIAN AMERICANS

Praised for their industriousness, heralded for their educational attainments, and lauded for their economic success, Asian Americans are often viewed as the **model minority.** Indeed, most Americans believe that the success of Asian Americans stems from a combination of industriousness and avoidance of discrimination (McQueen, 1991). But the history of Asian immigration tells a very different story, and the persistence of negative stereotypes and acts of discrimination reflect past patterns that persist today, though in a more subtle and muted form (Matthaei and Amott, 1990; Takaki, 1989).

The first Asians to arrive in the United States in significant numbers were the Chinese, who initially worked in the gold mines of California in the 1850s and, later, in building the transcontinental railroad. By the early twentieth century, the Chinese were joined by increasing numbers of Japanese, Filipinos, Koreans, and Asian Indians. In the 1920s, this immigration decreased dramatically in reaction to a series of highly restrictive immigration laws enacted by the U.S. Congress that targeted immigrants from Asian countries. Later, in the period after World War II, these laws were liberalized, opening the door to a new wave of Asian immigration (Hing, 1993).

Asians made up 1.5 percent of the U.S. population in 1980, 4.2 percent in 2000, and almost 4 percent in 2008. Nearly 60 percent of the Asian American population is composed of Chinese, Filipinos, and Asian Indians, followed respectively by Vietnamese and Koreans (see Table 8.1).

The growth of the Asian American population between 2005 and 2008 is summarized in Table 8.2. Between 2005 and 2008 the Asian population grew by almost one million persons. From the data in the table, the Chinese population has grown the most, and the Japanese population has grown the least.

As noted earlier, people tend to lump Asians together because of their physical appearance, but each subpopulation has a distinct language, culture, and organizational pattern. Indeed, much of the subtle discrimination against Asians comes from the failure to recognize and appreciate their differences. Yet for our purposes it is useful to consider Asian Americans together in order

TABLE 8.1 Asian Subpopulations as a Percentage of Total Asian Population in the United States, 2008

Asian Subpopulation	Percentage of Total Asian Population	Percentage of U.S. Population*
Chinese	22.4%	0.99%
Filipino	18.1	0.80
Asian Indian	18.6	0.67
Vietnamese	10.68	0.47
Korean	10.02	0.39
Japanese	5.29	0.21
Cambodian	1.39	0.06
Hmong	1.28	0.05
Laotian	1.19	0.05
Pakistani	2.09	0.08
Thai	1.04	0.04
Other Asian	4.30	0.17

Source: 2008 American Community Survey.

TABLE 8.2 Growth of the Asian American Population by Major Ethnic Group, 2005–2008

Asian Ethnic Group	2005	2008	Change between 2005 and 2008
Total Asian Population	12.47*	13.41	0.94
Chinese	2.80	3.00	0.20
Asian Indian	2.32	2.50	0.18
Filipino	2.28	2.43	0.15
Vietnamese	1.42	1.43	0.01
Korean	1.25	1.34	0.09
Japanese	0.83	0.71	–0.12
Other Asian	0.27	0.58	0.31

*In thousands.
Sources: 2005, 2008 American Community Survey.

to describe what they all have in common—the experience of being victims of negative stereotyping, prejudice, and discriminatory practices directed at Asians living in America.

Resource Shares of Asian Americans

Impoverishment of Asian Americans   Table 8.3 summarizes the poverty rates for various Asian subpopulations. Overall, the rate of poverty for these Asian subpopulations is about the same as for the U.S. population as a whole, and considerably higher than that of non-Latino whites. More interesting, however, are the wide variations in the poverty rates for different Asian subpopulations. The lowest rate of poverty is for Filipino-origin Americans. The highest rates

TABLE 8.3 Poverty Rates for Asian Subpopulations, 2000

Asian Subpopulation	Percentage Who Are Poor
Chinese	13.5%
Filipino	6.3
Asian Indian	9.8
Vietnamese	10.9
Korean	16.0
Japanese	14.8
Cambodian	29.3
Hmong	37.8
Laotian	18.5
Pakistani	16.5
Thai	14.4
Other Asian	15.6
Total Asian population*	**12.6%**
Total U.S. population*	**12.4%**
Non-Latino white*	**7.4%**

*Figures vary slightly from Table 1.1 (p. 15) because the percentages here are from 2000 rather than 2008.
Source: U.S. Bureau of the Census, 2004d, Figure 14, p. 17.

are among Cambodian and Hmong refugee subpopulations who came to the United States in the aftermath of the Vietnam War. If only by poverty rates alone, it is clear that different Asian subpopulations have been subject to varying degrees and different kinds of discrimination. What is also clear is that the image of Asians as universally successful is contradicted by the different poverty rates and also by the fact that for most subpopulations of Asians, the poverty rate is higher than the national average of 12.4 percent poor.

Income of Asian Americans Table 8.4 summarizes the median household incomes of various Asian subpopulations. Overall, Asian household income is the highest in the United States, over $10,000 more than the average for all U.S. households and some $7,000 more than in non-Latino white households. But this overall rate hides the wide range of household income among different Asian ethnicities. As might be expected from the data on poverty, Cambodian and Hmong report the lowest median household income, which is about the same as Latino, Native American, and African American household income. Vietnamese, Laotian, Korean, and Thai incomes hover around the average for the total U.S. population. Chinese, Japanese, Filipino, Asian Indian, and Pakistani incomes are well above the national average, and Asian Indian and Japanese incomes are considerably higher than the non-Latino white median household income. Indeed, according to Wellner's (2002) analysis, Asian Americans have become the wealthiest ethnic group in the United States, with an estimated spending power of $300 billion per year. It is necessary to emphasize, however, that only *some* Asian Americans are wealthy, just as is the case for white Americans.

TABLE 8.4 Median Household Income for Asian Subpopulations, 1999–2000

Asian Subpopulation	Median Household Income
Chinese	$60,058
Filipino	65,189
Asian Indian	70,708
Vietnamese	47,103
Korean	47,624
Japanese	70,849
Cambodian	35,621
Hmong	32,384
Laotian	43,542
Pakistani	50,189
Thai	49,635
Other Asian	50,733
All Asian households*	**$63,642**
All U.S. households*	**$48,451**
Non-Latino white households*	**$52,375**

*Figures for these categories are from 2006; hence, they are not exactly comparable to the figure for Asian subpopulations in 1999–2000. However, since the median household incomes for all subpopulations declined during the recession of 2000–2001, they are roughly comparable to incomes in the years 1999–2000.
Sources: U.S. Bureau of the Census, 2004d, Figure 13, p. 16; U.S. Bureau of the Census, 2004a.

There are several reasons for the higher incomes, on average, of Asian households. One is that Asians as a whole are better educated than the general population, including non-Latino whites (see Table 8.6); and these educational credentials translate into better-paying jobs. Another reason for the higher incomes is that a higher proportion of spouses work in Asian households. Still another reason is that Asian children tend to live longer with their parents and contribute income to the household. And finally, Asian families are, on average, larger than the U.S. average, with more wage earners contributing to household income (Cabezas, Shinagawa, and Kawaguchi, 1990; Suzuki, 1989; U.S. Commission on Civil Rights, 1980, 1988). For example, for the most recent data available (DeNavas-Walt, Cleveland, and Roemer, 2001; U.S. Bureau of the Census, 1999a), 63 percent of Asian households have two or more income earners, compared to less than 60 percent for white Americans. Still, the larger number of individuals contributing to household income cannot explain, alone, the income differences between Asians and non-Asians. Education, entrepreneurial skills, economic capital, and other resources of Asian families and communities are also responsible for this income differential.

Occupational Distribution of Asian Americans As a whole, Asians are more likely than the U.S. workforce as a whole, including non-Latino whites, to hold managerial and professional jobs. The bottom of Table 8.5 summarizes the differences among Asians, the total labor force, and the non-Latino white labor

TABLE 8.5 Occupational Distribution of Asian Subpopulations, 2000

Asian Subpopulation	Percentage of Adults Employed in:					
	Management/ Professional	Service	Sales/ Office	Construction/ Extraction/ Maintenance	Production/ Transport/ Materials Moving	Fishing/ Farming/ Forestry
Chinese	52.3%	13.9%	20.8%	2.6%	10.4%	0.1%
Filipino	38.2	17.5	28.1	4.1	11.5	0.5
Asian Indian	59.9	7.0	21.4	2.1	9.4	0.2
Vietnamese	26.9	19.3	18.6	5.9	28.8	0.6
Korean	38.7	14.8	30.2	3.9	12.2	0.2
Japanese	50.7	11.9	26.9	4.3	5.9	0.4
Cambodian	17.8	15.9	23.5	5.5	36.8	0.5
Hmong	17.1	15.6	20.6	4.5	41.7	0.4
Laotian	13.4	14.5	19.1	5.8	46.6	0.5
Pakistani	43.5	8.4	30.3	3.6	14.1	0.1
Thai	33.4	25.9	22.6	3.6	14.3	0.2
Other Asian	39.8	15.6	27.7	4.1	12.6	0.3
Total Asian labor force	**44.6%**	**14.1%**	**24.4%**	**3.6%**	**13.4%**	**0.3%**
Total U.S. labor force	**33.6%**	**14.9%**	**26.7%**	**9.4%**	**14.6%**	**0.7%**
Non-Latino white	**36.6%**	**12.8%**	**27.2%**	**9.6%**	**13.2%**	**0.5%**

Sources: U.S. Bureau of the Census, 2004d, Figure 11, p. 14; U.S. Bureau of the Census, 2005c, Table 5, p. 6.

force in various occupational categories. Asians are clearly overrepresented in the management/professional categories and underrepresented in the construction/extraction/maintenance category, and in other categories they are distributed at about the same rate as the total labor force. Again, there is wide variation by specific subpopulations. Those with Chinese, Japanese, Asian Indian, and Pakistani ancestry are much more likely than the total population to be in the management/professional occupations, whereas those of Vietnamese, Cambodian, Hmong, and Laotian ancestry are much less likely than the general population to be in management/professional jobs. Filipinos, Koreans, Thai, and other Asians hold these higher-paying jobs at about the same level as non-Latino whites. According to occupational data for 2007, Asians have much greater rates of employment in management/professional jobs than other minorities, particularly Latinos, African Americans, Native Americans, and Pacific Islanders (see Table 1.4 on page 19).

The occupational success of the Asian American population, especially compared to other minority groups such as African Americans and Latinos, needs to be qualified, however. Hurk and Kim (1989) argue that the occupational accomplishments of Asian Americans create a "false consciousness" among Asian Americans that disguises their patterns of underemployment—that is, Asian Americans accept, to a degree, the stereotype that they are successful in light of their visibility in high-status occupations (doctors, engineers, scientists, entrepreneurs, etc.). As a result, they develop a false consciousness in believing that Asian Americans are more successful than they are unsuccessful (Gee, 1993; Wong et al., 1998). Yet, despite their representation in high-status occupations, most Asian Americans hold jobs in the *lower levels* of these professions (Duleep and Sanders, 1992; Osako, 1984; Sue, Zane, and Sue, 1985). For example, the placement of Asian Americans at lower levels in their professions has resulted in a noticeable pattern according to Ronald Takaki (1996:43): "This very image can produce a reinforcing pattern: Asian-American professionals often find they 'top out,' reaching a promotional ceiling early in their careers."

For example, in a study of Asian workers in management positions in local, state, and federal government agencies in the San Francisco area, Amado Cabezas found that most of the Asian American workers were at the bottom of the managerial tier, indicating that Asian Americans had lower salaries than their white counterparts (U.S. Commission on Civil Rights, 1979). Similarly, in a study of managers in U.S. corporations, "Asian descent" was found to have a negative effect on becoming a manager (Chiu, 1994:1089):

> The probability that an Asian man will become a manager is seven to eleven percentage points lower than for a white man. The study was adjusted for English-proficiency and was limited to American-born Asian Americans, so that language proficiency and cultural barriers could not account for these findings.

Thus, because of a "glass" or "bamboo" ceiling, many Asian Americans have not fully benefited from their mobility into the professional and management ranks (Equal Employment Opportunity Commission, 1985). Pat Chew (1996:37) has noted that even in occupations, such as law school faculty, where Asian Americans are relatively invisible, they find themselves channeled into certain professional roles because they are perceived as "foreigners, inarticulate, and nonadversarial."

The notion of a **glass or bamboo ceiling** refers to the perception held by Asian Americans that, because of negative stereotypes about them, they are limited, despite being qualified, for advancement in professional occupations. Some of these negative stereotypes are rooted in the perceptions that Asian Americans are unaggressive, have poor and/or limited communication skills in English, and are too technically oriented to be effective managers (Nguyen, 1993). As Chiu (1994:1090) has noted: "Asian Americans continue to be denied employment opportunities simply because they speak English with a foreign accent."

The overall occupational success of the Asian American population has reinforced the image of them as the model minority, an image that belies their difficulty in integrating fully in the professional world, especially its upper echelons (Kang, 1996; Thomas, 1995). Acceptance of the image by both Asian Americans and white Americans also creates the illusion that the entire Asian American population is not subject to social problems and does not need help

Asian Americans have achieved visibility in high-status occupations (such as doctors, engineers, scientists, and entrepreneurs), creating the stereotype of success. However, most Asian Americans hold jobs in the lower levels of these professions, held back by a glass or bamboo ceiling.

from either the state or the federal government (Hu, 1989; Lee, 1993). As Crystal (1989:405) has noted:

> In reality, the "model minority" myth has obscured many serious problems in the Asian community and has been used to justify omitting Asian Americans from federal funding and some special minority programs. Moreover, the Asian-American success story has been turned into a weapon against other minorities by persons who deny the existence of racism in America.

Educational Attainment of Asian Americans   Asian Americans are generally considered the most educated ethnic subpopulation in the United States, although Jewish and Arab Americans also reveal very high levels of educational attainment. As Table 8.6 documents, 44.1 percent of Asians, on average, have a college degree or more compared to only 24.4 percent of the total population and about 38 percent of non-Latino whites (U.S. Bureau of the Census 2003a, 2003b). The educational attainment is not only greater than for non-Latino whites, but even more dramatically so compared to other ethnic subpopulations: Only around 13 percent of Latinos, 17 percent of African Americans, 13 percent of Native Americans, and 49 percent of Asians fall into the category of college degree or more (see Table 1.5 on page 20). If the data are broken out by postgraduate

TABLE 8.6 Educational Attainment of Asian Subpopulations, 25 Years Old and Older, 2000

Asian Subpopulation	Less than High School	Percentage Who Have:		
		High School Graduate Only	Some College/ Associate's Degree	College Degree or More
Chinese	23.0%	13.2%	15.8%	48.1%
Filipino	12.7	14.9	28.6	43.8
Asian Indian	13.3	10.3	12.5	63.9
Vietnamese	38.1	19.1	23.4	19.4
Korean	13.7	21.6	20.9	43.8
Japanese	8.9	22.2	27.1	41.9
Cambodian	53.3	18.8	18.6	9.2
Hmong	59.6	16.1	16.8	7.5
Laotian	49.6	24.4	18.3	7.7
Pakistani	18.0	12.9	14.8	54.3
Thai	20.9	17.5	23.1	38.6
Other Asian	19.1	16.3	23.2	41.4
All Asians	**19.6%**	**15.8%**	**20.5%**	**44.1%**
Total U.S. population	**19.6%**	**28.6%**	**27.4%**	**24.4%**

Source: U.S. Bureau of the Census, 2004d, Figure 9, p. 12.

degree, 20 percent of Asians have graduate degrees, compared to around 11 percent of non-Latino whites, 6 percent of African Americans, 4 percent of Native Americans, 4 percent of Latino, and 4 percent of Pacific Islanders (2010 *Statistical Abstract*, Table 36).

As is the case with other resources, educational attainment varies by specific Asian ethnicities. Chinese, Asian Indians, Koreans, Japanese, Filipinos, Pakistani, Thai, and "other" Asians have college degrees or more at about the median or above for Asian Americans as a whole, whereas Vietnamese, Cambodians, Hmong, and Laotians fall considerably below the Asian median as well as the median for the total U.S. population. Thus, the aggregate figures conceal the large differences in educational attainment among diverse Asian subpopulations—with the extremes being Asian Indians at 64 percent receiving college or graduate degrees and only 7.5 percent of Hmong doing so. Variations among specific Asian subpopulations in educational attainment are equally dramatic at the other end of achievement: percentage of ethnic groups with less than a high school diploma. Of the Asian subpopulations listed in Table 8.6, only half of these populations meet or do better than the national average of 19.6 percent of adults who do not possess a high school degree. And some dramatically exceed this figure: 38 percent of Vietnamese, 53 percent of Cambodians, 59 percent of Hmong, and 49 percent of Laotians do not have high school degrees. These figures are matched only by Latinos. Some of this variation can be accounted for by the nature of these subpopulations, many of them displaced rural residents of nations ravaged by the Vietnam War. Still, the wide variations in educational attainment add an important point of qualification to the high levels of educational achievement evident for the total Asian American population (see Box 8.1).

Even for successful Asian ethnics, the figures on educational attainment do not expose subtle discriminatory practices against Asian Americans at colleges and universities. Asians are often victims of restrictive quotas that are informally applied to applicants to colleges and universities. For example, data from the 1980s reveal that while Asian applications to college increased by 70 percent, acceptance at any given college decreased by almost 80 percent (U.S. Commission on Civil Rights, 1992). To take another example, at Harvard, Brown, Princeton, Yale, Stanford, and the University of California, a pattern of lower admission rates for Asian American applicants was discovered, even though those applicants had academic qualifications equal to those of white applicants (Bunzel and Au, 1987; Nakanishi, 1988; Takagi, 1990). Interestingly, some college admission officers have contended that restrictive admission policies for Asian American applicants are important "because Asian American college admits would overshadow white college admits" (Takagi, 1990). This pattern of underadmitting qualified Asians has been justified as a way of overcoming "reverse discrimination" that would hurt qualified white applicants; in fact, it is a form of direct discrimination against Asian Americans, for whom "quotas" *limiting* (not increasing) their numbers apparently exist (Kang, 1996).

Box 8.1
Earnings and Education: A Dilemma for the Model Minority

One of the indicators used to gauge the success of a population is "returns of education." The table below shows that with the exception of persons with less than a high school education, the median earnings of the Asian American population are lower than the median earnings of equivalently educated white Americans. The discrepancy is more apparent for the category "4 or more years of college." While the proportion of the Asian American population in this category is greater than the proportion of the white population, the median earnings of whites are almost 10 percent greater than the median earnings of Asians. For Asian Americans, then, the returns of education are not comparable to those for white Americans.

	Less than High School		4 Years of High School		1–3 Years of College		4 or More Years of College	
	White	Asian	White	Asian	White	Asian	White	Asian
Median earnings*	$18,227	$19,625	$27,236	$24,703	$31,245	$27,764	$49,098	$41,626

*2004 year-round, full-time workers 25 years old and older.
Source: Current Population Survey: 2005 Annual Social and Economic Supplement.

TABLE 8.7 Asian College Student Enrollment in Select Schools

University	Percentage of Asians in the State	Percentage of Asians in the College Town
Cornell University (Ithaca, NY)	5.5%	13.7%
Penn State University (State College, PA)	1.8	8.8
University of Indiana (Bloomington, IN)	1.0	5.3
University of Wisconsin (Madison, WI)	1.7	5.8
Dartmouth College (Hanover, NH)	1.3	6.8
University of North Carolina (Chapel Hill, NC)	1.4	7.2
Texas A&M University (College Station, TX)	2.7	7.3

Source: Wellner, 2002.

Interestingly, according to data from the 2000 U.S. census, Asian Americans are concentrated in towns that have a major university (Wellner, 2002). Table 8.7 shows the college towns in which Asian Americans tend to be concentrated. The data show that Asians are overrepresented in college-town populations relative to their representation in the state's population. One interpretation of these data is that Asians locate in college towns to pursue academic careers or a college education (Wellner, 2002). As such, Asians bring diversity to both the college town and the campus.

Housing of Asian Americans The existence of "Koreatowns," "Little Tokyos," "Chinatowns," "Little Saigons," and "Little Manilas" indicates patterns of residential segregation among Asian American populations. Many Asian Americans have chosen to settle in large metropolitan areas in order to enhance their social, cultural, and economic development in U.S. society (Cabezas, Shinagawa, and Kawaguchi, 1986–87; Lyman, 1986; Wong, 1976); and as a consequence, their concentration in these areas produces a high degree of residential segregation (U.S. Bureau of the Census, 2002b).

Using a **segregation index** based on the percentage of the population that would need to move into white neighborhoods to achieve complete desegregation, the U.S. Commission on Civil Rights (1992) listed the results for five groups of Asian Americans: Japanese (42 percent), Chinese (52 percent), Filipino (55 percent), Korean (55 percent), and Vietnamese (69 percent). Based on the segregation index for each group, then, Japanese Americans are the least segregated and Vietnamese Americans are the most segregated. Researchers have suggested that the segregation index also reflects the groups' country of origin and length of residence in the United States (Langberg and Farley, 1985;

Montero, 1981). Japanese Americans have a lower segregation index because they tend to be American-born and have resided longer in the United States. In contrast, Vietnamese Americans have a higher segregation index because the majority are foreign-born and have resided in the United States for a shorter period of time. Moreover, some of the separation of whites and Asians may be self-segregation by Asians. Yet the separation of Asian and white Americans cannot be fully explained by self-selection, nativity, and length of residence. Discrimination is also involved, as we will see shortly. Unfortunately, the U.S. Census Bureau has not broken out data on residential segregation of specific Asian subpopulations, but the overall segregation index for all Asians and Pacific Islanders is high, indicating that 40 percent of Asians and Pacific Islanders would need to move out of their neighborhoods to have proportionate numbers in non-Asian neighborhoods within a city. Moreover, the index has increased slightly over the last two decades (U.S. Bureau of the Census, 2002c) (see Box 8.2).

Box 8.2

Discrimination in Metropolitan Housing Units: A Look at Asians and Pacific Islanders

The U.S. Department of Housing and Urban Development (HUD) sponsored a study conducted by the Urban Institute to measure patterns of racial and ethnic discrimination in urban housing markets across the United States. The methodology used in the HUD study is based upon rigorous paired tests, in which two individuals—one minority and the other white—pose as otherwise identical homebuyers or renters and visit real estate or rental agents to inquire about the availability of advertised housing units. This methodology provides direct evidence of differences in the treatment minorities and whites experience when they search for housing.

Random samples of advertised housing units were drawn from multiple advertising sources in each site on a weekly basis, and testers visited the sampled offices to inquire about the availability of these advertised units. Both minority and white partners were assigned income, assets, and debt levels to make them equally qualified to buy or rent the advertised housing unit. Test partners were also assigned comparable family circumstances, job characteristics, education levels, and housing preferences. They visited sales or rental agents and systematically recorded the information and assistance they received about the advertised unit and/or other similar units, including location, quality and condition, rent or sales price, and other terms and conditions. Test partners did not compare their experiences with one another or record any conclusions about differences in treatment; each simply reported the details of the treatment he or she experienced as an individual homeseeker.

The study's results for Asians and Pacific Islanders are based on a sample of 11 metropolitan areas that account for more than three quarters of all Asians and Pacific Islanders living in metropolitan areas nationwide. America's Asian and Pacific Islander populations are tremendously diverse, and different ethnic subgroups may

(continued)

face differing levels or forms of discrimination. However, producing rigorous estimates of discrimination for each subgroup would be extremely costly. As a result,
testers were recruited to represent the primary groups of Asians and Pacific
Islanders living in each of the sampled metropolitan areas, including people who
identify themselves as Chinese, Japanese, Korean, Filipino, Vietnamese and other
Southeast Asians, Native Hawaiian and other Pacific Islanders, and Asian Indians.

MAJOR FINDINGS OF THE STUDY

Asians and Pacific Islanders face significant levels of discrimination when they
search for housing in large metropolitan areas. For renters, patterns of adverse treatment are mixed; Asians and Pacific Islanders appear to be systematically favored
with respect to housing inspections. In general, the level of consistent adverse treatment against Asian and Pacific Islander renters is 21.5 percent—about the same as
the level for African American and Hispanic renters. In addition, Asian and Pacific
Islander homebuyers experience consistent adverse treatment 20.4 percent of the
time, with systematic discrimination occurring in housing availability, inspections, financing assistance, and agent encouragement. This level of discrimination is
comparable to the level experienced by African American homebuyers and significantly higher than the level of discrimination against Hispanics.

In an attempt to explore the effects of skin color on adverse treatment, the experiences of light-skinned Asians and Pacific Islanders were compared to those of
dark-skinned people. In general, the study found very little evidence that dark-
skinned Asians and Pacific Islanders experience higher levels of adverse treatment
than light-skinned Asians and Pacific Islanders. However, the study's findings suggest that dark-skinned renters face a greater disadvantage than homebuyers.

Source: Margery Austin Turner, Stephen L. Ross, Beata A. Bednarz, Carla Herbig, and Seon Joo Lee,
"Discrimination in Metropolitan Housing Markets: Phase 2—Asians and Pacific Islanders"
(Washington, DC: The Urban Institute, Metropolitan Housing and Communities Policy Center,
Final Report, March 2003).

Life Span of Asian Americans   There are negligible differences between
Asians and whites on factors associated with life and death (Lauderdale and
Kestenbaum, 2002). According to the National Center for Health Statistics
(1991), Asian Americans have a lower death rate from accidents and homicides
than do white Americans. For example, in 1990 the death rate per 100,000 population by accidents was 22 for Asians and 40 for whites, while the rate per
100,000 population for homicide was 29 for Asians and 49 for whites. See Box 8.3
for a summary profile of suicide and mental health in the Asian and Pacific
Islander population.

The Dynamics of Discrimination against Asian Americans

Like other ethnic subpopulations in the United States, Asian Americans are
victims of inaccurate perceptions (Lo, 2001; Sodowsky et al., 1991; Stephan and
Stephan, 1989; Thornton and Taylor, 1988). Stewart Kwoh, director of the Asian
American Legal Center, has observed:

Box 8.3
Suicide and Mental Health in the Asian and Pacific Islander Population

The perception that Asian Americans are the "model minority" obscures the problems they face. Suicide rates offer a useful illustration because the lower rates of suicide of Asian Americans masks other underlying problems.

Between 1999 and 2004, in the Asian American and Pacific Islander population:

- The suicide rate was 5.40 per 100,000, approximately half the overall U.S. rate of 10.75 per 100,000.
- The highest rate, 27.43 per 100,000, was found among adult males 85 and older.
- Suicide ranked as the eighth leading cause of death for Asians of all ages (compared to eleventh for the overall U.S. population).

    During the 1980s, the Asian and Pacific Islander population more than doubled in the U.S., making it the fastest growing racial/ethnic group, followed by Hispanics. Three-fourths of the Asian and Pacific Islander population growth has been due to immigration. This rapid growth is predicted to continue, doubling again by 2009.

- Elderly Asian American/Pacific Islander women had higher rates of suicide than whites or blacks. For women aged 75 and older, the suicide rate for Asian Americans/Pacific Islanders was 7.95 per 100,000, compared to the white rate of 4.18 and the black rate of 1.18.
- Asian American and Pacific Islander high school students were as likely as their black, Hispanic, and white counterparts to have attempted suicide.
- Suicide ranked as the second leading cause of death for among those who were ages 15 to 24 years old.

Asian Americans and Pacific Islanders are significantly less likely than Caucasians to mention their mental health concerns to a friend or relative (12 percent vs. 25 percent); a mental health professional (4 percent vs. 26 percent); or a physician (2 percent vs. 13 percent).

Asian Americans do not access mental health treatment as much as other racial/ethnic groups do, perhaps due to strong stigma related to mental illness. Emotional problems are viewed as shameful and distressing and this may limit help-seeking behaviors. Asian Americans also tend to rely on family to handle problems. Asian American concern about negatively affecting their social network and expectations of low effectiveness keep them from seeking help.

For nearly half of Asian Americans and Pacific Islanders, access to the mental health care system is limited due to their lack of English proficiency and to a shortage of providers with appropriate language skills.

Many Asian American and Pacific Islander cultures view the psychological and physical as highly interconnected, unlike the common view in Western cultures. Asian Americans and Pacific Islanders may be more likely to express emotional distress through physical problems and to believe that physical problems cause emotional disturbances.

(continued)

In Asian Americans, suicide risk increases with age. Some explanations for the increase are related to difficulties adapting to the U.S. culture. Elders are not treated with the level of respect of their native cultures and may feel that they impose a burden on their families. Many Asian American men who are in the U.S. without their families are isolated not just from family but also culture.

Confucianist, Buddhist, and Taoist beliefs may contribute to lower suicide rates among Asian Americans, since they emphasize interdependence and interconnectedness and the group over the individual. On the other hand, suicide may be condoned if it protects the family from shame or disgrace.

Source: Suicide Prevention Resource Center (SPRC), www.sprc.org, accessed May 25, 2008.

Asian Americans have been viewed as non-citizens. . . . Historically, we (Asians) have all been considered immigrants, temporary visitors, or foreigners. Even though we are not immigrants, Asian Americans, when they move out of Asian neighborhoods, are seen as new immigrants (U.S. Commission on Civil Rights, 1986:31–32).

As the number of Asian immigrants to the United States increases in the next decades, so will the perception that all Asians are recent arrivals to the United

Chinatown in New York City is a home to a sprawling ethnic Chinese community, with population estimates ranging from 150,000 to 350,000 residents, demonstrating the residential segregation among Asian Americans. Signs in Chinese are clearly visible on this rain-soaked Chinatown street.

States. The perception that Asian Americans are foreigners increases their visibility in U.S. society and reinforces negative beliefs and stereotypes that are used to legitimize discrimination (Chang, 2004; Lee, 1999; Thrupkaew, 2002; Tuan, 1998).

Identifiability of Asian Americans   In the United States, Asians are unique in their physical appearance. Their skin and hair color, as well as facial characteristics (especially the eye fold), make Asian Americans very noticeable. This identifiability, coupled with the misconception that Asian Americans are recent immigrants, has resulted in an anti-Asian climate. For example, the U.S. Commission on Civil Rights (1992) reports that anti-Asian slogans, signs, and slurs are widespread.

Negative Beliefs about Asian Americans   Stereotypes of Asian Americans have shifted from those characterizing them as sneaky, obsequious, or inscrutable to the stereotype of the model minority (Chun, 1980; Hurk and Kim, 1989). According to Lee (1999:8), at various points in U.S. history Asian Americans have been stereotyped as "The pollutant, the coolie, the deviant, the yellow peril, the model minority and the gook." Contemporary negative beliefs about Asian Americans draw from the historical representation of Asian immigrants as the "**yellow peril,**" or threats to Western civilization (Lee, 1999). At the turn of the nineteenth century, Asian immigrants were seen as an unsanitary race—the carriers of incurable diseases such as smallpox, syphilis, and bubonic plague (Mohr, 2005; Shah, 2001). In 2003, for example, there were widespread false rumors that Severe Acute Respiratory Syndrome (SARS) had broken out in Asian American communities in the United States. In response to the perceived threat posed by SARS, universities in the United States started banning Asian foreign exchange students even though non-Asian students from Asia were not subject to similar bans (Chang, 2003).

Can the model minority stereotype promote negative beliefs about Asian Americans? Asian Americans are portrayed as "model minorities" whose "success" is due to their ability to overcome discrimination, and its disadvantages, through determination, hard work, strong family ties, and education (Cheng and Yang, 1996; Lee, 1996). Although this stereotype seems positive, it can have negative implications, the most important of which is the perception that Asian Americans do not experience the same social and economic problems as other populations. Consequently, homelessness, poverty, domestic violence, unemployment, crime, and other problems of the Asian American population are often ignored (Abraham, 2000; Agbayani-Siewert and Flanagan, 2001; Crystal, 1989; Yoshihama, 2001).

Another negative belief about Asian Americans is that many are recent immigrants (Hosokawa, 1982; Lee, 1999; Tuan, 1998; Wang, 1988). For example, Asians are commonly asked, "Where did you learn English?" Diane C. Yu, a member of the California Commission on Racial, Ethnic, Religious, and Minority Violence, has noted that when acquaintances ask her where she was born, they are reluctant to accept "the United States" as a response; they are appeased when she mentions that her parents came from China (U.S. Commission on Civil Rights, 1986).

Portrayals in movies and television have also created persistent stereotypes (Delgado and Stefancic, 1992; Hamamoto, 1994; Lee, 1999; Wong, 1978). Asian Americans were portrayed in movies and television shows as perpetually foreign and never American. Asian and Asian American males were portrayed as effeminate and asexual whereas Asian/and Asian American women were portrayed in hypersexualized images of geishas, prostitutes, and submissive China dolls (Hamamoto, 1994; Lee, 1999). As anti-Asian sentiment grew, especially after the bombing of Pearl Harbor, Asian Americans were depicted as tricky and devious (Wong, 1978). During World War II, most movies promoted anti-Japanese sentiment by depicting Japanese as master criminals (the role of master criminal was usually played by a white actor in makeup). These stereotypes built on those created in 1919 by William Randolph Hearst who began an anti-Asian film serial that promoted the image of Asians as the "yellow peril."

In the public mind, Asian Americans are often regarded as "foreigners" because their status in U.S. society is associated with foreign policy between Asia and the United States (Schrieke, 1936; Takaki, 1993). As relations between Asia and America fluctuate, so does public sentiment in the United States toward Asian Americans. For example, when the Japanese automaking industry increased its share in the United States, segments of the population expressed anti-Asian sentiments. In some cases, anti-Asian sentiment has produced violent and tragic results. For example, the 1982 killing of Vincent Chin, a Chinese American, in Detroit was the result of his killers' resentment of Japanese automobile exports to the United States. As Asian automobile plants have been established in the United States, much of this intensity has receded, but the potential for a new wave of anti-Asian sentiment remains, as industries export jobs to lower-priced labor in Asian countries.

Even as excessively negative beliefs have moved some to violence against Asian Americans, a series of more subtle and invidious beliefs has emerged (Sodowsky et al., 1991). For example, the model minority becomes the "yellow peril" when Asian Americans are accused of taking jobs from white Americans, African Americans, and Latinos (Chang, 1993). Also, tensions between Japan and the United States have created various waves of "Japan bashing." Another negative belief stems from "Buy American" campaigns, which contain subtle anti-Asian messages, despite the fact that two of the three biggest trading partners with the United States are European.

Finally, Asians' occupational niche as a middleman minority group that sells to non-Asians has created the same kinds of negative beliefs that emerge against all middleman minority groups—that they are clannish, secretive, dishonest, and devious. The Chinese were labeled with these negative epithets early on, but in recent decades these beliefs have been revived with a new intensity as Asian Americans have established small businesses in the neighborhoods of other disadvantaged minority groups, particularly African Americans and Latinos. These beliefs have created a sometimes volatile mix of resentment that erupts into violence, as the Korean merchants learned in the Los Angeles riots of 1992.

Institutionalized Discrimination against Asian Americans   The model minority stereotype has obscured the issue of discrimination against Asian Americans (Aguilar–San Juan, 1994; Cheng and Yang, 1996). The model minority stereotype portrays American society as a fair, open society and a real land of opportunity for all those who work hard and possess the right values (Osajima, 1988). This stereotype, like so many other stereotypes, runs counter to the fact that prejudice and discrimination have been very much a part of the Asian experience in America.

Legal Discrimination   Legalized discrimination against Asian Americans is best exemplified by immigration legislation, most of which was designed to exclude Asian immigrants from competing with white Europeans and, at the same time, to perpetuate negative stereotypes about Asians.

Chinese Immigration   In 1848, the arrival of two men and one woman from China began a flow of Chinese immigrants that spanned three decades (Zo, 1978). The majority of Chinese immigrants were recruited as labor for the mining industry in the western United States and, later, for the building of railroads that would connect the west and east coasts. This massive immigration, however, produced a series of efforts to constrain social mobility and occupational opportunities (McKenzie, 1928; Miller, 1969):

- In 1855, California passed a law placing a fifty-five-dollar head tax on every Chinese immigrant. In 1858, a law was passed forbidding Chinese immigration into the state. In 1876 the U.S. Supreme Court ruled both laws unconstitutional.
- The U.S. Congress passed the **Chinese Exclusion Act of 1882.** The act suspended the immigration of Chinese laborers to the United States for ten years and prohibited persons of Chinese ancestry residing in the United States from obtaining U.S. citizenship after the effective date of the act. An 1888 amendment to the act applied the exclusion to all Chinese immigrants except merchants, students, teachers, tourists, and government officials. The act was extended for ten years in 1892, for two years in 1902, and indefinitely in 1904. The act was repealed in 1943 by Congress and replaced by a legislative agenda that established a quota system for Chinese immigrants.

Japanese Immigration   The Japanese began arriving in the United States, especially on the West Coast, at the turn of the twentieth century. Immediately upon their arrival, they were accused of taking jobs away from U.S. citizens, of working for very low wages, and of displacing white domestic and factory workers. Anti-Japanese sentiment quickly gained supporters from participants in the Chinese exclusion movement (Fukuda, 1980; Penrose, 1973). As the number of Japanese immigrants grew, the demand for a national policy restricting Japanese immigration increased. The United States tried to avoid enacting immigration legislation against the Japanese by reaching an accord with Japan called the **Gentleman's Agreement of 1907.** Under this compact, Japan agreed not to issue passports to skilled or unskilled workers, except for those already in the United States, or to wives or children of these workers. However, the agreement did not stem the tide of anti-Japanese sentiment:

- The **Immigration Act of 1917** was enacted in order to stop Japanese immigration as well as immigration from other Asian countries. The act barred admission of any person from "islands not possessed by the United States adjacent to the Continent of Asia" or the continent of Asia (excluding Persia and parts of Afghanistan and Russia).
- The **National Origins Act of 1924** was passed in order to stop the flow of Japanese immigrants. The act barred the immigration of Japanese wives even if their husbands were U.S. citizens, and it prohibited the immigration of Japanese aliens ineligible for U.S. citizenship. The act reinforced the legal decision in *Ozawa v. United States* (1922) that persons of Japanese ancestry could not become naturalized citizens.

Filipino and Korean Immigration Although immigration from Japan and China accounted for the bulk of Asian immigration to the United States prior to the 1920s, other Asian groups came in smaller numbers. Two of these groups were Filipinos and Koreans. Since the Philippine Islands were a territory of the United States in the 1920s, they were exempt from the 1917 Immigration Act and the 1924 National Origins Act. As a result, Filipinos were free to immigrate to the United States; they are now the second largest Asian ethnic population in America. Filipinos were recruited to work on sugar plantations in Hawaii and as field laborers in the California agricultural industry (Kitano, 1980; Knoll, 1982). However, as the number of Filipinos grew in California, riots between Filipinos and white Americans took place. The white rioters saw the Filipinos as another part of the "Asian horde" attempting to enter the United States. Partly in response to tensions between Filipinos and white Americans on the West Coast, the U.S. Congress passed, in 1934, the **Philippines Independence Act,** granting deferred independence to the Philippine Islands and imposing an annual quota of fifty Filipino immigrants to the U.S. mainland per year.

As early as 1885, Korean political exiles came to the United States (Kitano and Daniels, 1988). The first sizable wave of Korean immigrants went to Hawaii; between 1903 and 1905, approximately seven thousand Koreans immigrated there (Choy, 1979). By 1905, 1,000 Koreans were living in California. These immigrants expected to find better working and living conditions; instead, they found low wages and substandard housing. In an attempt to protect its citizens, the Korean government banned the entry of Koreans to the United States; as a consequence, Korean immigration did not reach noticeable proportions again until the passage of the Immigration and Naturalization Act of 1965.

The Internment of Japanese Americans Besides the use of immigration legislation to exclude and control Asian immigrants to, and within, the United States, the U.S. government manipulated the legal system to discriminate against Japanese Americans by placing them in **internment camps** after the bombing of Pearl Harbor on December 7, 1941. Immediately after the bombing, the FBI rounded up over 2,000 Japanese Americans suspected of aiding Japan's war effort. Not satisfied with the small numbers of incarcerated Japanese Americans, the Hearst press, through the column of Henry McLemore, rallied the cry of "Japs Must Go" (cited in Kitano, 1980:216):

> I am for the immediate removal of every Japanese on the West Coast to a point deep in the interior . . . let 'em be pinched, hurt, and hungry. Personally, I hate Japanese. And that goes for all of them.

Responding to mounting demands for anti-Japanese legislation, on February 19, 1942, President Franklin D. Roosevelt signed **Executive Order 9066,** which established restricted military areas and authorized the building of relocation camps. These camps were located in California, Arizona, Idaho, Wyoming, Colorado, Utah, and Arkansas. Interestingly, even though Executive Order 9066 did not specify that it applied to persons of Japanese descent, it was applied to them exclusively. The U.S. government argued that the relocation camps were vital to the national security of the United States.

The movement of Japanese Americans to the relocation camps began in March 1942. Anyone at least one-eighth Japanese was relocated. Of the approximately 127,000 Americans of Japanese descent living in the United States in 1940, 110,000 were placed in relocation camps (Peterson, 1971; Tsuchida, 1990).

Japanese and Japanese Americans from West Coast areas are evacuated under a U.S. army war emergency order. Here Japanese Americans are waiting to be registered.

Japanese Americans were forced to sell property and businesses at a fraction of their value—usually five cents on the dollar—and were allowed to bring to the camps only what they could carry. The relocation of Japanese Americans to the camps was generally smooth as a result of Japanese American cooperation; they responded to posted notices, gathered at designated departure areas, and boarded trains or buses for the trip to the camps.

Although things may have looked calm on the surface, there was turbulence underneath. Japanese Americans regarded the relocation camps as concentration camps (Daniels, 1971). At some camps, there were riots; at others, there were periods of silence between the Japanese Americans and the white guards; and in some camps anti-American slogans were painted on banners and buildings. In the cases of *Korematsu v. United States* (1944), *Yasui v. United States* (1943), and *Hirabayashi v. United States* (1943), Japanese Americans used the U.S. court system to question the legal status of the relocation camps. The U.S. Supreme Court upheld Executive Order 9066 in all cases (Bell, 1973).

Japanese Americans were officially released from the relocation camps on January 2, 1945. As might be expected, they wanted to know how the United States was going to redress their losses. According to the Commission on Wartime Relocation and Internment of Civilians (1983), the losses suffered by Japanese Americans interned in the camps—personal wealth, residences, businesses, and farms—were between $185 million and $400 million. In 1948, the U.S. Congress passed the **Japanese American Evacuation Claims Act,** which limited claims to a maximum amount of $2,500, with all claims to be submitted within eighteen months of the act's passage. The $131 million that Congress appropriated for the act paid ten cents for every dollar of actual loss. It took the federal government seventeen years to process all the claims submitted; in the end, the federal government paid out $38 million (in 1942 dollars, without interest) of the $131 million allocated by Congress.

In 1976, President Gerald Ford issued **Presidential Proclamation 4417,** which rescinded Executive Order 9066 and apologized to the Japanese American community. This proclamation created a new concern that victimization of Japanese Americans was being perpetuated by the government's failure to fully redress their losses during the internment period. In 1980, Congress created the **Commission on Wartime Relocation and Internment of Civilians** (1983) to examine the issue of uncompensated loss of income and property to Japanese Americans during the internment period. In 1983, the commission made the following recommendations:

1. The U.S. government must offer an "official apology" to Japanese Americans.
2. The U.S. government should pardon Japanese Americans convicted of violating Executive Order 9066.
3. The U.S. government should establish a $1.5 billion fund, from which $20,000 would be paid to each of the approximately 60,000 survivors of the relocation camps.

Prompted by the commission's recommendation, Congress passed the **Civil Liberties Act of 1988,** authorizing the $20,000 compensation payment for living survivors of the relocation camps.

The internment itself and the reluctance in its aftermath to apologize for suspending Americans' civil rights and to compensate for obvious damages afterward sent a clear message to all Asians: This can happen to you. Though this seemed implausible, it remained a subtle threat. More significantly, the willingness to suspend Asians' (but not Germans') civil rights reflected, and at the same time contributed to, a willingness to use the law to restrict Asian immigration and to threaten those who were already here with deportation or harassment. This legal threat persists today; although it is not as blatant as the one faced by Latinos, it is just as real, especially in a period when economic tensions between the United States and its Asian trading partners are high.

Economic Discrimination   Legal discrimination against Asian immigrants limits their economic opportunities. The driving force behind anti-Asian sentiment and negative beliefs is, and has been, fear that Asian immigrants would displace white workers. The ability of Asian immigrants to create economic opportunities for themselves through small-business activities was curtailed in the early decades of the twentieth century by stereotypes portraying them as dirty, immoral, unassimilable, sly, sneaky, and cheap. Such negative beliefs are typically applied to middleman minority groups, but they have been particularly intense when applied to Asian Americans because many white Americans, African Americans, and Latinos now believe that Asians want their jobs (Takaki, 1989).

These fears are codified into a set of social beliefs portraying Asians as a threat to the social and economic fabric of U.S. society (see Box 8.4). For example, according to the U.S. Commission on Civil Rights (1992), even though

---

Box 8.4
Asian Gangs and Legal Discrimination

Gangs are a part of the organizational structure of many Asian societies, linked to Asian organized crime (narcotics trafficking, prostitution, gambling, extortion, loan-sharking, and other illegal activities). Elements of this activity have been imported into the United States and adapted to ghetto life. Among the Chinese, for example, violent street gangs are linked to *tongs*, fraternal societies (sometimes called "clans") that control much of the internal activity in large urban Chinese enclaves in order to secure large profits from illegal activities. The gangs control territories, typically for one of the tongs.

The result of this gang activity is that all citizens in the affected areas feel threatened by violence. Many complain bitterly that the police do not attack this problem with the same zeal as they attack, say, Mafia activities in other ethnic enclaves. Few federal resources—FBI and special investigators and prosecutors—or local resources—organized crime units or drug enforcement units—are devoted to Asian ghettos, where it is presumed that residents "can take care of themselves." Inattention to gangs and organized crime in Asian communities represents a form of legal discrimination against the model minority.

Asian Americans are represented in greater numbers than other ethnic minorities in white-collar occupations in the United States, they suffer from discrimination that limits their mobility within these occupations. They eventually confront the glass ceiling: They are in, but they can go only so far. As noted earlier, the glass ceiling is partially attributed to stereotypical notions of Asian Americans—unaggressive, poor communicators in English, and unassimilated. Asian Americans in white-collar, especially management, occupations express their concerns as follows (U.S. Commission on Civil Rights, 1992:132):

- I am of the opinion that most Asian Americans are facing an insurmountable glass wall in the corporate world. As a matter of fact, most of us have given up hope of advancing up the corporate ladder. The more we think about it, the more frustrated, discouraged, and depressed we become. . . .
- I suspect that the minds of many corporate managers and the senior staff members who have direct control . . . are still in the 1960s. As a consequence, for most of them we Asians are a suspect class, and we usually have to prove that we are better in order to be equal. . . .
- Most of us have proved our technical capability. However, many major corporations tend to overlook the nontechnical side of many Asian Americans. Corporations pick pigeon holes for us. And what is worse, they believe that we are quite content staying in those technologically airtight pigeon holes.

Many Asian Americans perceive the glass ceiling as the product of attitudes held by white Americans. In a survey of Asian American professionals and managers in the San Francisco Bay Area, Cabezas et al. (1989) found that respondents regarded prejudice as the factor that limited their upward mobility. In particular, Asian respondents blamed prejudicial attitudes for excluding them from corporate network structures, creating an environment of management insensitivity, and inhibiting mentoring opportunities for them within the corporate organization. One economic result of these attitudes is limited upward mobility and, hence, loss of potential income for Asian American professionals and managers (Cabezas and Kawaguchi, 1990).

How real is the glass ceiling for Asian Americans? According to the U.S. Commission on Civil Rights (1988), Asian American men are less likely to be in management positions than white men with the same qualifications. In a study of the aerospace industry, the U.S. General Accounting Office (1989) found that Asian Americans were less successful in moving from professional to managerial positions than were either white Americans or other ethnic minority groups. A study of Asian American engineers found that they were less likely to be in management positions or to be promoted to management positions than were white engineers with the same qualifications (Tang, 1991). An analysis of managers in the aerospace industry also showed that while Asian Americans constituted a higher percentage of aerospace professionals than either African Americans or Latinos, they constituted the lowest percentage of managers (Chiu, 1994). A study of San Francisco's civil service found that because Asian Americans lacked opportunities for promotion, they tended to cluster in technical jobs (Der and Lye, 1989). Not only are Asian Americans clustered in some jobs in San Francisco's civil service, they are also underrepresented (13 percent) in the civil service relative to their number (28 percent) in San Francisco's population (Moore and Gunnison, 1994). This evidence confirms the existence of a glass ceiling for Asian Americans (see Box 8.5).

Box 8.5
Does a Glass Ceiling Exist for Asian Americans?

- An Asian American sales professional with an MBA in marketing and sales had worked with the same Fortune 500 company for well over a decade and received many sales achievement awards when he was promoted to regional sales manager for the San Francisco Bay Area. He had been working in that position for three years when a new management group came in. His new boss frequently used racial slurs against him. For instance, one time, when he was speaking to his boss, his boss said, "Slow down, I cannot write as fast as a Chinaman." Eventually he was demoted and transferred to a sales territory. When he asked his boss why he had been demoted, his boss told him that it was his "gut feeling" that he [the sales professional] was not a good manager and that he did not exhibit leadership qualities. The man subsequently filed a discrimination suit against his employer at the California Fair Employment and Housing Commission and was issued a right-to-sue letter. The suit was eventually settled out of court. He still works for the same company, but he has not been reinstated to his old position.
- A woman of Asian Indian descent was hired as the personnel manager for a midwestern city. She was the first woman and the first minority member ever to be hired in a managerial position by that city. As soon as she arrived at her job, she began encountering resistance from her staff, and when she brought their behavior to the attention of her boss, he told her that her staff was insubordinate because she was a woman of color. Almost a year after she started the job, despite receiving an above-average performance appraisal, she was abruptly fired without severance pay. A subsequent investigation by the city's human relations commission found that "substantial evidence exists to show that the Complainant was discriminated against because of her sex, female, and her face, Asian; her national origin, India; and her color, non-white, in the manner in which she was terminated/suspended and in the conditions under which she performed her job." Despite the human relations commission finding, the city did nothing to rectify the situation. In fact, city employees repeatedly told the woman's professional colleagues and others who called that she was under suspension for not performing up to par. As a result, the woman could not find another comparable job, suffered considerable mental anguish, and did not have the financial resources necessary to pursue her case in court.
- In early 1988, Angelo Tom, a fifth-generation Chinese American who had worked at the U.S. Department of Housing and Urban Development's (HUD) San Francisco regional office for nine years and become nationally recognized as the leading community planning and development analyst in the Bay Area, was turned down for promotion to the position of supervisor of his unit. The woman chosen

(continued)

to fill the job had less experience than Mr. Tom. At the time of Mr. Tom's rejection there were only three Asian Americans in middle-management positions at HUD's San Francisco office and none in upper management, and several qualified Asian Americans had repeatedly been rejected for management positions. After Mr. Tom filed a complaint, a HUD investigation found that he had been rejected for the position because he did not have leadership or interpersonal skills and was too technical for the job. Mr. Tom then requested and received a formal hearing in front of the U.S. Equal Employment Opportunity Commission (EEOC). At that hearing, witnesses refuted the HUD contention that he had poor leadership and interpersonal skills, and the EEOC administrative law judge agreed. He also held that a white man who was highly technically skilled would have been promoted with the confidence that he could develop the general outlook necessary to perform the management job. Mr. Tom was awarded back pay, a retroactive promotion, and attorney's fees.

Source: U.S. Commission on Civil Rights, 1992:134–35.

One result of the glass ceiling is that Asian Americans who have white-collar management and professional positions earn less than white Americans in similar positions (Cabezas and Kawaguchi, 1988). Limited upward mobility becomes a subtle but widespread form of economic discrimination, which reflects and reinforces negative beliefs held by top-level management in American corporations.

The arrest of Wen Ho Lee, a research scientist at the Los Alamos National Laboratory, on December 10, 1999, sent ripples throughout the Asian American community because it reinforced negative images of Asians in American society. The ripples merged into a tidal wave as the U.S. government increased its accusations that Lee was a spy for communist China (Loeb and Pincus, 2000). Lee's arrest portrayed Asian scientists as tools for the Chinese government's interest in stealing nuclear secrets from the United States (Bromwich, 1999). As such, the government's portrayal of Lee as a spy reinforced the stereotypic perception that Asians are sneaky and sly. A positive outcome of Lee's arrest, however, is that it caused Asian research scientists at the Lawrence Livermore National Laboratory to file bias complaints that they were paid less than white scientists and subject to racial harassment from white scientists (Kim, 1999). On September 13, 2000, Lee was released from custody when the U.S. government dropped its case against him. In dropping its case, the government admitted that 99 percent of the information Lee was accused of stealing was already available to the public and that the government's principal witness offered deceptive testimony (Locke, 2000).

Political Discrimination Despite their increasing numbers in the last two decades, Asian Americans are relatively absent from political offices and activities. Outside the state of Hawaii, few Asian Americans have been elected to political office. According to the U.S. Commission on Civil Rights, 10 percent of the California population is Asian American, yet only a few Asian Americans serve in Congress, only one has been elected to a state position, and Asian

Americans rarely serve in the California legislature. Political offices at the local level have also evaded Asian Americans (Karnow, 1992; Tamayo, Toma, and Koh, 1991). For example, in Daly City, California, where Asian Americans constitute over 42 percent of the population, no Asian American had ever been elected to the city council by the mid-1990s; in New York City, with an Asian American population of over a half million, no Asian American has ever been elected to the city council; and in Los Angeles, only recently have Asian Americans been elected to the city council. The relative absence of Asian Americans from the political scene has resulted in some revealing moments. For example, Senator Daniel Inouye of Hawaii was born in the United States and was a decorated soldier, having earned the Distinguished Service Cross during World War II. During the Iran-Contra hearings in the 1980s, however, he became the target of telephone calls and telegrams, often containing racial slurs, that told him to return to Japan.

The political underrepresentation of the Asian American population is largely the result of discriminatory political practices. Bai (1991:733–34) has identified the model minority stereotype as contributing to the political underrepresentation of the Asian American population:

> This popular preconception of Asian Pacific Americans as a politically silent "model minority" is just one of the many barriers facing Asian Pacific Americans who desire to enter the political process. . . . Obscured by the popular type which labels them as the "successful" minority, however, Asian Pacific Americans are viewed either as not warranting special protection from official discriminatory practices or as already participating greatly in the political process.

What are some of the other barriers to the political participation and representation of Asian Americans? They are discussed below.

Apportionment Policies　The potential political power of Asian Americans has been diluted by **gerrymandering** policies that split the Asian population of a community into several districts. In a study of how apportionment policies affect the political power of the Asian American population, Tamayo, Toma, and Koh (1991) have noted that Senate district boundaries split the Asian American community in San Francisco; and in Los Angeles, Koreatown, Chinatown, and Filipinotown each are split into several city council districts. As a result of gerrymandering, Asian Americans are not able to elect representatives from their own ranks because their voting power has been diluted.

Bilingual Election Materials　A provision of the Voting Rights Act of 1982 states that if 5 percent of a district's voting-age population is identifiable as a "single-language minority," then bilingual voting materials (that is, ballots) must be made available in the language of that minority. The linguistic diversity among Asian American populations and their lack of residential concentration prevent them from constituting 5 percent of a district's voting-age population (U.S. Commission on Civil Rights, 1992). As a result, the unavailability of bilingual election materials makes limited proficiency in English a barrier to the political participation of Asian Americans. For example, by 1980 over 100,000

Chinese Americans were of voting age in New York City, but the size of New York's population prevented this number from constituting the necessary 5 percent cutoff point for bilingual election materials. In an effort to incorporate Chinese Americans into the electoral process, federal legislation was passed in 1992 requiring bilingual ballots for Chinese American voters in parts of Manhattan, Brooklyn, and Queens (Dunn, 1994). However, two problems emerged in the effort to provide bilingual ballots: It is difficult to provide a transliteration of English names in Chinese characters, and ballot slots on voting machines are not big enough to accommodate both Chinese and English characters on the same ballot. Margaret Fung, executive director of the Asian American Legal Defense and Education Fund (quoted in U.S. Commission on Civil Rights, 1992:161), notes that:

> In Chinatown, four out of five voters have language difficulties. These voters stated . . . that they would vote more often if bilingual assistance were provided. Similarly in Queens, four out of every five limited–English proficient Asian American voters indicated that they would vote more if bilingual assistance were provided.

Political Party Snobbery   Both the Democratic and the Republican parties have ignored the Asian American population, creating a lack of political party identification among Asian Americans (Bai, 1991). In turn, Asian American candidates for political office have encountered difficulties in attracting support from the major political parties. In addition, these parties have failed to create agendas that incorporate Asian American concerns. For example, in a 1989 *Washington Post* article, Joel Kotkin and Bill Bradley (1989) chastised the Democratic party for not creating a political agenda that responds to Asian American concerns and to political rhetoric: "Yet to date, the Democrats have been remarkably resistant . . . to the idea of a less Eurocentric foreign policy. Perhaps the most ominous is the increasingly anti-Asian tone of Democratic rhetoric, all too clearly demonstrated in the 'Japan-bashing' and 'Korea-bashing' campaign ads." As preparation for the 1992 presidential election, Republicans established an outreach office in GOP national headquarters that targeted the recruitment of voters in the Asian American community (Awanohara, 1990). Republicans used the themes of anticommunism, antiwelfarism, and entrepreneurship to appeal to Asian American voters.

Educational Discrimination   The high levels of educational attainment by Asian Americans are often interpreted to mean that this ethnic group does not experience discrimination in education (Hsia, 1988; Peng, 1990; Wang, 1988). Yet considerable discrimination exists, especially in institutions of higher education. The higher level of Asian American enrollment in colleges and universities has resulted in strong anti-Asian sentiments (Chiu, 1994:1093):

> White college students rework college acronyms into biting commentary on Asian American presence. MIT becomes "Made in Taiwan," UCLA becomes "University of Caucasians Living Among Asians," and U.C. Irvine (UCI) becomes "University of Chinese Immigrants."

Let us review a couple of prominent cases that highlight the problem.

Brown University   Between 1980 and 1983 the Asian American admission rate at Brown University fell below the overall admission rate, even though the admission rate of Asian Americans had been historically higher than the overall admission rates. As a result, the Asian American Student Association of Brown University produced a report; its analysis of admission rates between 1979 and 1983 found the following:

- The Asian American admission rate dropped from 46 percent to 26 percent, while the overall admission rate declined from 27 percent to 24 percent.
- An analysis of academic qualifications between Asian American and white American applicants did not show significant changes for Asian Americans that would justify the decrease in their admission rate.
- The acceptance of the model minority stereotype by the university administration and admissions office resulted in reduced efforts to recruit Asian American students.

Brown University responded to the report's findings by establishing the Brown University Corporation Committee on Minority Affairs. After a review of the Asian American Student Association report, this committee admitted that Asian American applicants had been treated unfairly in the admissions process. The committee recommended that in order to rectify injustices against Asian American applicants, and minority applicants in general, the admission rate of minority applicants with academic qualifications comparable to those of nonminority applicants should be equal to the admission rate of nonminority applicants.

Berkeley   The Asian American Task Force on University of California Admissions was formed in 1984 to examine a decline in Asian American first-year student enrollment. In particular, the task force was concerned about the fact that as the pool of Asian American applicants grew between 1979 and 1984, the proportion of Asian American first-year students declined (Takagi, 1990). As the controversy intensified and attracted the attention of the California legislature, the auditor general of California (1987) completed a review of first-year admissions policies at Berkeley. The auditor general's report concluded that Asian American first-year applicants had been admitted at a lower rate than white American applicants despite a larger increase in the grade point average (GPA) of Asian American applicants than of white American applicants.

In 1989, the academic senate at Berkeley moved to examine the controversy surrounding Asian American first-year admissions by forming the Special Committee on Asian American Admissions. The committee reviewed admission policies, interviewed admissions personnel, and read application files. After its lengthy investigation, the committee produced a report that listed three factors responsible for the drop in Asian American first-year admissions:

1. The university's decision not to guarantee admission to applicants under the Educational Opportunity Program (EOP), and to exclude them from

affirmative action initiatives (that is, applicants who are from economically disadvantaged backgrounds but are not members of underrepresented groups), had a significant effect on Asian American first-year admissions because the majority (90 percent) of EOP applicants were found to be Asian Americans.

2. In the fall of 1984 the College of Letters and Science decided to raise the minimum GPA for admission but not the minimum scores on college entrance exams (for example, SATs). Applicants to Berkeley, at the time, could meet either the minimum GPA or the minimum test score for admission. Since Asian American applicants were more likely to gain admission to Berkeley on the basis of their GPA and white students on the basis of their test scores, the change in the minimum GPA discriminated against Asian American applicants: Asian American applicants had to meet higher standards than white applicants.

3. The Office of Admissions and Records announced on December 28, 1983, that applicants of "permanent alien" status not meeting a minimum SAT verbal score would be redirected to another UC campus. Even though this decision was reversed ten days later, the admissions office established a minimum score of 400 on the verbal part of the SAT for immigrant applicants only. The implementation of a minimum SAT verbal score was an obstacle to Asian American immigrant applicants.

Harvard   In 1988 the U.S. Office for Civil Rights, in response to concerns raised by the Asian American community at Harvard University, initiated a review of undergraduate admissions there. After two years of investigating undergraduate admissions, the Office for Civil Rights did not find discriminatory policies or procedures regarding Asian American applicants. Although the Office for Civil Rights cleared Harvard of discrimination charges, the review of applicant folders uncovered practices that some would deem discriminatory. In its review of applicant folders, the Office for Civil Rights found:

- Inequitable use of "ethnic readers" for Asian American applicant folders. Members of ethnic groups were used in the undergraduate admissions process to control for special cultural or ethnic factors. The Office for Civil Rights found that only a small number of Asian American applicant folders were read by Asian Americans. Consequently, it was possible that special cultural or ethnic factors pertaining to Asian American applicants were overlooked.
- Written comments stereotyping Asian American applicants. Some of these comments were "soft-spoken," "math oriented," "English-speaking difficulty," "shy," and "reserved." The Office for Civil Rights suggested that while the comments did not affect negatively the admission rate of Asian American applicants, they did reflect the operation of stereotypical beliefs about Asian Americans.

One can observe from the preceding retrospective examples that despite being labeled the "model minority," Asians have been the victims of educational discrimination. While institutional practices have been identified as discriminatory in the higher education of Asian students, Asian students have faced another form of discrimination in higher education—victimization through hate crimes. The National Asian American Pacific Legal Consortium (2002) conducted a ten-year audit of violent and hate crimes against Asian and Pacific Islander Americans. Here is a notable example from the audit (pp. 36–38) of the hate crimes experienced by Asian and Pacific Islander students in higher education.

> On February 27, 2000, four Asian Pacific American (APA) students were brutally attacked by three white members of the SUNY Binghamton wrestling team outside a dormitory. During the attack in which the wrestlers kicked, headbutted, and punched the APA students, two of the wrestlers shouted, "You damn chinks!" One of the victims, John E. Lee, suffered a fractured skull, hemorrhaging, and a concussion. As the assailants fled the scene they shouted, "This is what you get for being chinks!"
>
> The beating was classified as a racial hate crime. One of the assailants was indicted on a charge of misdemeanor third-degree assault. After plea-bargaining with the DA's Office, the remaining two assailants faced only minor criminal charges. On campus, the SUNY Binghamton administration expelled one of the students for his role in the attack, suspended a second student until the fall of 2002, and absolved the third student of all charges. The four APA victims retained legal assistance after the hate attack was treated leniently by the administration. The school's Asian Student Union (ASU) demanded apologies from the officials and a revision of school policies dealing with bias-motivated crimes on campus. Those negotiations broke down, and their attorneys and ASU called on the Department of Justice (DOJ) to probe the bias attack for federal civil rights violations.
>
> After the incident, one of the leading APA faculty members on the campus was personally threatened by the captain of the wrestling team (the hate crime was committed by his teammates). He tried by intimidation to stop the professor from speaking at a forum that night. Two witnesses, their attorneys, and a student were present. A police report was filed. A year later, the captain was nominated by a faculty, staff, and student committee to be the senior class commencement speaker. Despite objections, he was later chosen. This decision was approved and supported by the university. As a result, almost the entire faculty of color boycotted the graduation that year.

Housing Discrimination   A 1980 poll of white American attitudes toward Asian Americans found that the majority of white respondents (1) were against Asians moving into their neighborhoods, (2) believed that there were "too many" Asians in the United States, and (3) felt that Asians should have settled in other Asian countries (U.S. Commission on Civil Rights, 1986). At that time, in 1980, many white residents did not welcome Asian Americans into their neighborhoods, a situation that persists today. The U.S. Commission on Civil Rights (1986) documented the following examples of acts by white Americans who sought to discourage Asian Americans from living in their predominantly white neighborhoods:

- In San Francisco, white neighbors painted anti-Asian graffiti on the car of the only Asian American resident in the neighborhood.
- In Seattle, Washington, white neighbors fired gunshots at a home occupied by an Asian American family while the family was in the house.

- In Providence, Rhode Island, white neighbors painted "No Nips" on a house the day after an Asian family moved in.
- In 1987, anti-Asian flyers were distributed to mailboxes in the Bensonhurst and Gravesend neighborhoods of Brooklyn. These flyers urged the boycotting of Asian businesses and demanded that real estate agents not sell property to Asians in the neighborhoods. As a result of the flyers, Asian businesses and real estate offices that had sold property to Asians were vandalized (Giordano, 1987a, 1987b).
- In 1981, a Cambodian family that had bought a home in a white neighborhood in Maine was the target of racial bigotry. As the father played with his children in the snow, one of his white neighbors threw a snowball at him, a snowball containing a rock. The Cambodian man approached his neighbors, blood streaming down his face, to ask why they had hurt him. His neighbors responded: "Go back where ya came from, gook" (U.S. Commission on Civil Rights, 1989).
- In Massachusetts, arsonists set fire to an apartment building that left thirty-one Cambodians homeless (Yen, 1988).

The popular belief that Asians prefer to live "with their own kind" is weakened by the discrimination Asian Americans experience when entering non-Asian neighborhoods (see Box 8.6).

Typically, the model minority does not protest as loudly as other minorities in response to discriminatory treatment, but this treatment is a fact of life for Asian Americans today, over 100 years since they began immigrating to the United States. Chinatowns, Little Tokyos, Koreatowns, Little Manilas, and similar Asian enclaves exist for reasons other than the desire to live with "their own kind."

Stratification of Asian Americans

White American workers regarded early Asian immigrants as a threat to their jobs. In contrast, large-scale employers in agriculture and in the railroad industry viewed Asians as an inexpensive source of productive labor. Nevertheless, despite employers' views, when a majority of the working population sees a minority as a threat, negative beliefs are codified which, ironically, intensify the sense of threat. Such beliefs also legitimize discrimination. In the case of Asian immigrants, acts of violence and legal restrictions initially prevented them from fully realizing economic opportunities and gaining political power. Ghettoization ensued as a response to hostility in the host society. Yet Asian Americans made significant gains in education, which, in turn, opened opportunities in jobs, especially after the early fears of the "yellow peril" faded and the panic of Pearl Harbor abated with the victory over Japan in World War II. Education credentials coupled with middleman entrepreneurial skills enabled the descendants of these early immigrants to enter the middle classes but with restrictions on where they could live and how high on the corporate ladder they could climb. More recent tensions with Asian trading partners, along with a new wave of

Box 8.6
Violence against Asian Americans

Two murders of Asian Americans in the 1980s have been etched into the national consciousness as examples of the potential intensity of discrimination against Asian Americans: the murder of Vincent Chin in 1982 and the murder of Jim (Ming Hai) Loo in 1989. These killings are prominent examples, but they are not isolated incidents. Violence against Asians leading to injury and sometimes death occurs with disturbing frequency across the country and affects many different Asian groups.

VINCENT CHIN

The racially motivated murder of Vincent Chin and the inability of the American judicial system to bring his murderers to justice became a vivid symbol and source of outrage during the mid-1980s. The facts of the case are as follows.

On the evening of June 19, 1982, Vincent Chin, a 27-year-old Chinese American, met with some friends in a Detroit bar to celebrate his upcoming wedding. He was accosted by Ronald Ebens and Michael Nitz, two white automobile factory workers, who reportedly called him a "Jap" and blamed him for the loss of jobs in the automobile industry. Ebens and Nitz chased Chin out of the bar, and, when they caught up with him, Nitz held Chin while Ebens beat him "numerous times in the knee, the chest, and the head" with a baseball bat. Chin died of his injuries four days later.

Ebens and Nitz were initially charged with second-degree murder but subsequently were allowed to plead guilty to manslaughter. In March 1983 the defendants were each sentenced to three years' probation and fined $3,780 by Wayne Circuit County judge Charles Kaufman, who reasoned that the defendants had no previous history of violence and were unlikely to violate probation.

The U.S. Department of Justice brought federal civil rights charges against Ebens and Nitz to a federal grand jury, which indicted them on November 2, 1982. On June 18, 1984, Ebens was found guilty of interfering with Chin's civil rights, and on September 18, 1984, he was sentenced to twenty-five years in prison. However, Nitz was acquitted of the federal civil rights charges.

Ebens's conviction was overturned by the Sixth Circuit Court of Appeals in September 1986 for technical reasons, including issues pertaining to the admissibility of audiotapes and prosecutorial misconduct (overzealousness) in preparing witnesses. When Ebens came up for retrial in the Eastern District of Michigan, the defense moved for a change of venue on the grounds that Ebens could not get a fair trial in Detroit. The defense motion was granted, and the trial was moved to Cincinnati. The case was retried during the month of April 1987, and this time Ebens was acquitted.

The acquittal of Ebens in the second federal trial means that neither Ebens nor Nitz ever went to prison for Vincent Chin's killing. Some have speculated that the main reason the Cincinnati jury acquitted Ebens is that the jury could not comprehend the reality of anti-Asian bias. Whereas Detroit in the early 1980s was the scene of a massive media campaign against foreign imports, especially those from Japan,

(continued)

a campaign that inflamed anti-Asian sentiments in that city, there had not been the same type of campaign in Cincinnati. Also, there were very few Asians in Cincinnati, and anti-Asian sentiments were not widespread.

Others contend that the Cincinnati jury's acquittal of Ebens reflects a fundamental problem with current federal civil rights laws. Ebens was charged under federal criminal civil rights law Section 245(b), which prohibits (among other things) the racially motivated interference by force or threat of force with a person's use of public facilities, such as restaurants and bars. Some experts argue that the jury may have been confused about what had to be shown for there to be a civil rights violation under Section 245(b); even though the jury may have felt that the attack was indeed racially motivated, it might not have thought that Ebens specifically intended to interfere with Chin's use of a public facility (the bar).

JIM (MING HAI) LOO

Seven years after Vincent Chin's killing, another Chinese American was killed in Raleigh, North Carolina, under similar circumstances. Jim (Ming Hai) Loo, 24, had immigrated to the United States from China thirteen years before, was working in a Chinese restaurant, and was saving money so that he could attend college. On the evening of Saturday, July 29, 1989, during an altercation that began in a nearby pool hall, Loo was hit on the back of the head by a handgun held by Robert Piche. He fell into a broken beer bottle, which pierced his eye and caused a bone fragment to enter his brain, resulting in his death on July 31.

Loo and several Vietnamese friends had been playing pool in the pool hall, when Robert Piche, 35, and his brother, Lloyd Piche, 29, began calling them "gooks" and "chinks" and blaming them for American deaths in Vietnam. Lloyd Piche said, "I don't like you because you're Vietnamese. Our brothers went over to Vietnam, and they never came back," and "I'm gonna finish you tonight." Although the manager forced the Piche brothers to leave the pool hall, they waited outside for Loo and his friends and attacked them as they left the pool hall. Robert Piche and his brother first attacked one of Loo's friends, Lahn Tang, with a shotgun, but when Tang escaped, Robert swung a pistol at another of Loo's friends, Jim Ta. He missed his intended victim and hit Loo on the head instead.

Although Lloyd Piche made most of the racial remarks, he did not strike the fatal blow. He was sentenced to six months in prison for disorderly conduct and simple assault (on Tang), both of which are misdemeanors. In March 1990, Robert Piche was found guilty of second-degree murder and assault with a deadly weapon and sentenced to a total of thirty-seven years in prison. Although Judge Howard E. Manning, Jr., gave Piche a stiff lecture, the sentence was less than he could have meted out: Under North Carolina law, Piche could have been given life in prison.

MIJANURN RAHMAN

Mijanurn Rahman was killed in Brooklyn, New York, in 2002. He was from Bangladesh. In the aftermath of September 11, 2001, southern Asians who "looked Arab" may have been seen as fair targets. The killing was brutal. Rahman was beaten to death with baseball bats, hockey sticks, iron rods, and bamboo sticks. Curiously, the police proved reluctant to label the attacks as "racially motivated" and as a "hate crime," but the collective beating of a person can hardly be labeled anything else.

VIOLENCE AGAINST ASIANS IN HIGH SCHOOLS

In November 2005, harassment of Asian high school students was simply ignored by school administrators in Brooklyn, New York, and the problem became so acute that the U.S. Department of Justice stepped in, forcing the administrators of the high school to take serious measure to prevent the assaults and to address their underlying causes. This situation is not uncommon across the United States, and it is not confined to secondary schools, occurring in both primary schools and universities as well.

THREATS AND VIOLENCE IN UNIVERSITIES

Like several branches of the University of California, the Irvine branch has a very large Asian student population. For reasons that are not clear, except perhaps diffuse hatred of Asians, a threatening e-mail was sent to all "Asian-sounding" e-mail usernames. This e-mail was not acted upon, but violence has occurred at other university campuses. For example, at the State University of New York's Binghamton campus in 2000, four Asian American students were assaulted and seriously injured by three white students shouting racial slurs.

Lloyd Piche was indicted on eight counts of violating federal civil rights laws. On July 15, 1991, in a federal district court in Wilmington, North Carolina, Lloyd Piche was found guilty on all eight counts. On October 15, 1991, Lloyd Piche was sentenced to four years in prison and ordered to pay over $28,000 in restitution to the Loo family. Although the Justice Department had sought the maximum sentence under federal sentencing guidelines, Piche's sentence was less than the minimum sentence (six to seven and one-half years) under federal guidelines.

There are many similarities between the Loo and the Chin murders. In each case, the victim was a young man spending an evening relaxing with friends in a public facility (a bar in Chin's case, a pool hall in Loo's). In each case, an altercation began inside the public facility, and violence leading to murder erupted outside the facility. In each case, the victim was killed after being mistaken for or associated with Asians of other nationalities. In Chin's case, his killers were venting hostility against foreign Japanese, and in Loo's case, his murderers apparently mistook him for a Vietnamese. Thus, both Chin and Loo became victims simply because they were of Asian descent.

Together, the Chin and Loo murders underscore the harsh reality of ethnically motivated violence against Asians. They also signal in different ways the general public's lack of awareness of and to some extent indifference to anti-Asian discrimination. The three-year probation and almost nominal fines imposed by Judge Kaufman on Chin's murderers are suggestive of very little value being placed on an Asian American life. The ultimate failure of the American justice system to convict Ebens of civil rights charges, perhaps partly because of the Cincinnati jury's difficulty in believing in the existence of anti-Asian hatred, also implies that many Americans view racial hatred purely as a black–white problem and are unaware that Asian Americans are also frequently targets of hate crimes. Finally, neither murder was given much national prominence. Chin's killing did receive some national

(continued)

attention, but Loo's killing (in stark contrast to the murder of a young black man in Bensonhurst that occurred at roughly the same time) was hardly covered by the national media and raised no national sense of outrage.

HATE CRIMES, 2000–2005

Between 2000 and 2005, 199 hate crimes directed at Asians and Pacific Islanders were reported by the Federal Bureau of Investigation (FBI). A total of 9,035 hate crimes were reported by the FBI between 2000 and 2005, of which 252 or 27 percent were directed at Asians and Pacific Islanders. Of the hate crimes directed at Asians and Pacific Islanders, 17 percent were classified as aggravated assault, 29 percent as simple assault, and 54 percent as intimidation.

Sources: U.S. Commission on Civil Rights, 1992: 25–28; U.S. Department of Justice, Federal Bureau of Investigation, Uniform Crime Reports, *Hate Crime Statistics,* annual. See www.fbi.gov/ucr/hc2005/.

Asian immigrants, have rekindled old fears, intensified negative beliefs, and generated sporadic acts of discrimination against both newly arrived and established Asian American groups.

All these factors have sustained the subtle restrictions on this disproportionately middle-class minority. In time, these restrictions may diminish, but as long as Asian Americans remain readily identifiable in tight domestic job markets and in the context of tension-filled international trade with Asian nations, the potential for sustaining or even increasing barriers to full economic and political participation remains.

Responding to Discrimination

The Asian populations discussed in this chapter—Chinese, Japanese, Korean, and Filipino—are much more successful economically than the ethnic populations explored in other chapters. The percentage of Asian Americans who are middle class and white collar is much higher than comparable percentages in other subpopulations. However, the success of these established Asian immigrant groups has not been fully matched by newer immigrants. The hostility toward these new migrants creates a climate of prejudice and antagonism for the Asian American community as a whole.

The stereotype of Asian Americans as model minorities has rendered invisible the historical Asian American struggle against racism (Aguilar–San Juan, 1994). However, in the 1960s, inspired by various national liberation movements in Africa, Asia, Latin America, the Caribbean and Pacific Islands, and the Black Panthers and Young Lords in the United States, Asian American activists created "serve the people" organizations based on the Black Panther Party Survival Programs (Ho et al., 2000; Omatsu, 1994). Asian American youths initiated many of these organizations (Umemoto, 1989; Wei, 1993). In 1968, for example, Asian Americans were active members of the Third World Liberation Front

(TWLF)—a coalition of African American, Latino, American Indian, and Asian American campus organizations at San Francisco State University—which conducted the longest student strike in U.S. history (Omatsu, 1994; Umemoto, 1989). TWLF demanded the formation of a department of ethnic studies, open admissions, and the reorganization of the educational system. A decade later, in 1978, in response to the *Bakke* decision, Asian American and Pacific Islander student organizations on the West Coast formed the Asian/Pacific Student Union (APSU). The network of student organizations has fought for open admissions, affirmative action, and educational equality.

In 1969, I Wor Kuen (IWK), which means "Society of the Harmonious Righteous Fist," was formed as a revolutionary Chinese and Asian American collective in New York City (Ho et al., 2000). IWK was made up of radical students, workers, and working-class youth. IWK launched a door-to-door TB-testing campaign in Chinatown, initiated the first draft counseling program for Asian youth, and organized them to resist the draft. IWK also organized child care programs in schools. Similarly, in San Francisco, the Red Guard party was formed by mostly Asian American street youths to unite and politicize street youths and gangs who were constantly fighting the police and racist tourists, and who were fighting among themselves along with American-born and immigrant rival youth gangs (Ho et al., 2000). The Red Guard also organized Marxist reading groups, a free breakfast program for children, and a free lunch program for elderly persons.

In the 1980s, Asian American activists achieved successful campaigns at the grassroots level. Japanese Americans won redress and reparations. Chinese Americans mobilized community support for the pro-democracy struggle in China. Samoan Americans fought against police abuse in Los Angeles. At the same time, Asian American professionals were creating new coalitions and consortiums (Omatsu, 1994). However, in the 1990s, a wave of neoconservatism emerged among Asian Americans. In particular, these neoconservatives reject past struggles against racism. Most are proud to be Asian Americans, but they denounce the Asian American movements of the 1960s and 1970s or are not even aware that they existed. Most Asian American youth subscribe to the model minority myth (Lee, 1996). According to Park (1999), most Korean and Chinese youth believe that American society is an open society because of the entrepreneurial success of their parents. In other words, the rights and privileges of "social citizenship" are rooted in conspicuous consumption, in assimilating to the material structure of American consumer society.

The subtlety of much discrimination—for example, college admissions practices, corporate glass or bamboo ceilings, and gerrymandering of voting districts—along with the sporadic nature of acts of violence against Asian Americans by angry whites and disadvantaged minorities makes it difficult to mount a concerted corrective effort, especially by a politically passive model minority that is not perceived to have problems. Especially during the early years of the twenty-first century when considerable effort has been made by governmental and legal agencies to be more conscious of, and to correct for, past and present discrimination against African Americans, Latinos, and Native

Americans, we must view with some wonder the comparatively little effort that has been made on behalf of, or by, Asian Americans. Without protests and political mobilization by Asians, it is not likely that much will be done in the future—another cost of being the quiet, model minority.

The Precarious Situation for Asian Americans

Are Asian Americans really the model minority in the United States? On the surface, one could argue that their educational, occupational, and economic status is an indicator of success, especially in light of efforts to limit Asian American presence in, and assimilation into, mainstream American society. Asian Americans thus fit the model minority stereotype because many have overcome the odds and succeeded. Beneath the surface, however, the model minority image has negative repercussions for not only Asian Americans but other ethnic groups as well. For other ethnics, Hurk and Kim (1989:530) have noted:

> The dominant group's stereotype of Asian Americans as a model minority also affects negatively other minorities. Since the Asian Americans' "success" may be considered by the dominant group as a proof of openness in the American opportunity structure, there is a constant danger that other less successful minorities could be regarded as "inferior" and/or "lazy." These less achieving minorities may be blamed for their own failure and become victims of scapegoating ("Japanese have made it. Why can't they?").

The dominant group (that is, white society) can thus use the model minority image of Asian Americans as an ideological tool to maintain a pattern of unequal access to valued resources. To overstate the case in order to emphasize our point: Asian Americans succeed because they represent a small (though growing) percentage of the total population and, hence, pose less threat to the majority; other minority populations, such as African Americans and Latinos, are much larger and consequently pose more threat, which leads to more intense discrimination (Aguirre and Baker, 1988; Blumstein, 1982). With the model minority as a basis for comparison, these larger populations appear less successful—an unfair comparison because of the greater degree of discrimination experienced by these larger minority groups. Members of larger minority groups grow to resent Asian Americans whose success is used to highlight their failure. As the success of the model minority stereotype is used by white society to illustrate the "openness" of the American opportunity structure, other minority populations that have experienced far more discrimination will be blamed for their inability to take advantage of imagined opportunities. Yu (1980) has noted that many African Americans and Latinos resent Asian Americans because they believe that Asian Americans are the first to receive assistance in the United States. Similarly, Thornton and Taylor (1988) have found that many African Americans feel distant from Asian American populations and do not perceive Asian Americans as a minority group.

The model minority stereotype creates problems for Asian Americans as well, perpetuating the perception that poverty, homelessness, mental illness,

Resentment toward Asian Americans by many African Americans and Latinos was evident in the looting and destruction suffered by Korean American store owners in South Central Los Angeles during the riots that broke out in 1992 after four white police officers were acquitted in the beating of Rodney King. Although relations between Korean American store owners and their black and Latino customers have improved, this Korean American store owner works from behind protective glass.

crime, and other social problems do not exist among Asian Americans. As Crystal (1989:406) has noted:

> Rather than the "yellow peril" of the past, Asian Americans are currently viewed as an exemplary group of honest and hardworking citizens with low rates of juvenile delinquency and divorce. They are perceived as having few, if any, mental health problems and are thought to live in homogeneous communities composed of stable, close-knit families that "take care of their own" with little need of outside social services.

In reality, the lower rates of return on education, especially at the postsecondary level, and the existence of a glass ceiling in the job sector indicate that Asian Americans do indeed experience institutionalized discrimination and prejudice.

PACIFIC ISLANDERS: A SHORT EXPLORATORY NOTE

There is some evidence that people began to leave Asia many thousands of years ago to settle the distant islands of the Pacific. Some genetic markers suggest that Taiwan was the likely origin of these seafarers, who radiated all over

TABLE 8.8 Pacific Islander Subpopulations as a Percentage of Total
Pacific Islander Population in the United States, 2000

Subpopulation	Percentage of Total Pacific Islander Population	Percentage of U.S. Population
Native Hawaiian	36.8%	0.14%
Samoan	22.5	0.05
Guamanian	14.6	0.03
Tongan	7.3	0.01
Fijian	2.7	0.01
Marshallese	1.5	0.01
Other Pacific Islander	14.6	0.07
Total Pacific Islander population		**0.31%**

Note: Figures are for respondents who reported one and those who reported two ancestries.
Source: U.S. Bureau of the Census, 2005d, Table 1, p. 1, and Figure 1, p. 4.

the islands that are scattered both south and east from Asia. But since Pacific Islanders have been dispersed across the Pacific Ocean for so many millennia, it makes relatively little sense to lump them with people whose more recent ancestry is from the Asian continent—as had been the convention of the U.S. Census Bureau until very recently.

The total population of Pacific Islanders in the United States is very small, constituting only 0.31 percent of the total U.S. population, and this figure includes those who have listed another ancestry in addition to being a Native Hawaiian or a Pacific Islander. Those who report only one ancestry (as a Native Hawaiian/Pacific Islander) constitute only 0.13 percent of the total U.S. population. Table 8.8 documents the percentage of the total U.S. population, as well as the percentage of the Pacific Island population, of each prominent ethnic group whose origins are the Pacific Islands, including Hawaii. These figures, it should be noted, are for respondents reporting *both* one *and* two ancestries. Native Hawaiians, as might be expected, constitute the largest group, followed by Samoans, Guamanians, Tongans, Fijians, Marshallese, and "other" subpopulations from the Pacific Islands. Although the total population of Pacific Islanders is small, it is comparatively young, which means that as members enter childbearing years, the numbers of Americans with Pacific Island ancestry will grow.

Pacific Islanders in the United States come from areas where the United States has had political interests, particularly during World War II, and in several cases, the islands are protectorates of the United States. Although Pacific Islanders may "look similar" to each other (at least on the surface) in the eyes of the general population, they come from diverse cultures, widely separated in the Pacific Ocean. There may be some convergence among these cultures because of their common experiences with white European cultures, but as is often the case, the general public tends to place diverse peoples into one ethnic category—in this case, Pacific Islander.

Pacific Islanders have had a centuries-old history with European societies that first visited and then annexed various island groups as part of forming a global empire. The United States also took control of, or imposed protectorate status on, many Pacific Island societies, the most prominent being Hawaii but also

Guam and other islands in the Pacific. Once European-origin whites gained some economic and political control of island cultures, the indigenous population was forced to abandon many of its cultural traditions and modes of subsistence. As a result, islanders often had to become part of a lower-wage labor force, although many were also able to carve out small family business niches. When Pacific Islanders began to leave their homelands and migrate to Hawaii and California (see Box 8.7), they radiated into a number of occupational niches, mostly

---

Box 8.7
Pacific Islanders in California: A Case Study

The label "model minority" suggests that all Asians/Pacific Islanders are faring very well in U.S. society, and it's often assumed that they are doing better overall than the non-Latino white population. Pacific Islanders in California, however, are not faring as well as one might assume. A troublesome portrait of the Pacific Islander population in California emerges from the following data profile:

- Pacific Islanders increased from 0.4 percent to 0.7 percent of California's population between 1990 and 2003. In 2003, the Pacific Islander population in California numbered about 246,000.
- From 2000 to 2003, Asians had the fastest growth rate among the major racial populations in the San Francisco Bay Area (9 percent), and Pacific Islanders had the fastest growth rate in the Central Valley (24 percent) and Southern California (14 percent) regions.
- Contrary to the model minority stereotype, Pacific Islanders are not doing well on all fronts. They fare worse than average on a number of important measures of socioeconomic status: lower-than-average rate of home ownership (47 percent vs. 57 percent state average) and higher-than-average rates of living in overcrowded housing (26 percent of households vs. 15 percent state average) and of receiving public assistance income or welfare (7 percent vs. 5 percent state average).
- The Pacific Islander population lags behind other Californians on educational outcomes. In general, 22 percent of Pacific Islanders have not completed high school, and only 17 percent have a college degree. More specifically, 23 percent of all Californians have less than a high school education compared to 20 percent of Guamanians, 23 percent of Samoans, 34 percent of Fijians, and 38 percent of Tongans. Thirty-four percent of all Californians have a college degree compared to 22 percent of Guamanians, 18 percent of Samoans, 16 percent of Fijians, and 11 percent of Tongans.
- Pacific Islander groups have among the highest rates of poverty: Samoans (45 percent), Tongans (44 percent), and Fijians (34 percent). The Pacific Islander child poverty rate (20 percent) is more than twice that of white children (9 percent). The highest concentration of Pacific Islander poverty is found in the city of Compton, where a majority are in poverty and 63 percent of children are in poverty.
- Pacific Islander youth living in San Mateo County are more likely than any other racial group to be arrested, enter the juvenile justice system, and be detained in a locked facility.

Sources: Jocelyn Y. Stewart, "Data Reveal Hard Truths for Islanders," *Los Angeles Times* (Sept. 26, 2005): B1, B6; Asian Pacific American Legal Center, *The Diverse Face of Asians and Pacific Islanders in California* (Los Angeles: Asian Pacific American Legal Center, 2005).

lower-wage service, sales, and office work, although some entered blue-collar jobs as well. This history of subordination helps account for the fact that Pacific Islanders' shares of resources are less than those of whites, especially non-Latino whites.

Resource Shares of Pacific Islanders

Table 8.9 summarizes the rate of poverty for Pacific Islanders. In 1999–2000, the Census Bureau's special tabulation documented a very high rate of poverty: 17.7 percent. Indeed, only those of Fijian ancestry evidenced a rate below that of the total U.S. population. However, these figures must be qualified by noting the poverty rate for 2008 (see Table 1.1 on page 15) that shows a poverty rate for the Asian/Pacific Islander population of 8.1 percent for dual-headed families and 14.8 percent for female-headed families; and 10.2 percent for persons. In contrast, for white families and persons in 2008, the poverty rate was 9.4 percent for dual-headed families and 27.2 percent for female-headed families; and 11.2 percent for persons. Much of the discrepancy can be accounted for by the fact that the figures reported in Chapter 1 are only for those who reported *one* ancestry, as either Native Hawaiian or Pacific Islander, while the tables presented here include those who reported *two* ancestries (Native Hawaiian/Pacific Islander, plus another ancestry). The report from the Census Bureau is surprisingly ambiguous on what the data show, but the figures presented here include those reporting two ancestries. As is evident in Table 8.9 and subsequent tables, being a Pacific Islander and having another ancestry increases rates of poverty, lowers income, and decreases educational attainment—presumably because of discrimination against those of "mixed" ancestry. Pacific Islanders thus have very high rates of poverty. The Marshallese have a rate that may be higher than that of any other ethnic subpopulation in the United States.

As with the poverty rate, there is a discrepancy between earlier figures on median household income and the most recent data. Table 8.10 reports the earlier figures, for 1999–2000, which include respondents who listed two ancestries, and these figures show that Pacific Islanders lag behind the income of all

TABLE 8.9 Poverty Rates for Pacific Islanders, 1999–2000

Subpopulation	Percentage Who Are Poor
Native Hawaiian	15.6%
Samoan	20.2
Guamanian	13.7
Tongan	19.5
Fijian	10.5
Marshallese	38.3
Other Pacific Islander	21.4
All Pacific Islanders	**17.7%**
Total U.S. population	**12.4%**
Non-Latino whites	**7.8%**

Note: Figures are for respondents who reported one and those who reported two ancestries.
Source: U.S. Bureau of the Census, 2005d, Figure 14, p. 17.

TABLE 8.10 Median Household Income for Pacific Islanders, 1999–2000

Subpopulation	Median Household Income
Native Hawaiian	$49,686
Samoan	41,091
Guamanian	49,122
Tongan	46,261
Fijian	46,333
Marshallese	27,808
Other Pacific Islanders	41,165
All U.S. households	**$50,046**

Note: Figures are for respondents who reported one and those who reported two ancestries.
Source: U.S. Bureau of the Census, 2005d, Figure 13, p. 16.

families. In contrast, the 2003–2004 data indicate that Pacific Islanders, when reporting only one ancestry, have household incomes that are higher than those of the total U.S. population as a whole, and considerably higher than those for Latinos, African Americans, and Native Americans.

Table 8.11 summarizes the occupational distribution of Pacific Islanders. Here the overall figures correspond to the latest figures because they come from the same data set as those reporting two ancestries. All Pacific Islanders are underrepresented in managerial and professional occupations; and in fact, only Latinos reveal a lower percentage of individuals in these higher-paying occupations. As a whole, Pacific Islanders are overrepresented in lower-paying

TABLE 8.11 Occupational Distribution of Pacific Islanders, 2000

	Percentage of Adults Employed in:					
Subpopulation	Managerial/ Professional	Service	Sales/ Office	Construction/ Extraction/ Maintenance	Production/ Transportation/ Moving	Farming/ Fishing/ Forestry
Native Hawaiian	26.4%	20.9%	28.3%	10.1%	13.2%	1.1%
Samoan	18.6	18.8	31.4	9.3	21.2	0.06
Guamanian	26.4	18.1	30.2	8.8	15.7	0.8
Tongan	13.4	26.1	23.5	15.6	21.1	0.3
Fijian	19.0	28.6	28.5	7.1	16.5	0.3
Marshallese	9.4	22.2	16.6	6.8	43.5	1.5
Other Pacific Islander	23.9	21.9	28.5	7.9	16.8	1.0
All Pacific Islanders	**23.3%**	**20.8%**	**28.8%**	**9.6%**	**16.5%**	**0.9%**
Total U.S. population	**33.6%**	**14.9%**	**26.7%**	**9.4%**	**14.6%**	**0.7%**
Non-Latino whites	**33.6%**	**12.8%**	**27.2%**	**9.4%**	**13.2%**	**0.07%**

Note: Figures are for respondents who reported one and those who reported two ancestries.
Source: U.S. Bureau of the Census, 2005d, Figure 11, p. 14.

TABLE 8.12 Educational Attainment of Pacific Islanders, 25 Years Old and Older 2000

Subpopulation	Percentage Who Have:			
	Less than High School	High School Diploma Only	Some College/ Associate's Degree	Bachelor's Degree or More
Native Hawaiian	16.8%	36.5%	31.4%	15.2%
Samoan	24.2	36.2	29.1	10.5
Guamanian	22.2	29.9	33.7	14.3
Tongan	34.7	32.8	23.9	8.6
Fijian	33.2	29.5	28.6	8.8
Marshallese	32.3	38.5	24.0	5.1
Other Pacific Islander	23.3	38.5	32.5	17.9
All Pacific Islanders	**21.7%**	**33.7%**	**30.8%**	**13.8%**
Total U.S. population	**19.6%**	**28.6%**	**27.4%**	**24.4%**

Note: Figures are for respondents who reported one and those who reported two ancestries.
Source: U.S. Bureau of the Census, 2005d, Figure 9, p. 12.

service and sales/office jobs, while evidencing about the same percentage as the general population in construction/extraction/maintenance, production/ transportation/moving, and farming/fishing/forestry occupations. As is evident, there is some variation within the Pacific Islander population.

The poverty, income, and occupational distribution figures for Pacific Islanders can partially be accounted for by their lower levels of educational attainment. As is clear in Table 8.12, Pacific Islanders have a larger percentage of the adult population who did not receive a high school degree than the total population. More dramatically, the data also show a lower percentage of individuals who have received a bachelor's degree or more than the general population. Moreover, this figure for Pacific Islanders is slightly lower than that for Latinos and Native Americans, while being considerably lower than the figure for African Americans, Asians, and non-Latino whites. Interestingly, Pacific Islanders have a higher overall rate of "some college" than the general population, although much of this figure is the result of the rates for the two of the larger Pacific Islander populations (Native Hawaiians and Guamanians) that historically have had government-subsidized educational opportunities. Still, it is clear that a large percentage of those beginning college drop out, thus decreasing their opportunities in American society.

Identifiability of Pacific Islanders

Pacific Islanders display some features that distinguish them from other ethnic groups. Somewhat darker skin tones, wide faces, large torsos, and dark hair stand out in a society dominated by persons of European ancestry. Pacific Islanders often work to retain their ethnic heritage through religious worship, neighborhoods, intermarriage, language, and other cultural features. For example, almost

30 percent of Pacific Islanders do not speak English at home. This decision serves not only to sustain their culture but also to make them more distinctive. There is considerable variability in language fluency and use of a native language at home. Eighty-three percent of Native Hawaiians, for example, speak "only English" at home, compared to 17 percent of Tongans, 16.3 percent of Fijians, and 18.7 percent of Marshallese. Even more established Pacific Islanders, such as Guamanians and Samoans, do not speak English at home, thus preserving their ethnic identity and visibility to others (U.S. Bureau of the Census, 2005d:11).

Negative Beliefs about Pacific Islanders

Most Americans do not have wide exposure to Pacific Islanders because so many are concentrated in California and Hawaii, but in these states, subtle prejudices can be found. Most of these prejudices revolve around perceptions of ancestry from "more primitive" cultures—much like beliefs about the perceived characteristics of "peasants" from Europe in the nineteenth century and Latin America in the twentieth. Negative stereotypes may also include elements of Pacific Islanders not "assimilating," "keeping their old culture," and being "standoffish" in their own communities, thereby seeming "less American." In more recent years, however, some of these stereotypes have been mitigated by increased tolerance of diversity, especially in California and Hawaii. Still, these beliefs can quietly justify discrimination in school and work contexts, creating expectations about what Pacific Islanders can and cannot do.

Institutionalized Discrimination against Pacific Islanders

For many decades, Pacific Islanders were used as a low-wage workforce in Hawaii, but the profile of work has dramatically changed. Today, most Pacific Islanders are in service, office work, and small businesses. Newer immigrants to Hawaii and the mainland typically come without educational credentials or economic capital, and when this lack is coupled with subtle forms of informal discrimination, their economic options are limited. Moreover, because English is often not the dominant language at home, their children enter schools somewhat at a disadvantage. And, given residential segregation in ethnic neighborhoods and enclaves (reflecting a preference to be with fellow ethnics, economic realities, and subtle forms of housing discrimination), Pacific Islanders remain identifiable and, hence, potential targets of discrimination. Still, it is difficult to know *how much* actual discrimination occurs in schools, jobs, and the political arena, compared to the inevitable effects of self-selection into ethnic neighborhoods, lack of educational credentials of parents, and low levels of economic capital. Since this set of subpopulations is, as a total of the U.S. population, so small, systematic studies on discrimination are difficult to find. Community studies do reveal, however, informal discrimination in housing and, to a lesser extent, in schools and the job market.

Stratification of Pacific Islanders

The data on incomes, jobs, and educational attainment make clear that there is some degree of stratification of Pacific Islanders, and particularly so for recent immigrants who come with less capital and education than previous migrants to Hawaii and the mainland. Within specific communities, Pacific Islanders are often found in a limited range of jobs, suggesting that the full spectrum of jobs is not available to them. Still, it will be necessary to collect more data over the life course and across generations to be sure that there is a high degree of stratification among Pacific Islanders that is the equivalent of the stratification among African Americans, Native Americans, and Latinos.

SUMMARY

The first Asians came to America beginning in the 1850s and were instrumental in the development of the commercial, industrial, and agricultural infrastructure of the West. For many years Asian immigration was restricted, but these restrictions have been relaxed and the Asian population has doubled in size since 1980, although it is still quite small compared to the African American and Latino populations.

Asian Americans match or exceed white Americans in average family income, educational attainment, incumbency in managerial and professional occupations, and life span. Yet the signs of discrimination are evident along a number of fronts: Asian poverty rates exceed those of whites; returns on education to Asians are less than those for whites; and many Asians still remain segregated from non-Asians.

Asians are readily identifiable because of their distinctive eye fold and, to a lesser extent, color tones of their skin; hence, they are easy targets of discrimination. Although their success gives them the image of a "model minority" that has succeeded in spite of obstacles, lurking beneath the surface of this portrayal is a more sinister revival of the old "yellow peril" stereotype in which Asians are seen as foreigners who take jobs, admission slots in higher education, and business opportunities away from non-Asians. In the past, such perceived threats and their codification into negative stereotypes propagated considerable violence against Asians, but more significant has been the long legacy of open legal and political discrimination against them, which has abated only over the last few decades. Yet Asians still are subject to considerable violence from other minorities and whites. As the Asian population has increased, more subtle forms of discrimination have become evident: Asians frequently run up against a glass ceiling that keeps their careers in check despite successful performance and other qualifications. Asians rarely get elected to political office because of gerrymandering of their neighborhoods and because non-Asians are reluctant to vote for Asians. Asians are underrepresented in governmental appointments despite the fact that their educational credentials qualify them for these appointments in disproportionate numbers. Asians have been subjected to a quota system by elite colleges and universities, thereby denying opportunity to many qualified Asian students. And informal housing discrimination, often punctuated with white violence, is still evident in many communities. Historically, Asians have not been prone to visible protests, but in more recent years, legal and political challenges to all of these discriminatory practices have been mounted, indicating that Asians will no longer passively accept discrimination.

The recent decoupling of at least some data on Pacific Islanders from data on Asians will, in the future, allow researchers to track this small set of ethnic subpopulations. Hawaii and California have many people of Pacific Island ancestry, and like all minority subpopulations, they have been subject to prejudicial beliefs and some discrimination. Yet because Pacific Islanders are neither a large nor a resource-rich subpopulation, they likely pose less threat to other ethnics, and the discrimination they experience is less severe—at least in recent decades. Certainly, the takeover of Hawaii by whites and U.S. hegemony in the Pacific before and after World War II led to highly discriminatory practices in which land was confiscated and the indigenous populations reduced to a low-wage labor pool for white economic interests. Discrimination can still be found in Hawaii and in communities in California and elsewhere with a large Pacific Islander population.

POINTS OF DEBATE

Asian Americans are caught in a difficult bind: Their success engenders white hostility and, at the same time, is also used to condemn less successful minorities, thereby arousing increased hostility from disadvantaged minorities. Asians are caught in the middle of all manner of ethnic hostility, and as the percentage of Asians in the population increases, many intensely debated issues will surface.

1. Considering that Asian Americans are so successful, especially relative to other large minorities, should Asian complaints about subtle forms of discrimination limiting their further success be given the same attention as complaints from more disadvantaged minorities? Should programs to help Asians be of the same intensity as those to help less successful minorities? Should efforts at reducing ethnic discrimination be calibrated along a sliding scale, with those who are worse off getting most of the attention? The law would say no as an answer to all of these questions, but the policies of government always involve interpretations and selective implementations of the law. Is this desirable? Necessary? Inevitable in light of political realities?

2. As the Asian population grows in size and occupies many economic niches desired not only by whites but more significantly by other minorities, can hostility toward Asians be reduced, or will this tension, as manifested in the hostility of African Americans and Latinos toward Asian-owned businesses in their communities, become a chronic feature of the American landscape? If so, what is to be done to reduce this hostility?

3. Is American society in danger of hardening the lines of hostility among Asians, whites, Latinos, and blacks? If all are competing for the same scarce resources—jobs, income, education, housing—how is the tension to be mitigated? If America is on the path toward tension-provoking ethnic pluralism with each subpopulation viewing the other with considerable hostility, is this what most Americans want? If not, what is to be done?

KEY TERMS/KEY LEGISLATION

Chinese Exclusion Act of 1882, 245
Civil Liberties Act of 1988, 248
Commission on Wartime Relocation
  and Internment of Civilians, 248
Executive Order 9066, 247
Gentleman's Agreement of 1907, 245
gerrymandering, 253
glass or bamboo ceiling, 234
Hirabayashi v. United States
  (1943), 248
Immigration Act of 1917, 246
internment camps, 246

Japanese American Evacuation
  Claims Act of 1948, 248
Korematsu v. United States (1944), 248
model minority, 229
National Origins Act of 1924, 246
Ozawa v. United States (1922), 246
Philippines Independence Act of
  1934, 246
Presidential Proclamation 4417, 248
segregation index, 238
Yasui v. United States (1943), 248
yellow peril, 243

Visit our text-specific website at www.mhhe.com/aguirre7e for valuable resources for both students and instructors.

CHAPTER 9

Arab Americans

On September 11, 2001, Americans watched in horror as hijacked airliners crashed into the World Trade Center towers in New York. These acts, along with a less successful effort to destroy the Pentagon and a failed effort to target the White House, dramatically escalated Americans' sense of threat from an "enemy" arising from the Arab, Middle Eastern, and Muslim world. For decades, acts of terrorism had occurred all over the globe, and now, the United States was a clear target. In fact, Americans already had been targeted in the Middle East and Africa, and of course, in the earlier effort in February 1993 to blow up the North Tower of the World Trade Center from its underground parking facility. But the scale and drama of the September attack will be long remembered unless another effort is made to kill civilians on such a mass scale.

Almost immediately, the attack was blamed on "**Muslim or Islamic extremists**," which turned out to be a correct description of those who had hijacked the planes, but this label placed people of Arab ancestry, "Middle Eastern looking" persons, and followers of **Islam** in a precarious position—perhaps one that only Japanese Americans after the attack on Pearl Harbor could fully understand. Indeed, in the immediate aftermath of what has become known as "**9-11**," **hate crimes** against Arabs and Muslims escalated dramatically (Rubenstein, 2004), although such crimes have decreased somewhat over the last few years. Before 9-11, Arabs and Muslims had experienced hate crimes at rates below the three most targeted populations—gays, Jews, and African Americans—but in the months after 9-11, attacks on Middle Eastern persons exceeded, for a time, attacks on those long-standing targets of hate. Individuals from non–Middle Eastern backgrounds who "looked Arab or Middle Eastern" were also targeted, much as they had been in 1979–1981, when American hostages were taken and held in Iran. These hate crimes were only an extreme manifestation of a quieter prejudice that had long existed against individuals from the Middle East. In the minds of many Americans, people from the Middle East are to be viewed suspiciously, like all Americans of "color," but this biasing factor is further intensified by the perception of Middle Easterners and particularly "Arabs" as non-Christian and as "foreigners" within American society. Like so many prejudicial beliefs against minorities, those about Arab Americans are inaccurate. So before examining the dynamics of discrimination against Arab Americans, we need to gain some minimal insight about this much-maligned population.

This Arab American father and son joined more than a thousand Arab Americans at the Passaic (NJ) County Mosque following the World Trade Center disaster to pray for America and to donate blood for the wounded.

WHO ARE ARAB AMERICANS?

A Profile of Arab Americans

Americans tend to conflate "Arab," "Middle Eastern," and "Muslim," when, in fact, it is important to distinguish among these three labels. Islam is the second largest religion behind Christianity, but many Muslims live outside the Middle East. The largest number of Muslims in one society resides in Indonesia; societies across the top of Africa and in the southern regions of Europe and Asia also are home to many Muslims. The Middle East is, of course, predominately Muslim, although Jews, Christians, and Muslims have lived in this area for millennia. Not all Middle Easterners are Arab. Turks, Kurds, and Iranians, for example, do not define themselves as Arab, although a majority practice Islam. Indeed, the label "Arab" is somewhat elusive. Generally, if a person speaks Arabic, practices Islam, and identifies with the traditions of Arabic-speaking peoples, this individual can be classified as "Arab" (Touma, 1996). By these criteria, the countries listed in Table 9.1 can be classified as Arab, and Americans who have migrated from one of these countries could be labeled as having "Arab ancestry." The total Arab population in these societies is about the same size as the population of the United States—some 300 million persons.

Arab Americans, however, are not predominately Muslim. Only about 24 percent of Arabs in America are Muslim. The vast majority—some 66 percent—are

TABLE 9.1 Arab Countries

Algeria
Bahrain
Cosmoros
Djibouti
Egypt
Iraq
Jordan
Kuwait
Lebanon
Libya
Mauritania
Morocco
Oman
Palestine (Gaza Strip/West Bank)
Qatar
Saudi Arabia
Somalia
Sudan
Syria
Tunisia
United Arab Emirates
Yemen

Source: League of Arab States; Arab American Institute.
www.arab.de/arabinfo/league.htm.

TABLE 9.2 Religious Affiliation of Americans with Arab Ancestry, 2000

Religion	Percentage of Arab-Ancestry Families
Catholic	35%
Protestant	11
Orthodox	20
Total Christian	**66%**
Muslim	24
Other/no affiliation	13

Sources: Arab American Institute, 2005; Zogby International, 2000.

some version of Christian: 35 percent are Catholic, 20 percent are Eastern Orthodox, and 11 percent are Protestant. Table 9.2 details the religious affiliations of Americans of Arab ancestry.

Of the total number of Muslims in the United States, African Americans ("Black Muslims") represent 42 percent of all Muslims, followed by persons from South Asia, Africa, Iran, Turkey, and Southeast Asia, and European-origin whites. Table 9.3 lists the relative percentages of all Muslims in the United States and their regions of origin. As is evident, the vast majority of Muslims in the United States are not of Arab ancestry; indeed, only a comparatively small percentage—12.4 percent—of all Muslims in the United States have Arab origins.

TABLE 9.3 Muslim Population in the United States by Country of Origin/Ethnic Group

Ancestry	Percentage of Total Muslim Population
African American	42.0%
South Asian	24.4
Arab	12.4
African	5.2
Iranian	3.6
Turkish	2.4
Southeast Asian	2.0
Non-Arab white	1.6
Not determined	5.6

Source: Council on Islamic Education, 1995:5. See also Marvasti and McKinney, 2004:26.

Thus, many of the stereotypes among Americans that conflate Arabs, Muslims, and Middle Easterners are simply wrong. The overwhelming majority of Arabs in the United States are Christian, and the vast majority of Muslims do not have Middle Eastern ancestry. Fears among Americans about those of Arab ancestry being Islamic radicals are obviously overdrawn. Nonetheless, in the aftermath of 9-11, as a consequence of the conflation created by prejudicial beliefs, all "Arab looking" individuals and Middle Easterners, along with all Muslims, are viewed suspiciously by the American public and are potential targets of hate crimes.

There is considerable debate over how many persons of Arab ancestry reside in the United States. Where are the largest Arab American communities in the United States? For an answer to this question, see Box 9.1. The official census

A Muslim boy prays.

Box 9.1

Largest Arab American Communities in the United States

California	Los Angeles, Orange County, San Francisco, Marin County, San Diego, San José, Sacramento
Colorado	Denver, Aurora, Glendale, Arvada, Parker, Littleton, Golden, Louisville, Lafayette, Boulder, Colorado Springs
Connecticut	Hartford, Stanford, New Haven
Florida	North Miami Beach, Hallandale, Tampa, Fort Lauderdale, Coral Springs, Orlando, St. Petersburg, Daytona Beach
Georgia	Atlanta
Illinois	Chicago
Massachusetts	Boston, Newton, Brookline, Sharon, Lynn, Springfield, Framingham
Michigan	Detroit, Dearborn
Minnesota	Minneapolis, Hopkins, St. Paul, Woodbury, Minnetonka
Nevada	Las Vegas, Reno
New Jersey	Bergen County, Marlboro, Cherry Hill, Parsippany, Livingston, Manalapan, Matawan
New York	Brooklyn, Queens, Manhattan, Staten Island, Long Island, Westchester County, Rockland County, Albany, Rochester, Syracuse
Oregon	Salem, Woodburn, Portland, Oregon City, West Linn, Lake Oswego, Beaverton, Tigard, Tualatin
Pennsylvania	Philadelphia, Pittsburgh, Jenkintown
Texas	Houston, Dallas, San Antonio
Washington	Seattle, Bellevue, Redmond, Vancouver, Tacoma
Washington, DC	Baltimore, Bethesda, Rockville, Pikesville, Gaithersburg, Arlington, Fairfax

Source: www.allied-media.com.

figures indicate that a little under 1.2 million persons of Arab ancestry live in America, whereas data compiled by the Arab American Institute put the figure closer to 3 million. The difference in these two figures stems from the way Arabs have been classified by the Census Bureau. In the more recent categorizations by the Census Bureau, Arabs (and Middle Easterners) have been instructed to record their ethnicity as "white," which is somewhat ironic in light of the fact that the negative stereotypes about "Arab and Muslim terrorists" often include "racial" descriptions of their skin color and facial features. Still, the effect has been to undercount people from Arab backgrounds because many have followed instructions on census forms and simply recorded themselves as "white." And since it is only recently that the Census Bureau explicitly gathered data on Arabs, many whose families came to the United States generations ago simply fail to record their Arab ancestry on census forms. Whichever figure is used—1.2 million or 3 million—it is clear that the Arab population in the United States is very small, at best 1 percent of the total population or, more likely, only a fraction of 1 percent. Thus, the sense of threat experienced by Americans comes not from the numbers of Americans of Arab ancestry but from fears about Islam and extremists.

In Table 9.4, we have taken the lower census figure from the Census Bureau (2005a). As is evident, Lebanese constitute the largest country of origin; and as we will see shortly, Lebanese- and Syrian-origin Americans were among the first to immigrate to the United States in the late 1800s. Americans tend to forget that these countries of origin are very different in their culture and history; and coupled with the fact that most of the immigrants from these countries are *not* Muslim, stereotypes of a unified terrorist bloc of Muslim Arabs cannot possibly be true. Ironically, as we discuss later, discrimination against Arabs and Muslims has caused a certain amount of **ethnogenesis,** or the creation of an new pan-Arab ethnic identity as a defensive response to the hostility experienced daily by many Middle Easterners in the United States. Where Arabs have historically been divided by their religion and country of origin, their common plight has led to a new kind of **pan-ethnicity** among not only those of Arab

TABLE 9.4 Country of Origin among Arab Americans, 2000

Ancestry	Percentage of Arab Population
Lebanese	24.8%
Egyptian	14.5
Syrian	8.9
Palestinian	7.3
Jordanian	4.2
Moroccan	3.6
Iraqi	3.5
Arab "Arabic"	19.7
Other Arab	9.6

Note: Includes respondents reporting two ancestries. Total Arab American population is 1,189,731.
Source: U.S. Bureau of the Census, 2005a, Figure 1, p. 3.

ancestry but also those Muslims from Asia as well. In some ways, this emerging sense of ethnic identification is much like pan-Indianism among Native Americans who, for all their other differences, have been subject to similar patterns of discrimination.

A Short History of Arab American Immigration

From the mid-1500s to the mid-1800s, the first Muslims to come to the Americas were slaves from western Africa; thus, perhaps, it is not surprising that present-day African Americans might be attracted to Islam. The first Middle Easterners—many of them also Arabs—began to migrate to the United States in the late 1800s. Most of these were Lebanese and Syrians who were leaving the repressive conditions of the Ottoman Empire ruled by Turks (Hooglund, 1987; Khalaf, 1987; Marvasti and McKinney, 2004; Naff, 1985). These immigrants held Turkish passports, but they spoke Arabic and saw themselves as Syrians (Syria and Lebanon were not clearly distinct in the 1880s, and indeed, Syria still exerts considerable influence in Lebanon). Later, these immigrants viewed themselves as Lebanese because they came from the part of Syria that today is Lebanon. The hyphenated "Syrian-Lebanese" label was also common. These early migrants were divided by religion. Some were Muslim, others were Jewish, and a majority were Christian.

Unlike many immigrant populations who came to the United States in the nineteenth century, this first wave of migrants had some resources: (1) entrepreneurial and trading skills that could be applied to their new circumstances (many had been peddlers in rural areas of the Middle East), (2) modest amounts of capital from the sale of their homes in Syria/Lebanon, (3) and literacy. They also came with a **sojourner orientation,** hoping to make money in the United States and then return to their homeland. Many males came without their families on the presumption that they would eventually go back to the Middle East. These migrants often became **middleman minorities** and small shop owners in rural areas of the American heartland, a pattern of internal migration that facilitated the spread and assimilation of these Lebanese into the American mainstream. Yet like all middleman minorities, especially those who see themselves as sojourners, the owners of these small businesses faced pronounced hostility from non-Arabs. As a result, many of these early Arab immigrants moved into the wage-labor force, especially the automobile industry in the Midwest, in order to escape the hostility and persecution often experienced by middleman minorities (Naff, 1985).

World events upset these sojourners' efforts to get home, however. World War I isolated them in the United States; and after World War I, very restrictive immigration and emigration quotas kept them from returning home. As a result, this first wave of Arab migrants began to assimilate, emphasizing English at home, pushing their children to excel in school, and abandoning clothing and other cultural traditions that would identify them as Arab. Because these early immigrants were defined as "nonwhites," there was a constant debate in the courts over their rights to be citizens—much as many Latinos experience today.

But by making appeals to their Semitic ancestry, which made them "more white" than Europeans, these Lebanese/Syrians were eventually defined as "white"—a designation that persists to this day in the Census Bureau categorization of Arabs. Still, there was suspicion about the "whiteness" of Arabs and their rights to full citizenship well into the first decades of the twentieth century, suspicion that resurfaced in the wake of 9-11.

Today, about half of the current Arab American population is descended from this first wave of immigration. Because the **Immigration Act of 1924** put into place highly restrictive quotas for immigrants from Asia, the Middle East, and southern Europe, there was no second wave until after World War II; and because the key provisions of the Immigration Act of 1924 were not repealed until the late 1960s, the second wave came mostly in the late 1960s and 1970s. Those in this second wave were more evenly split between Christians and Muslims, although it appears that Muslims outnumbered Christians in these later migrations. And most were educated professionals seeking educational and economic opportunities in the United States. Unlike the first wave, they were not escaping persecution with the hope and expectation of returning to their homeland; rather, these new immigrants sought opportunities and planned to stay in the United States. As a consequence, Arab Americans are more integrated into the American mainstream than other minorities. They are less segregated in housing and are the most likely of all Americans to live in multiethnic neighborhoods; they have careers across a range of occupations and professions; and they have taken advantage of educational opportunities.

Because of restrictive quotas in place with the Immigration Act of 1924, there was little Arab American immigration from the mid-1920s until the late 1960s and 1970s. Many of the immigrants from this second wave of immigration are educated professionals and thus quickly integrated into the American mainstream.

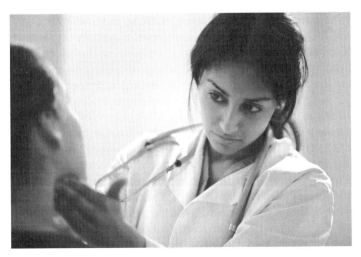

These Arab American women and their families are vulnerable to discriminatory acts from European-origin Americans because of fears of terrorism that arose following the September 11, 2001, attacks.

Yet the continuing tensions in the Middle East—the Arab oil embargo in the 1970s, the hostage taking at the Munich Olympics, the Iranian revolution and arrest of American marines guarding the U.S. Embassy in Teheran, the bombing of marines in Lebanon, terrorist acts against American targets overseas, the first World Trade Center bombing, and the spread of terrorism to American shores—have placed all Arabs in a difficult situation. The third and fourth generations from the first wave of immigrants before World War I, the second wave of the 1960s and 1970s, and the most recent immigrants are often painted with one prejudicial brush as Islamic fanatics who cannot be trusted. Because over 90 percent of Middle Easterners in general live in urban areas and because they are the least segregated of identifiable minorities, they are vulnerable to a wide variety of discriminatory acts, ranging from ethnic slurs to hate crimes.

As we have seen for other minority subpopulations, fear fuels prejudicial beliefs that, in turn, justify discrimination. Fears of terrorism have codified prejudicial beliefs among a significant portion of the European-origin majority, and this majority often sees all Arabs as members of one ethnic subpopulation when, in fact, they are diverse in their countries of origin and in their religious beliefs. Christian Arabs are often attacked for being Muslims. As a result, Arabs increasingly have retreated into a new kind of Middle Eastern ethnicity that emphasizes common cultural traditions. This new ethnicity is furthered by what have historically been relatively high intra-ethnic marriage rates among those with Arab ancestry. In effect, European-origin Americans, as well as other ethnic populations who hold prejudicial beliefs, have fulfilled their own prophecy by stereotyping all Middle Easterners *as if* they are the same and then acting on these stereotypes with acts of discrimination. In response, highly diverse members of the Arab American population are beginning to create a new ethnic identity, if only for their own defense in what has become a hostile world.

RESOURCE SHARES OF ARAB AMERICANS

Incomes of Arab Americans

Prejudice and discrimination have not had the same effect on Arab Americans as on other identifiable minorities. Indeed, by most measures of success, Arab Americans are comparatively successful. Median family income among Arab Americans is higher than that of the total population, including non-Latino whites. Table 9.5 shows that Arab family income was over $52,000 in 2000 compared to just over $50,000 for all U.S. families. As is evident in Table 9.5, however, income varies enormously among various Arab subpopulations; Lebanese, Egyptian, and Syrian family incomes are considerably higher than those of other Arab groupings. Persons of Lebanese and Syrian ancestry today are likely to be third- and fourth-generation members of the original Arab immigrants to the United States, whereas Egyptians are more typically the newer professional immigrants. The lower incomes of Arab/"Arabic" families stem from the fact that some of the newer immigrants to the United States have come without economic capital, educational credentials, and entrepreneurial skills.

Poverty among Arab Americans

The median family income figures disguise somewhat the fact that a larger number of Arab Americans are in poverty compared to the U.S. population as a whole, and especially to non-Latino whites. In Table 9.6, the percentage of Arabs in poverty is over 16 percent, a percentage that is considerably higher than the 12.4 percent rate for the total U.S. population and the 7.7 percent rate for non-Latino whites. Again, there is a great deal of variation in the poverty

TABLE 9.5 Median Household Income of Arab Americans, 2000

Population	Median Household Income
All Arabs	**$52,318**
Lebanese	$60,677
Egyptian	57,264
Syrian	58,204
Palestinian	49,940
Jordanian	45,659
Moroccan	41,277
Iraqi	44,272
Arab/"Arabic"	41,356
Other Arab	50,208
All U.S. families	**$50,046***

*Median income for all families is higher than other tabulations for 2000, since this tabulation is based on a sample. Median income has declined since 1999.
Source: U.S. Bureau of the Census, 2005a, Figure 13, p. 15.

TABLE 9.6 Percentage of Arabs in Poverty, 2000

Population	Percentage in Poverty
All Arabs	**16.7%**
Lebanese	10.8%
Egyptian	14.2
Syrian	11.3
Palestinian	17.1
Jordanian	16.1
Moroccan	18.4
Iraqi	26.4
Arab/"Arabic"	24.7
Other Arab	21.9
Total U.S. population	**12.4%**
Non-Latino whites	**7.7%**

Note: Poverty rates have gone up over the last five years to 14 percent, but we are using 2000 census figures in order to make comparisons with the data on Arab poverty in 2000. No more recent data are available at present for Arab Americans.
Source: U.S. Bureau of the Census, 2005a, Figure 14, p. 16.

rates for various Arab subgroups. Those of Lebanese ancestry are least likely to be in poverty, and those of Iraqi ancestry are most likely to be in poverty. The higher rates for some Arab subpopulations are equivalent to those evident among other minorities, such as African Americans, Native Americans, and Latinos, all of whom who have been victims of long-term discrimination.

Labor Force Participation among Arab Americans

As is evident in Table 9.7, the labor force participation rates of Arab males are higher than the rate of the total U.S. population, but labor participation rates for Arab females are lower than the overall female labor participation rate. Among

TABLE 9.7 Labor Force Participation Rates for Arab Men and Women, 16 Years Old and Older, 2000

Population	Percentage of Participation for Individuals of Arab Ancestry	
	Men	Women
All Arabs	**73.3%**	**45.5%**
Lebanese	73.7%	50.3%
Egyptian	76.7	49.2
Syrian	71.8	42.9
Palestinian	77.0	39.4
Jordanian	78.1	35.9
Moroccan	70.6	53.4
Iraqi	75.5	44.1
Arab/"Arabic"	70.7	36.9
Other Arab	69.2	45.6
Total U.S. population	**70.7%**	**57.5%**

Source: U.S. Bureau of the Census, 2005a, Figure 10, p. 12.

TABLE 9.8 Distribution of Arab Americans, Non-Latino Whites, and All Workers in Various Occupational Categories, 2000

Job Category	Percentage of Workers in Job Categories*		
	Arab Americans	Non-Latino Whites	All U.S. Workers
Managerial/professional	42.0	35.6	33.6
Service	11.7	13.4	26.7
Sales/office	30.2	27.0	30.3
Production/transportation/ materials moving	10.7	13.6	14.6
Construction/extraction/ maintenance	5.3	9.8	9.4
Farming/fishing/forestry	0.1	0.6	0.7

*Percentages vary for non-Latino whites from other tables in this book when Arab Americans, who are classified as "white," are removed for separate tabulation.
Source: U.S. Bureau of the Census, 2005a.

women, labor participation is lower across all Arab groupings. Thus, Arab women are less likely to work than women in the general population. As Table 9.8 documents, the occupational distribution of Arabs compared to that of all workers and of non-Latino whites reveals that Arab Americans are more likely to be employed in managerial and professional occupations. With 42 percent employed in managerial and professional jobs, Arabs exceed the participation rates not only of whites but also of Asians, who are overrepresented in these occupations (see Table 8.5 on page 233). Yet the occupational success of Arabs varies considerably among specific groupings.

Educational Attainment of Arab Americans

The occupational figures reflect the educational attainment of Arab Americans. As is evident in Table 9.9, persons of Arab ancestry are more likely to have a college degree than the general population (24 percent to 16 percent of adults over the age of 25), although those of Arab ancestry do not quite match the educational attainment of non-Latino whites (26 percent of whom have college degrees). But far more Arab Americans have graduate degrees (17 percent)

TABLE 9.9 Educational Attainment of Arab Americans, 25 Years Old and Older, 2000

Population	Percentage Who Have:			
	High School Diploma	Some College	College Degree	Postgraduate Degree
Arab Americans	84%	25%	24%	17%
Non-Latino whites	84	54	26	10
Total U.S. population	**80%**	**27%**	**16%**	**9%**

Sources: U.S. Bureau of the Census, 2003b, Table 21, p. 5; Arab American Institute, 2005.

compared to the total population (9 percent) and even to non-Latino whites (10 percent).

In sum, then, it is clear that Arab Americans come out well, on the whole, in the distribution of scarce resources. There is, however, considerable variation across the Arab population on how well families with different backgrounds fare in the distribution of valued resources. Yet, much like Asian Americans and Jews, Arab Americans—for all their relative success in America—still suffer from prejudice and discrimination, and even more so since 9-11. Thus, while Arabs have not been oppressed to the extent of some other ethnic subpopulations, they have had to endure a considerable amount of discrimination.

THE DYNAMICS OF DISCRIMINATION AGAINST ARAB AMERICANS

Identifiability of Arab Americans

Today, despite being officially classified as "white" (after decades of being classified as "nonwhite"), persons of Arab ancestry can still be identified by, on average, a somewhat darker skin than European-origin Americans, particularly those from northern Europe. Owing to "Middle Eastern" facial features and dark hair coloring, Americans perceive that they can identify Arabs, although hate crimes have been perpetrated against Latinos and even Italians who "look Middle Eastern." Among Muslim Arabs, clothing and religious practices can also serve as ethnic markers. And if Arabic or another Middle Eastern language is spoken in public, this too becomes a marker of "an Arab."

The fact that these markers are often exaggerated in political cartoons and Internet "jokes" cements in the public's eye the notion that Arabs are different from mainstream Americans. In fact, once ethnic stereotyping is in place, attention drawn to relatively minor traits like facial features and hair coloring make all members of an ethnic subpopulation vulnerable to discrimination. One study, for example, found that Arabs are portrayed in the media in highly derogatory ways that are very similar to the portrayal of Jews in Europe before Hitler and Japanese in America during World War II (Hasan, 2000:80–106). They are seen as "deceitful," "secretive," "enemies of God," and prone to "fanaticism." Thus, prejudicial beliefs not only make a minority more identifiable—at least in other people's minds—but also escalate the sense of threat attributed to persons with such undesirable traits.

Negative Beliefs about Arab Americans

Middle Easterners and Arab Americans are subject to many negative stereotypes, and these stereotypes are constantly reinforced by media images of events overseas and by opinion columns and cartoons that appear almost daily in the newspapers and over the Internet (Feagin and Feagin, 2003:325–27; Hasan, 2000; Marvasti and McKinney, 2004:41–66). One stereotype portrays

Arabs in general as being prone to violence, a view that is constantly reinforced by daily accounts of events in the Middle East and by U.S. government agencies such as the Pentagon and State Department. A related stereotype is that all Arabs are committed to **jihad** by Islamic law, when in fact the concept of jihad has several meanings not related to war. This stereotype of a propensity for violence among Arabs in the Middle East often targets Arab Americans, who are perceived, incorrectly, to be sympathetic toward, if not outright collaborators in, violence against Americans. In reality, Arab Americans have been among the minority populations in the United States who are *least* prone to violence.

Another stereotype is that terrorism represents a clash of civilizations and that Arabs are jealous of the affluence of the West (Huntington, 1996; Said, 1979). A variant of this belief is the notion that Arabs are antimodern. In both variants, Arabs wish to attack Western traditions that they see as violating the tenets of Islam. The view that Arab Americans are antimodern, however, flies in the face of their educational attainment and occupational distribution in the United States.

Another related variant of the clash-of-civilizations stereotype is the idea that the Arab Middle East is hostile to the West and seeks to undermine its institutions. Such hostility certainly exists, but Americans tend to forget that over the last 150 years, it is the West that has colonized and exploited the Middle East. Most of the national boundaries of Middle Eastern nations are the artifacts of decisions made by colonial powers rather than by the people living in these territories, and the dependence of Middle Eastern economies on oil production is at least partly the outcome of Western oil companies' early exploration for and exploitation of oil in Arab nations. Indeed, going even farther back, the Christian Crusades against the peoples of the Middle East were an early portent of later Western intervention. From the perspective of Middle Easterners, then, it is the West that is hostile to Arabs, and so, Westerners should not be surprised that this hostility is returned. Indeed, the U.S.-led invasion of Iraq has only reinforced this perception by many Arabs. Yet among American Arabs there is little hostility to the West. Americans of Arab ancestry monitor political events and support hot-button issues such as the formation of a Palestinian state, but they do not reveal hostility to the institutions of the West. Indeed, just the opposite is the case as they seek educational opportunities and managerial or professional jobs.

Yet another stereotype is that Arabs resist assimilation into the American mainstream. Only recently has the Middle Eastern–origin population in the United States become defensive and retreated into a pan–Middle Eastern community. But even here, Arabs' level of educational attainment and their occupational distribution undercut the notion that they are not part of the American mainstream. Add to this the facts that a majority of Arab Americans are Christian and less than 13 percent are Muslim, and it is difficult to sustain the fiction that Arab Americans resist becoming part of the core institutional systems in America—religious, educational, and occupational. Furthermore, Arab Americans generally speak English in public more than other minorities for whom English can be a second language (some 88 percent report speaking English well), a propensity that undermines the misperception that Arabs will not assimilate into the dominant culture. Also, Arab Americans are more likely than Jews, African Americans, Latinos, and Asians to donate to political campaigns (Kromkowski, 2001), and they are more likely to vote in elections than almost all other ethnic subpopulations—yet another indicator that calls into question the widely held assumption that Arab Americans have not assimilated (see Box 9.2 for a short list of prominent Arab Americans who clearly have assimilated into the mainstream).

Another stereotype is that Arab Americans support terrorism and thus cannot be trusted. Poll data on Arab American attitudes show exactly the opposite, and data from Arabs in the Middle East reveal that an overwhelming majority do not support terrorism, although the younger generations in Muslim countries (17–30 percent) did not agree to poll questions stating that the attack of 9-11 was unjustified (Marvasti and McKinney, 2004:62). Arabs in America, however, like all Americans, condemned the attack.

Still another stereotype is that Arabs oppress women. Although Arab women are less likely than the women in the general population to participate in the labor force, levels of educational attainment among Arab women remain high. Much of this stereotype about female oppression comes from assumptions that the clothing that many Muslim women wear signifies their subordination to men. There can be no doubt that Arab societies are patriarchal and that many Muslim women in the Middle East and in the United States are given fewer opportunities than their male counterparts (Roald, 2001), but it is not clear whether this "repression" is any greater than that advocated by fundamentalist Christians in America. Moreover, since most Arabs are Christians, the distribution of **patriarchy** among Arab Americans is probably about the same as among Christians in general, ranging from a high to a low degree.

All of these prejudicial beliefs are given visual expression in the media. Indeed, if African Americans or Latinos were so portrayed by the media, there would be immediate cries of outrage and charges of racism. But Arab Americans must endure constant portrayals of themselves as swarthy, hooded, big-nosed, and glowering fanatics who chant to Allah and are ready to do harm to others. There is, of course, no doubt that many Muslims around the world and even a handful in the United States do wish harm on Americans, but the percentage is very small among Arab Americans and is probably smaller than the proportion of European-origin whites who are neo-Nazis, white supremacists, and violent survivalists. Indeed, Americans often forget about the Oklahoma City bombings by European-origin whites; and in fact, if the bombings were portrayed as the work of "Christian extremists," many Americans would obviously be upset, but they might have a better sense of what Muslims in America must feel when reading the newspapers and watching the news. These negative stereotypes, constantly fueled by media reports and comments on events in the Middle East and on periodic orange and red alerts about the dangers of terrorism from the **Department of Homeland Security,** are used to legitimize discrimination. Indeed, the ethnic slurs against Arab Americans—"sand nigger" and "towel head," for example—give us a sense of the intensity of negative sentiment fueled by prejudicial beliefs.

Box 9.2
Prominent Arab Americans

Arab Americans are well integrated into the cultural mainstream of the United States. Here is a sampling of well-known Arab Americans in various social spheres.

POLITICS

Ralph Nader (presidential candidate)

John Sununu (U.S. senator)

Donna Shalala (former secretary of health and human services)

Helen Thomas (long-time dean of the White House press corps)

George Mitchell (former Senate majority leader)

SPORTS

Doug Flutie (NFL quarterback)

Jeff George (former NFL quarterback)

Rich Kotite (NFL coach)

Joe Robbie (former owner of Miami Dolphins)

Bobby Rahal (former race car driver)

BUSINESS

Jacques Nasser (former CEO of Ford Motor Co.)

Samir G. Gibara (board chair of Goodyear Tire Co.)

Dr. Joseph Jacobs (founder of Jacobs Engineering and former president of Occidental Petroleum)

Sam Moore (founder of Nelson Publishers, largest worldwide distributor of the Bible)

John Mack (CEO of Credit Suisse First Boston and former president of Morgan Stanley Dean Witter)

Roger Farah (chief operating officer of Polo Ralph Lauren)

Paul Orfalea (founder of Kinko's)

ENTERTAINMENT

Casey Kasem (radio disk jockey)

Paul Anka (one of America's first "teen idols")

Frank Zappa (rock artist)

Dick Dale (king of surf guitar)

Tiffany (pop star)

Paula Abdul (singer, former *American Idol* judge)

Jamie Farr (Corporal Klinger in *M*A*S*H*)

Danny, Tony, and Marlo Thomas (television actors and producers)

Tony Shalhoub (star of USA Network's *Monk*)

Kristy McNichol (costar of the former television sit-com *Empty Nest*)

Salma Hayek (movie actress)

Shannon Elizabeth (movie actress)

F. Murray Abraham (Oscar-winning movie actor)

FASHION

J. M. Haggar (founder of Haggar Clothing Co.)

J. M. Haggar III (CEO of Farah Brothers Clothing Co.)

Maloff brothers (manufacturers of Mode-O-Day women's dresses and owners of the Sacramento Kings NBA team and the Palms Hotel and Casino in Las Vegas)

MEDICINE AND SCIENCE

Dr. Michael DeBakey (inventor of the heart pump)

Dr. Ahmed Zewail (winner of the Nobel Prize in physics)

Dr. Elias Corey (winner of the Nobel Prize in physics)

Dr. Charles Elachi (head of the Jet Propulsion Laboratory)

Hassan Damel Al-Sabbah (scientist who helped invent solar energy panels and television tubes)

Christa McAuliffe (schoolteacher who died when space shuttle *Challenger* exploded)

Source: Kasem, 2005.

In related studies of media portrayals of Arabs in the United States, Zogby (2000) found that political cartoons portrayed Arabs in much the same way as Jews were viewed in czarist Russia and pre-Nazi German. The "fat, grotesque Jewish banker or merchant found its contemporary counterpart in the obese oil sheik, and the images of the Arab and Jewish terrorists differed only in their attire" (Zogby, 2000). Moreover, both Jews and Arabs were accused of not sharing Western values and of being prone to conspiracies against the institutions of the West. In another study of Arabs in entertainment programs on television, Zogby (2000) found that, much as in political cartoons, "the only presentation of Arab or Muslim characters were [*sic*] either as terrorists or oil sheiks."

In many ways, Arab Americans must live with the stigma of being associated with the new "world threat" that has replaced the "specter of communism" that previously dominated the American public's consciousness in the post–World War II period, up to the collapse of the Soviet Union in the early 1990s. Indeed, Zogby has argued that the tendency of Americans to see the world as either good or bad is much like the once popular view of "cowboys and Indians," with the former portrayed as "white hats" and "good" and the latter as "red savages." In some ways, Westerners are now the good cowboys and Arabs are the new Indians in this morality play. Even if this portrayal of the situation is too extreme, it is nonetheless the case that Arab Americans must constantly deal with negative stereotypes about Middle Easterners in general and Muslims in particular as hostile to the "American way" which, as we have seen, cannot possibly be the case in light of the data on the resource shares of Arab Americans.

Institutionalized Discrimination against Arab Americans

Discrimination against Arab Americans has not been as fully institutionalized as has been (and still is) the case for other minority subpopulations. Part of the reason for this is that the Arab-ancestry population in the United States is very small, about the size of the Native American population at best. Another part is that about half of the current Arab American population has immigrated over the last thirty years and hence does not have the same long history of discrimination as African Americans and Native Americans. Still, discrimination does occur, and its subtlety and informality give it an invidious character that makes it difficult to document. Indeed, having an "Arab sounding" name immediately raises suspicion and places Arab Americans on the defensive in nearly all key institutional spheres in American society.

Informal Discrimination   Arab Americans must constantly deal with informal acts by non-Arabs that make them feel uncomfortable in key institutional contexts. In newspapers, as noted earlier, they must see cartoons that depict their culture in highly negative, if not inflammatory, ways. Women who wear *hijab* (head coverings) in public are often victims of uncensored stares, and they are often ridiculed in schools and work for wearing this traditional style of dress. Moreover, women are very likely to be discriminated against in their search for jobs when wearing *hijab*. Ethnic slurs frequently occur in public places, from mass transportation and restaurant facilities through the work-place to school playgrounds. Because informal discrimination is just that—informal—it is very difficult to stop or to gain redress of grievances, but such informal discrimination has huge effects on its victims. They feel uncomfortable in public and basic institutional spheres, and as a result, they retreat into their own ethnic communities and thereby maintain the distinctiveness that makes them easy targets of discrimination. All ethnic minorities have had to deal, and still must deal, with informal discrimination. Arabs have always been viewed sus-piciously by the non-Arab majority (Jones, 2001), but in the aftermath of 9-11, rates of informal discrimination have increased. Moreover, even when individuals themselves have not directly experienced acts of prejudice and discrimination, instances of discrimination are reported by others and circulate through Arab communities. The result is for even those who have not actually been victims to develop fear, wariness, and other emotional reactions about what *may occur* to them in public places. To worry constantly about "what might happen" in public places and in key institutional spheres is a heavy bur-den for any individual to bear.

Legal Discrimination　Because early Arab migrants from Syria/Lebanon were defined as "nonwhite," laws and court interpretations of these laws worked against achieving full citizenship status. The key issue was the definition of "free white person"—a definition that was a holdover from the late 1700s and that entitled individuals (in the days of slavery) to citizenship. The **Naturaliza-tion Act of 1790** limited eligibility for U.S. citizenship to "free white persons," but this designation was not given to early Arab immigrants because they were not defined as "white." Later, some courts—for example, a ruling in South Carolina in 1915—ruled that even if Arabs could be considered Caucasian, they still did not meet the 1790 Naturalization Act's designation of "free white person"—an absurd contortion of all logic. Well into the twentieth century, formal rulings and informal practices worked against early immigrants' being granted citizen-ship status; and even when Arab immigrants were able to overcome these legal hurdles, the public still viewed Arabs suspiciously *as if* they were not entitled to the rights of citizens.

　International political forces have also worked against Arab Americans. The involvement of the United States in Middle East politics has led to fears of terrorism and immigration from the Middle East. Thus, the 1924 Immigration Act dramatically limited Arab American migration to the United States, while placing a stigma on Arab Americans already here and on the few who man-aged to come to these shores. More recently, the concern with terrorism has led to the enactment of a series of laws by the federal government that have in-creased the powers of the government to detain and interrogate immigrants who are "suspected" of having "links" to terrorism. The **Anti-Terrorism and Effective Death Penalty Act of 1996,** along with the **Illegal Immigration Act of 1996,** gave the government broad powers to suspend basic civil liberties. Such laws have a chilling effect on those who are likely to be defined as a "problem"; and this fear includes most Arab Americans, especially those who are Muslim or who have immigrated to the United States recently. The **USA Patriot Act of 2001** (its full title is "Uniting and Strengthening America by Providing Appropriate Tools Required to Intercept and Obstruct Terrorism Act") was rushed to enactment in the wake of 9-11. This legislation further extends the government's power to detain, question, and deport individuals without traditional civil rights protections granted by the Constitution. Again, as suspected sympathizers of terrorism are interrogated or even rounded up and detained, these events have a chilling effect on Middle Eastern communities, whose members recognize that the Patriot Act is primarily directed at them (see Box 9.3 for more details).

The events of 9-11 dramatically escalated the fears of all Americans, including Arab Americans, about the future. Hence, it is not surprising that rather severe laws were hastily enacted to "deal with" what was obviously a very real threat. Yet these laws undermine Arab American citizens' ability to feel "comfortable" in their own country. Indeed, much like Latinos who constantly must deal with law enforcement agencies—from the U.S. Border Patrol to the Highway Patrol—that are on the lookout for illegal immigrants, Arab Americans must endure surveillance and, potentially, harassment by the FBI and other law enforcement agencies. Escalated surveillance may well be prudent and necessary after the events of 9-11, but such extra caution has a discriminatory effect on all Arab Americans, many of whose families have been in the United States for generations.

Religious Discrimination   Even though a large majority of Arab Americans are Christians, all Middle Easterners tend to be typecast as Muslims. And to be seen—however incorrectly—as non-Christian in the United States invites discrimination, as Jews have learned in the United States and elsewhere in the world. The first slaves practiced (at least for a brief time) Islam, and some of the earliest Arab immigrants continued Muslim religious traditions. Because recent immigrants from Arab countries are likely to be Muslim, over the last few decades the number of mosques in the United States has increased dramatically, from less than 100 in 1950 to over 1,250 today (Arab American Institute, 2005). Coupled with Black Muslim activity, the profile of Islam has been greatly raised and, of course, dramatically so after the first World Trade Center bombing and, later, the 9-11 acts of terrorism. In the immediate aftermath of 9-11, some mosques were bombed, much like black churches in the South during the civil rights movement of the 1960s (see Box 9.4). As a result, Muslims must constantly worry that they could be subject to such assaults on their religious centers, a fear that encourages their retreat from the American mainstream.

The need for devout Muslims to pray toward Mecca five times a day often poses problems in schools and workplaces. Well over 95 percent of Arab children attend nonreligious schools—mostly public—but school administrators are unlikely to make accommodations for prayer under the presumption of separation of church and state (although prayer at school is often allowed by

Box 9.3
The USA Patriot Act and Justice

The USA Patriot Act gave the Department of Justice the tools it needed to investigate both citizens and immigrants from the Middle East (and others suspected of terrorist sympathies). Below are some of the outcomes of this Act:

- On September 20, 2001, the Department of Justice created an interim regulation that allowed for the detention of anyone suspected of terrorist connections without charge for forty-eight hours or "an additional reasonable period of time." Over 1,100 individuals were held in this way without an official charge—actions that clearly violate what had been traditional civil liberties guaranteed by the Constitution.
- An October 31, 2001, ruling allowed the government to eavesdrop on inmate–attorney meetings if there was reason to believe that ". . . a particular inmate may use communications with an attorney to further or facilitate acts of terrorism."
- Under a November 9, 2001, directive of the Attorney General, over 5,000 men between the ages of 18 and 33 were to be interviewed (interrogated) because they had non-immigrant visas and came from countries defined as harboring terrorists.
- Homes and offices of individuals in fourteen Muslim organizations were raided in March 2002. Officers entered at gunpoint, handcuffed individuals, hauled off boxes of materials, and, according to eyewitness accounts, destroyed property. Yet, no arrests were made, nor were any of the organizations shut down.
- Visas of individuals from particular countries were put on hold, which had the effect of dramatically limiting foreign students from coming to the United States and, for those who did, requiring the schools to constantly monitor each student's presence and to report to the FBI and Justice Department.
- Workers such as mail carriers and utility workers were given encouragement to monitor households and report anything suspicious to the FBI or Justice Department.
- Advisories have been issued to landlords to monitor their tenants to see if terrorists might be in their midst.

It is perhaps understandable that these kinds of actions were taken as a result of the fear generated by 9-11. Still, they conflict with the civil liberties guaranteed by the Constitution, and they place all "Arab looking" Americans under a blanket of suspicion. They also give police officers powers that they have never been allowed to have before. Because the Patriot Act is still in force and, indeed, has been renewed with relatively little substantive reduction in its scope, these powers remain—thus ensuring that Arab Americans will be viewed suspiciously by their government and by the citizens who have been "deputized" to spy on the government's behalf.

Sources: Akram and Johnson, 2002; Taylor, 2002.

Box 9.4
Hate Crimes against Arabs and Muslims
after September 11, 2001

British sociologist Frank Furedi argues that the image of the half-crazed third-world terrorist with a bomb in hand, ready to die for some incomprehensible cause, has taken hold of the Western imagination. The terrorist attacks of September 11, 2001, on the World Trade Center in New York City served as a catalyst for reinforcing negative stereotypes in popular thinking of Arab Americans and Muslims as terrorists. According to Human Rights Watch, Arabs and Muslims in the United States—including persons perceived to be Arab or Muslim—became victims of a severe wave of backlash violence after 9-11 that included murder, beatings, arson, vandalizing mosques, shootings, and verbal threats. According to Human Rights Watch, more than 2,000 hate crimes after 9-11 were committed against Arabs, Muslims, and those perceived to be either Arab or Muslim. Hate crimes committed against Arabs and Muslims increased seventeenfold after September 11, 2001.

Human Rights Watch has documented at least seven murders resulting from anti-Arab and anti-Muslim hatred after 9-11. More than 300 assaults occurred between September 11 and the first week of February that were related to anti-Arab and anti-Muslim hatred. During the first week after September 11, more than 100 bias incidents were reported involving vandalism and arson of mosques and worshippers being threatened with violence. Among the bias incidents reported in the United States are the following:

- On September 29, 2001, Abdo Ali Ahmed, a 51-year-old Yemini Arab and Muslim, and father of eight, was shot and killed while working at his convenience store in Reedley, California. The cash in two registers was left untouched.
- On September 15, 2001, Adel Karas, a 48-year-old Arab and Coptic Christian, and a father of three, was shot and killed at his convenience store in San Gabriel, California. No money was taken from the cash register.
- On November 19, 2001, four teenagers burned down the Gobind Sadan, a multifaith worship center in Oswego, New York, because they believed the worshippers to be supporters of Osama Bin Laden. On September 23, 2001, the St. John's Assyrian American Church was set on fire in Chicago. The church's pastor said that the person who he believed set the fire had asked a local resident whether the church was a mosque.
- On August 24, 2002, federal authorities in Tampa discovered a plan by a doctor to bomb and destroy approximately fifty mosques and Islamic cultural centers in south Florida.

It is clear that Arabs and Muslims became identifiable targets for hatred and violence as a result of 9-11. More important, the context of hatred and violence that developed after 9-11 is indicative of a long-standing problem in American society: the persistence of hate crimes in the social fabric. The anti-Arab and anti-Muslim hatred expressed since September 11, 2001, has its roots in a historical context of hate—the Rodney King beating, the burning of African American churches, the murders of James Byrd, Yusef Hawkins, and Matthew Shepard, and the 1993 Long Island Railroad shooting spree.

Sources: Furedi, 1994; Human Rights Watch, 2002.

school clubs, and the Pledge of Allegiance uttered each day includes reference to God). In the workplace, where such constitutional issues are less relevant, employers have been slow to make accommodations for prayer; indeed, the need for such activities can be used as an excuse to avoid employing followers of Islam.

More pernicious is the fact that Muslims will always be viewed suspiciously by those in key administrative positions in the government, economy, and schools. Most administrators will be Christian, and some will be Jews; and together, they must overcome the prejudices of their own religious beliefs to be tolerant of Muslims. It is, of course, illegal to discriminate on the basis of religion in the United States, but informal practices of discrimination are difficult to monitor, and the burden of proof (including the costs of litigation) is almost always placed on the victims of discrimination.

In recent years, there have been concerted efforts among religious leaders in communities to break down the barriers of mutual suspicion among Christians, Arabs, and Jews (and other religions). These are early and halting efforts, but over the longer term, they may work to reduce the informal discrimination that Muslims must endure today.

Educational Discrimination The vast majority of Arab parents send their children to public schools. As Table 9.9 documents, Arabs are better educated than the general population, a fact that reflects the long emphasis in the Middle East on education as well as the professional, managerial, and business success of Arab parents who, like all successful persons, emphasize education as the key to success. The major problem that Arab children encounter in schools is basic ignorance about Middle Eastern culture or Islam among teachers, administrators, and fellow students. Arab children come from very diverse cultural backgrounds, a fact that is often lost on school personnel, who tend to paint all Arab children with the same brush. Another problem that often has discriminatory consequences is that events in the Middle East have large effects on American public opinion, which, in turn, are transferred to students, teachers, and administrators who may themselves develop prejudices based on political events or, if not actually developing prejudices, are not fully prepared to deal with them in others. As a result, Arab schoolchildren and, indeed, adults in colleges and universities must constantly be on guard for negative beliefs about and actions against them as the politics of the Middle East or fears of terrorism heat up. And if Arab children evidence distinctive dress, demeanor, and speech, they become even more likely targets for slurs and other discriminatory acts that many teachers and administrators are unprepared or unwilling to combat. Still, the success of Arab children in schools attests to their capacity to overcome these informal practices, although these negative experiences create anxiety about what they will encounter not only in schools but elsewhere whenever they must be among the non-Arab population.

Economic Discrimination Because the Arabs who first immigrated to the United States often possessed entrepreneurial skills, many became small-business owners, opening fruit stands, small grocery stores, dry-goods establishments, and other businesses that serviced both urban and rural populations

(Naber, 2000). Another large group entered the industrial labor force when Henry Ford increased wages (to five dollars per day!) for workers in his large automobile plants. Yet unlike many other immigrant populations, Arab Americans did not enter a broad spectrum of the industrial labor force. Their entry was largely confined to the automobile industry around Dearborn and Detroit, Michigan. Indeed, this area has the largest concentration of Arab-ancestry persons outside of the Middle East; some 300,000 Arab Americans live in metropolitan Detroit (David, 1999; U.S. Bureau of the Census, 2005a).

Later immigrants came with educational degrees or sought them in the United States, and as a result, they are much more likely to be in the professional labor force. Still, there are signs that Arab Americans have been excluded from some categories of jobs. For example, Arab Americans are far less likely than other minorities to be employed in government jobs (Zogby, 2000), although the Arab American Institute (2005) reports increases in elected and appointed positions in government over the last three decades. Moreover, as is reported in Table 9.8, Arab Americans are more likely than the general population to be employed in managerial and professional occupational categories as well as sales. They are, however, less likely than non-Latino whites and the general population to be employed in the industrial jobs that have served as the springboard for so many generations of immigrants to the United States.

Arab Americans today are much more likely to experience informal job discrimination. Indeed, an "Arab sounding" name is often sufficient to get an applicant rejected from a job interview. And, as noted earlier, Arab Americans must endure jokes and slurs in the workplace from their non-Arab colleagues, while always having to "explain themselves" and their Arab ancestry to others who are fearful in the post 9-11 era. Still, much of the occupational distribution of Arabs is the result of self-selection and preferences for small-business ownership and a limited range of professions. Blatant and highly institutionalized economic discrimination against Arabs has been far less pronounced than discrimination against African Americans, Latinos, and Native Americans. The discrimination that has been endured is subtle and invidious, revolving around the hostility often given to middleman minorities owning small businesses and prejudicial stereotypes leading to slurs and jokes in the workplace about Arabs in managerial and sales jobs. Such informal practices create a tension that is chronic, often forcing individuals to retreat into safe ethnic enclaves and, as a consequence, denying Arab Americans access to the full range of economic opportunities in the United States.

Political Discrimination   Because many early Arab immigrants were sojourners and, hence, oriented to returning to their homelands, they had little incentive to become politically involved in the United States. Moreover, because Arabs were not initially classified as "free whites," they could not be citizens and vote, so political involvement seemed pointless. And, coupled with the hostility that often comes with small-business owners selling to the non-Arab majority, Arab Americans like their Asian counterparts in the early decades of the twentieth century were likely to shy away from civic engagements that would arouse hostility.

Even though the Immigration Act of 1924 effectively altered the orientations of Arab Americans from sojourners to committed citizens, there was a considerable lag in their political participation at all levels of government. No doubt much of this lack of officeholding was the result of fears about the reactions of non-Muslim voters. The result was that aside from a few officeholders in the 1930s, Arab Americans were not involved significantly in state and national politics until the 1950s. In 1958, the first Arab American was elected to the U.S. House of Representatives. Not until 1980 was the first Arab American, James Abourezk from South Dakota, elected to the U.S. Senate. By 2000, only four Arab Americans had served in the Senate (including George Mitchell, who was Senate majority leader for a time), and only a handful are now serving in the House (Arab American Institute, 2005; Marvasti and McKinney, 2004).

Today, Arab Americans are among the most politically engaged groups in the United States according to several indicators. They are more likely than any other minority group to donate to political campaigns; they are more likely to have listened to presidential debates than the population as a whole; and they are more likely to vote than the population as a whole. And increasingly, Arab Americans have assumed elected and appointed governmental positions at the local, state, and federal levels. (The Arab American Institute keeps a running account of these trends; see www.asiusa.org.) In rough terms, Arab Americans are evenly divided among Democrats, Republicans, and independents; and although the number of Arab American voters is small on a national scale, their concentrations in a few states—Michigan, California, New York, Florida, and New Jersey (see Table 9.10)—make them a potential swing vote in close elections. In general, Arab Americans are conservative on crime and punishment and liberal on health care and social issues.

TABLE 9.10 Size of Arab American Population in Key Electoral States

State	Number of Arab Americans
California	650,000
New York	410,000
Michigan	400,000
Florida	270,000
New Jersey	250,000
Texas	190,000
Illinois	180,000
Ohio	160,000
Massachusetts	160,000
Pennsylvania	150,000
Virginia	140,000
Maryland	60,000
New Hampshire	60,000

Source: Arab American Institute, n.d., p. 5.

On international issues, the opinions of Arab Americans deviate somewhat from those of the general population. Although the overwhelming majority of Arab Americans oppose any form of terrorism anywhere in the world, over 74 percent see U.S. policy in the Middle East as biased toward Israel, and 82 percent want to see an independent Palestinian state. Still, 63 percent believe that U.S. policies show respect for Islam (Zogby International, 2000).

Much like the attitude of early Asian immigrants, Arab Americans' reluctance to be politically involved has lessened. Fears about backlash from non-Arabs have dissipated, and Arab Americans not only are voting in large numbers but also are seeking elective office. Although there are some fears about non-Arab majorities' reactions to Arab-ancestry candidates, it is clear that more and more Arab Americans are willing to confront these prejudices and seek to exert political influence.

RESPONDING TO DISCRIMINATION: ETHNOGENESIS

It is ironic that a minority population that has been relatively successful and active in the American mainstream now finds itself in retreat to the point of creating a new sense of ethnicity. Arab Americans come from many different countries and are split between Christian and Muslim religious affiliations, but the aftermath of 9-11 exposed a quiet suspicion by the American public toward Middle Easterners in general and Arab Muslims in particular. International events and terrorism have made the public's concerns more explicit, often to the point of prompting hate crimes and informal discrimination. Prejudices appear to have codified into a set of beliefs that justify, at least for some, discrimination against Arab Americans. In the face of this obvious hostility, some Middle Easterners as well as Muslims from other parts of the globe, such as those from Pakistan and Indonesia, are in the middle of creating a new kind of ethnicity based on shared experiences and traditions—whether a common language, history, or religion. Even some third- and fourth-generation families of Arab ancestry have joined this movement for a new Arab ethnic identity.

When individuals feel insecure in a society, they tend to band together, particularly when their common ancestry—for all its diversity—is the basis for discrimination. But ethnogenesis only makes individuals more identifiable as they adopt symbols of their commonality (language, dress, religion, and rituals), which in turn make them easier targets of discrimination. As long as terrorism remains a condition of the modern world and as long as Americans remain fearful, it is likely that prejudice and discrimination—informal and invidious as it may be—will be experienced by those Arab Americans who "stand out," whether by language, dress, religion, or some other marker of their Arab origins. The end result will be one more fault line of ethnic tension in America.

SUMMARY

Individuals from the Middle East began to immigrate to the United States in the 1880s. Most of these migrants came from what today is Lebanon and parts of Syria, and the vast majority were Christian. Immigration laws and policies isolated them in the United States, forcing many who had come as sojourners to settle permanently and, after considerable conflict over their rights, to become citizens. These early migrants often became small entrepreneurs and middleman minorities in both urban and rural areas in the United States, although some moved into the industrial labor force of the expanding automobile industry. These ethnics had some resources, entrepreneurial skills, literacy, and a concern for education, and so it is not surprising that they and their descendants have done well in securing resources in America. About one-half of all Arabs in the United States today are descendants of this first wave of immigration. The second wave did not really begin until the 1960s and 1970s. Migrants in this wave were more likely to be Muslim, and they came with, or in search of, educational and occupational skills. As a result, they too have done well in securing resources in the United States, although many remain poor.

By all measures of success, Arab Americans have the incomes, education, and jobs of a successful minority population. Moreover, in recent years, Arab Americans have become more politically active, securing both appointed and elected positions in government, although Arab Americans are still underrepresented in other forms of government employment. Despite their success, highly negative stereotypes of Arabs in general have worked to stigmatize Arab Americans and to legitimize informal acts of discrimination. These stereotypes have been fueled by long-standing conflicts in the Middle East and, more recently, by acts of terrorism abroad and in the United States. A constant barrage of negative images—media reports, editorial cartoons, Internet blogs—portrays Arabs as prone to violence and as hostile to American interests. These images run counter to the actual accomplishments of Arab Americans, but they are nonetheless used to paint all Arab Americans with the same brush.

After the dramatic events of 9-11, prejudice and discrimination against Arabs often escalated into hate crimes; and although these have faded somewhat, the memory of these attacks on persons and mosques has prompted a defensive reaction among Arab Americans who find comfort in those traditions that they have in common. This emerging ethnogenesis makes Arab Americans more identifiable and fuels prejudicial beliefs that Arab-ancestry citizens are not really Americans and, hence, cannot be trusted. Indeed, Arab Americans are caught in a very strange litmus test: If they retreat, this cultural ghettoization may seem to confirm that they have not assimilated and cannot be trusted. But if they seek to remain in the mainstream, non-Arabs may view them with suspicion as "up to something" that could harm the United States as the hijackers of 9-11 did. Thus, Arab Americans are caught in a double bind from which it is not easy to escape.

Historically, Arab Americans have been the victims of various laws that have worked against them. First, immigration laws and holdover statutes from slavery kept them, for a time, from becoming citizens. More recently, laws intended to control terrorism have left Arab Americans vulnerable to searches, seizures, and detention in violation of what most Americans consider their basic civil rights. In view of informal patterns of discrimination—ethnic slurs, public stares, rejection of job applications because of an "Arab sounding" name, ridicule of women and girls who wear head coverings and other "Arab look-ing" clothing, hate crimes, mosque burnings, and many other events that make Arab Americans feel threatened and unwelcome—it is not surprising that they have retreated into a newfound ethnicity that minimizes the big differences in the backgrounds of Arab Americans and provides comfort for what they share in common, namely, Arab traditions and a common fear of how the non-Arab population in America sees them.

POINTS OF DEBATE

Terrorism along with other events in the Middle East have put to a test Americans' commitment to civil liberties. Fears about further acts of terrorism have led to the enactment of laws and to administrative decisions by the Departments of Justice and Homeland Security that clearly violate traditional interpretations of Americans' civil rights. Because most citizens are not the intended victims of these efforts to find terrorists, they have remained conspic-uously silent. But for those who must endure the effects of the concern about terrorists, some important questions can be asked and debated.

1. If some classes of citizens can have their civil liberties violated while others stand by, what are the long-run prospects for the traditional constitutional guarantees that have been the basis for social movements and legal actions against ethnic discrimination?
2. If existing laws are extended into the indefinite future as (justified) fears of terrorism persist, what are the long-run consequences for the traditional constitutional guarantees for all citizens, not only those who are now tar-geted by these new antiterrorism laws and policies? Will the United States become more authoritarian, and will citizens lose certain rights that have been the hallmark of American freedoms?
3. If Arab Americans further retreat from the American mainstream—at least culturally—how are they to avoid being perceived as somehow "not American" when in fact they are among the most successful of all ethnic subpopulations? And if they continue to enter the mainstream, how are they to avoid being perceived as "up to something" that requires govern-mental monitoring?
4. If Arab-origin Americans are allowed to be monitored by government, what is to prevent other ethnic subpopulations from being monitored for real or manufactured "threats to national security"? Once the slippery slope

of government eavesdropping, search and seizure, and detention of "suspects" is approached, where will it end? And who will be its next victim? Will any ethnic group that protests its situation also be vulnerable to the government's concern for "national security"?

KEY TERMS/KEY LEGISLATION

Anti-Terrorism and Effective Death
   Penalty Act of 1996, 293
Department of Homeland
   Security, 289
ethnogenesis, 280
hate crimes, 275
Illegal Immigration Act of 1996, 293
Immigration Act of 1924, 282
Islam, 275

jihad, 288
middleman minorities, 281
Muslim or Islamic extremists, 275
Naturalization Act of 1790, 293
9-11, 275
pan-ethnicity, 280
patriarchy, 289
sojourner orientation, 281
USA Patriot Act of 2001, 294

Visit our text-specific website at www.mhhe.com/aguirre7e for valuable resources for both students and instructors.

CHAPTER 10

The Future of Ethnicity in America

Changes in the ethnic composition of a society are always accompanied by tensions between declining populations and those that are growing. In the nineteenth and early twentieth centuries, dramatic changes in the composition of white ethnics occurred, the first wave of Asian immigration arrived, and African Americans migrated from the South to the North. These demographic transformations were highlighted by extreme prejudice and discrimination. Now, America is experiencing a similar transformation of the population. The numbers of Latinos are dramatically increasing, whites are moving toward minority status, and Asian populations are beginning to grow again.

The Bureau of the Census makes projections into the future on the relative size of ethnic subpopulations, and the demographic shift is dramatic. Non-Latino whites will go from about 68 percent of the population today to 46 percent in 2050, whereas Latinos will rise from 15 percent to 30 percent of the population by 2050. African Americans will grow from about 12 percent of the population today to about 15 percent; Asian Americans/Pacific Islanders will almost double from 5 percent to 9 percent in 2050; and Native Americans/Alaska Natives will remain unchanged at a bit less than 1 percent of the population. Thus, there is potential for ethnic tension in such a large shift in the relative numbers of various ethnic subpopulations. Those whose relative numbers are declining will often experience a sense of threat, causing them to hold prejudices about, and discriminate against, those whose numbers are increasing.

THE NEW IMMIGRANTS

Changing Patterns of Immigration

The sense of threat is compounded by patterns of immigration. First, the absolute number of immigrants has increased, and absolute numbers matter because there are so many more immigrants who are increasingly spread across most regions of the United States. Currently there are 37.9 million foreign-born immigrants in the United States (U.S. Bureau of the Census, 2008), making it

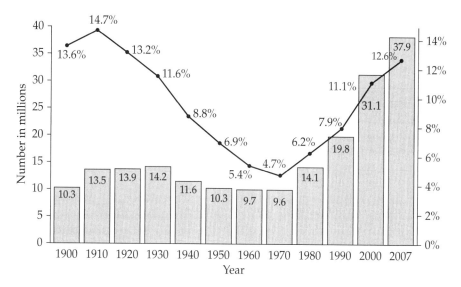

FIGURE 10.1 The size* of the immigrant population, 1900–2007.
*The absolute size of the immigrant population is inside the bars, while the immigrant population as a percentage of the total population is marked on the trend line.
Source: U.S. Bureau of the Census, 2007 Community Population Survey (March) and 2000 Census.

virtually impossible for people to avoid the recognition that the numbers of other ethnics is increasing. Second, the percentage of the total population that is foreign born is rising, and rapidly so. At one of the peaks of immigration at around 1910, 14.7 percent of the total population was composed of foreign-born immigrants; in 2007, the percentage has risen from a low of 4.7 percent in 1970 to 12.6 percent of the total of the 300+ million people in the United States. Figure 10.1 documents the decline of immigration during much of the twentieth century, as well as the rapid rise in the percentage of foreign-born immigrants in the last three decades of the twentieth century and the first decade of the twenty-first century. Such a rapid rise is, once again, threatening to some in communities across America, thereby fueling prejudice and discrimination. It is very difficult to extrapolate from trends like that from 1970 to 2007, given that the data in noncensus years are obtained from surveys that, if anything, undercount immigrants because so many are illegal and undocumented. Still, it is likely that the current slope in the curve from 1970 onward will remain relatively steep, with an even larger number and percentage of the total population being foreign-born immigrants in just the next two decades. This is the reality of American society today and into the future, but it is always an unsettling reality to those who feel threatened.

A third pattern to the immigration is that those migrating to the United States are settling in more communities than before. In 1995, 69 percent of the foreign-born population resided in the top-five states; this percentage had declined to 66 percent by 2000; and by 2007, it had declined further to 61 percent of the foreign-born. These figures signal that settlement patterns of immigrants are more dispersed. For example, the immigrant population between 2000 and 2007 increased 152 percent in Georgia, 160 percent in Tennessee, 143 percent in Alabama, 121 percent in South Carolina, 125 percent in Mississippi, 105 percent in Arkansas, 180 percent in Wyoming, and 115 percent in Montana; and while these growth rates reflect increases from a small immigrant population base, the fact that the immigrant population has more than doubled in just seven years is significant. Even states where the immigrant population was already large have experienced high growth rates, which means that there is also more dispersion of these new immigrants into new communities within these states. For instance, in the seven-year period between 2000 and 2007, Texas experienced a 33 percent increase in its immigrant population, New Jersey a 46 percent increase, Arizona a 29 percent increase, and California a 10 percent increase (while this latter percentage seems small, it signals dramatic growth to the already large immigrant population of 9 million persons in 2002; a 10 percent increase thus means that the immigrant population grew by almost a million people in California over a seven-year period). More and more communities across America, then, have become destinations for new waves of immigrants, with the result that a sense of threat can be found in most communities.

A fourth pattern of immigration is the comparatively high rate of "illegal" and undocumented immigration. In the Census Bureau's Current Population Survey, 11.3 million of the 37+ million foreign-born are undocumented, with 6.9 million of these working mostly in unskilled jobs. These immigrants are less educated than legal immigrants (as defined by not completing high school). For native-born members of American society, these "illegals" pose a threat because the number of unskilled jobs in the United States has declined as a proportion of all jobs, but for those unskilled natives who need such jobs, competition from illegal immigrants is likely to breed resentments, prejudices, and discrimination. Their fears can easily be played upon by anti-immigration political groups and ideologues and, thus exaggerated, but there is also a grim reality for the unskilled and poor in America: fewer low-skilled jobs and more competition among the less educated members of various ethnic subpopulations for these jobs—a formula that is sure to feed prejudice and discrimination. Illegals now represent close to 30 percent of the foreign-born population, and in some states, they can be found in even higher numbers. Table 10.1 lists the states with the largest proportion of illegal immigrants (up to 30 percent of all foreign-born) as a proportion of the total population in each of these states. Thus, for example, 9 percent of the total population in Arizona is illegal, 8 percent in California (and 10 percent in Los Angeles County), 4 percent in Colorado, 6 percent in Florida, and so on down the list. Two-thirds of these individuals are seeking jobs, mostly in low-skill and low-wage labor markets, and this fact can be highly threatening to native-born who have few job skills in what are now highly competitive labor markets.

In Figure 10.2, the country of origin of the ten largest immigrant populations (as a total of all foreign-born) is displayed. Well over one-half of all foreign-born individuals come from these countries, with 30 percent coming from Mexico alone. Table 10.2 expands upon Figure 10.2 by listing the top twenty-five countries of birth among the immigrant population, while Table 10.3 summarizes the regions from which foreign-born immigrants have come.

TABLE 10.1 Estimated Illegal Immigrants as a Percentage of the Total Population and Workers in Selected States*

	Illegals as Share of Total State Population	Illegals as Share of Workers in a State
Arizona	9%	12%
California	8	10
L.A. Country	10	14
Colorado	4	4
Florida	6	7
Georgia	5	7
Illinois	4	5
Maryland	5	6
Massachusetts	3	4
Nevada	6	9
New Jersey	5	6
New York	3	4
North Carolina	4	6
Texas	7	9
Virginia	3	4
Washington	4	5

*This list of states represents 30 percent of the foreign-born population of 11.3 million individuals.
Source: U.S. Bureau of the Census, 2007 Current Population Survey.

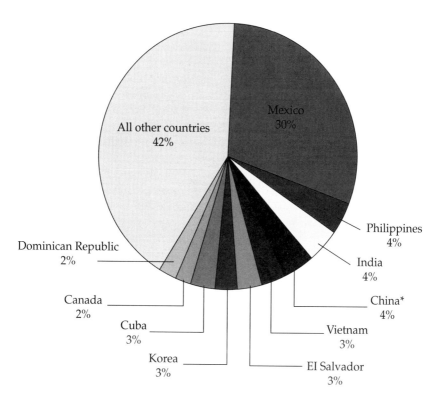

FIGURE 10.2 Top ten countries of immigrants to the United States, 2008.
Source: U.S. Bureau of the Census, 2008 American Community Survey.

TABLE 10.2 Top Twenty-Five Countries of Birth for Immigrants* in 2007

Country of Birth	Numbers in Millions	Percent Who Are Citizens
Mexico	11,671	19.8%
China	2,007	52.3
India	1,704	38.5
Philippines	1,665	60.3
Vietnam	999	68.8
El Salvador	998	25.8
Cuba	980	47.6
Former USSR	973	54.7
Korea	906	43.4
Dominican Republic	856	40.1
Canada	699	43.2
Guatemala	681	17.4
Columbia	669	42.7
United Kingdom	590	41.0
Jamaica	550	60.4
Germany	514	62.6
Haiti	514	54.0
Honduras	439	20.3
Poland	427	51.1
Italy	418	76.3
Ecuador	111	37.2
Iran	371	75.8
Peru	354	39.0
Brazil	338	24.9
Japan	286	28.0
World Total	37,280	39.0%

*Data include all immigrants who were born in another country who have come to the United States over the last six decades.
Source: Center for Immigration Studies, March 2007. Data based upon U.S. Bureau of the Census, 2007 Current Population Survey.

TABLE 10.3 Region of Birth for all Immigrants,* 2007

	Share of All Immigrants	Number of Immigrants
All Latin America	54.6%	20,372
Mexico	31.3	11,671
Caribbean	9.1	3,379
South America	7.3	2,725
Central America	7.0	2,597
East/Southeast Asia	17.6	6,558
Europe	12.5	4,646
South Asia	5.5	2,044
Middle East	3.5	1,310
Sub-Saharan Africa	2.8	1,030
Canada	1.9	699
Not Given/Oceana	1.7	621
Total	**100.0%**	**37,280**

*Regardless of year of entry.
Sources: Center for Immigration Studies. Data Source: U.S. Bureau of the Census, 2007 Current Population Survey.

As Table 10.3 documents, Latin America is the area of origin for 54.6 percent of the foreign-born population; Eastern and southeast Asia account for 17.6 percent of immigrants, and South Asia adds another 5.5 percent (making the Asian total 23.1 percent); Europe is the country of origin for 12.5 percent of immigrants, followed by 3.5 percent from the Middle East, 2.8 percent from Sub-Saharan Africa, 1.9 percent from Canada, and 1.7 percent from Oceana (or not given). Thus, the Latino immigrants can pose threats because their numbers are so large—over 20 million—as can Asians (of a wide variety of ethnicities) at 6.7 million. Other populations, such as those from the Middle East, do not pose so much of a threat from their numbers but from American concerns and fears about terrorism. Latin Americans are mostly white (except for Caribbean immigrants), and thus the threat comes from their large numbers and the large proportion who have immigrated illegally, whereas the Asian immigrants are often labeled as a "race," and coupled with their larger numbers and higher levels of education, they can pose a different kind of threat to more middle-class Americans who have to compete with them for jobs. Sub-Saharan African immigrants who, as documented in Chapter 4, tend to be well educated are often lumped with the descendants of slaves, and thus they too can be seen to pose threats based upon prejudicial beliefs about "this race." The same is true for less-well-educated blacks from the Caribbean. Thus, the source of threat to native-born Americans varies, but the critical point is that these immigrants are, like their counterparts 100 years earlier, rapidly changing the ethnic makeup in the United States. Change of any kind is always threatening to some segments of an indigenous population, and change of this magnitude and speed can be doubly threatening, with the result that the dynamics of threat, prejudice, and discrimination will inevitably be set into motion.

The shifting patterns of immigration can be brought into greater focus by looking at longer-term profiles of regions of immigrant origins. In Table 10.4, the shifting profile of immigrants from 1951 to 2007 is summarized. The data for 2007 are reported in Table 10.3, but Table 10.4 gives us a longer historical view (Rolph, 1992; U.S. Bureau of Census 1995, 1997, 2001a, 2008; U.S. Department of Justice, 1991a). In 1951, almost 68 percent of immigrants came from Europe and Canada, slightly over 6 percent from Asia, and almost 25 percent from Latin America and the Caribbean. Fifty-six years later, these numbers have changed

TABLE 10.4 The Shifting Profile of Immigrants to the United States, 1951–2006

Area of Origin	1951–60	1961–70	1971–80	1981–90	1991–93	1997	2000	2007
Europe and Canada	67.7%	46.3%	21.6%	12.5%	13.1%	18.4%	17.8%	14.4%
Asia	6.1	12.9	35.5	37.5	30.0	26.5	25.5	23.1
Latin America and the Caribbean	24.6	39.2	40.3	47.1	49.9	61.5	51.0	54.0

Sources: Rolph, 1992; U.S. Department of Justice, 1991a; U.S. Bureau of the Census, 1995; U.S. Bureau of the Census, March 1997 Current Population Survey (Internet release date: October 15, 1999); U.S. Bureau of the Census, 2001a; U.S. Bureau of the Census, 2008 *Statistical Abstract*, Table 43.

dramatically: 14.4 percent now come from Europe and Canada, 23.1 percent from Asia, and 54.6 percent from Latin America and the Caribbean. In a very brief time frame, then, the pattern of immigration has been turned upside down; change of this magnitude means that the native-born have had to make adjustments to new kinds of immigrants. Moreover, since these new immigrants do not come from countries in the Anglo-Saxon core (Canada and Europe), there are often greater differences in culture between the new and older post–World War II immigrants. Thus, when significant shifts in the origins of immigrants take place, both the native-born and immigrants must make large adjustments, which are rarely easy and which can often feel threatening.

The significant increase in numbers of immigrants over the last decades represents one level of adjustment (see Figure 10.1), but perhaps even more important are the cultural differences between native- and foreign-born. These differences are probably the greatest for Asian immigrants, and while immigrants from Latin America represent a mix of European cultures (mostly Spanish but other European countries as well) and the indigenous native populations of North and South America, there are still significant cultural differences—if only by language which, to English-speaking Americans, can be seen as threatening. Some of these differences are mitigated by the dramatic globalization that has occurred during this period when the origins of immigrants shifted away from the older European core. Global capitalism, coupled with the export of the culture of capitalism, has reduced—to a degree—cultural differences across the industrial nations of the world. Still, as new immigrants, speaking non-English languages, enter communities, the culture and structure of these communities must change. The demography of school enrollments (especially among high-fertility immigrants), the composition of neighborhoods, the nature of local businesses catering to diverse ethnics, the balance of power in politics (especially if immigrants become citizens), and many other features of a community will never be quite the same, and often these kinds of local changes are highly threatening to the descendants of European immigrants. Prejudice and discrimination thus become more likely as the demography, ecology, institutional order, and culture of communities are altered.

Immigration, Birth Rates, and Changing Composition of Ethnic Populations

Today, non-Hispanic whites constitute 68 percent of the population, Latinos 15 percent, African Americans 12 percent, Asians/Pacific Islanders 5 percent, and Native Americans/Alaska Natives less than 1 percent (U.S. Bureau of the Census, 2008). As is emphasized in the tables and figures presented thus far, immigration is increasing and dramatically changing the ethnic mix of American society. One important consequence of new patterns of immigration is wide variation in the rates of fertility among ethnic subpopulations. As high-fertility ethnics enter the United States, their numbers will accelerate compared to most domestic-born ethnics as well as other immigrant ethnics who evidence lower rates of fertility. Thus, the doubling of the Latino population over the next four decades is the result of more than immigration—both legal and illegal—but also of the comparatively high birth rates of immigrants from Mexico, Latin America, and the Caribbean. Asians and Pacific Islanders have widely varying rates of reproduction, but some subpopulations have high rates of fertility, especially those from the South and Southeast, and the result is that they too will grow as a consequence of their patterns of fertility. This acceleration of growth of some ethnic subpopulations with high birth rates always poses a threat to those whose relative size is declining or remains unchanged; thus, non-Hispanic whites and African Americans often feel threatened by the higher birth rates of Latinos and some Asian populations because their numbers are increasing rapidly within a particular community, thereby changing the ethnic composition of schools, neighborhoods, and workplaces. For example, from 1980 to 2000, the total population of the United States grew by 24 percent, but the non-Latino white population grew by only 8 percent, the African American population by 31 percent, and the American Indian/Alaska Native population by 74 percent. Except for non-Latino whites, the growth rates of these native-born ethnics were higher than the overall average and seem robust, but when compared to the growth rates of Asians/Pacific Islanders (204 percent) and Latinos (141 percent), the differential rate of growth can be threatening to ethnics revealing lower rates of growth. The upswing in immigration accounts for part of this differential rate of growth, but much of it is due to variations in fertility rates of various ethnic subpopulations. And since high birth rates bring young children to a community, they have large impacts on local, community systems—schools, housing, jobs, recreation, welfare, politics, and the like. As a result, individuals living in a community experience firsthand the changing ethnic composition of their community and, often as a consequence, feel threatened.

Reasons for the Shift in Immigration Patterns

This shift in immigration patterns is, to a great extent, the result of changes in immigration laws over the last four decades. Rolph (1992) has suggested that much of the shift is due to the **Immigration Act of 1965,** which eliminated country-specific quotas that had favored European countries and, simultaneously, allowed immediate family members of U.S. citizens the opportunity to enter the country without numerical restriction. In addition, prior to 1965, immigrants from European countries had entered the United States largely through a program that gave visas to persons in professions and occupations that were in short supply. The Immigration Act of 1965 placed a 20 percent ceiling on these visas. Thus, as Rolph (1992:10) notes: "Removal of country-specific quotas and the new preference system designed to facilitate family reunification had been . . . responsible for substantial changes in the ethnic composition and skill level of the immigrant pool over the years."

The growth of immigrant populations from Asia, Latin American, and Caribbean countries between 1981 and the present is related to two additional

---

Box 10.1
Why Do Mexicans Come to the United States?

Why do Mexicans come to the United States? Is it the promise of riches or fame? Is it the perception of the United States as a paradise? The historical survey of Mexican immigration to the United States in Chapter 7 (pp. 204–205), identified social conditions in Mexico and the need for cheap labor in the United States as the "push-pull" factors behind Mexican immigration to the United States. Although these socioeconomic indicators may explain the circumstances behind Mexican immigration, do we know what reasons Mexicans offer for Mexican immigration to the United States?

Aguirre (1993) conducted a study regarding the association between English-language and U.S.-origin communication media and how Mexicans perceive Mexican social issues. He found that Mexicans have definite perceptions as to why Mexicans immigrate to the United States. In order of decreasing importance, Aguirre found that Mexicans believe that Mexicans immigrate to the United States for the following reasons:

1. There is no employment in Mexico (59 percent).
2. Mexicans want to earn more money (38 percent).
3. The standard of living is higher in the United States (36 percent).
4. There are better employers in the United States (32 percent).
5. Mexicans like adventure (28 percent).

Source: Aguirre, 1993.

---

pieces of immigration legislation. The first, the **Refugee Act of 1980,** encouraged immigration from Asian countries—especially from Vietnam, Laos, and Cambodia. In the aftermath of the Vietnam War, Congress enacted the Refugee Act in an attempt to regulate the flow and number of refugees who qualified for admission to the United States. A **refugee** was defined as anyone who held a "well-founded fear of persecution in their home country." At the same time, **asylees** (persons who petition for legal status in the United States because they fear persecution in their country of origin) were given the same statutory recognition as refugees. The Refugee Act of 1980 resulted in the arrival of large numbers of immigrants from Vietnam, Laos, and Cambodia as either refugees or asylees.

The second piece of legislation, the **Immigration Reform and Control Act (IRCA) of 1986,** targeted two immigrant groups: **long-term undocumented residents (LTUR)** and **special categories of agricultural workers (SCAW)** who had entered the United States illegally. The primary purpose of the IRCA was to curb undocumented immigration, but it also sought to protect those persons already in the United States from being uprooted and deported. The implementation component of the IRCA was an amnesty program that offered legal status to persons (1) who had resided continuously in the United States since January 1, 1982, and (2) who could demonstrate that they had worked ninety days or more in designated agricultural labor between May 1985 and May 1986. Since the vast majority of immigrants from Latin America were most likely to enter the agricultural labor force in the United States, the IRCA resulted in an increase of immigration from Latin America between 1986 and 1990 (Hollmann, 1992; Vernez, 1990).

The effects of immigration policy on the ethnic composition of the U.S. population are summarized in Table 10.5. The largest percentage of refugees entering the United States in 2006 came from Latin America and the Caribbean. In contrast, the smallest percentage of refugees in 2006 came from East Asia. As can be seen, these 2006 figures represent a dramatic reversal of earlier trends.

In response to public pressure and to a mixture of lobbying interests, the 1990 Immigration Act allowed immigration to increase substantially. The act encouraged immigration of more skilled workers and those from Europe, but it also sought to limit numbers of immigrants in the future. The full effect of this law is hard to estimate, but, as reported above, the reality for the next half century is that the U.S. population will include more Latinos and more Asians because of the continued effects of the 1965 and 1986 acts.

Settlement Patterns of the New Immigrants

Where do recent immigrants live? Table 10.6 reports where immigrants have settled, by state and region (see also Table 10.1). California is the state most heavily populated by immigrants; in 2005, 27 percent of immigrants settled there, especially in southern California along the Long Beach–Los Angeles and Anaheim–Santa Ana metropolitan corridors. Currently, states where immigrants locate are forced to carry the financial burden of managing these immigrants' transition into U.S. society (Vernez and McCarthy, 1996).

Because foreign-born immigrants to the United States do not settle evenly across the country, their impact on particular regions, states, and metropolitan areas is much greater than their numbers often suggest. As a result, those already residing in areas of heavy immigration will experience an escalated sense of threat that, in turn, can fuel prejudicial beliefs and discrimination, which can spread across the nation. Although the labor force increased by 14.4 million jobs between 1990 and 2002, 41 percent of these jobs were taken by foreign-born immigrants (Kritz and Gurak, 2005). But since immigrants have tended to migrate to a limited number of states and metropolitan regions, they take a much larger portion of the new jobs in these destinations than the aggregate figure of 41 percent for the whole nation would suggest. In Miami, for example, over one-half of the population in the metropolitan area and 63 percent of its labor force is foreign-born. In California, another prominent example, 25 percent of the population and 30 percent of the labor force is foreign-born. Some of these jobs may be perceived as undesirable by the native-born, but it is still likely that immigrants displaced some workers (Kritz and Gurak, 2005). And even if jobs have not been taken, immigrants change the makeup of housing markets and neighborhoods, the availability of social services, the composition of schools, and health care services. The

TABLE 10.5 Percentage of Total Refugee Arrivals in the United States by Area of Origin, 1990–2006

						Percentage from Each Area					
Area of Origin	1990 (N = 109,078)	1991 (N = 96,587)	1992 (N = 114,498)	1993 (N = 107,926)	1994 (N = 109,593)	1995 (N = 98,520)	1996 (N = 74,791)	1997 (N = 69,276)	2000 (N = 65,941)	2002 (N = 126,084)	2006* (N = 205,903)
Africa	3%	5%	5%	6%	5%	5%	10%	9%	3%	11%	22%
East Asia	35	39	30	36	37	36	25	11	11	13	10
Eastern Europe and Soviet Union (former)	52	47	56	48	46	46	55	70	41.9	39	17
Latin America and Caribbean	5	4	3	4	6	8	5	4	23.6	22	33
Near East	5	5	6	6	6	5	5	6	6.7	15	18

*Individuals granted asylum are included in 2006 data.
Sources: U.S. Department of Homeland Security, 2007; U.S. Department of Justice, 2001; Office of Immigration Statistics, 2006 Yearbook of Immigration Statistics.

TABLE 10.6 Patterns of Immigrant Settlement by Selected States and Metropolitan Areas, 1995–2005

	Percentage of Population Made Up of Immigrants					
	1995	1996	1997	1998	2000–02	2005
State						
California	23%	22%	26%	26%	26.4%	27.2%
New York	18	17	16	15	21.0	21.4
Florida	9	9	10	9	18.5	18.5
Texas	7	9	7	7	14.2	15.9
New Jersey	6	7	5	5	18.6	19.5
Metropolitan Area						
New York, NY	16%	15%	14%	12%	13.9%	17.0%
Los Angeles–Long Beach, CA	8	7	8	9	11.3	17.2
Chicago, IL	4	4	4	5	3.4	4.5
Miami, FL	4	5	6	4	5.0	6.6
Washington, DC–MD–VA	4	4	4	4	5.3	7.4

Sources: Camarota, 2002; U.S. Bureau of the Census, 2005 American Community Survey; U.S. Department of Justice, 1999a.

result is an escalated sense of threat, the ultimate force behind ethnic discrimination.

As noted earlier, this sense of threat is becoming more dispersed because immigrants are moving to all areas of the country. While immigrants are still disproportionately settled in a few key states and metropolitan areas, as Table 10.6 documents, there is more dispersion of immigrants than a generation ago. The result is that many more communities, often rather small ones, must adapt to their changing demographics—a task that almost always fills the longer-term residents of any community with fear and threat.

Other Characteristics of the New Immigrants

Table 10.7 summarizes some of the characteristics of the immigrants who came to the United States after 1983. Regarding educational attainment, several differences are evident. First, compared to other populations, a noticeable proportion of Latinos have not graduated from high school. Second, on average, almost one-fourth of Latinos and Europeans have completed four years of high school. Third, more than one-third of the Asian population has completed four years or more of college. In 2000, the college completion rate of the Asian population was four times that of the Latino population. The data on educational attainment in Table 10.7 support observations by researchers that Asian and Latino immigrants arrive in the United States with high educational aspirations (Gray et al., 1996; Vernez and Abrahamse, 1996).

As it is evident from Table 10.7, the majority of foreign-born Asians, Latinos, and Europeans are employed in the United States. Interestingly,

TABLE 10.7 Characteristics of Foreign-Born Persons, Age 14 Years Old and Older, in the United States, 1983–2006

Characteristic	Asian, %							Latino, %							European, %						
	1983	1986	1988	1994	1997	2000	2006	1983	1986	1988	1994	1997	2000	2006	1983	1986	1988	1994	1997	2000	2006
Educational Attainment																					
Not high school graduate	26.5%	26.6%	23.9%	12.9%	16.0%	16.2%	13.2%	60.1%	58.0%	58.8%	40.9%	64.6%	50.4%	48.6%	40.2%	33.3%	30.5%	33.0%	34.7%	18.7%	13.7%
4 years of high school	20.5	23.6	21.5	30.8	26.2	21.8	21.2	22.8	23.4	23.6	24.3	36.1	24.9	26.5	31.7	34.1	35.3	31.4	34.3	25.0	28.6
4 years or more of college	36.6	34.7	36.3	34.0	44.5	44.9	50.6	7.8	7.8	6.7	6.1	5.6	11.2	11.9	15.2	18.3	19.1	13.6	24.5	25.8	37.7
Labor Force Status																					
Employed	55.2%	56.4%	60.7%	53.6%	65.1%	64.0%	—	54.0%	60.9%	63.4%	52.2%	63.0%	64.9%	—	44.7%	48.9%	49.9%	50.6%	52.5%	55.8%	—
Unemployed	5.7	4.9	3.1	4.0	4.4	3.5	—	10.1	6.3	4.5	6.4	8.6	7.3	—	4.0	2.3	1.5	5.2	5.9	2.3	—
Residence																					
In poverty area	7.2%	10.5%	16.5%	18.0%	15.0%	12.8%	11.9%	18.8%	27.5%	37.0%	31.7%	32.0%	21.9%	20.7%	5.5%	4.0%	6.0%	24.1%	13.0%	9.3%	9.3%
Not in poverty area	92.8	89.5	83.6	82.0	85.0	87.2	88.1	81.2	72.5	62.9	68.3	68.0	78.1	79.3	94.5	96.0	94.0	75.9	87.0	90.7	90.7
Citizenship Status																					
Naturalized	39.3%	41.2%	45.4%	51.7%	44.3%	47.1%	56.3%	30.0%	29.7%	31.4%	38.3%	15.7%	28.3%	30.7%	71.1%	65.1%	66.4%	69.2%	53.3%	52.0%	58.3%
Not a citizen	58.7	57.6	52.1	48.3	55.7	52.9	43.7	68.3	67.6	66.2	61.7	84.3	71.7	69.3	27.0	31.7	31.4	30.8	46.7	48.0	41.7

Sources: Schmidley, 2001; U.S. Bureau of the Census, 1991d; March 1994 Current Population Survey: The Foreign-Born Population: 1994; U.S. Bureau of the Census, "Profile of the Foreign-Born Population in the United States, 1997"; U.S. Bureau of the Census, 2008 *Statistical Abstract*, Tables 43, 44.

A Latino couple poses with their daughter.

both Asians and Latinos have higher employment rates than Europeans presumably because spouses in European families may choose not to work. This influence is confirmed by the fact that Latinos tend to have a higher unemployment rate, followed by Asians and Europeans, respectively. The vast majority of Asians, Latinos, and Europeans live in nonpoverty areas. Latinos have a higher rate of living in poverty areas than either Asians or Europeans.

Finally, among the three populations, the group born in Europe has generally had the highest naturalization rate. This statistic is consistent with Rolph's (1992) suggestion that U.S. immigration policies have historically favored persons of European origins. The larger proportion of noncitizens among the Asian and especially the Latino populations may suggest something about their accommodation in U.S. society. Asians and Latinos tend to locate within residential or geographical areas where they are the majority population. For example, many settle in areas where their native language is dominant—in the neighborhood, the workplace, and the home (Portes and Rumbaut, 1990; Wallace, 1989; Wilson and Portes, 1980). Settlement within areas of shared ethnic identity may curtail interest in becoming naturalized citizens (see Chavez, Flores, and Lopez-Garza, 1990; Greenwell, DaVanzo, and Valdez, 1993; and Jaret, 1991). In a sense, the structural accommodation of Asians and Latinos in the United States may facilitate their participation in, but not their absorption into, mainstream social institutions (see Box 10.2 on the economic progress of immigrants).

Box 10.2

Economic Progress of Native-Born and Foreign-Born Workers in the United States

---

How do foreign-born workers fare in the economic marketplace? A comparison of median earnings for native-born and foreign-born workers in the United States shows the following:

- In 2006, 24.7 percent of foreign-born workers and 18.0 percent of native-born workers earned less than $25,000.
- Among foreign-born workers, the proportion earning less than $25,000 ranged from 35.3 percent of those from Central America to 14.5 percent of those from Europe.
- A higher proportion of native-born workers (57.3 percent) than foreign-born workers (46.7 percent) earned $50,000 or more. Among foreign-born workers, the proportion earning $50,000 or more ranged from 65.1 percent for those from Asia to 28.2 percent for those from Central America.
- Foreign-born workers from Asia and Europe, respectively, were more likely to earn $50,000 or more than native-born workers.

Household Income by Nativity and by World Region of Birth, 2006

	Percentage Who Earn:		
	Less than $25,000	$25,000 to $49,999	$50,000 or More
Total native-born	18.0%	24.7%	57.3%
Total immigrants	24.7	28.6	46.7
By Nativity			
Europe	14.5%	24.4%	61.1%
Asia	16.7	18.1	65.1
Latin America	32.0	35.1	32.9
Caribbean	27.5	32.4	40.1
Central America	35.3	36.5	28.2
South America	19.6	31.1	49.3

In general, the data in the table suggest that immigrant workers from Europe and Asia are almost at parity with native-born workers. Immigrant workers from Latin America and Central America are more likely than other immigrant workers to earn less than $25,000. In addition, immigrant workers from Latin America and Central America are less likely than other immigrant workers to earn $50,000 or more.

Sources: U.S. Bureau of the Census, 2008 *Statistical Abstract*, Table 42, Table 43.

THE IMMIGRATION DILEMMA

Despite the fact that most Americans are the descendants of immigrants, recent immigrants are not welcomed by a majority of the American public (Morganthau, 1993). These immigrants have sparked debate over such questions as who can come; how many can come; who is to pay for their needs; how can institutions like the schools and the economy absorb them; and will they adopt the tenets of the Anglo-Saxon core culture (Trueba, 1989; Valdez et al., 1993; Vernez, 1993). Table 10.8 illustrates the changes in public opinion concerning immigration, to the United States in general and to heavily populated states such as California and Florida in particular. Over 50 percent of Americans—up from one-third in 1965—now want immigration reduced; the number of those who want immigration to remain "about the same" decreased noticeably between 1965 and 2002; the percentage of those who have "no opinion" dropped by 75 percent. These data indicate that immigration is now a priority issue on the American political agenda. The tragic events of September 11, 2001, may have increased anti-immigrant sentiment in the United States (see Box 9.3 on page 294).

Part of the reason for this hardening of public opinion is, no doubt, the result of the recent shift in composition of the immigrant population from mostly European to mostly Latin American, Caribbean, and Asian. This shift has aroused suspicion and fears not only among those of European ancestry but also among those of Latino ancestry. The Latino National Political Survey—the most extensive

TABLE 10.8 Public Opinion on Appropriate Levels of Immigration to the United States

Survey Year and Scope	Immigration Levels Should Be:			
	Increased, %	Kept the Same, %	Reduced, %	No Opinion, %
1965 (U.S.)[a]	8%	39%	33%	20%
1977 (U.S.)[b]	7	37	42	14
1982 (Calif.)[c]	5	31	62	2
1984 (U.S.)[d]	8	38	40	14
1987 (Calif.)[e]	8	38	40	14
1988 (Fla.)[f]	6	24	67	3
1990 (U.S.)[g]	9	29	48	14
1992 (U.S.)[h]	5	28	59	8
1992 (Calif.)[h]	8	18	63	11
1999 (U.S.)[i]	10	41	44	5
2000 (U.S.)[j]	17	26	54	3
2002 (U.S.)[k]	15	27	55	3
2003[l]	12	28	47	13

[a]George H. Gallup, *The Gallup Poll: Public Opinion, 1935–1971*, vol. 3 (New York: Random House, 1972), p. 1953.
[b]George H. Gallup, *The Gallup Poll: Public Opinion, 1972–1977*, vol. 2 (Wilmington, DE: Scholarly Resources, Inc., 1979), p. 1050.
[c]California Opinion Index, "Immigration" (mimeo), Field Institute, San Francisco, June 1982.
[d]Jonathan Alter and Joseph Contreras, "Closing the Door?" *Newsweek*, June 25, 1984, p. 18. Average of responses to immigration level.
[e]California Opinion Index, "Immigration" (mimeo), Field Institute, San Francisco, October 1987.
[f]*Atlanta Journal*, January 31, 1988.
[g]*Los Angeles Times*, June 5, 1990, p. A23 (Roper Organization poll).
[h]*American Attitudes toward Immigration* (New York: The Roper Organization, April 1992).
[i]Gallup Poll (March 8, 1999 release).
[j]Gallup Poll (September 6, 2002 release).
[k]www.worldviews.org.
[l]www.fairus.org.

effort to date to measure Latino attitudes—found considerable hostility toward new immigrants, who represent economic competition for those already here (de la Garza et al., 1992). Perhaps the growing sentiment against immigrants extends to many ethnic subpopulations who perceive the same threat. (See Box 10.3.)

Much of the energy and vitality of the United States lies in its immigrant subpopulations. If the American public now wants to close the borders, will such restrictions damage the engine that has driven America? In some respects this question is rhetorical because, legally or illegally, immigrants will continue to arrive in the United States.

The dilemma is this: Will the inevitable influx of immigrants set in motion the dynamics of discrimination and ethnic antagonism that will undermine the structure and integrity of American society? Could this relatively recent broad-based resentment of non-European immigrants escalate the intensity of these dynamics to a new, disintegrative level? As we close our review of American ethnicity, these questions are worth consideration.

Box 10.3
Factoids That Generate Fear and Fuel Prejudice

The average American generally does not analyze deeply why they fear the changes brought about by immigration of new ethnic populations to the United States. Rather, personal experiences, gossip, news media, talk shows, political debates, and other sources of information typically generate a cognitive list of "facts" that form the basis of prejudicial beliefs. Even when the facts are essentially correct, their meaning can be distorted by people's fears about immigration and its consequences for their lives. Below are listed facts that are basically correct, at least to the extent that the Census Bureau's tabulations are correct, but in listing these as "factoids," the combined effect can strike fear and fuel prejudices. Read them quickly and see how you feel.

The nation's immigrant population is close to 38 million, which is a record number.

Since 2000, 10.3 immigrants have arrived, making this the highest period of immigration to the United States. More than half of these post-2000 arrivals are estimated to be illegal immigrants.

Nearly one in three immigrants is an illegal alien. One-half of Mexican and Central American immigrants and one-third of South American immigrants are illegal.

The total increase in the American population by 2060 will be 167 million, with 63 percent of this increase coming from current immigrants, those who are still to come, and their descendants.

If annual net immigration was reduced by 300,000, future immigration would add only 25 million people to the population by 2060, a reduction of 80 million from what will be the case if current trends continue.

Among adult immigrants, 31 percent have not completed high school, compared to 8 percent of native-born Americans.

The share of immigrants and native-born with college degrees is approximately the same, but this situation reverses an older pattern where immigrants were more likely than natives to be college graduates.

Thirty-three percent of immigrant households in the United States rely on some form of welfare compared to 19 percent of native-born households.

Immigrants and their U.S.-born children account for 71 percent of the increase of those not having health insurance.

The poverty rate for immigrants and their U.S.-born children (under 18 years of age) is 50 percent higher than for native-born and their children.

Immigrants make progress over time, but even those in the United States for over 20 years are more likely than natives to be in poverty, to lack health insurance, and to use welfare.

The primary reason for the preceding fact is low levels of education rather than either immigrants' legal status or work ethnic.

Of immigrant households, 82 percent have at least one worker compared to 73 percent of native-born households.

Immigration accounts for most of the increase in enrollment of children in public schools. In 2007, there were 10.8 million children from immigrant families.

Immigrants and native-borns reveal converging rates of entrepreneurship—13 percent for natives and 11 percent for immigrants who are self-employed.

Strung together "factoids" like these paint a picture of immigrants that comes close to the beliefs of most Americans. The factoids are empirically true, at least to the degree that census data provide an accurate picture of immigrants. Yet, these feed into what can become prejudicial beliefs because they do not document the contributions of immigrants to communities and the society as a whole; such contributions are not easily measured by census takers, and so they are underemphasized in public discourse, private talk, media outputs, talk radio, and political debates. Rather, factoids tend to be selected to affirm prejudicial beliefs. An interesting exercise is to accept the preceding facts as true, but then to construct a list of other factoids about the impacts of ethnic immigrants on American society.

Source: Facts taken from Camorota, 2008.

THE FUTURE DYNAMIC OF DISCRIMINATION

The shift in the ethnic composition of American society over the next fifty years will increase the Latino, Asian, and African American subpopulations. Most of the Latino population will consist of Mexican Americans, plus significant numbers of Puerto Ricans, Central and South Americans, and Spanish-speaking Caribbean Islanders (Mahler, 1995; Pessar, 1995). The Asian population will be of diverse origins; Filipinos are likely to be the most numerous, followed by Chinese, Vietnamese, Koreans, and Asian Indians (Freeman, 1995; Lessinger, 1995). The predominant segment of the African American population will be the descendants of slaves, supplemented by some recent Caribbean and African immigrants.

If we refer to the theoretical model presented in Chapter 2 and delineated in Figures 2.1 and 2.3, on pages 47 and 53, we can make some predictions about the future of ethnic relations in the United States. The key variables in the model are the following:

1. The size of an ethnic population
2. The entrepreneurial and educational resources of a population
3. The distinctiveness and identifiability of a population
4. The sense of threat experienced by other ethnic groups, especially the dominant ethnic subpopulations
5. The intensity of negative and prejudicial stereotypes
6. The degree of discrimination against a subpopulation
7. The resource shares of a subpopulation
8. The level of stratification, or confinement to a particular social class
9. The salience of egalitarian values and beliefs

We have seen how these variables have structured the lives of ethnic groups discussed in Chapters 5 through 9. Let us now assess how these variables will influence the lives of recent immigrants within these groups.

Latinos and the American Future

As the largest minority in the future, Latinos will not be able to fill middleman-minority niches and positions. The sheer size of this subpopulation, along with its average lower levels of education, job skills, and financial resources, will continue to limit the entrepreneurial opportunities available to most Latinos. The sense of threat generated by the growing size of the Latino population will increase and generate considerable negative stereotyping. The movement of many Latinos back and forth to their country of origin will ensure the survival of barrios, patterns of intragroup marriage and reproduction, native language use, and other cultural traditions. These cultural ties not only will sustain identifiability but also will increase the sense of threat to a diminishing white majority and an African American population who will have to compete with Latinos for jobs.

These negative effects of increasing numbers and low socioeconomic position eventually will be neutralized by a number of factors: (1) Most Latinos are less physically identifiable than either Asian Americans or African Americans. (2) Latinos are likely to intermarry with other ethnic groups in relatively large numbers because of their physical and cultural similarities with the white population. (3) The Latino population will continue to concentrate in the Southwest and, by virtue of their numbers, will acquire access to political power. (4) Latinos will obtain academic credentials in significant numbers and, hence, will have access to nonmenial jobs and higher incomes. Coupled with these factors are the effects of civil rights laws, which can, and will, be used to redress many of the law enforcement abuses of the past. Moreover, affirmative action extensions of these laws—or those that survive current efforts to eliminate them—will also be used to facilitate educational attainment and job placement. These large numbers of Latinos will continue to infiltrate the Anglo mainstream, even as a large mass remains ghettoized in barrios.

Despite these mitigating factors, the large size of the Latino population and its concentration in the Southwest as well as in the larger cities of the Northeast and south Florida will continue to fuel the hostility and resentment of white Americans who believe that their majority status is threatened and who feel forced to accommodate a "foreign culture" in ways never before experienced in the United States. Such hostility will translate into discrimination. If economic pressures continue to limit the number of available jobs and the flow of tax revenues to schools and other institutional structures, then considerable conflict and antagonism will ensue. The flash points will be symbolic issues such as bilingual education, language use in general, or highly visible stratification issues such as gang violence. The underlying tension will emanate from the threat that a large Latino population poses to the integrity of white American culture, job security, education, public services, and control of political power. As we saw in Chapter 7, the antagonism has been great as Latinos approached 8 percent of the U.S. population; as the Latino population surpasses 20 percent of the general population and over 50 percent in much of the Southwest, the antagonism will increase.

Asian Americans in the Future

The Asian population is highly diverse, immigrating from many different societies and cultures. Currently the largest Asian American population is the Chinese (2.3 million), followed by Filipinos (1.8 million), Asian Indians (1.7 million), Vietnamese (1.1 million), Koreans (1.1 million), and Japanese (0.80 million) (U.S. Bureau of the Census, 2002a). Except for the Japanese, these populations have been growing rapidly over the last decade. Individually, no Asian subpopulation will ever constitute more than 1 to 1.5 percent of the total population, but as a whole and adding Cambodians, Hmong, Laotians, Thailanders, Indonesians, Malaysians, Okinawans, Pakistanis, Sri Lankans, and a dozen or so Pacific Islander subpopulations to this list, Asians may constitute as much as 11 to 12 percent of the U.S. population.

This increase in the aggregate numbers of Asian Americans may pose an increased threat to white Americans, especially if world competition with China and other Asian economic powers creates economic hardships for non-Asian workers. Most Asian Americans are likely to move into middleman minority and professional niches because many bring with them education (or an education ethic), entrepreneurial skills, and systems for pooling capital. Different Asian ethnic groups may seek somewhat different middleman minority niches, although considerable competition among Asians may occur in certain metropolitan areas (Whitmore, Trautmann, and Caplan, 1989). Equally likely, younger Asians will secure those academic credentials that will place them in middle- and upper-middle-class professions and occupations. Their growing numbers in higher education and occupations formerly dominated by white Americans will cause considerable hostility and discrimination. Moreover, Latinos and African Americans will resent Asians who take advantage of opportunities in small business, higher education, and middle-class professions and positions. As a result, negative stereotypes of Asians will be used to justify discrimination, primarily of the informal and subtle kind that Asian Americans experience today (see Chapter 8).

Mitigating these discriminatory forces are counterforces: (1) Significant numbers of Asian Americans will intermarry with white Americans, thereby blurring the lines of physical distinction. (2) Asian American communities will continue to use their resources to promote success in business and education, two arenas in which positive interaction with white Americans frequently occurs. (3) Large numbers of Asian Americans living in the metropolitan areas will use their financial resources to mobilize political and legal resources to combat discrimination. (4) Young Asian Americans will use their academic credentials to penetrate all types of middle-class economic positions, thereby breaking the cycle of Asian confinement to middleman minority activity.

Asian American success will generate hostility among those who are less successful. Asian Americans who do not have academic credentials or other resources will remain in menial jobs within Asian ghettos or will enter the labor market and compete with Latinos and African Americans in a declining pool of lower-skilled and semiskilled jobs.

It is likely that Asian Americans will continue to use their resources to overcome discrimination. History has shown that when broad-based anti-Asian sentiments emerge, Asian Americans tend to come out of their "cultural shell" and fight discrimination aggressively. Yet we predict that within the next fifty years, relatively peaceful relations will prevail among diverse Asian subpopulations and mainstream America.

African Americans in the Future

If African Americans approach 16 percent of the population in the future as some predict, many of the problems that confront them today will persist. The size of the population prevents African Americans from filling only middleman minority niches, unless Asian Americans abandon these niches because of African American and, to a lesser extent, Latino hostility and violence. Negative stereotypes will perpetuate hostility from as well as toward African Americans. Moreover, as poorer African Americans and Latinos compete for the decreasing number of low-skilled and semiskilled jobs, tensions, mutual stereotyping, and hostility between these populations may increase (Graham, 1990).

The economic future of the African American population will be both bitter and sweet. As a result of affirmative action and other programs, many African Americans have escaped poverty, and the proportion of African Americans in the middle class will continue to increase. African Americans have increased their average years of education, violent crime in slums has decreased, literacy skills have increased, and drug use has declined (Jencks, 1991:5). However, the drop in male college enrollment may hinder further upward mobility for many males. Also, trends toward a dramatically expanded black middle class will emphasize the socioeconomic differences within the black population. Many poor black families are headed by single mothers and their relatives; these caretakers must raise children without the benefit of a father at home, often in substandard housing located in violent and crime-infested neighborhoods. Under these conditions, the jobless rate for young males has increased; many have simply withdrawn from the labor market, and some have drifted into gangs. Those who do not join the expanding middle class are likely to find it harder to rise above poverty, and their offspring will carry the legacy of poverty into adulthood. This scenario will become reality if the national economy declines and if the American public does not address the social problems with dollars from both the public and the private sectors. In the future, African Americans will be overrepresented in the lowest socioeconomic strata without enough resources to correct this imbalance. Tension between poor African Americans and other ethnic groups will persist as a result of a combination of factors: competition for jobs and government resources, resentment over long-term poverty and discrimination, and the incursion of other ethnic groups into entry-level, menial jobs.

Although black culture and its icons—celebrities in sports, music, movies, and television—will continue to penetrate the Anglo-Saxon cultural core, the general population of blacks will experience discrimination owing to skin color and other cultural differences. In most cases this discrimination will be informal and subtle but very real. Moreover, despite a growing African American middle class becoming more integrated with white and Asian Americans in jobs, housing, and education—with a concomitant reduction in the intensity of established stereotypes and blatant forms of discrimination—the problems of those left behind will foster new levels of threat, new negative stereotypes, and new forms of discrimination.

These predictions are based on attributes shown in the discrimination model, which applies to African Americans living in poverty: large in number, easy to identify, threatening to other populations, negatively stereotyped, low on the socioeconomic ladder, lacking in resources, and persistent targets of discrimination. The white Americans' sense of threat in the perception that affirmative action programs as well as government aid programs diminish their own well-being will discourage many from making resources available to the black community and, thereby, from redressing this long-standing American dilemma.

NEW PATTERNS OF ETHNIC MIXING

The 2000 census allowed individuals to list more than one ethnic/racial ancestry (U.S. Bureau of the Census, 2005b). The result was that 7.2 million respondents indicated at least two ancestries or "races," which represents a bit over 2.5 percent of the total U.S. population. The most common mix was white and "some other race," followed by white and Native American/Alaska Native, white and Asian, white and black, black and "some other race," and Asian and "some other race." Other possible combinations represented less than 200,000 cases. It should not be surprising, of course, that a society as ethnically diverse as the United States would have many people who are offspring and descendants of more than one ethnic/racial subpopulation. More interesting is these individuals' prospects for garnering resources in American society.

In general, these "mixed ancestries" are worse off than whites alone and the general population as a whole. Respondents who recorded "two or more races" on the census form reveal less educational attainment than the total population, with higher high school dropout rates and fewer receiving a college degree or more (U.S. Bureau of the Census, 2005b:13). These persons are less likely than the general population to be in managerial and professional occupations and more likely to be in lower-wage service jobs (U.S. Bureau of the Census, 2005b:14). They have a median family income that is over $10,000 less than that for all U.S. families (U.S. Bureau of the Census, 2005b:16). They are more likely to be in poverty. And they are 20 percent less likely than the rest of the population to own a house (U.S. Bureau of the Census, 2005b:18).

If one of the ancestries in these combinations of two or more "races" is white, however, the prospects for resource shares increase, but they do not reach the level of the general population. And when the combination of races is nonwhite, mixing of nonwhite ethnics appears to work against receiving resource shares, although some nonwhite combinations are more disadvantageous than others. Thus, the white European core, when combined with another "race," works to raise resource shares.

Because these mixed-"race" persons are, on average, younger than the general population, their numbers will grow in the years to come as the children of today enter childbearing age over the next decade. Also, if a decrease in prejudice and discrimination encourages marriage among partners from different ethnic groups, this dual-ancestry population will grow even more. Still, there appears to be a "penalty" for nonwhite mixing of "race"— ample testimony, perhaps, to the continued influence of the Anglo-Saxon core on the distribution of valued resources in American society.

THE PROBLEMATIC NATURE OF A MULTICULTURAL AMERICA

No large-scale society has ever successfully integrated all of its ethnic subpopulations, nor has any ever eliminated the tensions among ethnic populations. The United States has done better than most societies along these lines, primarily because it was created through immigration to a land where genocide had been practiced on the indigenous population, thereby opening the land for settlement (Takaki, 1993). The most enduring problems are the plight of African Americans who cannot escape the legacy of slavery and Native Americans who have not overcome the effects of their conquest and attempted genocide. The most visible new problem in the future is the growth of the Latino population and the challenges that this poses to the Anglo-Saxon cultural core.

As our speculative scenario has emphasized, the enduring problems of a large black population and the explosive growth of the Latino population ensure tension in the future. Added to these two fault lines are the growth of diverse Asian ethnics, the continued plight of Native Americans, and the declining size of the white ethnic subpopulation relative to other ethnic subpopulations. Just how these points of cleavage will play out cannot be known for sure, but the salience of ethnicity will increase in the decades to come.

Some people celebrate ethnic diversity, but it should be noted that no large-scale society with highly diverse and entrenched ethnic subpopulations has been stable (Gold, 1995). Historically, ethnic tensions have torn societies apart. The collapse of the Soviet empire along roughly ethnic lines, the brutality of hostility in what was once Yugoslavia, the festering conflicts in the "United" Kingdom over Northern Ireland, the ethnic hostilities among diverse Muslim sects in most countries of the Middle East, the state of tension between Indians and Pakistanis, and the "wars" of ethnic liberation all over the world today illustrate that conflict becomes intense when ethnicity runs deep.

Thus, ethnic pluralism must revolve around relatively weak ethnic identification; otherwise, it becomes a focal point for societal disintegration (Trueba, 1993). It is now politically *in*correct to question pluralism or, worse, to extol the virtues of integration of ethnics into an Anglo-Saxon cultural core—at least within academia. But if there is no cultural core to which each wave of immigrants adjusts, or if ethnic populations of any size refuse to or cannot adjust, then

These schoolchildren mirror the racial and ethnic diversity in American society.

societal integration will be tenuous. It is for this reason that discrimination is such a harmful force: It often forces ethnics to sustain deep-seated ethnic patterns at odds with the cultural core. Discrimination is, of course, inevitable when some feel threatened by the presence of other ethnics, but if the discrimination can be only temporary and, in fact, serve to decrease differences between ethnics as its victims seek to reduce their identifiability and, hence, their vulnerability to discrimination, then something positive comes of discrimination. But when discrimination is intense, is long-term, and inhibits assimilation, then it creates cleavages along ethnic lines, and such cleavages are among the most volatile forces of human organization. So if discrimination over the next decades prevents African Americans, Latinos, and Asian Americans from adopting the cultural core and from fully participating in the society, and at the same time heightening their ethnic identity, it will increase the level of ethnic tension in America, perhaps to the point of societal disintegration.

Such is not likely to be the case, because of powerful values and beliefs emphasizing equality and because these cultural tenets have been codified into laws and enforcement procedures. These can be used to mitigate discrimination and to weaken the intensity of people's diverse ethnic identities. At the same time, the reality of a declining proportion of the population from Anglo-Saxon European stock can, perhaps, force some changes in the Anglo-Saxon cultural core, not to the point of its destruction, which would only deepen ethnic boundaries, but to the point of inclusion of new cultural elements from African, Latino, and Asian cultures. Such inclusion has always occurred, but the ethnics involved were white and European. In particular, whether the same inclusion can occur for the descendants of black slaves and for the returning descendants of those who were pushed off their land in the Southwest is the real problem of the future. These are the most volatile cleavages; others also exist, but the populations involved are too small to disintegrate the society. If these points of antagonism among whites, blacks, and browns in America can be reduced in the next century, then the United States will have been unique in the history of the world.

CONCLUSION: THE ONGOING STRUGGLE FOR SOCIAL JUSTICE IN U.S. SOCIETY

U.S. society portrays itself as rooted in a pluralist framework that promotes access to opportunity for all its citizens. However, in previous chapters we documented that racial and ethnic populations do not have equal access to resources in American society. Unequal resource shares create contexts of inequality that often enhance the saliency of race and ethnicity in determining quality of life in society. Ironically, U.S. society entered the twenty-first century cloaked with institutionalized forms of discrimination that limit the life chances of racial and ethnic minority populations.

We noted in Chapter 5 that the social struggles of the 1960s served as an opportunity for the formalization of social policy interventions intended to promote equal opportunity for socially oppressed groups. These social interventions were designed to alter societal contexts of inequality that restricted the access of racial and ethnic minorities to resource shares in U.S. society. For example, income maintenance programs were utilized to alleviate the economic hardships of the working poor; Head Start programs were introduced as vehicles for improving access to educational opportunity among poor—especially minority—households; and affirmative action was designed to increase the chances that racial and ethnic minority populations could compete for resource shares. Interestingly, the most controversial social policy initiative from the 1960s, and the one that continues to pose a serious challenge to the distribution of resource shares in American society, is affirmative action.

Discussions of affirmative action quite often result in moral arguments about who "merits" access to resource shares or technical discussions of "who" determines access to resource shares (Aguirre, 2000). We noted in Box 2.2 (see p. 55) that the American public holds ambivalent views of how affirmative action can be practiced without challenging general notions of equality, merit, and opportunity. Can affirmative action serve as an intervention strategy for increasing the access of underserved populations to resource shares in U.S. society without challenging ideological notions of equality? As an intervention strategy, affirmative action is controversial because it challenges the social production of *merit* by trying to "close the gap" between the privileged and underprivileged in U.S. society (Greenberg, 2002). Affirmative action is also controversial because it attacks unequal access to opportunity in order to remove the "lingering effects" of discrimination against minority (nonwhite) persons (Cunningham, Loury, and Skrentny, 2002).

The controversy surrounding affirmative action has unfortunately **racialized** affirmative action in the minds of the American public as a social policy that seeks to give racial and ethnic minorities resource shares by taking them away from white persons. Not surprisingly, affirmative action is viewed by white Americans as a policy of reverse racism that victimizes them in initiatives to redress the unequal access of racial and ethnic minorities to resource shares in U.S. society (Platt, 1997). Affirmative action is perceived as a social policy of **reverse discrimination** by white Americans because they regard it as an excuse for racial and ethnic minorities to avoid playing by the rules that "hard work, assimilation, and virtue can overcome any adversity, including racism" (Vargas, 1998:1502).

Caught in the vortex of the civil rights movement of the 1960s, affirmative action continues to challenge the principles about equality and opportunity that operate as the ideological framework for U.S. society (Delgado, 1995; Morris, 1984). Supporters of affirmative action argue that it is vital to increasing the representation of racial and ethnic minorities in the social fabric of American society, especially within societal institutions that structure pathways to resource shares. Supporters of affirmative action also argue that it is vital to a society whose social fabric is becoming increasingly diverse in its racial and ethnic composition (Bell, 1997). In a sense, affirmative action is a vehicle for including racial and ethnic minorities in mainstream social institutions and for enhancing their participation within those institutions. (See Box 10.4 for one future.)

Box 10.4
Where Multiculturalism Succeeds

To the east of Los Angeles a series of ethnic suburbs are emerging, and minorities are moving in. Walnut, California, is perhaps unique among these previously all-white communities, because it has undergone two dramatic transformations in the last few decades: (1) from agricultural to suburban and (2) from predominately white to multiethnic. At the high school prom, couples of very different ethnic backgrounds can be found on the dance floor together. "Race" and ethnicity do not seem to matter as much as they do in other communities; indeed, African Americans dance with Asians, Anglos with Latinos, Latinos with African Americans, Anglos with African Americans and Asians, and just about any combination possible in light of the demographics of Walnut, which has become 36 percent Asian and Pacific Islander; 34 percent non-Latino white; 24 percent Latino; and 7 percent African American. The city has had African American, Anglo, and Asian mayors; and neighborhoods are, for the most part, fully integrated.

Is Walnut a harbinger of America's future? By 2050, the U.S. Bureau of the Census estimates that non-Latino whites will constitute only 52 percent of the U.S. population; and in California, there will be no majority. Indeed, such is the case now or in the very near future for California, as the 2000 census reported. Thus, California and much of the nation will be multiethnic, and the real question is, Can communities be like Walnut, or will they degenerate into patterns of residential segregation, hate crimes, and ethnic anxiety?

The transition to a peaceful multiethnic community was not always smooth in Walnut. There was a backlash as whites saw that they were soon to become just another minority. Many left. Others sought to protect themselves through subtle practices of discrimination, as when real estate agents guided blacks away from white neighborhoods or when a now disbanded Anglo-American club was formed. Yet other factors worked in favor of not just ethnic tolerance but real ethnic diversity and mutual understanding; and perhaps when these same conditions exist in other changing communities, they too can become like Walnut.

What were these factors? First, Walnut evolved into a community with ethnic balance among diverse groups, not just a dominant majority and a few minority populations. Second, Walnut is an affluent suburb; its residents have common economic aspirations, shared values, and similar orientations to housing standards and neighborhood quality. Third, people had a choice of whether or not to settle in Walnut; residence was not determined by history or a dominant industry, and in fact, many have moved to Walnut because of its multicultural profile and reputation for tolerance. Fourth, individuals are not in economic competition for jobs, as is the case in many urban communities, and as a result, they do not see in each other an economic threat to their well-being. Fifth, Walnut is a relatively new suburb and, hence, had little of the negative baggage of communities with longer histories of ethnic competition, ethnic politics, and ethnic neighborhoods.

The schools have also been particularly important in fostering ethnic tolerance. There are many ethnic clubs in the high school, but these do not seem to impose barriers. Moreover, there does not appear to be the same rigid hierarchy of social status typical of most American high schools, enabling all students to feel that they are "in" rather than "out"; and without the hostility that such hierarchies generate, students feel free to move about and mix, getting to know each other. Parents appear more worried about ethnic heritage than do their children, often encouraging study and participation in narrow ethnic activities, but such efforts tend to fail in the multi-ethnic mix of student friendships. The students' common orientation is more to youth culture than to ethnic heritage.

Thus, when ethnics do not see each other as threats, in an environment in which they can interact as equals, the engine of ethnic fear and discrimination is shut down. Not all communities can be Walnut; but in Walnut there is at least a demonstration that many of the typical patterns of ethnic tension in America can be broken down.

Source: O'Connor, 1999.

The U.S. Supreme Court's decisions in *Grutter v. Bollinger* and *Gratz v. Bollinger* identify the utility of affirmative action for including racial and ethnic minorities in higher education. (Box 10.5 summarizes court cases challenging the use of diversity measures in higher education.) On June 23, 2003, the U.S. Supreme Court decided *Grutter v. Bollinger* [539 U.S. 306 (2003)]. Justice O'Connor wrote in the majority opinion that the U.S. Constitution "does not prohibit the law school's narrowly tailored use of race in admissions decisions to further a compelling interest in obtaining the educational benefits that flow from a diverse student body." The court held that the law school's interest in obtaining a "critical mass" of minority students was indeed a "tailored use." O'Connor also noted in the majority opinion that "Race-conscious admissions policies must be limited in time. The Court takes the Law School at its word that it would like nothing better than to find a race-neutral admissions formula and will terminate its use of racial preferences as soon as practicable. The Court expects that 25 years from now, the use of racial preferences will no longer be necessary to further the interest approved today." In other words, Justice O'Connor was noting that in 25 years affirmative action would no longer be necessary to promote diversity. More importantly, the ruling in *Grutter* reinforced Justice Powell's argument for a **diversity rationale** in *Regents of the University of California v. Bakke*, which allowed race to be a consideration in admissions policy but held that quotas were illegal.

Gratz v. Bollinger [539 U.S. 244 (2003)] was heard in conjunction with *Grutter v. Bollinger*. In Gratz, the Court struck down the University of Michigan's more rigid, point-based undergraduate admission policy, which was essentially deemed a quota system. In writing the Court's decision, Chief Justice Rehnquist held that the university's point-based admission policy was unconstitutional and that "because the University's use of race in its current freshman admissions policy is not narrowly tailored to achieve respondents' asserted compelling interest in diversity, the admissions policy violates the Equal Protection Clause of the Fourteenth Amendment."

Box 10.5
Affirmative Action at the Crossroads

Justice Lewis Powell, Jr.'s opinion in *Regents of the University of California v. Bakke* [438 U.S. 265 (1978)] noted that ethnic diversity could be one factor in a range of factors that a university might consider in attaining a diverse student body. Justice Powell's opinion in *Bakke* was interpreted by institutions of higher education as identifying a diversity rationale that allows the use of race as a selective factor in admissions as long as racial quotas are not promoted. Unsurprisingly, institutions of higher education adopted admission policies that utilized race as one factor in determining an applicant's qualifications for admission and for diversifying the student body.

We describe here a series of court cases that have challenged the use of diversity measures in higher education and that frame the legal context regarding the diversity rationale in higher education.

UNIVERSITY OF CALIFORNIA V. BAKKE

Alan Bakke, a white male, challenged the validity of a special admissions program at the University of California at Davis School of Medicine after having twice been denied admission. The medical school filled 16 of its 100 slots in its entering class through a special admissions program open only to minority applicants who were compared among themselves and not with the overall applicant pool. Bakke's college grade point average and MCAT score were among the highest of all the applicants, and higher than those of all of the minority applicants admitted into the medical school through the special admissions program. In *Bakke,* the U.S. Supreme Court affirmed the California Supreme Court's decision that the special admissions program had violated the equal protection clause of the Fourteenth Amendment, directed that the plaintiff be admitted to the School of Medicine, and reversed the judgment prohibiting the defendant from considering race in its future admissions [*University of California v. Bakke,* 438 U.S. 265 (1978)].

HOPWOOD V. UNIVERSITY OF TEXAS

In 1992, Cheryl J. Hopwood and three other white plaintiffs filed suit against the University of Texas Law School alleging that they were denied admission as a result of procedures granting preferences to black and Mexican American applicants. The court paid deference to the U.S. Supreme Court precedent in *Bakke* and declined to declare the school's use of racial preferences in its admissions process unconstitutional [*Hopwood v. State of Texas,* 861 F. Supp. 551 (W.D. Tex. 1994)]. Instead, the court applied strict scrutiny to the law school's admissions process and found that the use of racial preferences for the purpose of achieving a diverse student body served a compelling state interest under the Fourteenth Amendment. The court also found that the use of racial classifications for overcoming the present effects of past discrimination served a compelling government interest. However, the court ultimately found that the law school's use of separate admissions procedures for minorities and nonminorities prevented any meaningful comparative evaluation among applicants of different races and was not narrowly tailored to achieve those compelling interests. Consequently, the court declared that the law school's 1992 admissions procedures violated the Fourteenth Amendment. In effect, the court ruled that the admissions procedures favored only black and Mexican American applicants.

The Fifth Circuit Court reversed and remanded the court's decision in part. It declared that the law school's use of racial preferences served no compelling state interests under the Fourteenth Amendment, and it directed the law school not to use race as a factor in admissions. The remanded part of the decision had to do with whether or not the plaintiffs would have been admitted to the law school in the absence of admissions procedures that take into account an applicant's race or ethnicity. The U.S. Supreme Court declined to hear appeals of the circuit court's decision, acknowledging that the 1992 admissions program had been discontinued and would not be reinstated.

GRATZ V. BOLLINGER (THE UNIVERSITY OF MICHIGAN—THE UNDERGRADUATE CASE)

In 1997, Jennifer Gratz and Patrick Hamacher filed a class-action suit on behalf of themselves and all others similarly situated against the University of Michigan, alleging that the university's College of Literature, Science and the Arts had violated Title VI of the Civil Rights Act of 1964 and the equal protection clause of the Fourteenth Amendment by using race as a factor in admissions decisions. The court ruled in favor of the plaintiffs and declared the admissions programs in existence from 1995 through 1998 unconstitutional on the basis that they were not narrowly tailored to meet the interest of diversity under the standard of strict scrutiny. However, the court found the admissions programs in existence in 1999 and 2000 to be constitutional [*Gratz v. Bollinger*, 122 F. Supp. 2d 811 (E.D. Mich. 2000)].

GRUTTER V. BOLLINGER (THE UNIVERSITY OF MICHIGAN—THE LAW SCHOOL CASE)

In 1997, Barbara Grutter filed suit against the University of Michigan Law School after having been denied admission in June of that year. Grutter alleged that she was discriminated against on the basis of her race (Caucasian—"a disfavored racial group") and that the law school violated the Fourteenth Amendment and Title VI of the Civil Rights Act of 1964, which prohibits recipients of federal funds from discriminating on the basis of race [*Grutter v. Bollinger*, 137 F. Supp. 2d 821 (U.S. Dist. 2001)]. In 1998, the University of Michigan sought to have this case designated as a companion to *Gratz v. Bollinger*. However, in a series of odd procedures involving an Order of Disqualification and Transfer by the chief judge of the district court and the nullification of an opinion by a two-judge panel, the cases were ultimately deemed not to be companion cases [16 F. Supp. 2d 797 (E.D. Mich. 1998)].

In *Grutter*, the district court found in favor of the plaintiff and against the law school. The court declared that the law school's use of race in its admissions decisions violated the equal protection clause of the Fourteenth Amendment and Title VI of the Civil Rights Act of 1964, and prohibited the law school from using race as a factor in its admissions decisions. The University of Michigan requested a stay of injunction and was denied by the district court. On May 14, 2002, a sharply divided

(continued)

Sixth Circuit Court of Appeals voted 5 to 4 to overturn the lower court's ruling that the admissions policy used by the University of Michigan's law school illegally discriminated against white applicants.

SMITH V. UNIVERSITY OF WASHINGTON

In 1997, Katuria Smith, Angela Rock, and Michael Pyle (collectively Smith) filed a class-action suit against the University of Washington Law School alleging that they and other white applicants had been denied admission on the basis of racially discriminatory admissions policies [*Smith v. Univ. of Washington*, 2000 WL 177045 (2000)]. In this case, the court followed the majority opinion rendered in *Bakke* and held that the law school's admissions program could consider race in the promotion of educational diversity, a compelling governmental interest, and that it met the demands of strict scrutiny of race-conscious measures. In 2001, the U.S. Supreme Court declined to hear the appeal despite the contradiction between this ruling and that in *Hopwood*. The court held that the issue was moot, since the University of Washington had discontinued using race, ethnicity, and national origin as factors in the admissions process following passage of Initiative 200. This Washington State Civil Rights Initiative was approved by voters in 1998. Modeled after California's Proposition 209, Initiative 200 prohibited the state from granting preferential treatment on the basis of race, sex, or national origin in the areas of public education, public contracting, and public employment.

JOHNSON V. UNIVERSITY OF GEORGIA

In 1999, Jennifer Johnson filed suit against the University of Georgia after she was denied admission to the freshman class for Fall 1999. Her complaint was later consolidated with the complaints of Aimee Bogrow and Molly Ann Beckenhauer, who were also denied admission in 1999. Johnson was offered admission to the University of Georgia after she had filed her lawsuit, but she declined to enroll at that time. The plaintiffs alleged that they were denied admission on the bases of race (Title VI) and gender (Title IX). The University of Georgia gave automatic preference in admissions to male applicants. The U.S. District Court for the Southern District of Georgia ruled in favor of the plaintiffs [*Johnson v. University of Georgia*, 106 F. Supp. 2d 1362 (S.D. Ga. 2000)]. The decision was upheld by the U.S. Court of Appeals for the Eleventh Circuit [263 F. 3d 1234 (U.S. App. 2001)].

POINTS OF DEBATE

As the United States becomes more pluralistic, and as lines of ethnic distinction harden, tensions will escalate. Such tensions and the conflicts that they generate will force all Americans to think seriously about a number of debatable issues.

1. Can any society remain integrated when ethnic identifications are strong, when the cultural core has eroded, and when ethnic conflicts are frequent? No society has yet done so; hence, all Americans need to consider whether the U.S. is on the road to permanent partitions and the conflicts that these divisions generate. Liberal ideologies preach the virtues of diversity, conveniently ignoring

the conflictual reality that they cause, whereas conservative ideologies demand rigid conformity to the cultural core and propose tension-producing, repressive means to ensure this conformity. Is there not some middle way—as exemplified by the case of past immigrants—to open the avenues of opportunity to the new immigrants, absorb portions of the immigrant culture into the cultural core, and eventually generate a revised core of old and new citizens? If this seems politically incorrect, or naive, or impossible, then what is the fate of America? Are we locked into inexorable and destructive ethnic conflict?

2. Can illegal immigration be stopped? This is the immigration that bothers and threatens Americans the most. Most discussions of this problem involve political and ideological posturing rather than concrete solutions to the problem. Thus far, simply adding border patrol agents, using new high-tech means of detection, massive deportations, and other procedures have not been particularly effective. Do we try more of the same thing? Do we dare entertain solutions that, historically, have proved effective, such as shooting those who cross a border? Or do we admit that repressive means are unacceptable to society and seek alternatives, such as the economic development of Mexico, Latin America, and the Caribbean, thus reducing incentives to immigrate? If the latter, how do we pay for such actions?

3. In a society where the unskilled, entry-level jobs are fast disappearing to labor markets overseas and to labor-reducing technologies, how are the new poor and unskilled immigrants to find work and to become part of the American mainstream? If there is no clear track for the unskilled to make it in America—as their predecessors did in the past—then what is to be done? Who will support them? How are the pathologies of despair—crime, drug use, gangs, welfare dependency—to be avoided?

4. Can the United States cut off immigration without destroying the vital source of energy it has provided both culturally and economically since the country's beginnings? Can it encourage limited and selective immigration in the face of rampant illegal immigration? If the answer is no to both questions, then what does this mean for America's future?

KEY TERMS/KEY LEGISLATION

asylee, 312
diversity rationale, 331
Immigration Act of 1965, 311
Immigration Reform and Control Act
 (IRCA) of 1986, 312
long-term undocumented residents
 (LTUR), 312

racialize, 329
refugee, 312
Refugee Act of 1980, 312
reverse discrimination, 329
special categories of agricultural
 workers (SCAW), 312

 Visit our text-specific website at www.mhhe.com/aguirre7e for valuable resources for both students and instructors.

Glossary

abusive practices Patterns of action against the victims of discrimination by members of other ethnic groups and particularly by those charged with law enforcement.

accommodation stage of assimilation According to Robert Park, the stage of assimilation in which immigrants and their descendants are forced to change and adapt to their new environment. During this unstable stage, there is some degree of stabilization of relations between immigrants and those in the host society, even if this accommodation forces migrants into lower social strata.

active bigots Robert Merton's term for people who are prejudiced and quite willing to discriminate against members of other racial or ethnic groups.

affirmative action The civil rights laws of the 1960s, as interpreted by Executive Order 11246, required organizations doing business with, or receiving funds from, the government to increase minority representation in those organizations. In practice, these government mandates applied primarily to businesses receiving (directly or indirectly) government contracts and to schools, especially colleges and universities.

Alaska Native Claims Settlement Act (1971) Legislation that ended the sovereign status of Indian nations in Alaska by incorporating them into the United States. Approximately 44 million acres of Native American land, including the oil beneath and the timber on top, became U.S. assets.

all-weather liberals Robert Merton's term for people who are not prejudiced and do not discriminate against members of other racial or ethnic groups.

American Indian Movement (AIM) An organization representing a more radical movement to organize Native American nations to pursue political goals.

Anglo-Saxon An ethnic complex consisting of northern European ethnic stock with light, "white" skin; Protestant religious beliefs; Protestant-inspired values based on individualism, hard work, savings, and secular material success; and English cultural traditions (e.g., language, laws, and beliefs) and institutional structures (e.g., politics, economics, and education). Also known as *WASP* (white Anglo-Saxon Protestant).

anti-Semitism Hostility or discrimination against Jews as an ethnic group.

Anti-Terrorism and Effective Death Penalty Act Legislation enacted in 1996 to deter terrorism by making terrorism a federal crime punishable by death.

Community Service Organization A community-based organization formed in Los Angeles to encourage Mexican American participation in local, state, and national elections.

competitive phase of assimilation According to Robert Park, the stage of assimilation in which ethnic populations compete over resources (e.g., jobs, living space, and political representation).

Conservative Jews Jews who adhere to the traditional customs of Judaism, but who also accept modern interpretation of their religious texts.

Council of Energy Resource Tribes (CERT) An organization formed in 1975 with the goal of creating an OPEC-like cartel to coordinate the development of, and perhaps manipulate the market for, the resources on reservation land.

cultural assimilation Assimilation that occurs when the values, beliefs, dogmas, ideologies, language, and other systems of symbols of the dominant culture are adopted.

Dawes Act of 1887 Legislation designed to break up the collective ownership of Indian lands by requiring Indians to identify themselves by means of a **blood quantum measure.** Under the act, "full-blood Indians" received the deeds to land parcels over which the U.S. government exercised control for twenty-five years, and "mixed-blood Indians" received "patents in fee simple"—basically, land rental agreements—and were forced to accept U.S. citizenship. Also known as the **General Allotment Act.**

Department of Homeland Security Federal agency in charge of preventing and responding to terrorist attacks and natural disasters.

discrimination The process by which an individual, a group, or a subpopulation of individuals acts in ways that deny another individual, group, or subpopulation access to valued resources.

diversity rationale The opinion of U.S. Supreme Court Justice Lewis Powell, Jr., expressed in *Regents of the University of California v. Bakke* (1978), that race can be used as a selective factor in admissions as long as racial quotas are not promoted.

egalitarianism American core values stressing that people should be treated equally and given equal opportunities.

"English as the official language" movement A powerful political movement in the 1980s advocating a constitutional amendment to make English the official language of the United States and the elimination of bilingual ballots and bilingual education. Two major "official English" organizations are U.S. English and English First.

entrepreneurial resources The occupational skills, education, money, and organizational abilities that an ethnic population possesses.

environmental racism The dumping of toxic wastes in neighborhoods inhabited by poor and relatively powerless ethnic groups. Waste-disposal sites are generally located in poor and minority neighborhoods.

equality of results A situation in which differences among a group of individuals have been eliminated in order to create a more level playing field.

ethnic cleansing Systematic attempts to eliminate an ethnic or religious group from a society. The attempts by the Serbs to "cleanse" the former Yugoslavia of Muslims and ethnic Albanians is an example.

ethnic discrimination The process by which the members of a more powerful and dominant ethnic subpopulation deny the members of another, less powerful and subordinate ethnic population full access to valued resources—for example, jobs, income, education, health, prestige, power, or anything else that the members of a society value.

ethnic group   A subpopulation of individuals who are labeled and categorized by the general population and, often, by the members of the group itself, as being of a particular type of ethnicity. They reveal a unique history as well as distinctive behavioral, organizational, and cultural characteristics; and, as a result, they are often treated differently by others.

ethnic population   See **ethnic group.**

ethnic prejudices   Beliefs and stereotypes about designated subpopulations who share certain identifying characteristics—biological, behavioral, organizational, or cultural—or at least are perceived to share these identifying characteristics.

ethnic stratification   The location of an ethnic subpopulation within the stratification system of a society. It reflects several interrelated processes: (1) the amount, level, and type of resources (e.g., jobs, education, health, money, power, and prestige) that an ethnic subpopulation receives; (2) the degree to which these resource shares locate most members of an ethnic subpopulation in various social hierarchies; (3) the extent to which these resource shares contribute to the distinctive behaviors, organizations, and cultural systems that provide justification to the dominant group for making members of the ethnic subpopulation targets of discrimination. See **stratification theories.**

ethnic subpopulation   See **ethnic group.**

ethnicity   A socially constructed conception of a subpopulation of individuals who are perceived to reveal shared historical experiences as well as unique organizational, behavioral, and cultural characteristics.

ethnogenesis   The process of creating a distinctive ethnicity as a means of adapting to discrimination, even as some degree of assimilation occurs. See **pluralism theories.**

ethny   A cluster of kinship circles created by endogamy (in which mate selection is confined to specific groups) and territoriality (physical proximity of its members and relative isolation from nonmembers).

exclusion   The pattern of discrimination that denies members of an ethnic group certain positions, independent of the effects of segregation.

Executive Order 9066   The order signed by President Franklin D. Roosevelt on February 19, 1942, that established restricted military areas and authorized the building of relocation camps to house Japanese Americans.

expulsion   The act of exiling members of an ethnic subpopulation from a country. Expulsion can take the form of direct coercion, or it can be indirect. It is a common form of discrimination.

external colonialism   The process by which one nation controls the political and economic activities of another, less developed and less powerful society.

Fifteenth Amendment (1870)   The amendment to the U.S. Constitution that extended suffrage to African Americans.

fish-ins   Protests by the American Indian Movement and its supporters against government interference in traditional Native American fishing areas.

Fourteenth Amendment (1868)   The amendment to the U.S. Constitution that provided equal protection for all people under the law. It was an extension of an earlier civil rights act designed to overrule the emerging **black codes.**

General Allotment Act   See **Dawes Act of 1887.**

Indian–white miscegenation laws Laws prohibiting marriage between Indians and whites.

individualism American core values stressing that people get ahead through their own efforts and hard work.

institutionalized discrimination Discrimination that exists when cultural values, beliefs, laws, and norms allow acts by individuals to deny others access to valued resources. These acts or practices are part of the way a social structure normally operates and are pervasive and persistent features of interaction between people.

internal colonialism Theory that views the history of ethnic relations in America as involving the establishment of internal colonies of people who are not white and who are dominated by descendants of the original Anglo-Saxon Protestant colonists. The motivation behind internal colonialism in the United States was twofold: (1) the need for cheap labor to increase profit and (2) the desire to take and control land, first from the Native Americans and later from the Mexicans.

internment camps Camps to which Japanese Americans were forced to relocate by the U.S. government during World War II. Over 120,000 Japanese Americans were placed in internment camps after the bombing of Pearl Harbor on December 7, 1941. Japanese Americans were forced to sell their personal property and businesses at a fraction of their value.

Islam Literally meaning "submission to the will of God," this is a monotheistic religion, with the world's second largest number of followers, in which members adhere to the belief that Allah is God and Muhammad was his prophet.

Japanese American Evacuation Claims Act (1948) Legislation that limited Japanese Americans' claims to a maximum of $2,500 and required all claims to be submitted within eighteen months of the act's passage. It took the federal government seventeen years to process all the claims submitted; in the end, only $38 million (of the $131 million appropriated by Congress) was paid out.

Jewish Lobby An all-encompassing term used to describe the real or perceived power and influence of Jews in America over the government, media, and industry.

jihad An Islamic term with several meanings, one of which is used to suggest a military effort furthering the cause of Islam, and another of which is an introspective struggle of spiritual determination.

Jim Crow practices Discriminatory practices that began roughly in the late 1890s, when southern states began systematically to codify (or strengthen) in law and state constitutional provisions the subordinate position of African Americans in society. African Americans were denied access to jobs, education, and housing. Jim Crow also aimed to separate the races in public spaces, such as public schools, parks, accommodations, and transportation.

Jones Act of 1917 Legislation that allowed Puerto Ricans free access to the U.S. mainland.

Keyes v. Denver School District No. 1 (1973) The U.S. Supreme Court ruled that evidence of governmental action to maintain segregation (e.g., site selection for schools or manipulation of attendance zones) was sufficient to require desegregation using busing and other means.

kin selection The concept that family structures are a strategy allowing males and females to maximize their fitness by keeping as much of their genetic material as possible in the gene pool; also known as *inclusive fitness*.

Korematsu v. United States **(1944)**   U.S. Supreme Court decision that upheld the constitutionality of the internment of Japanese Americans.

La Raza Unida   Organization established in 1970 at a meeting of 300 Mexican Americans at Campestre Hall in Crystal City, Texas, to bring greater economic, social, and political self-determination to Mexican Americans in Texas, where they held little or no power in many local and county jurisdictions although they were often in the majority. José Ángel Gutiérrez and Mario Compean, who had helped found MAYO (the Mexican American Youth Organization) in 1967, were two of the principal organizers.

Latinos   A term that includes Mexicans, Puerto Ricans, Cubans, and Central and South Americans. It does not denote a unified ethnic population.

League of United Latin American Citizens (LULAC)   Organization founded in 1929 by Mexican Americans who chose to refer to themselves as "Latins" in order to reinforce their loyalty to the United States.

long-term undocumented residents (LTUR)   Undocumented persons who have resided continuously in the United States since January 1, 1982.

Major Crimes Act (1885)   Legislation that allowed the United States to extend its jurisdiction into Native American territories. Since the sovereignty of Native American territories was defined by treaty, this act nullified the treaties' purpose, which had been to permit Native Americans to exercise their own jurisdiction within their own territories.

Manifest Destiny   The philosophy that legitimated the seizing of Indian lands by whites. European Americans believed that they had the right, through divine ordination and natural superiority, to seize and occupy all of North America.

marginal participation   Participation by subordinate ethnic subpopulations in a niche where their creative resources allow them to prosper. Marginal participation tends to be most successful when the minority population is small and does not enter areas dominated by the majority.

Mariel boatlifts/Marielitos   In 1980, Fidel Castro released about 125,000 people from Cuban prisons and mental hospitals, beginning the Mariel boatlifts. The Marielitos were different from the earlier wave of Cuban refugees. The majority of the Marielitos were single, black adult males with a criminal background. The United States processed them at Eglin Air Force Base in Florida. When riots broke out, federal troops were called in. Much of this population ended up either deported or imprisoned for crimes or for what the Bureau of Prisons terms "temporary detention," but many were released into the community, boosting local unemployment rates from 5 percent to 13 percent.

marital assimilation   Assimilation that occurs when there are high rates of intermarriage between immigrants and dominant ethnic groups.

middleman minorities   Members of an ethnic subpopulation who have middle—or moderate—levels of resources and serve as distribution links between producers and buyers of goods.

middleman minority theories   Theories arguing that certain minorities bring to a host society entrepreneurial skills and perhaps some capital, that these attributes pose a threat to dominant groups, and so these minorities are excluded from many middle-class positions and are allowed to operate only businesses that serve their own ethnic group, other oppressed ethnics, and, occasionally, more elite ethnic groups.

References

Abraham, Margaret. 2000. *Speaking the Unspeakable: Marital Violence among South Asian Immigrants in the United States.* New Brunswick: Rutgers University Press.

Acuña, Rodolfo. 1981. *Occupied America: A History of Chicanos,* 2d edition. New York: Harper & Row.

Adams, Karen, and Daniel Brink (eds.). 1990. *Perspectives on Official English: The Campaign for English as the Official Language of the USA.* Berlin: Mouton de Gruyter.

Agbayani-Siewert, Pauline, and Alice Yick Flanagan. 2001. "Filipino American Dating Violence: Definitions, Contextual Justifications, and Experiences of Dating Violence." In *Psychosocial Aspects of the Asian-American Experience: Diversity within Diversity,* edited by N. G. Choi, pp. 115–33. New York: Haworth Press.

Aguilar–San Juan, Karin. 1994. *The State of Asian America: Activism and Resistance in the 1990s.* Boston: South End Press.

Aguirre, Adalberto, Jr. 1980. "The Sociolinguistic Situation of Chicano Adolescents in a California Border Town." *AZTLAN: International Journal of Chicano Studies Research* 10:55–67.

———. 1982. "The Political Economy Context of Language in Social Service Delivery for Hispanics." In *Ethnicity and Public Policy,* edited by Winston Van Horne, pp. 89–104. Madison: University of Wisconsin Press.

———. 1984. "Language Use in Bilingual Mexican American Households." *Social Science Quarterly* 65:565–72.

———. 1988. "Language Use and Media Orientations in Bilingual Mexican-Origin Households in Southern California." *Mexican Studies/Estudios Mexicanos* 4:115–30.

———. 1990. "Poverty in the United States: Race, Ethnic, and Gender Differentials." In *Income and Status Differences between White and Minority Americans: A Persistent Inequality,* edited by Sucheng Chan, pp. 101–12. Lewiston, NY: Edwin Mellen Press.

———. 1993. "Communication Media and Mexican Social Issues: A Focus on English-Language and U.S.-Origin Communication Media." *International Journal of Comparative Sociology* 34:231–43.

———. 1995a. "Nativist Feeling and Immigrant Workers: An Interpretive Note." *Latino Studies Journal* 6:48–62.

———. 1995b. "Ethnolinguistic Populations in California: A Focus on LEP Students and Public Education." *The Journal of Educational Issues of Language Minority Students* 15:77–91.

———. 2000. "Academic Storytelling: A Critical Race Theory Story of Affirmative Action." *Sociological Perspectives* 43:319–39.

House Committee on Indian Affairs. 1934. U.S. Department of the Interior Hearings on HR7902, 73rd Congress, 2d Session. Washington, DC: U.S. Government Printing Office.

Hsia, Jayjia. 1988. *Asian Americans in Higher Education and at Work.* Hillsdale, NJ: Lawrence Erlbaum Associates.

Hu, Arthur. 1989. "Asian Americans: Model Minority or Double Minority?" *AMERASIA* 15:243–57.

Hughes, Mark, and Janice Madden. 1991. "Residential Segregation and the Economic Status of Black Workers: New Evidence for an Old Debate." *Journal of Urban Economics* 29:28–49.

Human Rights Watch. 2002. *We Are Not the Enemy: Hate Crimes against Arabs, Muslims, and Those Perceived to Be Arab or Muslim after September 11.* New York: Human Rights Watch.

Humphrey, Norman. 1941. "Mexican Repatriation from Michigan: Public Assistance in Historical Perspective." *Social Service Review* 15:497–513.

Hunt, Mathew O. 2007. "African American, Hispanic, and White Beliefs about Black/White Inequality, 1977–2004." *American Sociological Review* 72:390–415.

Huntington, Samuel P. 1966. "Political Modernization: America vs. Europe." *World Politics* 18:147–48.

Huntington, Samuel P. 1996. *Clash of Civilizations and the Remaking of World Order.* New York: Simon and Schuster.

Hurk, Won, and Kwang Kim. 1989. "The 'Success' Image of Asian Americans: Its Validity and Its Practical and Theoretical Implications." *Ethnic and Racial Studies* 12:512–38.

Hurtado, Albert. 1982. "Hardly a Farm House—A Kitchen without Them: Indian and White Households on the California Borderland Frontier in 1860." *Western Historical Quarterly* 13:245–70.

Huskisson, Gregory. 1988. "Enough Is Enough: Blacks Protest Redlining." *Black Enterprise* (October): 22.

Imhoff, Gary. 1990. "The Position of U.S. English on Bilingual Education." *The Annals* 508:48–61.

Institute for Women's Policy Research. 2007. *The Status of Women in the United States: Wide Disparities by Race, Ethnicity, and Region.* Downloaded November 2007 from www.iwpr.org.

Isaacs, Julia B. 2007. *Economic Mobility of Black and White Families.* Washington, DC: The Brookings Institution.

Jackson, Aurora. 1993. "Black, Single, Working Mothers in Poverty: Preferences for Employment, Well-Being, and Perceptions of Preschool-Age Children." *Social Work* 38:26–35.

Jaffe, A., Ruth Cullen, and Thomas Boswell. 1980. *The Changing Demography of Spanish Americans.* New York: Academic Press.

Jaimes, M. Annette. 1992. "Federal Indian Identification Policy: A Usurpation of Indigenous Sovereignty in North America." In *Native Americans and Public Policy,* edited by Fremont Lyden and Lyman Legters, pp. 113–35. Pittsburgh: University of Pittsburgh Press.

Jaret, Charles. 1991. "Recent Structural Change and U.S. Urban Ethnic Minorities." *Journal of Urban Affairs* 13:307–36.

Jarvenpa, Robert. 1985. "The Political Economy and Political Ethnicity of American Indian Adaptations and Identities." In *Ethnicity and Race in the U.S.A.: Toward the Twenty-first Century,* edited by Richard D. Alba, pp. 29–48. New York: Routledge.

Jaynes, Gerald David, and Robin Williams (eds.). 1989. *A Common Destiny: Blacks and American Society.* Washington, DC: National Academy Press.

Jencks, Christopher. 1991. "Is the American Underclass Growing?" In *The Urban Underclass,* edited by C. Jencks and P. E. Peterson, pp. 28–102. Washington, DC: The Brookings Institution.

Jet. 2000. "Annual Poll Shows That Most People Believe Racial Profiling by Cops Is Common." *JET* (Jan. 10): 6.

Johnson, James, Karen Johnson-Webb, and Walter Farrell. 1999. "Newly Emerging Communities in the United States: A Spatial Analysis of Settlement Patterns." In *Immigration and Opportunity: Race, Ethnicity, and Employment in the United States,* edited by Frank Bean and Stephanie Bell-Rose, pp. 263–310. New York: Russell Sage Foundation.

Johnson, Kevin. 2000. "The Case against Racial Profiling in Immigration Enforcement." *Washington University Law Quarterly* 78:675–736.

Joint Center for Political Studies. 1977. *Profiles of Black Mayors in America.* Washington, DC: Author.

———. 1996. *Blacks and the 1996 Elections: A Preliminary Analysis.* Washington, DC.

Jones, Eugene. 1988. *Native Americans as Shown on the Stage, 1753–1916.* Metuchen, NJ: Scarecrow Press.

Jones, Jeffrey M. 2001 (Sept. 28). "Americans Felt Uneasy toward Arabs Even before September 11." *The Gallup Poll* (www.gallup.com): 1.

Jones-Correa, Michael, and David Leal. 1996. "Becoming 'Hispanic': Secondary Panethnic Identification among Latin American–Origin Populations in the United States." *Hispanic Journal of Behavioral Sciences* 18:214–54.

Jordan, Winthrop D. 1962. "Modern Tensions and the Origins of American Slavery." *Journal of Southern History* 28:18–30.

———. 1968. *White over Black: American Attitudes toward the Negro, 1550–1812.* Chapel Hill: University of North Carolina Press.

Juarez, José. 1995. "The American Tradition of Language Rights: The Forgotten Right to Government in a 'Known Tongue.'" *Law and Inequality* 13:443–642.

Kamin, Leon J. 1974. *The Science and Politics of I.Q.* New York: Wiley.

Kang, Jerry. 1996. "Negative Action against Asian Americans: The Internal Instability of Dworkin's Defense of Affirmative Action." *Harvard Civil Rights–Civil Liberties Law Review* 31:1–47.

Karnow, Stanley. 1992. *Asian Americans in Transition.* New York: Asia Society.

Kasem, Casey. 2005. *Arab Americans: Making a Difference.* Washington, DC: Arab American Institute Foundation. Retrieved March 2006 from www.aaiusa.org/PDF/Cas.Broch .(AAIFV).pdf.

Keller, Gary. 1985. "The Image of the Chicano in Mexican, United States, and Chicano Cinema: An Overview." In *Chicano Cinema: Research, Reviews and Resources,* edited by Gary Keller, pp. 13–58. Binghamton, NY: Bilingual Review Press.

Kelly, Lawrence. 1975. "The Indian Reorganization Act: The Dream and the Reality." *Pacific Historical Review* 44:291–312.

Khalaf, Samir. 1987. "The Background and Causes of Lebanese/Syrian Immigration to the United States before World War I." In *Crossing the Waters: Arabic-Speaking Immigration to the United States before 1940,* edited by Eric J. Hooglund. Washington, DC: Smithsonian Institution Press.

Kim, Ryan. 1999. "Livermore Scientists File Bias Claims." *San Francisco Examiner* (Dec. 24): A1.

Kinder, Donald, and Lynn Sanders. 1990. "Mimicking Political Debate with Survey Questions: The Case of White Opinion on Affirmative Action for Blacks." *Social Cognition* 8:73–103.

Kitano, Harry. 1980. *Race Relations.* Englewood Cliffs, NJ: Prentice-Hall.

Kitano, Harry, and Roger Daniels. 1988. *Asian Americans: Emerging Minorities.* Englewood Cliffs, NJ: Prentice-Hall.

Kluegel, James R., and Lawrence Bobo. 1993. "Opposition to Race-Targeting: Self-Interest, Stratification Ideology, or Racial Attitudes?" *American Sociological Review* 58:443–64.

Kluegel, James R., and Eliot R. Smith. 1986. *Beliefs about Inequality in America.* Hawthorne, NY: Aldine de Gruyter.

Kluger, Richard. 1975. *Simple Justice: The History of Brown v. Board of Education and Black America's Struggle for Equality.* New York: Vintage Books.

Knobel, Dale T. 1986. *Paddy and the Republic.* Middletown, CT: Wesleyan University Press.

Knoll, Tricia. 1982. *Becoming Americans: Asian Sojourners, Immigrants, and Refugees in the Western United States.* Portland, OR: Coast to Coast Books.

Kotkin, Joel, and Bill Bradley. 1989. "Democrats and Demographics; Asians, Hispanics and Small Business Are the Party's Future." *Washington Post* (Feb. 26).

Kousser, J. Morgan. 1974. *The Shaping of Southern Politics: Suffrage Restrictions and the Establishment of the One-Party South, 1880–1910.* New Haven, CT: Yale University Press.

Kritz, Mary M., and Douglas T. Gurak. 2005. *Immigration and a Changing America.* Washington, DC: Population Reference Bureau.

Kromkowski, J. (ed.). 2001. "Arab Americans: Protecting Rights at Home and Promoting Peace Abroad." In *Race and Ethnic Relations, Annual Editions 2002/2003.* Guilford, CT: McGraw-Hill.

Krueger, Alan, and Jonathan Orszag. 2002. "Hispanics and the Current Economic Downturn: Will the Receding Tide Sink Hispanics?" Washington, DC: PEW Hispanic Center.

Kunitz, Stephen. 1971. "The Social Philosophy of John Collier." *Ethnohistory* 18:213–39.

LaDuke, Winona. 1981. "Indian Land Claims and Treaty Areas of North America: Succeeding into Native North America." *CoEvolution Quarterly* 32:64–65.

Lander, Ernest McPherson. 1969. *The Textile Industry in Antebellum South Carolina.* Baton Rouge: Louisiana State University Press.

Langberg, Mark, and Reynolds Farley. 1985. "Residential Segregation of Asian Americans in 1980." *Sociology and Social Research* 70:71–75.

Langley, Lester. 1988. *MexAmerica: Two Countries, One Future.* New York: Crown.

La Piere, Richard T. 1934. "Attitudes vs. Actions." *Social Forces* 13:230–37.

Lauderdale, Diane, and Bert Kestenbaum. 2002. "Mortality Rates of Elderly Asian American Populations Based on Medicare and Social Security Data." *Demography* 39:529–41.

Learsi, Rufus. 1954. *The Jews in America: A History.* Cleveland, OH: World.

LeClere, Felicia, Richard Rogers, and Kimberly Peters. 1997. "Ethnicity and Mortality in the United States: Individual and Community Correlates." *Social Forces* 76:169–99.

Lee, Moon. 1993. "Asian Americans Don't Fit Their Monochrome Image." *Christian Science Monitor* (July 27): 9, 10.

Lee, Robert G. 1999. *Orientals: Asian Americans in Popular Culture.* Philadelphia: Temple University Press.

Lee, Sharon. 1998. "Asian Americans: Diverse and Growing." *Population Bulletin,* vol. 53, no. 2. Washington, DC: Population Reference Bureau.

Lee, Stacey J. 1996. *Unraveling the "Model Minority" Stereotype: Listening to Asian American Youth.* New York: Teachers College Press.

Lessinger, Johanna. 1995. *From the Ganges to the Hudson: Indian Immigrants in New York City.* Boston: Allyn and Bacon.

Lestschinsky, Jacob. 1955. "Economic Development of American Jewry." In *The Jewish People,* vol. 4, pp. 131–56. New York: Jewish Encyclopedic Handbooks.

Lewis, Ronald L. 1979. *Coal, Iron and Slaves: Industrial Slavery in Maryland and Virginia 1715–1865.* Westport, CT: Greenwood Press.

———. 1989. *Black Workers: A Documentary History from Colonial Times to the Present,* edited by Philip S. Foner and R. L. Lewis. Philadelphia: Temple University Press.

Leyburn, James G. 1962. *The Scotch-Irish.* Chapel Hill: University of North Carolina Press.

Lieberson, Stanley, and Mary C. Waters. 1988. *From Many Strands: Racial and Ethnic Groups in Contemporary America.* New York: Russell Sage Foundation.

Lipset, Seymour Martin. 1987. "Blacks and Jews: How Much Bias?" *Public Opinion* 10 (July/August): 4–5, 57–58.

———. 1991. *Equality and the American Creed: Understanding the Affirmative Action Debate* (Washington, DC: Progressive Policy Institute, 1991).

Litwack, Leon F. 1961. *North of Slavery: The Negro in the Free States, 1790–1860.* Chicago: University of Chicago Press.

Lo, Kwai-Cheung. 2001. "Double Negations: Hong Kong Cultural Identity in Hollywood's Transnational Representations." *Cultural Studies* 15:4–26.

Locke, Michelle. 2000. "Scientist Celebrates Turning 61 as a Free Man." *Associated Press Wire* (Dec. 21).

Loeb, Vernon, and Walter Pincus. 2000. "Judge: Lee Can Be Freed on Bail." *Washington Post* (Aug. 25): A1.

Lopez, Alfred. 1973. *The Puerto Rican Papers.* Indianapolis, IN: Bobbs-Merrill.

Lopez, Manuel. 1986. "Su Casa No Es Mi Casa: Hispanic Housing Conditions in Contemporary America, 1949–1980." In *Race, Ethnicity, and Minority Housing in the United States,* edited by Jamshid Momeni, pp. 127–45. New York: Greenwood Press.

Lopez-Garza, Marta, and David Diaz (eds.). 2001. *Asian and Latino Immigrants in a Restructuring Economy: The Metamorphosis of Southern California.* Stanford, CA: Stanford University Press.

Lopreato, Joseph. 1970. *Italian Americans.* New York: Random House.

Lummins, Charles. 1968. *Bullying the Hopi.* Prescott, AZ: Prescott College Press.

Lyman, Stanford. 1986. *Chinatown and Little Tokyo: Power, Conflict, and Community among Chinese and Japanese Immigrants in America.* Milwood, NY: Associated Faculty Press.

———. 1990. "Race, Sex, and Servitude: Images of Blacks in American Cinema." *International Journal of Politics, Culture and Society* 4:49–77.

Macias, Reynaldo. 1993. "Language and Ethnic Classification of Language Minorities: Chicano and Latino Students in the 1990s." *Hispanic Journal of Behavioral Sciences* 15:230–57.

Mahler, Sarah. 1995. *Salvadorans in Suburbia: Symbiosis and Conflict.* Boston: Allyn and Bacon.

Major, Aline, and Arien Egley. 2002. "2000 Survey of Youth Gangs in Indian Country." *National Youth Gang Center Fact Sheet #01* (June).

Maldonado, Rita. 1976. "Why Puerto Ricans Migrated to the United States in 1947–1973." *Monthly Labor Review* 9:7–18.

Maldonado-Denis, Manuel. 1972. *Puerto Rico, A Socio-historic Interpretation,* translated by E. Vialo. New York: Random House.

Marger, Martin. 2000. *Race and Ethnic Relations: American and Global Perspectives,* 5th edition. Belmont, CA: Wadsworth.

Marquez, Benjamin. 1993. *LULAC: The Evolution of a Mexican American Political Organization.* Austin: University of Texas Press.

Martinez, Ramiro, Jr. 1996. "Latinos and Lethal Violence: The Impact of Poverty and Inequality." *Social Problems* 43:131–46.

Martinez, Tomás. 1969. "Advertising and Racism: The Case of Mexican Americans." *El Grito* 2 (Summer): 13–31.

Marvasti, Amir, and Karyn D. McKinney. 2004. *Middle Eastern Lives in America.* Lanham, MD: Rowman and Littlefield.

Massey, Douglas. 1983. *The Demographic and Economic Position of Hispanics in the United States: The Decade of the 1970s.* Washington, DC: National Commission for Employment Policy.

Massey, Douglas, and Nancy Denton. 1988. "The Dimensions of Residential Segregation." *Social Forces* 67:281–315.

Matthaei, Julie, and Teresa Amott. 1990. "Race, Gender, Work: The History of Asian and Asian-American Women." *Race and Class* 31:61–80.

Maxwell, Bill. 2004. "On Campus, Grim Statistics for African-American Men." *St. Petersburg Times* (Jan. 4): B1.

Mazon, Mauricio. 1984. *The Zoot-Suit Riots: The Psychology of Symbolic Annihilation.* Austin: University of Texas Press.

McAdam, Doug. 1982. *Political Processes and the Development of Black Insurgency, 1930–1970.* Chicago: University of Chicago Press.

———. 1988. *Freedom Summer.* New York: Oxford University Press.

McCarthy, Cameron. 1990. *Race and Curriculum.* New York: Falmer Press.

McCarthy, Kevin, and R. Valdez. 1986. *Current and Future Effects of Mexican Immigration in California.* Santa Monica, CA: RAND Corporation.

McDonnell, Janet. 1991. *The Dispossession of the American Indian 1887–1934.* Bloomington: Indiana University Press.

McKenzie, R. 1928. *Oriental Exclusion.* Chicago: University of Chicago Press.

McKinney, Scott, and Ann B. Schnare. 1989. "Trends in Residential Segregation by Race: 1960–1980." *Journal of Urban Economics* 26:269–80.

McQueen, Michel. 1991. "Voters' Responses to Poll Disclose Huge Chasm between Social Attitudes of Blacks." *Wall Street Journal* (May 17): A16.

McWilliams, Carey. 1968. *North from Mexico: The Spanish-Speaking People of the United States.* New York: Greenwood Press.

Medina, Marcell, Jr. 1988. "Hispanic Apartheid in American Public Education." *Educational Administration Quarterly* 24:336–49.

Mendoza Report. 1978. *Access of Non or Limited English Speaking Persons of Hispanic Origin to the New York City Department of Social Services.* Washington, DC: U.S. Department of Health, Education, and Welfare.

Merrell, James. 1984. "The Indians' New World: The Catawba Experience." *William and Mary Quarterly* 41:537–65.

Merton, Robert K. 1949. "Discrimination and the American Creed." In *Discrimination and National Welfare,* edited by R. H. MacIver, pp. 99–126. New York: Harper and Row.

Messner, Steven F., Robert D. Baller, and Matthew P. Zevenbergen. 2005. "The Legacy of Lynching and Southern Homicide." *American Sociological Review* 70:633–55.

Meyer, Doris. 1978. "Early Mexican-American Responses to Negative Stereotyping." *New Mexico Historical Review* 53:75–91.

Meyer, Melissa. 1991. " 'We Can Not Get a Living as We Used To': Dispossession and the White Earth Anishinaabeg, 1889–1920." *American Historical Review* 96:386–94.

Miller, Cynthia, and Kristin Porter. 2007. "Barriers to Employment among Out-of-School Youth." *Children & Youth Services Review* 29: 572–587.

Miller, Kerby A. 1985. *Emigrants and Exiles.* New York: Oxford University Press.

Miller, Stuart. 1969. *The Unwelcome Immigrant: The American Image of the Chinese, 1785–1882.* Berkeley: University of California Press.

Minerbrook, Scott. 1993. "Blacks Locked Out of the American Dream." *Business and Society Review* 87:23–28.

Miranda, Leticia. 1991. *Latino Child Poverty in the United States.* Washington, DC: Children's Defense Fund.

Mohr, James C. 2005. *Plague and Fire: Battling Black Death and the 1900 Burning of Honolulu's Chinatown.* New York: Oxford University Press.

Montero, Darrel. 1981. "The Japanese Americans: Changing Patterns of Assimilation over Three Generations." *American Sociological Review* 46:829–39.

Mooney, James. 1928. *The Aboriginal Population of America North of Mexico.* Washington, DC: Smithsonian Institution Miscellaneous Collections, vol. 80, no. 7.

Moore, Theresa, and Robert Gunnison. 1994. "Blacks and Asians Say the System Is Insensitive." *San Francisco Chronicle* (Mar. 3): A4.

Morales, Armando. 1972. *Ando Sangrando (I am Bleeding): A Study of Mexican American-Police Conflict.* La Puente, CA: Perspectiva Publications.

———. 1973. "Police Deployment Theories." In *Voices: Readings from El Grito,* edited by Octavio Ignacio Romano-V., pp. 167–80. Berkeley, CA: Quinto Sol Publications.

Morales, Julio. 1986. *Puerto Rican Poverty and Migration: We Just Had to Try Elsewhere.* New York: Praeger.

Morganthau, Tom. 1993. "America: Still a Melting Pot?" *Newsweek* (Aug. 9): 16–23.

Morris, Aldon. 1984. *The Origins of the Civil Rights Movement: Black Communities Organizing for Change.* New York: Free Press.

Morris, Glenn. 1992. "International Law and Politics: Toward a Right to Self-Determination for Indigenous People." In *The State of Native America: Genocide, Colonization, and Resistance,* edited by M. Annette Jaimes, pp. 55–86. Boston: South End Press.

Moses, Marion. 1993. "Farmworkers and Pesticides." In *Confronting Environmental Racism: Voices from the Grassroots,* edited by Robert Bullard, pp. 161–78. Boston: South End Press.

Mozo, S. Montes, and J. Garcia Vasquez. 1988. *Salvadorian Migration to the United States: An Exploratory Study.* Washington, DC: Georgetown University Center for Immigration Policy and Refugee Assistance.

Mulvey, Sister Mary. 1936. *French Catholic Missionaries in the Present United States, 1604–1791.* Washington, DC: Catholic University of America Press.

Munoz, Carlos, Jr. 1989. *Youth, Identity, Power: The Chicano Movement.* New York: Verso.

Murguia, Edward. 1975. *Assimilation, Colonialism, and the Mexican American People.* Monograph Series No. 1. Austin: University of Texas at Austin Center for Mexican American Studies.

Naber, Nadine. 2000. "Ambiguous Insiders: An Investigation of Arab-American Invisibility." *Ethnic and Racial Studies* 23:39–47.

Naff, Alixa. 1985. *Becoming American: The Early Arab Immigrant Experience.* Carbondale: Southern Illinois University Press.

Nakanishi, Don. 1988. "Asian Pacific Americans and Selective Undergraduate Admissions." *Journal of College Admissions* 118:17–26.

National Academy of Public Administration. 1999. *A Study of Management and Administration: The Bureau of Indian Affairs.* Washington, DC: Author.

National Asian Pacific American Legal Consortium. 2002. *Audit on Violence Against Asian Pacific Americans.* Washington, DC: NAPALC.

National Center for Education Statistics. 2007. *Status and Trends in the Education of Racial and Ethnic Minorities.* Washington, DC: U.S. Department of Education.

National Center for Health Statistics. 1991. *Health: United States, 1990.* Hyattsville, MD: Public Health Service.

———. 2002. *Deaths: Final Data for 2000.* Washington, DC: U.S. Government Printing Office.

———. 2004. *Health: United States, 2004.* Hyattsville, MD: Public Health Service.

———. 2006. *Health: United States, 2006.* Hyattsville, MD: Public Health Service.

National Puerto Rican Coalition. 1985. *Puerto Ricans in the Mid '80s: An American Challenge.* Washington, DC: National Puerto Rican Coalition.

National Vital Statistics Reports. 2002. Volume 50, no. 15. "Deaths: Final Data for 2001." Washington, DC: Department of Health and Human Services.

National Vital Statistics Reports. 2004. Volume 52, no. 13. "Deaths: Preliminary Data for 2002." Washington, DC: Department of Health and Human Services.

———. 2007. "United States Life Tables, 2004." Washington, DC: Department of Health and Human Services.

Nelson, Candace, and Marta Tienda. 1985. "The Structuring of Hispanic Ethnicity: Historical and Contemporary Perspectives." *Ethnic and Racial Studies* 8:49–74.

Newton, James E., and R. L. Lewis (eds.). 1978. *The Other Slaves: Mechanics, Artisans and Craftsmen.* Boston: G. K. Hall.

Nguyen, Beatrice Bich-Dao. 1993. "Accent Discrimination and the Test of Spoken English: A Call for an Objective Assessment of the Comprehensibility of Nonnative Speakers." *California Law Review* 81:1325–61.

Noriega, Jorge. 1992. "American Indian Education in the United States: Indoctrination for Subordination to Colonialism." In *The State of Native America: Genocide, Colonization, and Resistance,* edited by M. Annette Jaimes, pp. 371–402. Boston: South End Press.

O'Connor, Anne-Marie. 1999. "Learning to Look Past Race." *Los Angeles Times* (Aug. 25): A1.

O'Connor, John. 1980. *The Hollywood Indian: Stereotypes of Native Americans in Film.* Trenton, NJ: New Jersey State Museum.

Olzak, Susan. 1986. "A Competition Model of Collective Action in American Cities." In *Competitive Ethnic Relations,* edited by S. Olzak and J. Nagel, pp. 17–46. Orlando, FL: Academic Press.

———. 1992. *The Dynamics of Ethnic Competition and Conflict.* Stanford, CA: Stanford University Press.

Omatsu, Glenn. 1994. "The 'Four Prisons' and the Movements of Liberation: Asian American Activism from the 1960s to the 1990s." In *The State of Asian America: Activism and Resistance on the 1990s,* edited by K. Aguilar–San Juan, pp. 19–69. Boston: South End Press.

Ortego, Philip D. 1973. "The Chicano Renaissance." In *Introduction to Chicano Studies,* edited by L. I. Duran and H. R. Bernard, pp. 568–84. New York: Macmillan.

Osajima, Keith. 1988. "Asian Americans as the Model Minority: An Analysis of the Popular Press Image in the 1960s and 1980s." In *Reflections on Shattered Windows: Promises and Prospects for Asian American Studies,* edited by G. Y. Okihiro, pp. 165–174. Seattle: Washington State University Press.

Osako, Masako. 1984. "Japanese-Americans: Melting into the All-American Pot?" In *Ethnic Chicago,* edited by Melvin Holli and Peter Jones, pp. 69–76. Grand Rapids, MI: William B. Eerdmans.

Osborne, Stephen. 1989. *Indian-Hating in American Literature, 1682–1857.* Unpublished doctoral dissertation, University of Michigan, Ann Arbor.

Pace, David. 2001. "Indian Casinos." *IRE Journal* 24:8–10.

Padilla, Felix. 1987. *Puerto Rican Chicago*. Notre Dame, IN: University of Notre Dame Press.

Padilla, Raymond, and Alfredo Benavides (eds.). 1992. *Critical Perspectives on Bilingual Education Research*. Tempe, AZ: Bilingual Press/Editorial Bilingue.

Page, Bryan. 1980. "The Children of Exile: Relationships between the Acculturation Process and Drug Use among Cuban Youth." *Youth and Society* 11:431–47.

Palm, Risa. 1985. "Ethnic Segmentation of Real Estate Agent Practice in the Urban Housing Market." *Annals of the Association of American Geographers* 75:58–68.

Paredes, Raymond. 1977. "The Mexican Image in American Travel Literature, 1831–1869." *New Mexico Historical Review* 52:5–29.

Park, Kyeyoung. 1999. "I Really Do Feel I'm 1.5!: The Construction of Self and Community by Young Korean Americans." *Amerasia Journal* 25(1): 139–145.

Park, Robert E. 1916. "The City: Suggestions for the Investigation of Human Behavior in an Urban Environment." *American Journal of Sociology* 20:577–612.

———. 1950. *Race and Culture*. Glencoe, IL: Free Press.

Park, Robert E., and Ernest W. Burgess. 1924. *Introduction to the Science of Sociology*. Chicago: University of Chicago Press.

Parker, Linda. 1989. *Native American Estate: The Struggle over Indian and Hawaiian Lands*. Honolulu: University of Hawaii Press.

Passel, Jeffrey. 1976. "Provisional Evaluation of the 1970 Census Count of American Indians." *Demography* 13:397–409.

———. 1993. "Discussion: Racial Identity/Classification and Its Effect on the Undercount." In *Proceedings of the Bureau of the Census 1993 Research Conference on Undercounted Ethnic Populations*, pp. 345–53. Washington, DC: U.S. Bureau of the Census.

Passel, Jeffrey, and Patricia Berman. 1986. "Quality of 1980 Census Data for American Indians." *Social Biology* 33:163–82.

Pear, Robert. 1998. "Black and Hispanic Poverty Falls, Reducing Overall Rate for Nation."*The New York Times* (Sept. 25): A1.

Pedraza-Bailey, Silvia, and Teresa Sullivan. 1979. "Bilingual Education in the Reception of Political Immigrants: The Case of Cubans in Miami, Florida." In *Bilingual Education and Public Policy in the United States,* edited by Raymond Padilla, pp. 376–94. Ypsilanti: Eastern Michigan University Department of Foreign Languages and Bilingual Studies.

Peng, Samuel. 1990. "Attainment Status of Asian Americans in Higher Education." In *Contemporary Perspectives on Asian and Pacific American Education,* edited by Russell Endo, Virgie Chattergy, Sally Chou, and Nobuya Tsuchida, pp. 56–77. South El Monte, CA: Pacific Asia Press.

Penrose, Eldon. 1973. *California Nativism: Organized Opposition to the Japanese, 1890–1913*. San Francisco: R & E Research Associates.

Perez, Lisandro. 1980. "Cubans." In *Harvard Encyclopedia of American Ethnic Groups,* edited by Stephan Thernstrom, pp. 256–61. Cambridge, MA: Belknap Press.

———. 1986. "Immigrant Economic Adjustment and Family Organization: The Cuban Success Story Re-Examined." *International Migration Review* 20:4–20.

Perez, Sonia, and Deirdre Martinez. 1993. *State of Hispanic America 1993: Toward a Latino Anti-Poverty Agenda*. Washington, DC: National Council of La Raza.

Pessar, Patricia. 1995. *A Visa for a Dream: Dominicans in the United States*. Boston: Allyn and Bacon.

Peterson, William. 1971. *Japanese Americans: Oppression and Success*. New York: Random House.

Pew Research Center. 2007. *Blacks See Growing Values Gap Between Poor and Middle Class: Optimism about Black Progress Declines.* Washington, DC: Pew Research Center for the People and the Press.

Pinkney, Alphonso. 1969. *Black Americans.* Englewood Cliffs, NJ: Prentice-Hall.

———. 1984. *The Myth of Black Progress.* New York: Cambridge University Press.

Pitt, Leonard. 1966. *The Decline of the Californios.* Berkeley: University of California Press.

Platt, Anthony. 1997. "End Game: The Rise and Fall of Affirmative Action in Higher Education." *Social Justice* 24(2):103–18.

Pohlmann, Marcus D. 1990. *Black Politics in Conservative America.* New York: Longmans.

Portes, Alejandro. 1990. "From South of the Border: Hispanic Minorities in the United States." In *Immigration Reconsidered: History, Sociology, and Politics,* edited by V. Yans-McLaughlin, pp. 160–84. New York: Oxford University Press.

Portes, Alejandro, and Dag MacLeod. 1996. "What Shall I Call Myself? Hispanic Identity Formation in the Second Generation." *Ethnic and Racial Studies* 19:523–47.

Portes, Alejandro, and Ruben Rumbaut. 1990. *Immigrant America: A Portrait.* Berkeley: University of California Press.

Price, John. 1978. *Native Studies: American and Canadian Indians.* New York: McGraw-Hill/Ryerson Limited.

Proctor, Bernadette, and Joseph Dalaker. 2002. *Poverty in the United States: 2001.* Washington, DC: U.S. Bureau of the Census.

Proctor, Bernadette, and Joseph Dalaker. 2003. *Poverty in the United States: 2002.* Washington, DC: U.S. Bureau of the Census.

Rable, George C. 1984. *But There Was No Peace: The Role of Violence in the Politics of Reconstruction.* Athens: University of Georgia Press.

Ramirez, Roberto, and Patricia G. de la Cruz. 2003. *The Hispanic Population in the United States: March 2002.* Washington, DC: U.S. Bureau of the Census.

Reed, Ishmael. 1993. *Airing Dirty Laundry.* Reading, MA: Addison-Wesley.

Reisler, Mark. 1996. "Always the Laborer, Never the Citizen: Anglo Perceptions of the Mexican Immigrant during the 1920s." In *Between Two Worlds: Mexican Immigrants in the United States,* edited by David G. Gutierrez, pp. 23–43. Wilmington, DE: Scholarly Resources.

Ricketts, Erol R., and Isabel Sawhill. 1988. "Defining and Measuring the Underclass." *Journal of Policy Analysis and Management* 7:316–25.

Roald Anne Sofie. 2001, *Women in Islam: The Western Experience.* New York: Routledge.

Robbins, Rebecca. 1992. "Self-Determination and Subordination: The Past, Present, and Future of American Indian Governance." In *The State of Native America: Genocide, Colonization, and Resistance,* edited by M. Annette Jaimes, pp. 87–121. Boston: South End Press.

Robinson, Cecil. 1963. *With the Ears of Strangers: The Mexican in American Literature.* Tucson: University of Arizona Press.

Rodriguez, Havidan. 1992. "Population, Economic Mobility and Income Inequality: A Portrait of Latinos in the United States, 1970–1991." *Latino Studies Journal* 3:55–86.

Roediger, David R. 1991. *The Wages of Whiteness: Race and the Making of the American Working Class.* New York: Verso.

Rogg, Eleanor. 1974. *The Assimilation of Cuban Exiles: The Role of Community and Class.* New York: Academic Press.

Rolph, Elizabeth. 1992. *Immigration Policies: Legacy from the 1980s and Issues for the 1990s.* Santa Monica, CA: RAND Corporation.

Romo, Ricardo. 1989. "The Urbanization of Southwestern Chicanos in the Early Twentieth Century." In *Race and Culture in America,* edited by Carl Jackson and Emory Tolbert, pp. 235–49. Edina, MN: Burgess International Group.

Ross, Thomas. 1990. "Innocence and Affirmative Action." *Vanderbilt Law Review* 43:297–336.

Rowan, Carl T. 1993. *Dream Makers, Dream Breakers: The World of Justice Thurgood Marshall.* New York: Little, Brown.

Rubel, Arthur. 1966. *Across the Tracks.* Austin: University of Texas Press.

Rubenstein, William B. 2004. "The Real Story of U.S. Hate Crime Statistics: An Empirical Analysis." *Tulane University Law Review* 78:1–39.

Rubio, Mercedes, and David R. Williams. 2004. "The Social Dimensions of Race." In *Race and Race Research,* edited by B. M. Beech and M. Goodman. Washington, DC: American Public Health Association.

Rumbelow, Helen. 2002. "Dreaming of Homes on the Reservation." *Washington Post* (Oct. 13): A3.

Russell, James. 1994. *After the Fifth Sun: Class and Race in North America.* Englewood Cliffs, NJ: Prentice-Hall.

Russell, Katheryn. 2001. "Racial Profiling: A Status Report of the Legal, Legislative, and Empirical Literature." *Rutgers Race & The Law Review* 3:61–81.

Russell Sage Foundation. 1999. *The Multi-City Study of Urban Inequality.* New York: Russell Sage Foundation.

Rydgren, Jens. 2007. "The Power of the Past: A Contribution to a Cognitive Sociology of Ethnic Conflict." *Sociological Theory* 25:225–44.

Saenz, Rogelio. 2004. *Latinos and the Changing Face of America.* New York: Russell Sage Foundation.

Safire, William. 2002. "Non-Indians Benefit Most from Casinos." *Seattle Post-Intelligencer* (Dec. 15): G2.

Said, Edward W. 1979. *Orientalism.* New York: Vintage Books.

Sanchez, George. 1951. *Concerning Segregation of Spanish-Speaking Children in the Public Schools.* Inter-American Education Occasional Paper No. 9. Austin: University of Texas Press.

San Miguel, Guadalupe, Jr. 1987. *"Let All of Them Take Heed": Mexican Americans and the Campaign for Educational Equality in Texas, 1910–1981.* Austin: University of Texas Press.

Santiago, Anne M., and Margaret G. Wilder. 1991. "Residential Segregation and Links to Minority Poverty: The Case of Latinos in the United States." *Social Problems* 38:492–515.

Schaefer, Richard T. 1990. *Racial and Ethnic Groups,* 4th edition. Glenview, IL: Scott Foresman/Little, Brown.

Schafer, Daniel. 1993. "A Class of People Neither Freemen nor Slaves: From Spanish to American Race Relations in Florida, 1821–1861." *Journal of Social History* 26:587–609.

Schiavo, Giovanni. 1934. *The Italian in America before the Civil War.* New York: Vigo Press.

Schmidley, A. Dianne. 2001. *Foreign-Born Population in the United States: 2000.* Washington, DC: U.S. Bureau of the Census.

Schneider, Mark, and Thomas Phelan. 1990. "Blacks and Jobs: Never the Twain Shall Meet?" *Urban Affairs Quarterly* 26:299–313.

Schrieke, B. 1936. *Alien Americans: A Study of Race Relations.* New York: Viking.

Select Committee on Aging. 1992. "Farmworkers' High Mortality: Government Neglect?" Washington, DC: U.S. Government Printing Office.

Selzer, Michael. 1972. *"Kike"—Anti-Semitism in America.* New York: Meridian Press.

Senate Committee on Housing and Urban Affairs. 2002. "Capital Investment in Native American Land." Washington, DC: U.S. Government Printing Office.

Shah, Nayan. 2001. *Contagious Divides: Epidemics and Race in San Francisco's Chinatown.* Berkeley: University of California Press.

Shively, J. 1992. "Cowboys and Indians: Perceptions of Western Films among American Indians and Anglos." *American Sociological Review* 57:725–34.

Shorris, Earl. 1992. *Latinos: A Biography of the People.* New York: Avon Books.

Shrier, Arnold. 1958. *Ireland and the American Emigration, 1850–1900.* Minneapolis: University of Minnesota Press.

Simmons, Ozzie G. 1973. "The Mutual Images and Expectations of Anglo-Americans and Mexican Americans." In *Introduction to Chicano Studies,* edited by Livie Duran and H. Russell Bernard, pp. 112–20. New York: Macmillan.

Singleton, Royce, and Jonathan H. Turner. 1975. "Racism: White Oppression of Blacks in America." In *Understanding Social Problems,* edited by D. Zimmerman and L. Weider, pp. 130–60. New York: Praeger.

Sissons, Peter. 1979. *The Hispanic Experience of Criminal Justice.* New York: Hispanic Research Center at Fordham University.

Sklare, Marshall. 1971. *American Jews.* New York: Random House.

Smith, Geoffrey. 1992. "There's No Whites Only Sign But . . ." *Business Week* (Oct. 26): 78.

Smits, David. 1991. "Squaw Men, Half Breeds, and Amalgamators: Late 19th Century Anglo-American Attitudes toward Indian-White Race-Mixing." *American Indian Culture and Research Journal* 15:29–61.

Snipp, C. Matthew. 1986. "The Changing Political and Economic Status of the American Indians: From Captive Nations to Internal Colonies." *American Journal of Economics and Sociology* 45:145–57.

———. 1989. *American Indians: The First of This Land.* New York: Russell Sage Foundation.

Sodowsky, Gorgi, Edward Lai, and Barbara Plake. 1991. "Moderating Effects of Socio-cultural Variables on Acculturation Attitudes of Hispanics and Asian Americans." *Journal of Counseling & Development* 70:194–204.

Spalter-Roth, Roberta, Terri Ann Lowenthal, and Mercedes Rubio. 2005. *Race, Ethnicity, and the Health of Americans.* ASA Series on How Race and Ethnicity Matter. Washington, DC: American Sociological Association. Downloaded August 2005.

Spinden, Herbert. 1928. "The Population of Ancient America." *Geographical Review* 18:640–60.

Stampp, Kenneth M. 1956. *The Peculiar Institution: Slavery in the Ante-Bellum South.* New York: Vintage Books.

Staples, Robert. 1975. "White Racism, Black Crime, and American Justice: An Application of the Colonial Model to Explain Crime and Race." *Phylon* 36:14–22.

Starobin, Robert S. 1970. *Industrial Slavery in the Old South.* London: Oxford University Press.

Stedman, Raymond. 1982. *Shadows of the Indian: Stereotypes in American Culture.* Norman: University of Oklahoma Press.

Steele, Shelby. 1990. *The Content of Our Character.* New York: St. Martin's Press.

Stephan, Walter, and Cookie Stephan. 1989. "Antecedents of Intergroup Anxiety in Asian-Americans and Hispanic-Americans." *Journal of Intercultural Relations* 13: 203–19.

Stewart, Omer. 1987. *Peyote Religion: A History.* Norman, OK: University of Oklahoma Press.

Stockton, Ronald. 1994. "Ethnic Archetypes and the Arab Image." In *The Development of Arab-American Identity,* edited by E. McCarus. Ann Arbor: University of Michigan Press.

Stoddard, Ellwyn R. 1973. *Mexican Americans.* New York: Random House.

Sue, Stanley, Nolan Zane, and Derald Sue. 1985. "Where Are the Asian American Leaders and Top Executives?" *PLAAMARC Research Review* 4:13–15.

Suh-Ruu, Ou. 2008. "Do GED Recipients Differ from Graduates and School Dropouts?" *Urban Education* 43:83–117.

Suleiman, Michael W. 1999. "Introduction: The Arab Immigration Experience." In *Arabs in America: Building a New Future,* edited by Michael W. Suleiman, pp. 1–9. Philadelphia: Temple University Press.

———. 2004. "The Arab Immigrant Experience." In *Rethinking the Color Line,* edited by Charles Gallagher. Boston: McGraw-Hill.

Suzuki, Bob. 1989. "Asians." In *Shaping Higher Education's Future: Demographic Realities and Opportunities, 1990–2000,* edited by Arthur Levine and Associates, pp. 87–115. San Francisco: Jossey-Bass.

Swinton, David. 1989. "The Economic Status of Black Americans." In *The State of Black America,* pp. 9–39. New York: National Urban League.

Tajfel, Henri, and J. C. Turner. 1979. "An Integrated Theory of Intergroup Conflict." In *The Social Psychology of Intergroup Relations,* edited by W. G. Austin and S. Worchel, pp. 94–109. Monterey, CA: Brooks Cole.

Takagi, Dana. 1990. "From Discrimination to Affirmative Action: Facts in the Asian American Admissions Controversy." *Social Problems* 37:578–92.

Takaki, Ronald (ed.). 1987. *From Different Shores: Perspectives on Race and Ethnicity in America.* New York: Oxford University Press.

———. 1989. *Strangers from a Different Shore: A History of Asian Americans.* Boston: Little, Brown.

———. 1993. *A Different Mirror: A History of Multicultural America.* Boston: Little, Brown.

———. 1996. "The Myth of the 'Model Minority.'" In *Taking Sides: Clashing Views on Controversial Issues in Race and Ethnicity,"* 2d edition, edited by Richard Monk, pp. 41–47. Guilford, CT: Dushkin.

Takougang, Joseph. 2007. "Contemporary African Immigrants to the United States." w.w.w. africamigration.com/archive_02/j_takougang.htm.

Terazas, Aaron. 2009. "African Immigrants in the United States." http://migrationinformation.org/Usfocus.cfm?id=719.

Tamayo, William, Robin Toma, and Stewart Koh. 1991. *The Voting Rights of Asian Pacific Americans.* Los Angeles: University of California at Los Angeles Asian American Studies Center.

Tang, Joyce. 1991. *Asian American Engineers: Earnings, Occupational Status, and Promotions.* Paper presented at the Annual Meeting of the American Sociological Association, Cincinnati, OH.

Taylor, Marie. 2002. "Immigration Enforcement Post-September 11: Safeguarding the Civil Rights of Middle Eastern-American and Immigrant Communities." *Georgetown Immigration Law Journal* 17:63–113.

Taylor, Marylee. 1998. "How White Attitudes Vary with Racial Composition of Local Populations: Numbers Count." *American Sociological Review* 63:512–35.

Taylor, Ronald. 1973. *Sweatshops in the Sun—Child Labor on the Farm.* San Francisco: Earthwork.

Thomas, Gail. 1995. "Notes on Asian American Employment." In *Race and Ethnicity in America: Meeting the Challenge in the 21st Century,* edited by Gail Thomas, pp. 265–68. Washington, DC: Taylor & Francis.

Thomas, R. Roosevelt, Jr. 1990. "From Affirming Action to Affirming Diversity." *Harvard Business Review* 68:107–17.

Thompson, Laura, and Alice Joseph. 1944. *The Hopi Way.* Ann Arbor: University of Michigan Press.

Thornton, Michael, and Robert Taylor. 1988. "Intergroup Attitudes: Black American Perceptions of Asian Americans." *Ethnic and Racial Studies* 11:474–88.

Thrupkaew, Noy. 2002. "The Myth of the Model Minority." *The American Prospect* 13:38–42.

Tinker, George, and Loring Bush. 1991. "Native American Unemployment: Statistical Games and Coverups." In *Racism and the Underclass: State Policy and Discrimination against Minorities,* edited by George W. Shepherd, Jr., and David Penna, pp. 119–44. New York: Greenwood Press.

Titiev, Misha. 1944. "Old Oraibi." Papers of the Peabody Museum of American Archaeology and Ethnology, vol. 22, no. 1. Cambridge, MA: Harvard University Press.

Tolnay, Stewart E., and E. M. Beck. 1992. "Racial Violence and Black Migration in the American South, 1910–1930." *American Sociological Review* 57:103–16.

Tomasi, Silvano, and Madeline Engel (eds.). 1970. *The Italian Experience in the United States.* New York: Center for Migration Studies.

Torres, Maria de los Angeles. 1988. "From Exiles to Minorities: The Politics of Cuban Americans." In *Latinos and the Political System,* edited by F. Chris Garcia, pp. 81–98. Notre Dame, IN: University of Notre Dame Press.

Touma, Habib Hassan. 1996. *The Music of the Arabs,* translated by L. Schwartz. Portland, OR: Amadeus Press.

Trennert, Robert. 1982. "Educating Indian Girls at Nonreservation Boarding Schools, 1878–1920." *Western Historical Quarterly* 13:271–90.

Treviño, Fernando, M. Moyer, R. Valdez, and Christine Stroup-Benham. 1991. "Health Insurance Coverage and Utilization of Health Services by Mexican Americans, Mainland Puerto Ricans, and Cuban Americans." *Journal of the American Medical Association* 265:233–37.

Trueba, Henry. 1986. *Success or Failure? Learning and the Language Minority Student.* New York: Newbury House.

———. 1989. *Raising Silent Voices: Educating the Linguistic Minorities for the 21st Century.* New York: Newbury House.

———. 1993. "Race and Ethnicity: The Role of Universities in Healing Multicultural America." *Educational Theory* 43:41–54.

Tsosie, Rebecca. 1999. "Privileging Claims to the Past: Ancient Human Remains and Contemporary Cultural Values." *Arizona State Law Journal* 31:583–677.

Tsuchida, Nobuya. 1990. "The Evacuation and Internment of Japanese Americans during World War II: An Invaluable Lesson on the American Judicial System." In *Contemporary Perspectives on Asian and Pacific American Education,* edited by Russell Endo, Virgie Chattergy, Sally Chou, and Nobuya Tsuchida, pp. 160–91. South El Monte, CA: Pacific Asia Press.

Tuan, Mia. 1998. *Forever Foreigners or Honorary Whites? The Asian Ethnic Experience Today.* New Brunswick: Rutgers University Press.

Turner, J. C. 1975. "Social Comparison and Social Identity: Some Prospects for Intergroup Behaviours" *European Journal of Social Psychology* 5:5–34.

Turner, J. C., M. A. Hogg, P. J. Oaks, S. D. Reieher, and M. S. Wetherell. 1987. *Rediscovering the Social Group: A Self-Categorization Theory.* Oxford, UK: Blackwell.

Turner, Jonathan H. 1992. "Inequality and Poverty." In *Social Problems in America,* edited by G. Ritzer and C. Calhoun, pp. 73–138. New York: McGraw-Hill.

Turner, Jonathan H., and Edna Bonacich. 1980. "Toward a Composite Theory of Middleman Minorities." *Ethnicity* 7:144–58.

Turner, Jonathan H., and Alexandra Maryanski. 1993. "The Biology of Human Organization." *Human Ecology* 3:1–36.

Turner, Jonathan H., and Pedro Payne. 2002. "Power, Politics, and African Americans." In *Sociological Views on Political Participation in the 21st Century,* edited by Betty A. Dobratz, Timothy Buzzell, and Lisa K. Waldner, pp. 139–69. New York: JAI Press/Elsevier.

Turner, Jonathan H., and Royce Singleton. 1978. "A Theory of Ethnic Oppression." *Social Forces* 56:1001–8.

Turner, Jonathan H., Royce Singleton, and David Musick. 1984. *Oppression: A Sociohistory of Black-White Relations in America.* Chicago: Nelson-Hall.

Umemoto, Karen. 1989. "'On Strike' San Francisco State College Strike 1968–69: The Role of Asian American Students." *Amerasia Journal* 15:3–41.

U.S. Bureau of the Census. 1973a. *U.S. Census of Population: 1970 (PC2–1D).* Washington, DC: U.S. Government Printing Office.

———. 1973b. *1970 Census of Housing and Population (Subject Report PC2–1F).* Washington, DC: U.S. Government Printing Office.

———. 1975a. *Historical Statistics of the United States: Colonial Times to 1970.* Washington, DC: U.S. Government Printing Office.

———. 1979a. *The Social and Economic Status of the Black Population in the United States: An Historical Overview, 1790–1978 (P-23-No. 80).* Washington, DC: U.S. Government Printing Office.

———. 1983a. *U.S. Census of Population: 1970 (PC80–1).* Washington, DC: U.S. Government Printing Office.

———. 1983b. *1980 Census of Population (PC80–51–10).* Washington, DC: U.S. Government Printing Office.

———. 1983c. *America's Black Population: 1970 to 1982, A Statistical View (PIO/POP-83-1).* Washington, DC: U.S. Government Printing Office.

———. 1989a. *Money, Income and Poverty Status in the United States: 1987 (P-60-No. 161).* Washington, DC: U.S. Government Printing Office.

———. 1991a. *Current Population Reports, The Hispanic Population of the U.S. Southwest Borderland (P-23-No. 172).* Washington, DC: U.S. Government Printing Office.

———. 1991b. *Current Population Reports, The Hispanic Population in the United States: March 1990 (P-20-No. 449).* Washington, DC: U.S. Government Printing Office.

———. 1991c. *The Black Population in the United States: March 1990 and 1989 (P-20-No. 448).* Washington, DC: U.S. Government Printing Office.

———. 1991d. *Studies in American Fertility (P-23-No. 176).* Washington, DC: U.S. Government Printing Office.

———. 1993a. *1990 Census of Housing—Detailed Housing Characteristics: American Indian and Alaska Native Areas (1990 Ch-2-1A).* Washington, DC: U.S. Government Printing Office.

———. 1993b. *Statistical Abstract of the United States: 1993.* Washington, DC: U.S. Government Printing Office.

———. 1994a. *The Hispanic Population in the United States: March 1993 (Series P20-475).* Washington, DC: U.S. Government Printing Office.

———. 1995. *Statistical Abstract of the United States: 1995.* Washington, DC: U.S. Government Printing Office.

———. 1999a. *Poverty in the United States: 1998.* Washington, DC: U.S. Government Printing Office.

———. 1999b. *Asian and Pacific Islander Population in the United States: March 1998.* Washington, DC: U.S. Government Printing Office.

———. 1999c. *Population of the United States by Age, Sex, Race, and Hispanic Origins: 1995–2050.* Washington, DC: U.S. Government Printing Office.

———. 2001a. *Profile of the Foreign-Born Population in the United States: 2000.* Washington, DC: U.S. Bureau of the Census.

———. 2001b. *Overview of Race and Hispanic Origin.* www.census.gov. July 2005.

———. 2001c. *Statistical Abstract of the United States: 2001.* Washington, DC: U.S. Government Printing Office.

———. 2002a. *The Asian Population: 2000.* Washington, DC: U.S. Bureau of the Census.

———. 2002b. *Money Income in the United States: 2001.* Washington, DC: U.S. Bureau of the Census.

———. 2002c. *Racial and Ethnic Residential Segregation in the United States: 1980-2000.* Washington, DC: U.S. Bureau of the Census.

———. 2002d. *Demographic Trends in the 20th Century.*

———. 2002e. *Census 2000 Brief. The American Indian and Alaska Native Population: 2000.* Downloaded August 2005.

———. 2003a. *School Enrollment: 2000.* Downloaded August 2005.

———. 2003b. *Educational Attainment: 2000.* Downloaded August 2005.

———. 2003c. *Occupations: 2000.* Downloaded September 2005.

———. 2004a. *Income, Poverty and Health Coverage in the United States: 2004.*

———. 2004b. *We the People: Hispanics in the United States.*

———. 2004c. *Ancestry: 2000.* Downloaded August 2005.

———. 2004d. *We the People: Asians in the United States.* Downloaded July 2005.

———. 2005a. *We the People of Arab Ancestry in the United States.* Downloaded September 2005.

———. 2005b. *We the People of More Than One Race in the United States.* Downloaded August 2005.

———. 2005c. *Income, Poverty, and Health Insurance Coverage in the United States: 2004.* Downloaded August 2005.

———. 2005d. *We the People: Pacific Islanders in the United States.* Downloaded October 2005.

———. 2007. *American Community Survey.* Washington, DC: U.S. Government Printing Office. Downloaded November 2007.

———. 2008. Statistical Abstract 2008. Washington, DC: U.S. Bureau of the Census Publications.

———. 2009. 2007–2009 American Community Survey. Washington, DC: U.S. Government Printing Office.

U.S. Commission on Civil Rights. 1972. *The Excluded Student: Educational Practices Affecting Mexican Americans in the Southwest.* Washington, DC: U.S. Government Printing Office.

———. 1976. *Puerto Ricans in the Continental United States: An Uncertain Future.* Washington, DC: U.S. Government Printing Office.

———. 1979. *Civil Rights Issues and Asian and Pacific Americans: Myths and Realities.* Washington, DC: U.S. Government Printing Office.

———. 1980. *Success of Asian Americans: Fact or Fiction?* Washington, DC: U.S. Government Printing Office.

———. 1986. *Recent Activities against Citizens and Residents of Asian Descent.* Washington, DC: U.S. Government Printing Office.

———. 1988. *The Economic Status of Americans of Asian Descent: An Exploratory Investigation.* Washington, DC: U.S. Government Printing Office.

———. 1989. *Civil Rights Issues in Maine.* Washington, DC: U.S. Government Printing Office.

———. 1992. *Civil Rights Issues Facing Asian Americans in the 1990s.* Washington, DC: U.S. Government Printing Office.

———. 1996. *Briefing on Efforts to End Discrimination in Mortgage Lending: Executive Summary.* Washington, DC: U.S. Commission on Civil Rights.

U.S. Department of Health, Education and Welfare. 1976. *A Statistical Portrait of the American Indian.* Washington, DC: U.S. Government Printing Office.

U.S. Department of Homeland Security. Office of Immigration Statistics. 2007. *2006 Yearbook of Immigration Statistics.* Washington, DC: Author.

U.S. Department of Housing and Urban Development. 1991. *Housing Discrimination Study.* Washington, DC: U.S. Department of Housing and Urban Development.

U.S. Department of Justice. 1980. *National Hispanic Conference on Law Enforcement and Criminal Justice.* Washington, DC: U.S. Department of Justice Law Enforcement Assistance Administration.

———. 1991a. *1990 Statistical Yearbook of the Immigration and Naturalization Service.* Washington, DC: U.S. Government Printing Office.

———. 1991b. *Teenage Victims: A National Crime Survey Report.* Washington, DC: U.S. Government Printing Office.

———. 1991c. *School Crime: A National Crime Victimization Survey Report.* Washington, DC: U.S. Government Printing Office.

———. 1995. *Bureau of Justice Statistics Sourcebook of Criminal Justice Statistics—1994.* Washington, DC: U.S. Government Printing Office.

———. 1997. *1996 Statistical Yearbook of the Immigration and Naturalization Service.* Washington, DC: U.S. Government Printing Office.

———. 1999a. *Legal Immigration, Fiscal Year 1998.* Washington, DC: U.S. Government Printing Office.

———. 1999b. *Refugees, Fiscal Year 1997.* Washington, DC: U.S. Government Printing Office.

———. 2001. *2000 Statistical Yearbook of the Immigration and Naturalization Service.* Washington, DC: U.S. Government Printing Office.

———. 2002. *Criminal Victimization 2001.* Washington, DC: U.S. Government Printing Office.

U.S. Department of Labor. 1991. *Preliminary Report on Discrimination in the Workplace and the Existence of the "Glass Ceiling."* Washington, DC: U.S. Government Printing Office.

U.S. General Accounting Office. 1989. *Equal Employment Opportunity: Women and Minority Aerospace Managers and Professionals.* Washington, DC: U.S. Government Printing Office.

———. 2002. *Native American Housing. GAO Report GAO-02-654.* Washington, DC: U.S. General Accounting Office.

Urban Institute. 2004. Overcoming Challenges to Business and Economic Development in Indian Country. Washington, DC: Urban Institute.

Valdez, R. Burciaga, Julie DaVanzo, Georges Vernez, and Mitchell Wade. 1993. "Immigration: Getting the Facts." RAND Issue, Paper #1. Santa Monica, CA: RAND Corporation.

Van Ausdale, Debra, and Joe R. Feagin. 2001. *The First R: How Children Learn Race and Racism.* Boulder, CO: Rowman and Littlefield.

———. 1981. *The Ethnic Phenomenon.* New York: Elsevier.

Vargas, Sylvia. 1998. "Deconstructing Homo[geneous] Americanus: The White Ethnic Immigrant Narrative and Its Exclusionary Effect." *Tulane Law Review* 72: 1493–1596.

Vernez, Georges. 1990. *Immigration and International Relations: Proceedings of a Conference on the International Effects of the 1986 Immigration Reform and Control Act (IRCA).* Santa Monica, CA: RAND Corporation and the Urban Institute.

———. 1993. *Needed: A Federal Role in Helping Communities Cope with Immigration.* RP-177. Santa Monica, CA: Program for Research on Immigration Policy.

Vernez, Georges, and Allan Abrahamse. 1996. *How Immigrants Fare in U.S. Education.* Santa Monica, CA: RAND Corporation.

Vernez, Georges, and Kevin McCarthy. 1990. *Meeting the Economy's Labor Needs through Immigration: Rationales and Challenges.* Santa Monica, CA: RAND Corporation.

————. 1996. *The Costs of Immigration to Taxpayers: Analytical and Policy Issues.* Santa Monica, CA: RAND Corporation.

Villareal, Roberto. 1988. "The Politics of Mexican-American Empowerment." In *Latino Empowerment: Progress, Problems, and Prospects,* edited by Roberto Villareal, Norma Hernandez, and Howard Neighbor, pp. 1–9. New York: Greenwood Press.

Vitucci, Jeff. 1999. "The State of Hispanic Health." *Hispanic Business* 21:40–42.

Wagenheim, Kal (ed.). 1973. *Puerto Ricans: A Documentary History.* Garden City, NY: Doubleday, Anchor.

Wallace, Steven P. 1989. "The New Urban Latinos: Central Americans in a Mexican Immigrant Environment." *Urban Affairs Quarterly* 25:239–64.

————. 1990. "Race versus Class in the Health Care of African-American Elderly." *Social Problems* 37:517–34.

Wang, L. Ling-chi. 1988. "Meritocracy and Diversity in Higher Education: Discrimination against Asian Americans in the Post-Bakke Era." *The Urban Review* 20:183–209.

Warner, W. Lloyd. 1941. "Introduction." In *Deep South,* edited by Allison Davis, Burleigh Gardner, and Mary Gardner, pp. 1–6. Chicago: University of Chicago Press.

Warner, W. Lloyd, and Leo Srole. 1945. *The Social Systems of American Ethnic Groups.* New Haven, CT: Yale University Press.

Webster, Bruce N., and Alemayehu Bishaw. 2007. *American Community Survey Reports, ACS-08: Income, Earnings, and Poverty.* Washington, DC: U.S. Government Printing Office. Downloaded October 2007.

Wei, William. 1993. *The Asian American Movement.* Philadelphia: Temple University Press.

Weinberg, Meyer. 1977. *A Chance to Learn: The History of Race and Education in the United States.* New York: Cambridge University Press.

Welch, Susan. 1990. "The Impact of At-Large Elections on the Representation of Blacks and Hispanics." *Journal of Politics* 52:1050–76.

Welch, Susan, J. Gruhl, and C. Spohn. 1984. "Dismissal, Conviction, and Incarceration of Hispanic Defendants: A Comparison with Anglos and Blacks." *Social Science Quarterly* 65:257–64.

Wellner, Alison. 2002. "Beyond City Limits: Asian Americans Are More Likely Than Ever to Call the Suburbs, or Even Small Towns, Home." *American Demographics* 22:2–5.

Whetstone, Muriel. 1993. "The Story behind the Explosive Statistics: Why Blacks Are Losing Ground in the Workforce." *Ebony* (Dec.): 102–4.

White, John. 1985. *Black Leadership in America: From Booker T. Washington to Jesse Jackson.* New York: Longmans.

Whitmore, John, Marcella Trautmann, and Nathan Caplan. 1989. "The Socio-Cultural Basis for the Economic and Educational Success of Southeast Asian Refugees (1978–1982 Arrivals)." In *Refugees as Immigrants: Cambodians, Laotians, and Vietnamese in America,* edited by David W. Haines, pp. 121–37. Totowa, NJ: Rowman & Littlefield.

Wildavsky, Ben. 1990. "Tilting at Billboards: Butts (et al.) vs. Poutts." *New Republic* (Aug. 20): 19–20.

Williams, David, and Chiquita Collins. 2001. "Racial Residential Segregation: A Fundamental Cause of Racial Disparities in Health." *Public Health Reports* 11:404–17.

Williams, Robert. 1990. *The American Indian in Western Legal Thought: The Discourses of Conquest.* New York: Oxford University Press.

Williamson, Joel. 1984. *The Crucible of Race: Black/White Relations in the American South since Emancipation.* New York: Oxford University Press.

Wilson, Kenneth, and Alejandro Portes. 1980. "Immigrant Enclaves: An Analysis of the Labor Market Experience of Cubans in Miami." *American Journal of Sociology* 86: 295–319.

Wilson, William J. 1987. *The Truly Disadvantaged.* Chicago: University of Chicago Press.

Wirth, Louis. 1945. "The Problem of Minority Groups." In *The Science of Man in the World Crisis,* edited by R. Linton, pp. 347–72. New York: Columbia University Press.

Wong, Bernard. 1976. "Social Stratification, Adaptive Strategies and the Chinese Community of New York." *Urban Life* 5:33–52.

Wong, Eugene. 1978. *On Visual Media Racism: Asians in the American Motion Pictures.* New York: Arno.

Wong, Paul, Chienping Lai, Richard Nagasawa, and Tieming Lin. 1998. "Asian Americans as a Model Minority: Self-Perceptions and Perceptions by Other Racial Groups." *Sociological Perspectives* 41:95–119.

Wood, Andrew. 2001. "Anticipating the Colonias: Popular Housing in El Paso and Ciudad Juarez, 1890–1923." *Journal of the Southwest* 43:493–505.

Woodward, C. Vann. 1966. *The Strange Career of Jim Crow,* 2d edition. New York: Oxford University Press.

Wound, Barbara Bad. 2000. "American Indian Youth Outnumber Others in Justice System." *The Aboriginal Youth Network* (August). Available at: www.ayn.ca/news.

Wright, Bobby, and William Tierney. 1991. "American Indians in Higher Education: A History of Cultural Conflict." *Change* 23:11–18.

Yen, Earl. 1988. "Flames Leave Massachusetts Cambodian Families Homeless." *Asian Week* (Dec. 2).

Yoshihama, Mieko. 2001. "Model Minority Demystified: Emotional Costs of Multiple Victimizations in the Lives of Women of Japanese Descent." In *Psychosocial Aspects of the Asian-American Experience: Diversity within Diversity,* edited by N. G. Choi, pp. 201–24. New York: Haworth Press.

Yu, Jin. 1980. *The Korean Merchants in the Black Community.* Elkins Park, PA: Philip Jaisohn Foundation.

Zambrana, Ruth, and Claudia Dorrington. 1998. "Economic and Social Vulnerability of Latino Children and Families by Subgroup: Implications for Child Welfare." *Child Welfare* 77:5–28.

Zambrana, Ruth, and Laura Logie. 2000. "Latino Child Health: Need for Inclusion in the U.S. National Discourse." *American Journal of Public Health* 90:1827.

Zelio, Judy. 2005. "Tribes Bet on Gaming," *State Legislatures* 31:26–29.

Zo, Kil. 1978. *Chinese Emigration into the United States, 1850–1880.* New York: Arno.

Zogby, James. 2000. "Are Arab Americans People Like Us?" Retrieved March 2006 from www.aaiusa.org/zogby/InTheNews/people_like_us.htm.

Zogby International. 2000. Poll commissioned by the Arab American Institute. www.aaiusa.org.

Zweigenhaft, Richard L., and G. William Domhoff. 1982. *Jews in the Protestant Establishment.* New York: Praeger.

Photo Credits

Index